MAKING SENSE OF INDIAN DEMOCRACY

Making Sense of Indian Democracy

THEORY IN PRACTICE

YOGENDRA YADAV

in association with

Published by

PERMANENT BLACK

'Himalayana', Mall Road, Ranikhet Cantt,
Ranikhet 263645

perblack@gmail.com

in association with

Distributed by

ORIENT BLACKSWAN PRIVATE LTD

Bangalore Bhopal Bhubaneshwar Chandigarh Chennai
Ernakulam Guwahati Hyderabad Jaipur Kolkata
Lucknow Mumbai New Delhi Patna
www.orientblackswan.com

ISBN 978-81-7824-638-3

Typeset in Adobe Garamond Pro
by Guru Typograph Technology, Crossings Republic,
Ghaziabad 201009

Printed and bound by Manipal Technologies Limited, Manipal

to

MY PARENTS

for imparting
the spirit of democracy and the idea of India

Contents

Acknowledgements ix

Introduction xiii

HISTORICAL OVERVIEW

1 The Creolisation of Indian Democracy: Making Sense of National Politics 1947–1997 1

2 From Hegemony to Convergence: Party System and Electoral Politics in the Indian States 1952–2002 40

COMPARATIVE OVERVIEW

3 "Nation State" or "State Nation"? India in Comparative Perspective 108

4 Democratic Paradox: Political Representation in Contemporary India 166

5 What is Distinctive About Indian Elections? A Hypothesis 193

6 The Decline of Political Judgement: Comparing Regimes and Parties 203

7 How Good is the Rise of States? Ten Theses on State Politics 213

THEORY AND METHOD

8 On the Necessity of Politics 233

9 On Theories of the Indian State: A Review Essay 236

10 On Rajni Kothari: The Enigma that is *Politics in India* 249

11 On Election Forecasting: Polls, Predictions, Psephology 262

12 On Sample Surveys: Reflections on the State of Survey Research on Politics in Most of the World 271

13 On Ethnography: What Work Does "Fieldwork" Do in the Field of Elections? 300

REFORM AND ACTION

14 A Radical Agenda for Political Reforms: What is Not to be Done? 325

15 An Agenda for Political Action in Our Times: What is to be Done? 347

Index 367

Acknowledgements

MORE THAN A DECADE ago, Mahesh Rangarajan suggested that I put together some of my essays into a volume. Rukun Advani resumed this conversation a few years ago and turned it into a serious chase in 2017, assisted by Raja Mujeeb, his "resident representative". If the book has seen the light of day, it is a tribute to Rukun's infinite patience, gentle perseverance, and firm editorial judgement. My laptop folder calls this book "rukun volume". And that is what it is.

The essays collected here were written over three decades. I was fortunate to work with several scholar-editors who invited me to write many of these essays and persisted despite my procrastination. But for Harsh Sethi and Tejbir Singh at *Seminar,* I might not have written half of what I have published. Philip Oldenburg, Nilkantha Rath, Pratap Mehta, and Niraja Jayal commissioned and nurtured some of these essays to fruition.

During much of this period (1993–2016), the Centre for the Study of Developing Societies (CSDS) was my institutional home. A continuous conversation with colleagues at the CSDS, especially its Lokniti programme and the Lokniti network through the country, informs these pages. Many other institutions also hosted me during this period: Panjab University, Chandigarh; Wissenschaftskolleg zu Berlin; University of Michigan, Ann Arbor; Columbia University, New York; and Brown University, Providence.

Suhas Palshikar is the co-author of much of what may be of value in this book, even when he is not formally mentioned as one. Thinking, arguing, and writing with him have been among the most cherished associations of my academic life. The essay I wrote with my guru Kishen Pattanayak (I was merely a scribe) is a badge of honour for me. Writing with Alfred Stepan and Juan Linz, both giants of political science, was an education.

Much of what I have written on Indian politics is a virtual conversation with Rajni Kothari and real-life dialogues with D.L. Sheth, who seconded me to the CSDS and initiated me into its traditions. The writings here also bear the stamp of what I have learnt from my teachers Sudipta Kaviraj and Rajeev Bhargava, as also from John Dunn, Ashis Nandy, and Charles Taylor.

Over the years, I have benefited from conversations with Abhay Dube, Abhijit V. Banerjee, Aditya Nigam, Ajit Jha, Alistair McMillan, Anindo Saha, Apurba Baruah, Aseema Sinha, Ashutosh Varshney, Avik Saha, Bishnu Mohapatra, B.S. Brar, Christophe Jaffrelot, Donal Cruise O'Brien, Gopal Guru, Hilal Ahmed, James Manor, Javeed Alam, John Keane, Joachim Nettlebeck, Jorge Heine, Kanchan Chandra, K.C. Suri, Larry Diamond, Madhu Kishwar, Marta Lagos, Meena Dhandha, Mukulika Banerjee, Nazima Parveen, Niraja Jayal, Nivedita Menon, Partha Chatterjee, Peter deSouza, Pradeep Kumar, Pratap Mehta, Pritam Singh, Rajiv Lochan, Rajendra Vora, Sandeep Shastri, Sanjay Kumar, Sanjay Ruparelia, Sanjeer Alam, Satish Saberwal, Sunil Khilnani, Subrata K. Mitra, V.B. Singh, Vijay Pratap, Ujjawal Kumar Singh, and Yehuda Elkana. At different points, Banasmita Bora and Ashish Ranjan provided invaluable research support.

Madhulika Banerjee, my wife, and also my intellectual and political companion, saw me through this journey from the life of an academic to that of a political worker. I could also fall back upon the warmth and support from my family, especially from both sets of sisters – Neelam and Poonam-jiji, and Mukulika and Krittika. Our children, Sufi and Sahaj, have shared this journey, first as victims and now, hopefully, as fellow-travellers. Madhulika persuades me that my academic writings are still of some value. Hence this book.

Essay 1, "The Creolisation of Indian Democracy: Making Sense of National Politics 1947–1997", was first published as "Politics" in Marshall Bouton and Philip Oldenburg, eds, *India Briefing: A Transformative Fifty Years* (New York: M.E. Sharpe, 1999).

Essay 2, "From Hegemony to Convergence: Party System and Electoral Politics in the Indian States, 1952–2002", is co-authored with Suhas Palshikar and was first published in the *Journal of Indian Institute of Political Economy*, XV (1&2), January–June 2003.

Essay 3, "'Nation State' or 'State Nation'? India in Comparative Perspective", was first published in Shankar Bajpai, ed., *Democracies and Diversity: India and the American Experience* (Delhi and Oxford: Oxford University Press, 2006).

Essay 4, "Democratic Paradox: Political Representation in Contemporary India", was first published as "Political Representation in Contemporary India" in Pratap Mehta and Niraja Gopal, eds, *Oxford Companion to Politics in India* (Delhi: Oxford University Press, 2010).

Essay 5, "What is Distinctive About Indian Elections: A Hypothesis", is a revised version of a talk titled "What is Distinctive About Indian Elections", delivered at the Wissenschaftskolleg, Berlin, in 2010, as the concluding presentation of a year-long fellowship.

Essay 6, "The Decline of Political Judgement: Comparing Regimes and Parties", was first published as "The Decline of Political Judgement" in *Seminar*, Annual Number, January 2011.

Essay 7, "How Good is the Rise of States? Ten Theses on State Politics", is coauthored with Suhas Palshikar and was first published as "Ten Theses on State Politics" in *Seminar*, November 2008.

Essay 8, "On the Necessity of Politics", is co-authored with Kishen Pattanayak in response to an editorial in the *Lokayan Bulletin* titled "Between Idealism and Pragmatism – Non-Party Formations and Political Parties" and first published in the *Lokayan Bulletin*, July–August 1994.

Essay 9, "On Theories of the Indian State: A Review Essay", was first published as "Theories of the Indian State" in *Seminar* 367, March 1990.

Essay 10, "On Rajni Kothari: The Enigma that is *Politics in India*", was first published as a review essay on Rajni Kothari's *Politics in India* in *Studies in Indian Politics*, 1(1), 1 June 2013.

Essay 11, "On Election Forecasting: Polls, Predictions, Psephology", was first published as "Polls, Predictions, Psephology" in *Seminar* 385, September 1991.

Essay 12, "On Sample Surveys: Reflections on the State of Survey Research on Politics in Most of the World" was delivered as the Adiseshiah Memorial Lecture, Madras Institute of Development Studies, Chennai, November 2008.

Essay 13, "On Ethnography: What Work Does Fieldwork Do in the Field of Elections?" was first published as "What Work Does 'Fieldwork' Do in the Field of Elections?" in M.N. Srinivas and A.M. Shah, eds, *The Grassroots of Democracy: Field Studies of Indian Elections* (Delhi: Permanent Black, 2007).

Essay 14, "A Radical Agenda for Political Reforms: What is Not to be Done", was first published as "A Radical Agenda for Political Reforms" in *Seminar*, 506, October 2001.

Essay 15, "An Agenda for Political Action in Our Times: What is to be Done", was first published as "What is to be Done" in *Seminar*, November 2017.

Introduction

India's First Republic 1950–2019

THIS VOLUME BRINGS together some of my essays on what now appears to be the first phase in the history of Indian democracy: India's "first republic", as it were.

The essays I have gathered here were written over the time when I was trying to make sense of not just the vicissitudes of Indian democracy but also the concept of democracy and the idea of India. Looking back at them, I see two selves at work behind this collection: first, a researcher gathering evidence for theorising the specificity of Indian democracy, and second, an activist seeking to reform and transform the political arena. As a body of work the essays seem to contain mixed if not contradictory feelings: pride in what India has achieved despite all the odds; optimism over the prospects of democratic politics; a desperate keenness for political reforms; and, given where we seem to have reached, despair at where we are headed.

The end point of a journey is in many ways the perfect vantage point from which to look at its entire course, its twists and turns, and take stock of where we have arrived. The question that must torment every student of Indian politics in 2020 is this: What happened to the famous "Indian system"? As one institution after another caves in, as every constitutional check and balance gives way, as democratic elections become an exercise in sanctioning majoritarian rule, as opposition leaders and organisations turn irrelevant to the politics of resistance, and as ideas are reduced to being the mere shadows of power games, all those who, only a short while ago, took pride in Indian democracy must ask themselves some very hard questions:

Were we, all this while, deluded in celebrating the achievements of Indian democracy? Was this precipitous decline and fall written into the very fabric of our democratic politics? If not, are we living through a bad dream? Were the electoral results of 2014 and 2019 only aberrations? In this short introduction I attempt to outline an answer to these difficult questions, following a brief description of the travels that brought me here.

The book is divided into four parts. The first part contains two long essays that offer historical overviews of the working of Indian democracy and of India's party system for the first five decades of the "first republic". The second part is thematic. It contains international as well as intra-national comparative generalisations on the uniqueness of India's "state-nation" model of handling diversities, the specificity of elections, political representation and political judgement in India, and patterns of politics across Indian states. My engagement with Indian democracy has also resulted in some reflections on theory and method, which are collected in the third part. The last part of the volume contains two essays – one on political reforms and the other on political action – that represent my quest for not just interpreting the world but changing it too.

II

My personal and professional journey happened to coincide with the journey of Indian democracy. I was brought up during the heyday of the "Congress system" and was first exposed to politics just before, during, and after the Emergency. I can in fact date my interest in democracy to 21 March 1977, the day I found myself in the middle of an electrifying crowd celebrating the defeat of Indira Gandhi in that historic post-Emergency election. In the joy of that moment lay the seeds of an inchoate political sense that perhaps made me turn to Political Science for my post-graduation.

My two years at Jawaharlal Nehru University (JNU) did not attract me to marxist theory or communist politics; I turned instead towards the Gandhi–JP–Lohia tradition of democratic socialism for my politics, and to Rajni Kothari for analysis of Indian politics (chapter 10 is my assessment of his intellectual legacy). The ensuing years were a time of disenchantment with the Janata experiment, of coping with the horrors of the 1984 Sikh massacre, and of coming to terms with Rajiv Gandhi's massive Congress victory immediately thereafter. I started teaching political theory at the Panjab University, Chandigarh, focusing my research on the history of socialist ideas in India and away from the study of Indian politics.

My shift from that direction towards making sense of Indian democracy began three decades ago, during the Lok Sabha elections of 1989. This was the era popularly known as "Mandal, Mandir, and Market". By then I had developed an amateur interest in election forecasting, thanks to Prannoy Roy's *Compendium of Indian Elections* (1984; co-authored by David Butler and Ashok Lahiri), which had next to nothing to do with my formal training in Political Science. This side interest, almost a private hobby, allowed me to make a transition from the study of political theory to some of the ground realities of Indian politics.

A lazy but good forecast of the 1989 elections, and a fluke success in an exit poll for the Chandigarh constituency in 1991, completed the transition (some early lessons in "psephology" are summarised in chapter 11). For the next twenty years, and until I formally announced my retirement from pollstering in 2012, I was involved in survey-based analyses of elections (chapters 12 and 13 reflect on the strengths and limits of survey research and ethnographic method, respectively, in the study of non-Western democracies). A faculty position at the Centre for the Study of Developing Societies (CSDS) in 1993 and the formation of the Lokniti network in 1995 provided me the institutional base for these analyses.

It was an exciting time to study politics. The decline of Congress and the rise of new regional political formations had signalled a political reconfiguration. This was accompanied by a structural shift: state politics now came centrestage and the "second democratic upsurge" led to the deepening of electoral participation by disadvantaged social groups. Alongside my colleagues in Lokniti, it seemed to me that to study elections was to study the changing character of Indian democracy. In place of the abstract theorisation and ideological judgements that dominated the field then, we were committed to an empirically grounded and theoretically oriented study of Indian politics. And in this quest, survey research provided the base-line data required for making sense of Indian democracy.

What may have appeared from the outside as innocuous "election study" in fact contained four different sub-fields in the study of politics: election prediction, the post-mortem of elections, the analysis of public opinion, and general political analysis. We were engaged in the business of election forecasting only in the narrowest sense, even though it was what grabbed public attention most (and irked professional colleagues most). We were really far more focused on post-mortems of electoral verdicts, looking at popular preferences, assessing the performance of governments, and analysing the social basis of voting. We combined these with an analysis of the aggregate data from official results. Much of this kind of work is now mainstream election analysis in India (chapter 11).

This engagement with election forecasting via post-poll surveys was driven by the need to create a large data archive that did not exist beyond some early forays in the 1960s and 1980s. With the revival of the National Election Study in 1996, we managed to create a more or less unbroken data archive that enabled us to study public opinion, attitudes, and behaviour. This led to some methodological innovations and reflections, besides empirically informed theorisation about the patterns of electoral participation and the legitimacy of democracy. These specific forms of inquiry were all linked to the fourth and final field of general analysis of Indian democracy (chapter 9 was the starting point). Professor Suhas Palshikar and I were involved in proposing a series of middle-level generalisations about India's changing party system (chapter 2), the nature of electoral contestations, and the patterns of state politics (chapter 7).

Underlying our effort was not just an attempt to understand Indian democracy but also to change it. My exposure in my university days to the socialist movement and Kishen Pattanayak had connected me to the world of activism (See chapter 8 for an initial formulation inspired by Kishen-ji). From the mid-1980s I was involved with political organisations such as the Samata Sangathan and the Samajwadi

Janparishad, and associated with various peoples' movements. So, while trying to understand Indian democracy, I was also involved in attempts to change its course through radical political reforms and alternative politics (chapter 14 suggests an approach). This led me into being one of the founders of the Aam Adami Party in 2012, and subsequently to Swaraj Abhiyan in 2015 and Swaraj India in 2016. Now, as a full-time political worker, my tryst with making sense of Indian democracy takes a different form. Confronted with the dismantling of democratic institutions, reclaiming the republic is at the heart of my current political quest (chapter 15 outlines a roadmap). The present volume brings together some bits and pieces that seem to retain significance from my three-decade-long journey; my hope is that shoring these fragments of my past from ruin will help make sense of the current crisis of Indian democracy.

III

The current state of Indian democracy is neither just a bad accident in an otherwise perfect journey nor its inevitable destination. The rise of Modi to power was anything but a freak phenomenon. The Ramjanmabhoomi movement had signalled this possibility twenty-five years ago. That was foreshadowed by Congress' victory in the wake of the Sikh massacre and followed by Modi's victories in the Gujarat assembly elections, held in the wake of the anti-Muslim pogrom of 2002. We should have known about the dark side of Indian democracy. At any rate, we are no longer now looking at Modi's victory in 2014 as a single incident: his popularity thereafter and even bigger victory in 2019 is enough to make it clear that we are looking at something deeper than one individual, one election, one incident.

At the same time, the victory of a Modi-led BJP was not the only possible outcome of India's political trajectory (chapter 1 offers a more optimistic reading of this trajectory). The political logic of Indian democracy, the economic logic of a neo-liberal state, the social logic of a caste system under transformation, and the cultural logic of India's own modernity still left open several possibilities. Modi's rise to power in Gujarat, his ascendance within the BJP, and his nationwide electoral victory were not preordained. Plausible counterfactuals come to mind: it is not hard to imagine a very different course of history had the Anna Hazare movement not delegitimised the UPA regime, had the Congress leadership not proved itself so utterly inept, had the Pulwama attack not happened as and when it did. So, I think it is best to see the current crisis of Indian democracy as the outcome of a "democracy capture" that was at once contingent and determined. We need to understand how a political leader seized upon a very difficult chance and converted it into a personal triumph – and how it is that he now manages to do so repeatedly. At the same time, this democracy capture could not have happened without some structural weaknesses within the Indian democratic enterprise. A student of democracy must focus on the conditions that made this kind of capture possible (written much before the "capture", chapters 1, 2, 4, and 6 offer many clues to these conditions).

Understanding this democracy capture requires rewriting democratic theory. The dominant orthodoxy on democracy presents us with a neat definition of democracy, a universal normative standard which allows every political regime to be pigeonholed into a democracy/non-democracy binary. It supplies us with an institutional checklist that can be used across the globe to operationalise this ideal of democracy. And it weaves a lovely tale of the nation's utopian transition to, consolidation of, and culmination in a finished-product democracy. This is a highly stylised and selective version of what has in fact been the contingent path that democracy has taken in a tiny but dominant part of the globe. Making sense of democracy in most other parts of the world in the twenty-first century demands that this orthodoxy be challenged on multiple grounds.

First of all, we need to widen the conceptual apparatus of "democracy" to include diverse ways – languages, idioms, theories – in which democracy has been understood all over the world. Second, it requires enriching the normative standards embedded in the idea of democracy by taking into account the many histories and traditions of democratic thinking across the world. Third, we need to expand the repertoire of institutions, conventions, and practices that go into the making of democracy in societies that are often quite different from each other. And fourth, we need to rewrite the history of actually existing democracies, both in the global north and the global south, to reflect their radically different experiences and trajectories.

While challenging democratic theory is a global challenge today – besides Narendra Modi, we live in the age of Donald Trump, Boris Johnson, Recep Tayyip Erdogan, and Vladimir Putin – the task is certainly essential if we are to make sense of Indian democracy, for the dominant narrative fails to understand both the successes and the failures of our specific variety of this broad template called democracy. If we go by the dominant understanding of the preconditions of democracy – namely, some degree of affluence, and widespread literacy – India should never have been a democracy in the first place. If we insist on oscillations of power within a muti-party competitive framework, the "Congress system" should not be characterised as democratic. If we stick to the idea of an overlap between the cultural boundaries of a nation and the political boundaries of a state, independent India with its deep diversities should never have survived beyond its first decade and made a transition to a democratic nation-state. If we believe in a balance between participatory urge and institutional depth, Indian democracy should not have taken off in the 1960s; and having taken off, it should not have suffered the crisis that it did during the Emergency; and, once its institutional fragility had been as exposed as it was during that episode, Indian democracy should not have survived the Emergency. The rise of identity politics – region-, caste-, and religion-based mobilisation through the 1980s and 1990s – should not have led to a consolidation of democracy. And, once democracy became "the only game in town" and was buttressed by an unprecedented rate of economic growth, Indian democracy should not have faced its worst crisis – the one it faces today.

Clearly, students of Indian democracy need a fresh pair of glasses. We need to see the democratic enterprise in India as an open-ended journey with no predetermined starting point, fixed route, and given destination. The journey has its origins in a freedom struggle that stapled the ideal of democracy to the goal of national independence. The formal journey began as a joint enterprise: building a self-reliant and self-governing nation, alongside the building of democratic institutions for the new nation. And yet in this joint journey, in which democracy had been so intertwined with the nation-state, the imperative of nation-building and state-building began to take precedence over the requirements of building a democracy. Democracy featured here as a necessary aid, a mechanism that allowed the masses to be mobilised, peoples' preferences to be ascertained, their legitimate representatives to be identified, and faultlines to be repaired – all for building a successful nation-state. Alternatively, democracy featured as an impediment, as a road block necessitating consultations, procedures, and consensus-building – all resulting in slowdowns that could ignite pre-existing faultlines and lead to explosions. This journey developed into one within which we cleared the path as we moved along: there was no ready-made road, no given end point. What made this journey so exciting was that it was so indeterminate, always full of promise and danger.

The democracy capture that we face today is one such danger, always lurking round the corner. To call it "democracy capture", rather than, say, "authoritarian capture of democracy" or "crisis of democracy" is to remember that democracy is both the object and the subject of this capture. The apparatus being seized is democracy, a constitutionally sanctified and ideologically legitimised form of governance. The means being deployed for this capture are also democratic, at least seemingly so – by way of an electoral majority attained in "free and fair" elections. It is to remind us that the formal procedures of democracy have been used to subvert the substance of democracy. This subversion is not just an accident in an otherwise well-planned journey. Nor is it the end point in the inevitable decline and fall of Indian democracy.

IV

In order to make sense of this trajectory, and to understand how and why this democracy capture has happened, let me map four different dimensions to the story of Indian democracy. Our journey of democracy, I argue, required four elements. One, it needed *people*, both ordinary citizens and leaders, to be mobilised. Two, it needed *institutions*, both formal as well as informal, to streamline people and co-ordinate their actions. Three, it had to tackle *structural obstacles*, social as well as economic, inherited as also self-generated, that could impede the journey. Finally, it needed *ideas*, both formal ideologies as well as popular beliefs, that could serve as a compass in this journey.

The story of India's democratic journey is not of failure in all these respects. What makes the Indian story interesting is that it succeeded, in some ways, in each of these (see chapter 1). Yet each success left chinks, cracks, or bigger gaps in the democratic enterprise and exposed it to the dangers of a capture. It took a determined political player and a constellation of events to string these vulnerabilities and turn a dire possibility into calamitous reality.

Let me outline these elements and see how each of these successes contributed to the present democracy capture in the life of India's first republic. The first dimension involved expansion: the story here is of *peoples'* mobilisation through the routines of electoral democracy. In this respect, Indian democracy was a truly spectacular and rather surprising success story. Over the decades, voters' participation in elections deepened and widened in ways that were unexpected. Electoral turnouts in India were robust, defying the global trend of voter fatigue. The enlarged participation was particularly obvious in local-level elections: the lower the tier of democracy, the higher citizens' participation. The lower orders of society – the poor, marginal communities, rural populations – showed a greater appetite for electoral democracy than did socio-economically privileged sections. By global standards, Indian democracy enjoyed a fairly high level of popular legitimacy. In a minimal sense, most Indian elections could be called free and fair. Democratic elections came to be the mandatory and sanctified form for transfers of power. Democracy, howsoever understood, had come to be the only game in town.

Yet this success came with a cost. While the electoral arena attracted large-scale mobilisation, the system failed to offer real choices, empower people, or deliver substantive outcomes. It provided representation without effective voice in decision-making (chapter 4). This could have resulted – though it did not – in frustration with or alienation from elections. Instead, it produced impatience with the procedural aspects of democracy and led to the search for a strong leader in and through elections.

The centrality of elections as the principal and only functioning mechanism for democratic participation meant that it became the sole locus of democratic legitimacy (chapter 5). The result was the according of sanctity to electoral democracy without any securing of substantive outcomes or the assurance of procedural safeguards. This paved the way for India's own distinctive style of majoritarianism based on communities. In this situation, electoral victory by any means became the proxy for democratic legitimacy. Election capture became an effective route for democracy capture.

The second dimension of the journey of democracy involved entrenchment: protecting it against structural impediments. When India began its democratic journey, the odds were heavily stacked against its survival. Going by the conventional understanding, this nascent democracy faced too many social, ethnic, communal, and economic faultlines waiting to tear it apart. Negotiating these faultlines was no mean achievement. Yet diffusing each of these potential divisions also meant a disconnect with the potential energy that each of them contained. This disconnect also paved the way for democracy's capture.

If we were to look for a textbook example of democratic "entrenchment", India's handling of regional-linguistic cleavages would be a good candidate. The country's vast size, huge population, deep linguistic diversities, and ethnic-racial differences, superimposed on regional divisions, presented almost a perfect case for balkanisation. India's nation-builders responded to this challenge with a unique "state-nation" approach (chapter 3). Instead of the assimilationist "nation-state" approach followed in Europe, India admitted all its deep diversities in from the front door. Linguistic differences were acknowledged through the formation of linguistic states. Regional political parties were given free play to appeal to regional identities and to mobilise on regional lines. A potentially disruptive energy was channelised into a cementing force.

The downside of this instant normalisation of regional politics was the absence of a strong federal ideology. Regional politics found an effective expression in the electoral domain, leading to the formation of many state governments led by regional parties. Soon, the logic of electoral alignment brought these regional forces in negotiation with centrist forces, thus strengthening India's unity and at the same time diluting the regional sentiment. The situation played a positive role during the "Third Electoral System", when state politics emerged as the centrestage of national politics (chapter 7). But it also paved the way for the next stage, when national and state-level elections were separated. Regionalism was confined to state elections and local governance, without becoming a player in reshaping the nation. A robust defence of the federal division of power could have been a bulwark against democracy capture, but the democratic accommodation of regional sentiment made it compatible with centralisation. This is what allowed the BJP to get regional parties to endorse the ex-parte abrogation of Article 370 and erasure of the state of Jammu and Kashmir. National politics was now available for capture by a unitary and homogenising vision of India.

Given deep economic inequalities and a vast segment of the population living below the poverty line, class-based violence was an obvious challenge for the Indian republic, especially in the first three decades when the global and domestic political climate favoured class-based revolutionary politics. Eventually, this was contained through appropriation and suppression. As the Congress adopted a "socialist" charter and an aggressive rhetoric of "*garibi hatao*", the communist and socialist parties were squeezed out into the margins of politics. Leftists who did not join the game of electoral politics were suppressed with a heavy hand. This successful tackling of the challenge of class divisions also meant an erasure of class issues, or at least the disconnection of class mobilisation from the agenda of socialism or any egalitarian vision.

The handling of caste-based divisions was very different. These were neither erased not suppressed. Caste politics was domesticated and turned into a quotidian and harmless routine of democratic politics. In the process, the caste question lost both its threat and promise. Instead of caste capturing politics, it was politics that controlled caste. At the same time, the caste issue was uncoupled from the ideology of social change. The normalisation of caste also meant the normalisation of caste inequalities and injustice. Any party, including the BJP, could and did accommodate the aspirations of hitherto excluded castes and communities. Thus the potential of "bahujan" politics for checking religious mobilisation was blunted.

Unlike caste, religious faultlines could not be domesticated except in states like Kerala and Punjab where religious communities functioned practically as castes. Through the first four decades, the Hindu–Muslim faultline was also partly normalised. But the history of Hindu–Muslim strife and a blood-soaked Partition left open the possibility of igniting communal faultlines. An exceptionally imaginative and energetic politics was needed to keep such a possibility at bay. For a time, the politics of secularism stuck to this difficult and principled path. However, soon the politics of conviction gave way to the politics of convenience, and eventually to a conspiracy to keep Muslims electorally hostage to supposedly secular parties. The success in creating a Muslim vote bank made possible the improbable political project of creating a highly diverse Hindu community into a vote bank. It was only a matter of time before secular politics capitulated to the weight of majoritarianism.

Thus, insulating democracy from structural faultlines proved to be a double-edged sword. While it saved a young republic from sudden death and disintegration, it also delinked the power of these cleavages from ideas like socialism, social justice, federalism, and secularism, thus paving the way for democracy capture.

The third dimension in the journey of democracy involves entrapment: this is the story of institutions, more specifically the story of the fragility of formal institutions that left democracy vulnerable to a sudden capture. Here, too, we often fail to notice that this failure is premised on a success, the unprecedented rise of a powerful modern state. Ever since independence, India has witnessed a massive expansion in the footprint of the modern state and a steady accretion in state capacity. So, the crisis of democratic institutions is not that modern political institutions failed to take root. Rather, the crisis is that the outer shell got stronger while the inner core of institutions – where the requirement was autonomy – did not; that institutions were only formally erected without being provided the cultural, administrative, and functional bases that could sustain them. Instead of serving any of the real objectives for which they were set up, these institutions turned supinely self-serving and made themselves ripe for mobilisation by self-serving rulers. Seven decades after independence, the country's institutions were simultaneously stronger and weaker than they were when founded. Unlike those of our neighbours, our institutions were stronger in their reach and weight. But they were weaker in their ability to exercise autonomous decision-making and mediation. Large and powerful institutions that enjoyed constitutional protection did not manage to develop the capacity to resist capture by a powerful and rampaging executive. The purely formal façade of a democratic institutional set-up was, in fact, a "set-up": it entrapped Indian democracy.

The weakness of formally democratic institutions of governance shifted a lot of the actual burden of governing to political processes and practices. The institution of the Indian political party has in a very short time been amazingly successful. Parties have become omnipresent, and have come to possess an unprecedented mobilisational capacity. Yet the weakness of institutions has affected these political parties too: they have frequently been hollowed out from within, showing little capacity for egalitarian and non-hierarchical functioning, internal democratic dissent, and the independent processing of claims (chapter 2). Social movements and non-party political formations have moved in to fill the vacuum left by political parties. The hollowness of political parties has also been exploited by organised vested interests, especially crony corporates and capitalists, to capture democratic politics. The institutional edifice of a constitutional liberal democracy has thus been in no position to push back a determined assault on democracy by a powerful and popular leader.

The fourth and final dimension of the journey of democracy is characterised by entropy: this is the story of the thinning and erosion of ideas that went into the making of the democratic enterprise. The success of electoral democracy meant that more and more ordinary people were participating in the business of making political judgements of their own. Rapid strides in formal education, the easy access to instant communication, and the ubiquity of the mass media has equipped vast swathes of the population with information and the self-confidence to arrive at their own judgement. Public opinion has begun to weigh more, as it should in a democracy. At the same time, neither the country's education system nor the media has enhanced people's capacity for informed choices. The mass media, predominantly owned and/or controlled by massive business conglomerates, has seemed more and more vulnerable to majoritarian capture and in a position to sway the growing power of public opinion in directions of its choosing. The social-media revolution has intensified this process by expanding the pool of opinion makers while either diminishing or eliminating any truth filters that existed at all. Under these conditions, a political actor that could capture media could capture democracy as well.

These transformations in the field of ideas were accentuated by a sudden collapse in the elite frame that structured public opinion. Modern Indian political thought provided ideas that nourished Indian democracy: it was an intellectual corpus that supplied concepts and a vocabulary, it suggested frameworks with which to absorb new information, it provided filters to check truth claims. This intellectual pool dried up abruptly after independence. Between the 1960s and 1970s we have experienced what can only be called the sudden death of modern Indian political thought as a living and continuous intellectual tradition. Academic political science is no substitute for this tradition of engaged reflection, disconnected as academia is from ordinary people, their language and culture. So, instead of intense – even if misplaced – ideological debates, we have been left with fragments of political understanding floating around amidst the fossils of twentieth-century ideologies. Unlike the freedom struggle, there is little capacity to adapt Western ideas to our needs or to create new universal ideals of our own, and to connect ideas to political practices. This loss underpins the sheer poverty of political judgement that informs our politics, the lack of political perspective in public policy now, and the debasement of public debate (chapter 6). Ironically, this disfiguration of high ideologies has made possible the disempowerment of people; the proliferation of information has enabled a higher degree of thought control; more vociferous and loud-volume debates have facilitated fewer templates of opinion; and the greater democratisation and expression of public opinion has led India's democratic journey into a cul-de-sac.

The story of India's first republic no doubt demands a more detailed and careful delineation of these four trajectories, of how each has overlapped or crisscrossed with the others, than the sketchy outline offered above. The argument developed here merely suggests an approach to writing the story of democracy capture. More than grasping the past, it is an attempt to get to grips with the present and to develop a sense of the future.

Clearly, now is not the first time Indian democracy has faced the real danger of a democracy capture. It could have been attempted in the mid-1960s, in the aftermath of the Sino-Indian war, or at the death of Nehru and the subsequent severe crisis, including famine. It happened and nearly succeeded during the Emergency, being thwarted largely by Indira Gandhi's self-goal, when her overweening self-confidence and misjudgement about her popularity led to her calling the elections of 1977. Arguably, the intersection of Mandal and Mandir with the sudden collapse of Congress and the economic crisis, all around 1990, offered yet another possibility for democracy capture. But, as so often happens in history, two roads diverged and there was a road not taken. In each of these instances a possibility that existed did not turn into an occurrence. Not that such good fortune worked to the country's advantage. Instead of turning its good luck into enduring solutions through long-term institutional reform, Indian democracy lurched on from one crisis to another. Political reforms were either postponed, or else the very agenda of political reform was captured by anti-democratic rhetoric. This was the context in which an improbable chance was seized upon to mark the end of India's first republic.

V

What is likely to replace the first republic? When? How? Can we still save the republic? What is to be done?

These are the most critical and difficult questions of our time that political sense and political science must confront. They do not admit of a "correct" answer, at least as long as history admits the inescapability of contingency. Let me only, in conclusion, sketch three possible courses that the journey of democracy may take in the near future, without assigning probabilities.

The first route leads to a long Indian summer. We may be witnessing a quick transition from the first "socialist, secular, democratic republic" to a quasi-democratic, firmly majoritarian, and crony-capitalist republic. We could date the inauguration of the second republic to 2014, when the BJP started consolidating its electoral, ideological, and coercive power into a new one-party dominance system. Unlike the famous Congress system of consensus, the new "BJP system" is based on a concentration of power, a sectarian ideology, and the social exclusion of minorities. This second republic need not have a new constitution for as long as the Modi regime can define and redefine the threshold of tolerance for deviations from constitutionally mandated procedures. The constitutional form of parliamentary democracy may remain untinkered with, yet for all practical purposes India could become a Latin American-style presidential democracy where the supreme leader draws power from the people and is answerable only to them. The public could be continuously mobilised to undo the republic.

In such a new dispensation our political system, while retaining the label "democracy", would in practice be describable as "competitive authoritarianism". Elections would be held without fail, but only in order to affirm the supreme leader's popularity. Instead of being one among many episodes in a representative democracy, elections might then become the only available democratic episodes. Any form of political contestation outside the electoral arena – dissent, protests, and human-rights struggle or civil-society activism – would be ruthlessly suppressed. For its survival and popular endorsement, the second republic's ruling dispensation would depend on occasional electoral endorsement, a massive propaganda machine, formal and informal regimentation of the "independent" media, indirect control of the judiciary and other "autonomous" institutions, continuous crusades against "internal enemies", and regular military adventures, especially preceding an election.

India may never formally be declared a Hindu Rashtra. It would be unnecessary, for the second republic is likely to be a non-theocratic majoritarian state with a de facto hierarchy of religious communities. An American style "melting pot" model could be tried in India, with the pot bearing a distinct Hindutva stamp. We are unlikely – or so I hope despite the Delhi riots of February 2020 – to witness large-scale anti-minority pogroms, in part because the regime would like to avoid the international outcry that is bound to follow such violence. In any case, since the need of the day in our second republic would be to reduce the minorities, mainly Muslims and Christians, to the status of second-rung citizens, quotidian put-downs and symbolic violence would suffice. Dalits and adivasis may not face the same kind of onslaught, because the ruling regime in the second republic would be cognizant of the political benefits of accommodating them, at least symbolically. To grind their noses into the dust would in any case seem unnecessary, given a de facto hegemony of upper-caste Hindus. In our New India the politics of social justice would effectively have taken a back seat, with any expression of Dalit or Adivasi upsurge being nipped in the bud or tamed. While the imposition of Hindi on non-Hindi states would be deemed an unnecessary upsetting of the apple cart, cultural homogenisation in all other respects would be the state's agenda. Our second republic may not be quite the Hindu Rashtra of Savarkar's dreams, but as close to its 21st-century version as required and feasible.

And now to consider the second possible route. This would involve a period of uncertainty, a no-man's land between the first and the second republic. It may result from simultaneous movements in both directions, preventing either a firm hegemony or its effective reversal. The counterbalancing could come from various directions. The BJP might keep losing power in the states while continuing its success story at the centre. The regional forces might, belatedly, offer effective resistance to the BJP's political hegemony and its drive for cultural homogenisation. Or the BJP might lose national power in 2024, only to bounce back sooner or later, as Indira Gandhi did quite soon after her defeat in 1977. This might delay the transition to the second republic. Though unlikely, opposition might even come from within. An intense power struggle within the BJP, however inconceivable it seems at the moment, might possibly defer or deter this transition. We cannot rule out another version of this internal challenge: a party other than the BJP might use the template of nationalism and Hindutva, or its milder versions, to defeat the BJP in elections. As a popular advertisement has it, "Impossible is Nothing".

There are other possibilities as well. The balancing might come from a hidden hand outside the electoral-political domain. Attempts to smother diversities could trigger resistance from other social cleavages, such as caste and language, that the regime might find difficult to overlook or polarise to its advantage. Or, while the regime continues to dominate elections and public opinion, its success might be undermined by abject failure with handling the economy. Signs of such failure are in evidence already: an economic slowdown that does not look just cyclical; farm distress triggered by an agrarian crisis and accentuated by climate change; the highest recorded rate of unemployment, and rising inflation. So far, the regime's handling of the economy has been amateurish at best; its attempts with data suppression and impatience with ideologically unaligned economic advisers have, to put it euphemistically, raised eyebrows everywhere. It is possible, therefore, that the large numbers of those at the bottom of the pile will begin to connect their economic distress and absence of hope on the horizon with an incompetent government and punish it. Popular movements could channelise such disaffection. Even as the institutions of democracy keep collapsing, powerful movements might, as they have in the past, fill the vacuum for a time and retrieve some democratic balance. Any or all of these counterweights to the BJP might temporarily halt or slow the hegemonic march of the BJP, but not challenge its fundamentals. For all we know, in real life this might be the most optimistic scenario.

A third route, a mirage for the moment, promises a reversal of hegemony and reclamation of the republic by the public. This route too involves a radical transition: there can be no return to the *ancien regime* represented by parties like the Congress. In this route, the second republic would show a new configuration of power, a renewal of the idea of India, a new social contract. It may be hard to visualise what such a transition might entail, let alone how it can be brought about. The last essay in my book (chapter 15) tries to respond nevertheless to this all-important question: "What is to be done?" The strategy suggested there (in 2017) remains relevant in its broad outlines. The immediate focus should be on mass movements on the economic front, mainly involving distress-affected farmers and unemployed youth. In the medium run, a political reconfiguration involving existing parties and social movements would be needed. In the long run, there can be no escaping the battle of ideas that necessitates a reaffirmation of nationalism, the recovery of pluralist religious traditions, and a reconnection with our languages.

The strategy and the tactics of this third, counter-hegemonic, route need constant fine-tuning. But two lessons are already clear. First, a struggle to rescue Indian democracy cannot be separated either from the battle to save the Indian model of a diverse nation, or from the need to resurrect the promise of an inclusive welfare state. A single point "save democracy" or "save constitution" movement is unlikely to succeed. The political battle has to go hand in hand with struggles in the economic and cultural spheres. And second, the electoral arena may not be central to the historic mission of reclaiming the republic. We are unlikely to witness a repeat of 1977 when an authoritarian ruler quietly stepped down after an electoral defeat. Mass mobilisation and popular resistance outside the electoral arena are going to be prerequisites for any effective reversal of the hegemonic power.

The ongoing anti-CAA movement of 2020 offers a glimmer of what such resistance might look like. It is hard to anticipate how this movement might appear in the mirrors of the future, or even by the time this book is published. It might well turn out to be a short-lived protest of the north-east and the Muslim community. In any case, such a movement is unlikely to become the fulcrum of a counter-hegemonic politics. And yet the dynamics of this movement does have all the elements of what a dramatic turnaround might involve: the outpouring of masses on the street; an outburst of new ideas, slogans, and poems; the sudden fusing of issues and social groups; the evaporation of fear in the face of state repression.

Such hopes appear romantic today. But if democracy is about instituting uncertainty into the heart of public life, there are perhaps no reasons powerful enough to snuff out all hope.

1

The Creolisation of Indian Democracy

Making Sense of National Politics 1947–1997

Two events drew international attention to Indian politics in the year when India officially celebrated the fiftieth anniversary of its Independence from the British empire. The first was the outcome of the twelfth general election to the Lok Sabha, the popular chamber of the Indian Parliament, held in March 1998. For the fourth time in succession, it was a "hung" parliament with no single party securing a majority. But it was clear that the Bharatiya Janata Party (BJP) – usually described to foreign audiences as a party of right-wing Hindu fundamentalists – and its numerous recently acquired regional allies had done better than others. After years of inching towards it, the BJP had finally come to power at the centre. The event was noted even outside India with concern, for it aroused fear that some of the achievements of plural democracy in India would be rolled back. To many, India appeared yet another third world state on the slippery slope of ethnic majoritarian politics.

The second event came soon thereafter. The new and rather shaky BJP government decided to end India's 24-year-old nuclear ambiguity by conducting five nuclear tests in May 1998, declaring that India was a nuclear weapons state, and demanding entry to the exclusive nuclear club. The club was not amused, and a spate of economic sanctions and abuse followed. "Just when you thought the world was safe . . . India's Nukes . . ." proclaimed the cover story of *Time* magazine, depicting India as a rogue state. Friends of India bemoaned the fact that the country had decided to go against the current of history. The fact that the tests enjoyed considerable popular support in the country strengthened doubts about the future of India as a moderate liberal democracy.

These two events were probably not the two most significant landmarks in the history of Indian politics. They were certainly not the events most representative of the larger trends of democratic transition in the 1990s. Yet the logic of short attention spans reserved for countries like India ensures that, for a long time to come, the "global" image of Indian democracy will be formed by the television footage associated with these two events. In the current international information (dis)order, democracies outside the first world are routinely judged by norms drawn from the history and present contingencies of democracies in the West. From its inception, Indian democracy has had to respond to an agenda that bears only a tangential relationship to its inner trajectory and has had to account for its life in a register kept to write someone else's history. A fair assessment of India's democratic experience must, therefore, be anchored in an understanding of the Indian model of democratisation in its specificity. I begin by describing that model. I then map how it fared in what I see as the three phases of India's democratic politics. Finally, I come back to a synoptic assessment of its success, its distortions, its inherent weaknesses, and the challenges that confront it.

The Indian Model

Fifty years ago when India began its journey, it was easier to describe the destination and the route, for the privilege of describing these lay without much contestation with a small section of India's westernised elite. All of them did not think alike, but their differences were not unbounded. There was a significant overlap in the various ideologies and social contexts. The model of Indian democracy was founded on that consensus. Since then, the number of those who wish to participate in the process of defining the Indian model has increased phenomenally, thanks, no doubt, to the success of the processes initiated by the original inheritors of the legacy of the British Raj. Moreover, our awareness of the complexities of mass ideologies and the crooked logic of collective action has rendered the question of the meaning of the Indian model less amenable to a confident answer.

At first sight, the initial design of the Indian democratic enterprise might not look original at all. Many of the attempts to articulate the vision of democracy in an independent India appear to result from a desire to imitate the experience of liberal democracy in the West. The speeches and writings of the nationalist leadership and the debates of the Constituent Assembly are full of fond references to democracies in the West. Indeed, the basic design of the Indian constitution was consciously borrowed from the European and American traditions. The parliamentary system governing the relationship between the executive and the legislature; the federal structure for governing the interaction between the centre and the states; the idea of fundamental rights; an independent judiciary to safeguard those rights; and the constitution itself – it would sound familiar to students of the constitutional history of the West. A large number of the provisions of the constitution retained verbatim the corresponding provisions in the Government of India Act of 1935, the political design set by the colonial rulers.

Yet, the Indian constitution was not a simple imitation of the British model or of any existing constitution, for no attempt at copying can be free of some modification. Elements picked up from various Western models – such as the parliamentary system from Britain, the judicial system and the Bill of Rights from the United States, the Directive Principles from Ireland – were combined in a unique mix. Besides, various specifically Indian elements were introduced by way of "redefinition" of some of the familiar Western ideas and institutions. Community as much as the individual was acknowledged as a basis of citizenship in the affirmative action policies of the state. Secularism was redefined in a specifically Indian manner. These and many other examples demonstrate that creativity in the garb of imitation has been the preferred mode of political innovation in modern India. Right from the beginning, the Indian model of democracy involved selective usage and subtle adaptation of the language of modern liberal democracy.

The constitution, however, was not the main aspect of India's innovative path to democratisation. The essence of that path lies in the unwritten political model that has informed the practice of democracy over the last five decades. The Indian model, as its most shrewd interpreter Rajni Kothari argued in his magnum opus *Politics in India*, involved the *primacy* of the political and a redefinition of the *boundaries* of the political. Politics was not just one of the areas that the Indian elite sought to transform; it was at the heart of India's tryst with modernity. In a bold move that broke from the political models available at that time, the Indian elite chose to pursue multiple goals simultaneously: to make democracy work, to create a single political community in a large and diverse society, to pursue Western-style economic development, and to bring about fundamental changes in society.

They opted for political democracy, more specifically the constitutional-representative-democratic-republican form of government, in a society that lacked any historic precedent of such governance at the scale they confronted. By opting for democracy, they also made themselves subject to radical egalitarian expectations of a political community of equals, a community in which the people were self-ruling. Some of them realised that this was a distant ideal from the form of government they had established.

The second goal was built into the first: the survival of democracy in the face of the amazing diversities that defined India required the creation of a single political community across the recently acquired political boundaries of the Indian state. The lessons of the partition of territory between India and Pakistan were too painful a reminder of the need for what was then called "national integration" and later "nation building". The creation of a modern public sphere required bringing together a huge number of communities that had little to do with each other. The modern public sphere also provided the resources for meeting this requirement.

In the realm of the economy, the Indian elite opted for Western-style development in the hope that the path to development would be open to anyone who cared to step in. They may not have hoped for a miraculous entry into the world of consumer goods for everyone, but they did expect substantial and speedy economic growth in aggregate terms. Their economic goals included a reduction in the historical gap between India and the developed world and a substantial trickle down of the gains of economic growth to the worst-off.

Finally, the Indian elite aimed at bringing about fundamental changes in the structure of the society they had inherited. Even those who did not share the radical desire for the abolition of the traditional social hierarchy and its inequities looked forward to mitigating the worst effects of the caste system. At any rate, the goal of social modernisation that would transform the traditional, "parochial" beliefs of the masses into modern, "cosmopolitan" values was widely shared.

Democracy was not just one of the goals; it was also the principal instrument of realising all the goals simultaneously. The power of a modern state, the mobilising capacity of universal adult franchise, the dynamics of competitive politics, the firm grip of a system of political institutions, and the vision of an enlightened elite were the main elements in the politics-centred approach to modernisation adopted by India. The colonial state had expanded considerably the boundaries of the political and had annexed for politics the crucial privilege of deciding the boundaries of the political. The nationalist movement expanded the political domain further by including within it various social and economic issues that colonial power had avoided. The modern Indian state was to exercise power over this wide arena and bring about the social transformation necessary to the realisation of the fourfold goal mentioned above. Its reach was to be made effective by a wide range of bureaucratic apparatuses, while the constitutional institutions would ensure that the game was played according to the rules. The introduction of the universal adult franchise was meant to draw a hitherto unprecedented number of participants into the game of governance as well as to secure their acceptance of its outcome. Open electoral competition was the dynamo expected to harness the energy of the political actors, while political parties were to channel this energy towards creative political change. The enlightened political elite was supposed to steer the way, keeping its gaze fixed on the larger, if distant, goals.

All this was not spelled out anywhere, at least not in the formal text of the constitution. When we look back from a distance of fifty years, it is easy to read a clear design in what must have been a mix of prudent judgements, half-examined convictions, and sheer hope. The above formulation of the "Indian model" draws heavily upon Kothari's subtle interpretation of the working of democratic politics in the first two decades of Independence. Kothari insisted that the historical trajectory of Indian politics must be assessed against this "model". In arguing that the Indian model should be the starting point of the discussion, he had already parted company with the then dominant mode of thinking about democracy in non-Western societies. Cast in a somewhat simplistic universal framework of modernisation, the dominant approach measured political development by the extent to which a traditional society had come to resemble the political system of the advanced societies of the West. Western democratic theory has changed considerably since then, but the checklist approach to democracy that expects non-European societies to take the same route as the West still persists. To that extent, the approach implicit in Kothari's work still provides a useful starting point for any attempt to assess the experience of the last fifty years.

At least some of the designers of this Indian model were acutely conscious of the fact that they were stepping into uncharted territory, that they were attempting something for which there was no precedent. The Indian elite had already done to the received Western models of democracy what the Indian masses were to do to the elite's own model. By selective adoption and adaptation, they had already begun the creolisation of the idea of democracy, a process that was to have profound historical implications.

The Story of India's Democracy

Establishment of democracy was an invitation by the Indian elite to ordinary Indians to join them in playing a new game. It is true that the invitation must not have come as a surprise to keen observers of nationalist politics in the decades prior to Independence. In opposing British rule, the nationalist leaders drew upon the most progressive strands of modern European thinking. It is no wonder that democracy was an article of faith for them. Besides, the last two decades before Independence were marked by intensification of popular movements that gave rise to expectations of self-rule among the lower orders of society. All this left a very narrow range of options for the Indian elite when it came to choosing the form of government. Yet those options were more than is realised now. Pakistan's choice of what in effect was a viceroy system illustrates the range of options open then. The establishment of democracy in India was undoubtedly a bold invitation, for the rules and the possible consequences of this game were not entirely clear to the elite, and, more important, they did not know the players they had invited to join very well.

The history of Indian politics since Independence is the story of how Indians accepted the invitation and discovered this new game, at first with hesitation and amusement and then with a fierce obsession. It is a history of what this encounter did to them and to the game itself. What happened afterwards is not difficult to understand. After the initial unease, the guests felt at home in their new setting and then changed the rules to suit their taste. For the first few years, everyone felt guilty about demanding that language be the basis of political reorganisation of the federal map of India, but very soon it became an indisputable principle. The invited players now turned their backs on the hosts and started enjoying themselves. The game was different now. It took on a life of its own and was played for purposes substantially at variance with the intentions of the original hosts. Devi Lal, the farmer leader from Haryana and the deputy prime minister during 1989–90, was frank enough to admit in a press conference that he had not read the election manifesto of his party. Although not everyone had read, or even cared about, their party manifesto in the past, decades ago this admission would have been a major political scandal. That this news appeared as no more than a small diary item indicated the sea change in India's political culture. It indicated that the consequences of the game of democracy were turning out to be radically different from what anyone had intended or anticipated, presenting a new set of opportunities and constraints for which there were no well-known precedents in the history of democracy in the West.

It is a comment on the imaginative charms of the original model that Indian politics is still understood as a series of deviations from it and that every deviation is seen as a sign of decline and disorder. This tendency contributes to the predominant way of telling the story of Indian politics. It goes something like this: The first decade and a half were a golden period when a charming prince called Jawaharlal Nehru ruled this country. His rule saw economic growth, rule of law, political institutionalisation, secular policy, and a far-sighted foreign policy. His death in 1964 was followed by a steady and then rapid decline during the reign of his progeny, real and otherwise. The reign of his daughter, Indira Gandhi, was characterised by institutional decay, a growing authoritarian streak, intolerance towards ethnic minorities, and the beginning of an aggressive and narrow foreign policy. Finally, in the third phase, local chieftains and thugs took over, leading to complete chaos and continuous crises. Democratic institutions are in tumult, regional powers have gained at the expense of national parties, and sectional demands and exclusivist politics dominate the political agenda. The rise of the BJP to power, in tandem with the latest series of nuclear explosions, in a sense completes the story of an impending political crisis, of a dream lost.

The storyline is simple but powerful. Like all stories of its kind, it has the power to give meaning to any event, big or small, and to serve as a yardstick that distinguishes normalcy from deviation. Like all stories, it looks at things from one vantage point and whispers a moral in our ears. Thanks to its charms and the English-speaking upper-caste origins of those who publicly articulate ideas about Indian democracy, this narrative continues to dominate the imagination of all political analysts, academic or otherwise. Implicit in this dominant story of Indian democracy, or for that matter in contemporary democratic theory, is what may be called a "hardware" approach to democracy: democracy is above all an institutional mechanism that can be made to work properly in any setting, given the right conditions of installation.

I think the story of Indian democracy can be told differently. In fact, the challenge of understanding India at fifty requires that we tell this story differently. It requires that we treat democracy like a language or a software that cannot even begin to work without the establishment of a firm protocol of shared symbols with its users. If it is to have a life, democracy must exist in and through the minds of ordinary people; it must learn to work its way through the beliefs and values they happen to have. We must change our approach, for the "palace-eye view" of politics has hidden from us for far too long the story of popular opposition to designs imposed from above, of the participatory upsurge of the lower orders of society, and of the less-known attempts to weave dreams of social emancipation in the language of modern democracy. It is crucial to contest the dominant story, for its moral is deeply, if subtly, anti-political.

India's Democratic Politics

The First Phase: The Congress System

The first phase, the famous "Congress system" of the 1950s and 1960s, was characterised by a wide gulf that separated the assumptions of all-powerful westernised elite from popular beliefs. In this period, the Indian National Congress, the party that led the national movement, dominated the political scene: it won all the national and practically all the state-level elections. India was undoubtedly a democracy, for the rulers were being elected by the people in a system of open and fair competition among different political parties. But in the realm of ideas, it hardly respected the democratic principle of equal respect. "Guided democracy" was a euphemism used by leaders like Mohammad Ayub of Pakistan and Sukarno of Indonesia to describe their versions of semi-authoritarian regimes in the post-colonial setting. That, of course, did not apply to the decision-making structure of Indian democracy. But in terms of ideas, Indian democracy was firmly guided in the first phase.

The democratic invitation, which meant an invitation to participate in the new spectacle of elections, was accepted by an ever-growing number. The turnout jumped from 46 per cent in the first general election, in 1952, to 55 per cent in the third election, in 1962, and to 61 per cent in the fourth one, in 1967. The new entrants had begun to defeat the English-speaking inhabitants of the Indian state, with serious political consequences. The idea of "linguistic states" was forced down Nehru's throat in the mid-1950s. Charan Singh, the farmer leader from Uttar Pradesh, successfully defied Nehru's proposal for Soviet-style co-operative farming.

Yet the structure of the game basically followed the rules set by the hosts. There were deviations and distortions. The enquiry against Pratap Singh Kairon, Nehru's favourite chieftain in the Punjab, revealed the extent to which corruption had already been institutionalised. But on balance the game was manageable, or at least recognisable. The first Backward Classes Commission recommended reservations on caste basis, but its chairman Kaka Kalelkar bent over backwards to ensure that its recommendations were not implemented. The matter could be silently buried in the parliamentary records. There was no dearth of political opposition to Congress rule. There were the Socialists and the Communists as well as the right-wing opposition parties. The Communists actually managed to come to power in 1957 in the state of Kerala, which was the first time a Communist party anywhere in the world won a democratic mandate and the first time the central government of India shamelessly dismissed a legitimately elected government in a state. But, barring some followers of Gandhi and of the indigenous socialism advocated by Ram Manohar Lohia, there was little challenge to the vision of democracy shared by India's English-speaking elite.

Nehru's schoolteacher-like mannerisms symbolised the didactic relationship between the political elite and ordinary people in this first phase. If we focus on the flow of ideas, it was clearly a one-way traffic. Ordinary citizens were autonomous in this realm only to the extent to which they misunderstood, deliberately or otherwise, the ideas they received from above – a dubious privilege that the lower orders of society have enjoyed throughout history. From a certain vantage point, it was a fairly satisfactory state of affairs. If you were born in the right kind of family, took care to keep away from the heat and dust of this country, and took a telescopic view of things, Indian democracy could appear very much like an authentic or at least a "developing" liberal democracy.

The insulation of democracy from popular beliefs gave it a certain breathing space, an initial settling-in period for the new set of institutions. The legacy of nationalism meant that the new regime enjoyed a high level of popular legitimacy even if the people did not quite understand what they were supporting. Thanks to these favourable conditions, the modern Indian state not only inherited the powers of the colonial state but could also expand considerably the scope of its activities to cover what was regarded earlier as the private or the societal domain. Rather than being dictated by the relations of production, politics was very much in a position to fundamentally alter property relations. In the first decade after Independence, the Indian government passed a series of land reform laws aimed at changing the pattern of landownership. There already was, to be sure, micro-level collusion of the politically powerful with the dominant economic interests, but there were very few overt macro- or structural-economic limits to politics. Thus the smooth transfer of power in 1947 brought into existence something that appears as an astonishing accomplishment in retrospect. Without much fuss, it signalled the beginning of an era of centrality of politics in the public sphere. It is amazing to see the extraordinary power modern political agencies have come to occupy in a society characterised by the absence of a political centre, where politics was heretofore a limited and self-limiting activity. A future historian might remember these fifty years not for the more noticeable political events but for the creation of the space in which these events took place.

Behind this appearance, however, the content had already begun to change. If one takes cognizance of what the actors thought they were doing, rather than going by an external description of their behaviour, it is clear that a new and unfamiliar life was being infused into the formal structures of liberal democracy. The few field studies of local politics and the fictional accounts available through contemporary literature in the Indian languages provide sufficient proof that patron–client networks and systems of reward distribution were already in place in the first decade after Independence. And what is worse, most of these were based on criteria other than those of which liberal democracy could approve. Competitive politics had already formed linkages with the pre-existing social divisions. Caste acquired a new salience in political mobilisation. This development, initially condemned as casteism in politics but later theorised as the politicisation of caste, was to have enduring effects both on democracy and on the institution of caste.

The fact that the basic building blocks of competitive politics in India are not individuals or groups based on ideas and interests but communities based on birth has been something of a scandal in the eyes of commentators, analysts, and some elite practitioners of Indian politics, irrespective of their ideological preferences. It has been interpreted as the Indian corruption of the ideal of liberal democracy. This sense of shame informs the dominant story of Indian politics. It may not be out of place here to remember that this gap between the self-image and the reality of liberal democracy is not specific to India. A comparison, for example, with the history of democracy in the United States in the nineteenth century shows that this gap lies at the very heart of the practice of liberal democracy. The problem is not that real life has failed to live up to theoretical ideals, but that theory has failed to take into account the nuances of real life. A more sensitive theory would have noticed that this gap may have actually helped the growth of democracy, for its articulation through the pre-existing social divisions helped competitive politics take firm root in society and assume something like an organic growth. A closer look at the interaction between caste and politics would have shown that the basic building blocks were never really the product of "primordial loyalties". Before becoming the basis of politics, units such as caste or community underwent a secular process of packaging in which interest, and to some extent ideology, mattered as much as it did anywhere else.

The workings of the famous "Congress system" in the first phase should be viewed in this context. The one-party-dominance system, in which both governmental and effective oppositional roles were performed by the different factions of the Congress, served as a nursery of the multiparty system. There was very little ideological polarisation, except on the very extremes of the political spectrum, as the Congress occupied a wide range of middle positions through which different interests could be articulated. At the macro level the diverse character of the Congress ensured that its support was evenly spread across different sections of society, a feature mirrored by its major opponents.

The composition of the political elite was heavily biased in favour of the upper caste, the upper class, and the English-educated.

Occasionally, the game threatened to break down, for popular beliefs refused to be tamed, at least on some questions. One such question proved to be that of "linguistic states". The British division of the country into administrative subunits has not respected the natural cultural divisions. At the time of Independence, Indian rulers kept those divisions more or less intact, despite the fact that more than two decades earlier Gandhi had already reorganised the Congress party on the principle of the linguistic state. The resultant resentment formed the basis of the first organised political movement in a large number of states for redrawing the federal units on the basis of language. After initial reluctance based on the typical secular suspicion of such "primordial" sentiments, Nehru conceded the demand by setting up the States Reorganisation Commission and accepting its recommendations in most cases. Skilful political handling routinised and thus rendered harmless the legitimate political expression of regional diversity. As has already been observed, popular self-identities in terms of local communities were also granted back-door entry by all the parties through a process of politicisation of castes.

A combination of good design, skilful execution, and fortune thus ensured that the new democracy did not create alienation or face deep-seated hostility from those sections of the population whose beliefs did not find much play in the system. It is true that these sections were not very active in the first phase of electoral politics. Consequently, the first two – in some cases the first three – elections witnessed a relatively low level of popular participation and competitiveness. But this actually helped the structure of competitive politics take root and thus contributed to early institutionalisation. The electoral system, party organisations, legislatures, the judiciary, and the bureaucracy got a grace period in which their capacities were not subjected to the strenuous test of popular democracy.

The Nehruvian phase of Indian democracy is widely seen, and rightly so, as a period of consolidation. The achievements of this phase, and of Nehru in giving a long-term institutional base to democracy in a fragile moment, must not be undervalued. But it must be remembered that these achievements were made possible by a discursive chasm between the elite and the masses. Such a reminder is necessary, for a loudly proclaimed nostalgia for Nehruvian democracy is a common refrain in Indian politics. Often this desire to recreate Nehru's India reflects a longing for an infinite extension of the time when politics was not spoiled by the entry of commoners. It barely conceals a desire to save democracy from the people.

The Second Phase: The Coming of Age

The second phase of Indian democracy can be said to have begun with the fourth general election held in the year 1967. In this election, the monopoly of the Congress party's power was broken for the first time. In an election marked by higher turnout and intense participation of the "backward" communities, the Congress was voted out in many states, although it managed to retain a thin majority at the centre. Congress stalwarts like Kamaraj and S.K. Patil lost elections. The Congress party was not finished – its reincarnation was to win an unprecedented majority in the next election – but the Congress system came to an end. It was also the culmination of a series of political developments – the Kamaraj Plan to shift some of the Congress heavyweights to organisational work, the rise of the "syndicate" of regional bosses and the beginnings of "backward class" politics in the south – that brought about a qualitative change in the chemistry of power.

A weaker candidate for the beginning of the second phase is 1969, the year in which the Congress faced its first major split. The legislative wing, under the leadership of the prime minister Indira Gandhi, broke from the organisational wing that was led by many regional stalwarts. It was also the year of the beginning of the Naxalite movement, the extreme left-wing protest movement that was to attract a new generation of radical youth and address itself to the question of inequality of landownership. Alternatively, the break was in the year 1971, when Indira Gandhi scored a decisive electoral victory on the plank of poverty removal. It was the first of the four "wave" elections, in which one party swept the polls with the help of a massive swing of votes cutting across various states, that changed the electoral geography of India. But none of this created the kind of world-turned-upside-down feeling that was generated by the results of the 1967 elections.

Whatever the exact cut-off point, it is clear that after about two decades of the initial phase of installation and incubation, the nature and the character of Indian democracy changed significantly. This second phase of Indian democracy is recalled as signalling the failure of the system, as the beginning of its regrettable decline. Yet, it is at least equally plausible to read this phase as the natural outcome of the first phase of successful installation and consolidation. It marked the coming of age of Indian democracy. The infant was now taken out of the incubator and placed into the more natural though also more risky environment. Far from being a result of the failure of the system, it was a direct consequence of the extraordinary success of democratic politics in drawing new sections of the population into the political arena.

As more and more participants came to see the game as their own, they brought their own expectations, demands, and beliefs. At least some of the sections hitherto excluded from centres of power thought it was time they had a say in framing the rules of the game. The most notable group among these were the peasant-proprietors belonging to the middle castes, well below the "twice-born" (*dwija*) castes but distinctly above the ex-Untouchables. Traditionally involved in agriculture and handicrafts, this group of castes had lagged behind the upper castes in education and other dimensions of the modern public sphere. They were, however, the first ones to take advantage of the opening offered by democratic politics. Benefiting from their relatively secure economic background, these castes staked their claim to political power. This phenomenon took the form of new political parties like the Bharatiya Kranti Dal in Uttar Pradesh, the Dravida Munnetra Kazhagam (DMK) in Tamil Nadu, and the Vishal Haryana Party in Haryana. In most cases, their rise was facilitated by the major parties. The Congress itself acted as the agent of mobility of the "backward castes" in southern states like Karnataka and Kerala, while the reluctance of the Congress to play that role in the north meant that the Socialist parties, especially the Samyukta Socialist Party (SSP), led the entry of the "backward" into mainstream politics.

This second phase was marked by the beginning of an interaction between elite ideologies and popular belief systems. As political competition grew more intense, political actors were forced to pay attention to the tastes and preferences of ordinary voters: Charan Singh blew a hole in the ideology of industrialised development by exposing the neglect of the agrarian sector in particular and rural India in general. The Socialists in the north and parties like the DMK in the south made the empowerment of "backward castes" the leading plank in their critique of the Congress. The Naxalites, and then the youth movements in Gujarat and Bihar, gave expression to the frustration of the new generation. The grace period was over, and generalised pleas for hope in an incomprehensible ideological language were simply insufficient.

The first casualty of the new compulsions of the political market was the edifice of borrowed high ideologies for both the government and the opposition. These had to be quietly and quickly replaced by homespun, or rather homemade, patchwork ideologies. Gandhi replaced Nehruvian socialism with the more attractive if vacuous slogan of "Garibi Hatao" or "Get rid of poverty". Highly visible policy initiatives like the nationalisation of all the major private banks as well as of the coal industry, and the abolition of the "privy purse" of ex-princely families, accompanied the new rhetoric. The Socialist parties translated their ideology in terms of social justice to the lower castes. The Jan Sangh, the parent party of the present-day BJP, moved towards the middle position and formally adopted "Gandhian socialism" as its ideological self-description by the time of its reincarnation in 1980. The Communists stuck to a pure ideology but paid the price in terms of their political containment. The Swatantra Party, the party of the political right in the pure sense, also failed to innovate and simply disappeared.

The overall impact on the ideological map was admittedly shabby: stitched in haste by tailors of varying skills, the new clothes did not quite fit the customer. English-speaking analysts and pure ideologues interpreted these developments as the decline or demise of ideology in politics. Yet a paradigmatic change had taken place. Everyone, save the die-hard ideological purists, came to recognise that the clothes must fit the customer, and not the other way round. Indeed, much of the political innovation was taking place through the back door, in response to the "regrettable compulsions of practical politics". None of the innovators had the audacity to call the innovation by name; usually the tendency was to dissimulate, to deny that these changes were at all significant.

The immediate result of this paradigmatic shift was the rise of populism as the dominant political ideology. The label needs to be understood carefully, for it has become an abused word in commentaries on Indian politics. Populism is equated with political irresponsibility, with short-sighted measures meant to appease the people without really helping them. As such, it has come to be seen as pure evil and a sign of ideological corruption. Such a reading fails to understand the role of these non-standard ideological packages in the process of democratisation. Populist ideologies bridged the gap between popular aspirations and the language of high ideology without formally displacing the latter from its dominant position. Gandhi's ideology of "Garibi Hatao", the Janata Party's redistributive policies, Charan Singh's demand for remunerative prices for agricultural products, N.T. Rama Rao's policy of supplying cheap rice and saris to the poor, and Devi Lal's decision to waive farmers' outstanding loans all illustrate various versions of populism. Not many of these schemes proved successful, and indeed the motives behind them were far from noble. Yet these "corrupt" versions made the language of democracy accessible to the newly enfranchised and reduced the yawning gap between the theory and the practice of politics. At the same time, populist ideology did not necessarily reflect popular beliefs, let alone rework high ideology in light of popular aspirations and needs. At this stage, it was not easy for ideas to travel from the bottom upward.

The Indian version of populism involved a selective appropriation of the language of socialism, which had been incorporated in the political mainstream following the official adoption in 1956 by the Congress of the "socialist pattern of society" as its goal. Socialist symbols and rhetoric served to package substantive policies that had little to do with either pure socialist doctrine or an egalitarian agenda. If anything, mainstream politics grew less sensitive to the real needs of the people, at least to those needs that did not lend themselves to easy aggregation. Yet, insofar as rhetoric tends to restrict the actors, the language of socialism set limits to what could be defended and legitimately argued in the political arena. First used to reap electoral harvest in 1971, populism continued to be the reigning ideology of Indian politics until the end of the 1980s. Different political brands were worked out by recombining familiar elements under the socialist label.

Elections were now about whose claim to offer the same menu was found more credible by a nationwide electorate. This changed the character of elections. In the first phase, elections had been about electing a representative. The sum total of the local verdicts constituted the national verdict. But beginning with 1971, elections became something like plebiscites. The entire country was addressed as a single audience and was asked to give its verdict on a single issue. And they responded in the same spirit by voting for their Member of Parliament as if they were directly electing the prime minister. A regionally fragmented electorate gave way to a national electorate, whose swinging moods could cause a more or less uniform swing of votes across the country (or at least across the "Hindi heartland"), resulting in massive electoral waves from 1971 to 1984. It was not impossible to defeat the Congress, yet it continued to be the reference point around which other parties competed.

The picture at the state level looked somewhat different: the Congress was displaced from the ruling position in 1967 in most of the North Indian states. The party or, as in most cases, the coalition of parties that replaced it varied in their social base and ideological persuasion as well as in the duration for which they could replace the Congress. In most states the Congress came back to power by 1972, and its local fortunes fluctuated with the national fate of the Congress. But in the South Indian state of Tamil Nadu, the Congress had been reduced to a third force in the 1970s. In Bihar, the second-most populous Hindi-speaking state, the Congress returned to power but never regained the social base it had lost in the late 1960s. In West

Bengal, it lost power to the Communist parties in 1977 and has yet to reclaim it. The defeat of the Congress in the 1983 state assembly elections in Andhra Pradesh and Karnataka, its two remaining bastions in the South, completed the circle. By then, Maharashtra was the sole major state of the Indian Union where the Congress had not been ousted from power at least once. The rise of regional political parties like the Asom Gana Parishad and the Telugu Desam foreshadowed the political developments of the 1990s.

If the party system in the first phase was called the "Congress system", the second phase should be described as the Congress-opposition system. The Congress was still the only political party with a truly all-India spread. Yet it could not take electoral victories for granted. Ranged against it were a number of political parties with different ideologies and varying levels of political support: the ever splitting and reuniting versions of the Janata family of parties, mainly in the North; the right-wing BJP, the reincarnation of the Jan Sangh, moving from its traditional base in the North to the West; the two Communist parties, which were effectively contained by then to the three states of West Bengal, Kerala, and Tripura; and the regional parties. Political competition was organized along Congress versus non-Congress lines. Occasionally, all the non-Congress parties – routinely referred to as "the opposition" even when in power – would come together to defeat the Congress, as they did in 1977 and 1989. The system of one-party dominance in the first phase had by then given way to a system of one-party salience.

The Congress itself had been reinvented by Indira Gandhi following its split. The coalition of social forces that formed its support base was also reconstituted. It retained its capacity for cross-sectional mobilisation, but its support was no longer randomly scattered across all social groups: its core was now constituted by a rainbow coalition. It was a rainbow with thick edges: groups on the margins of society tended to vote for the Congress much more than anyone else. These included the dalits, or the 15–16 per cent of the population made up of ex-Untouchables at the bottom of the Hindu social hierarchy; the adivasis, or tribals, who lived outside the pale of the Hindu social order and made up 8 per cent of the population; and the minorities, mainly the 12 per cent of the population who were Muslim. The reinvention of the Congress and the occasional electoral success of the opposition resulted in a rapid turnover of the political elite and some enduring changes in the social composition of the political elite. Leaders from a non-upper-caste background had their first taste of power, especially in the South and the West. Their entry into the centres of political power accelerated the process of cultural encounter set in motion by the introduction of universal adult franchise.

This first encounter of Indian democracy with popular beliefs left it simultaneously deeper and weaker. It helped Indian democracy take root. Greater participation and more intense politicisation showed that the process of democratisation was continuing and that the system of representative democracy had greater acceptance among the people than was imagined at the beginning of India's democratic career. Repeated, almost ritual, alteration of government gave the people a sense of control and contributed to their sense of political efficacy. The social constituency of politics was considerably widened in the South as political power passed from the hands of the "twice-born" to the peasant-proprietors. The rise of the dominant Other Backward Classes (OBCs) in the South had some impact in the northern states of Uttar Pradesh and Bihar and in the western state of Gujarat. Although the tide was yet to turn in these states, an inexorable process of downward percolation of power had been set in motion.

This period also showed the weakness of political institutions exemplified in the Emergency. In some ways, it was a part of the larger crisis of political institutions. In this phase, the logic of imported liberal democratic institutions clashed with the cultural codes embedded in the everyday practice of Indian public life. Consequently, there began a process of erosion of political institutions, especially those that required functional autonomy. The Emergency was by no means the necessary outcome of this erosion, but it was surely one of the possible outcomes.

June 1975 was politically the most insecure moment for an inherently insecure person like Indira Gandhi, then prime minister. She used the internal emergency provisions of the Indian constitution to turn her personal crisis into a national emergency and suspended the basic human and political rights of citizens. The following nineteen months showed how fragile the institutional edifice was. Political opposition was silenced more easily than Gandhi may have thought. There were unmistakable elements of fascism as Gandhi's son became an unconstitutional centre of power, leading illegal demolitions of slums and campaigns of forced sterilisation. The civil services and the judiciary caved in even more willingly as there was considerable talk of the "committed" bureaucracy and judiciary. The record of the press and intelligentsia was far from heroic, notwithstanding later reconstructions. There were, of course, honourable exceptions in each of these categories. And yet, what brought India out of that phase was not heroism but something that must be described as the spirit of democracy. Something of that spirit continued to give Gandhi a bad conscience and ultimately forced her to call for general elections in 1977. It was the same spirit that translated into the loss of popular legitimacy of her regime, at least in the North, the epicentre of authoritarian excess.

The results of the Lok Sabha elections of March 1977 were astonishing, even for those who had hoped and worked for Gandhi's defeat. Her party was defeated in all but 2 out of the 226 parliamentary seats in the North Indian "Hindi heartland". The first non-Congress government came to power at the centre led by the Janata Party, a hastily put together combination of all the major non-Congress parties. In a limited respect, the Emergency demonstrated that Indian democracy had developed self-corrective mechanisms and could invent new anchors for itself in times of crisis.

Two decades of plebiscitary politics had considerably weakened the local character of democracy, encouraging the need to articulate issues that did not and could not find expression in mainstream politics. Since the fate of the representative did not depend on what he did or did not do, there was very little incentive to raise local demands at the centre. Besides, the organisational capacity of political parties shrank as leaders like Gandhi established direct relationships with the people, sometimes deliberately undermining their own parties. Governance became more remote than ever. Although the governments came to power with hitherto unprecedented majorities, they soon lost popular confidence. The failure of socialist rhetoric to deliver the goods also contributed to a deeply felt popular frustration. The gap between the people and the centres of power was filled by protest movements such as the Marxist–Leninist Naxalbari movement and the agitation by students in Gujarat and Bihar for a corruption-free public life. A large number of non-party political formations and some parties with a movement character like the Janata Party in 1977 or V.P. Singh's Janata Dal in 1989 filled a crucial gap in influencing the political agenda of the mainstream at a time when it was growing insensitive to popular demands.

If this phase led to the creation of a national political community, it also squeezed out some of the claims to power based on regional and ethnic diversity. The insensitive handling of two such claims in the states of Assam and the Punjab led to prolonged political crises. In Assam, a student movement protested against massive illegal migration into the state that threatened their culture and livelihood. In the Punjab, a movement for a part-regional, part-religious charter of demands nearly turned into a civil war in response to Operation Blue Star, an attack by the armed forces on the Golden Temple, the highest religious shrine of the Sikhs, in 1983. This was followed by the large-scale massacre of the minority Sikh population in 1984 in which the culprits were believed to have been shielded by the central government. The rise of regional parties restored something of the voice of diversity as well as faith in the self-correcting mechanisms of democracy.

By the mid-1980s, the stage was set for another political transition. However, Indira Gandhi's assassination in 1984 and the following general election blocked the natural flow of political events and postponed the arrival of the next phase by five years. For all its problems and weaknesses, the second phase had established that the people could not be kept out of the democratic process.

The Third Phase: Mandal, Mandir, and Market

The third and ongoing phase of democratic politics began somewhere around the turn of the decade with the almost simultaneous arrival of the three Ms on the domestic horizon and the collapse of the Soviet

Union, which silently but very effectively signalled the demise of the hegemony of the language of socialism in Indian politics.

The three Ms stood for Mandal, Mandir, and Market. Mandal was the chairman of the governmental commission formed in 1980 that recommended reservation of government jobs for OBCs to improve their social and educational conditions. In 1990 when the recommendations of the commission were suddenly implemented by the Janata Dal government, Mandal came to refer to the entire phenomenon of the OBC self-assertion movement. Mandir (temple) refers to the Hindu fundamentalist movement supported by the BJP in favour of the claim that the Babri mosque situated in the holy city of Ayodhya was actually occupying the site of a temple of Lord Rama. The movement culminated in the demolition of the Babri mosque by Hindu fundamentalists in December 1992. The third M, Market, stands for the policy of economic liberalisation and integration into the global economic regime. Now controlled by the World Trade Organization, that policy was sprung on unsuspecting Indians in 1991 by Manmohan Singh, then finance minister of a minority Congress government. After four decades of following a "socialist" path, admittedly with rapidly diminishing enthusiasm and almost no conviction, policymakers decided to make a U-turn without even forewarning the electors, let alone seeking a popular mandate on this question.

It can be argued that these changes were not as sudden as they appear. The first two years of Rajiv Gandhi's premiership signalled some of the changes. The first two budgets – presented, ironically, by V.P. Singh – gave the first indications of the economic "reforms" of the 1990s. It is also true that the beginnings of the three Ms had been present since the first phase: the assertion of the OBCs began in the southern states in the 1960s; the Hindu fundamentalist campaign against cow slaughter took place in 1966; and, in 1974, the government had to reverse its decision to nationalise the wholesale trade in wheat. Yet it was only in the 1990s that these tendencies came to dominate the political agenda nationwide.

What followed was a fundamental change in the terms of political discourse. Some of the changes in the ideology of the Communist parties, indisputably the purist practitioners of high ideology, illustrate the extent to which the terms of discourse had changed. Following the Mandal agitation, after decades of holding on to a doctrinaire belief in class, the Communist Party of India (CPI) accepted the reality of caste as a marker of social inequality in Indian society. Both of the Communist parties thought it necessary to turn to progressive elements within the Hindu religion to counter the BJP's position on the Mandir issue. Like all other state governments, irrespective of their stated ideology, the Left Front government in West Bengal actively pursued the policy of attracting foreign investment to promote industrial growth in the state. Other parties also made quick, if silent, amendments to their ideological postures. Notwithstanding its loud proclamations about nationalist economic policy, the BJP stuck faithfully to the economic agenda of the Congress. Despite fanning agitation against it, the BJP also officially accepted the Mandal report and has since made all possible efforts to accommodate the OBC upsurge within its organisation. Belatedly, the Congress also accepted Mandal; even the almighty Sonia Gandhi was forced to concede to the demands of the party's OBC MPs on the Women's Reservation Bill. The silence and inaction of the Congress government following the demolition of the Babri mosque also illustrated the attempt by the party to slip away from its established secular position. Within less than a decade, what are considered the norms of acceptable behaviour in the public arena have undergone a basic change.

These dramatic changes do not, however, rupture our story of the encounter of the language of democracy with popular imagination. The third phase takes this encounter a step further. The sudden ideological unsettling has created a context in which, for the first time, ideas from the lower orders can leave their imprint on high ideology. The removal of the token supremacy of socialism had both a liberating and a debilitating effect on democratic debate. Some of the new beliefs that have come into play in this phase are from the lower orders of society and articulate interests that could not be articulated under the previous ideological hegemony. This development liberated those like Kanshi Ram, the supremo of the Bahujan Samaj Party, a party mainly of dalits; or Laloo Yadav, a charismatic and controversial OBC leader from Bihar, from having to pack their sectional demands in the language of high ideology that had hitherto weighed against them.

It also made possible a reconfiguration of the "third force" to allow for a coalition of regional parties with the Left, something their fundamental ideological differences would not have allowed in the past.

This rising of ideas from the lower orders does not apply across the ideological dimensions. The New Economic Policy, with its ideology of privatisation and free trade, is by no means an influence from below. The price paid for the influence of the lower orders on the political discourse was the shrinking of the agenda itself. Economic policy no longer figures on the menu of political choices. Major economic decisions are now in the technical domain for experts to settle. Something of the extraordinary autonomy that politics had enjoyed since Independence has already been eroded in the current phase.

If the second phase had turned the ordinary voter into a customer whose tastes had to be taken into account by political entrepreneurs, the third phase has turned them into demanding and often discerning customers. In that sense, there is, for the first time, a two-way traffic in ideas. It is not surprising that a democratic upsurge is also taking place among hitherto disempowered sections. In this context, it is worth noting some of the findings of the two wide-ranging and representative national surveys of the Indian electorate conducted by the Centre for the Study of Developing Societies during the 1996 and 1998 general elections. The surveys report a dramatic upsurge in all forms in political participation, from voting to membership, in political parties among the dalits. There is the beginning of change among the adivasis, too, for their turnout recorded a sudden jump in the 1996 election, although a similar change is not evident in their other activities. For women, the increase in participation has affected all levels except voter turnout, which recorded only a marginal improvement in 1998. These are meaningful statistics. Also significant is that India is perhaps the only major democracy in the world where turnout and political activism are higher among the very poor than among the upper middle class. These are surely instances of participatory upsurge associated with the journey of the idea of democracy.

This radicalisation of the encounter of ideas does not, by itself, produce a radical agenda of politics. The erosion of the established language of high ideology and the inability to replace it with a homespun alternative have deprived political formations of the lower orders of any aggregating or screening ideological device. The beliefs brought to the centre of politics by the rise of the lower orders (especially the dalits and the OBCs) are often fragmentary in character, concerned with only one section and with a single issue. The Samajwadi Party (SP) and the Rashtriya Janata Dal, the two political expressions of the OBC upsurge, have not been able to evolve an agenda or an identity that speaks for all the OBCs. More often than not, these are seen as parties that look after the interests only of the Yadavs (agrarian caste). No wonder the SP reserves its fury not for the Congress or any other party of the upper caste but for the BSP, the party of the dalits.

The BSP's slogan, "*Vote hamara raj tumhara nahin chalega*" (Our vote and your rule no more), captures the evocative power and the narrow vision of these ideologies. On the one hand, it holds out the promise of liberation by asserting the democratic right to self-rule. At the same time, the "our" and "your" in this equation are defined in strictly sectional terms. "My rule" in this context means no more than the rule of those born in my community. Thinly wrapped in the language of liberal democracy, these sectional claims do not even attempt the task of ideological mediation of competing sectional claims, let alone provide an integrated vision for the polity. Although the BSP seeks to establish the rule of the bahujan, the majority, it has never attempted to reconcile the claims of the dalits with those of other victims of the caste system, the OBCs, or other oppressed groups such as the adivasis. What was achieved in the previous phases through mediation and accommodation within various parties is now attempted through political coalition among different parties by stapling together the different ideological fragments belonging to each. Thus, the mediation of the dalit and OBC claims takes place through the temporary and inherently fragile alliance between the BSP and the SP.

Politics in this phase represents the fuller working out of the logic of universal adult franchise. Electoral politics has now become the central arena of democratisation. It is marked by greater politicisation and higher participation, especially in the state- and local-level elections, of the lower orders of society. The urban upper middle classes have obviously not shared the participatory enthusiasm. While the political system continues to enjoy fairly high legitimacy, the legitimacy of the political agencies and actors has suffered a decline. If the second phase was accompanied by the first democratic upsurge, what we have seen in the last few years is best described as the second democratic upsurge.

The most noticed political development in this period has been the dramatic rise of the BJP to power. Facing the first general election after its rebirth, the party had managed to send only two MPs to the Lok Sabha in 1984. The number rose to 80 in the next election, in 1989, as the BJP rode piggyback on the success of the newly formed Janata Dal. The breakup with the Janata Dal only helped it further as the figure rose to 121 in 1991 in the wake of Mandal and Mandir. In the next election, in 1996, the BJP emerged as the single largest party in a fractured parliament, with 160 MPs. It accepted the presidential invitation to form the government but could not sustain the experiment beyond thirteen days; the United Front formed a new government that lasted eighteen months with outside support from the Congress. The BJP's long wait came to an end in the 1998 midterm poll, when it raised its strength to 180 MPs and surpassed 250 MPs if one included its regional allies.

Although the BJP has come to power, it has yet to win a popular mandate. With 25 per cent of the popular vote, it is technically the second largest party, just behind the Congress in the 1998 election. More importantly, the BJP has yet to fully overcome the three barriers that have historically blocked its bid for power. It is beginning to surmount the geographical barrier: it is unable to go beyond the North and the West, but much of its newly acquired vote in the South and the East is on loan from its allies, including the All India Anna Dravida Munnetra Kazhagam in Tamil Nadu, the Biju Janata Dal in Orissa, and the Trinamool Congress in West Bengal. The ideological barrier – its isolation from the mainstream – has also been partially overcome, thanks to its allies such as the Samata Party and the fact that the middle position itself has shifted towards the BJP in the last decade. The most important barrier that it still needs to cross is the social barrier – its inability to change its profile as a party of the socially privileged. The findings of the National Election Study in 1998 show that although support for the BJP has become broader than before, it is far from acquiring the kind of widespread support the Congress enjoyed in the past. The BJP continues to be the darling of upper-caste Hindus and the urban "middle classes", although it has also succeeded in getting a substantial vote from the OBCs. It still lags behind among the dalits and the adivasis. Despite marginal improvement in this respect, it has not even begun to win the confidence of the Muslims.

While the BJP has made a difference to the character of Indian politics, no less significant is the effect Indian politics has had on the BJP. The competition for power between the "forward" and the "backward" castes is as intense in the BJP as in any other party. While it succeeded in carrying out its hawkish line on the nuclear tests, it should be remembered that its enthusiasm for the tests was shared by every major political party in the last two decades. The bomb should not draw our attention away from the fact that in framing the National Agenda for Governance, the BJP had to give up various items of its aggressive agenda of cultural homogenisation in deference to the wishes of its regional allies. The party relinquished its demands for construction of a Ram temple at Ayodhya, withdrawal of the special status of Kashmir, and introduction of a uniform civil code.

The BJP's rise should be viewed as a part of the larger reconfiguration of the party political space. Although it may not be correct to speak of a realigning election in the Indian context – for there was no stable alignment to begin with – the changes brought about by elections from 1989 to 1998 show many similar features. Step by step, these elections have brought to an end the salience of one-party rule. At the national level, India seems to be moving towards a multiparty system. The Congress has been losing popular votes in every election since 1984 and is now just one among many parties. The decline of the Congress, or the move towards a post-Congress polity, is accompanied by a fresh outlining of the relationship between social divisions and political loyalties. If the Congress dominance in the first two phases was characterised by a rainbow coalition of social communities, its decline in the third phase has meant that the various stripes of the rainbow are coming apart. While the Congress has held on to a shrinking but more or less evenly spread rainbow, its major competitors are rather skewed in their social support. It is as if everyone is running away with a piece of the old rainbow. Even the Congress does not have the same social profile in all regions of the country. Wherever it faces the BJP, the Congress is a party of the lower segments of society. But in states like West Bengal and Kerala where it is pitted against the Communists, it is a party of the privileged. For the first time since Independence, political parties are developing macro-level identification with various communities. This is accompanied by a widening of the social base of political elites. The much-delayed transfer of political power to the OBCs has started taking place in northern India.

This national picture does not tell very much about perhaps the most salient aspect of the emerging political reality of the 1990s, namely, the decoupling of the national political arena from that of state politics. Throughout the 1970s and 1980s, state politics was often no more than a reflection of developments at the national level. Citizens voted in the state assembly elections as if they were electing their prime minister. Now the logic has almost reversed. Not only is the state arena largely free of the influence of national developments, but people now vote in the national election as if they are electing their chief minister. The emergence of state or region as the effective level of political decision making has changed the party system. While the national picture appears as if there is a multiparty system, a look at the state level shows the effective emergence of a two-party system. The emerging party system is best described as a system of multiple bipolarities. Practically every state is moving towards a bipolar political competition, but the pairs differ from state to state, thus creating the impression of a multiparty system.

It will take more time – yet another election, or perhaps even more than one – for the emerging picture of this latest phase of democratic politics to clarify. If the current coalition woes of the BJP continue unabated, the party may be forced to go for the next election very soon. However, one of the trends is already fairly significant and might, in retrospect, appear to be the defining characteristic of this phase. This is the erosion of the autonomy of politics, driven by economic globalisation and the sharpening of ethnic divisions. This process is most evident in the case of economic liberalisation. It has now been seven years since the economic policy took a U-turn, without any mention of such a change in the election manifesto or the campaign or any evidence of popular support for it either before or after its introduction. Since then India has seen two general elections and three new prime ministers. But there has been no serious political debate about these new policies. The same set of bureaucrats, all trained with the World Bank, continue to take all the important economic decisions with only cosmetic changes or occasional intervention by the political rulers. In the long run, however, this is bound to affect the quality of democracy. As the second democratic upsurge brings the hitherto disempowered into positions of state power, they might discover that history has cheated them once again, that there is little they can do with state power. This is perhaps the deepest irony in the story of the journey of the idea of democracy.

India's Established Democracy

Let me now leave this story and turn to an audit of the working of democratic politics in the last fifty years. Here one needs to distinguish between two different questions: Has India succeeded in establishing a democracy? And, has Indian democracy succeeded in achieving its goals? While the first is a question about what democracy is, the second is about what democracy does, or can be expected to do.

The first question allows a more cheerful answer, if only because of the sad record of most other post-colonial polities of which this question reminds us. Going by the baseline definitions of procedural democracy, India is, and is likely to remain so in the foreseeable future, a democracy. In other words, democracy has come to be "the only game in town". And that, as students of comparative democratisation never forget to remind us, is no mean achievement. This is recognised across the political spectrum in India, even by the system's harshest critics. A few years ago, when the CPI (Marxist Leninist) came above ground after years of underground violent anti-system politics and decided to contest elections, they were unwittingly paying a big compliment to Indian democracy.

To say that India is a democracy is not merely to make a statement about the formal constitutional structures of democratic governance that India has retained. More important, it is a statement about the presence of the language of democracy in India. India has, to use Shiv Visvanathan's memorable phrase, "by-hearted" democracy: this characteristically Indian English expression captures well how Indians have creolised the idea of democracy. They have accepted the Western idea of democracy as their own and then proceeded to take liberties with it as one does with one's own possessions. As a result, the idea of democracy has been localised and routinised. Note, for example, the frequency with which the virtually unlimited franchise election is used in settings that do not require it: from academic councils of universities, to managing committees of colleges, to the chairmanship of cooperative banks, to sports selection committees. The election has come to be the principal mode of settling competing claims to power in the entire public arena. Or witness the ubiquity of protest culture, from matters significant to trivial: collective public protest is an ever-present reminder of the belief in democratic rights. In its Indian version, the idea has come to shape ordinary Indians' beliefs about citizenship, their political rights, and the virtues of political participation. The idea of democracy has, above all, come to supply the only valid criterion for claims to legitimate rule and, correspondingly, the moral basis of political obligation.

The idea is embodied in political processes, which have on balance retained a certain dynamism, at least up to this point. The fundamental trend towards greater participation and more intense politicisation has continued to spread the idea of democracy both vertically and horizontally (except in the state of Jammu and Kashmir and some parts of the North-east). Competitive politics has retained its dynamic capacity to attract hitherto non-political segments, articulate cleavages, and build bridges. Thanks to its capacity to connect itself to pre-existing social cleavages and transform them, democracy has taken root in Indian society.

The idea of democracy also has powerful and reliable carriers by now. India has a wider pool for the recruitment of political elites than do most post-colonial polities. A rough estimate suggests that the number of elected political representatives, from the national to the village level, is no less than three million. Consequently, there is a large contingent of political actors (at least ten million including representatives, rivals, hopefuls, and "also-rans") whose instinct for self-preservation can be relied upon in defence of democracy. The logic of competitive politics has ensured that these active participants do not come only from within the traditional social elite, although this elite continues to enjoy a larger-than-proportionate share. Indeed, the number of registered political parties – 166 contested in the 1998 general election – is large, although their dynamic capacity and legitimacy has weakened somewhat over the last two decades. The idea of party is no longer a Western import; it has merged into the landscape of every village and found its way into practically every Indian language. Last but not least, there are the movement groups, non-party political formations, and various other organisations of civil society including many NGOs that have done much to deepen the idea of democracy in India. They have taken up causes that do not lend themselves to easy aggregation, demands of groups that are electorally non-viable, and issues that have yet to make their mark on the national political agenda. They have kept the spirit of democracy alive when the machinery of competitive politics has failed to nourish it.

Lest this description make democracy look more secure a possession than it actually is, let me also recall the aspects that cause concern for the future of democracy in the procedural sense, even if there is no immediate or imminent danger of its collapse. The formal institutional apparatus of Indian democracy has never been very strong; the institutions of liberal democracy did not undergo the kind of "by-hearting" that the idea of democracy did. It is true that these institutions are still stronger than their counterparts in other post-colonial polities, but they are not the strongest links in the democratic chain, and the very process of democratisation is weakening them further. Claims that cannot be processed in the electoral arena have not found anything close to adequate attention. The judicial apparatus has never been ready to take on the load of litigation thrust upon it. Notwithstanding the recent activism of upper levels of the judiciary, the judicial apparatus has become less effective over the years. The civil service has been politicised since colonial times. Democratisation has made it more politicised without the corresponding benefits of accountability, for the bureaucracy has still to outgrow its colonial legacy. The combined effect of these maladies is the denial of an effective rule of law to ordinary citizens.

Intermediary political institutions that were to act as a link between the people and the centres of power have declined considerably. The near-collapse of democratic procedures within political parties has left a major void that, of late, has been filled by managerial-style politics and criminalisation. The very autonomy of the political process, which lies at the heart of India's path to democratisation, faces encroachment as a result of the instrumental linkage of political power with the dominant economic interests and as a result of the structural limits created by the recent globalisation of the Indian economy. All these are not signs of the impending demise of democracy, as many radical democrats would have us believe. But if these trends continue to grow without adequate counter from within the political process, we could be moving slowly towards a "low-intensity democracy".

Successes and Failures of India's Democracy

As we move from a procedural to a more substantive definition of democracy, from a definition focused on a set of institutional inputs to one that demands a desired set of outcomes, the distinction between the two questions suggested above, between what democracy is and what democracy does, disappears. At this level, it also becomes difficult to sustain a "universal checklist" definition: democracy cannot be defined without reference to the historically specific dreams and ideals that were articulated through the label. This brings us back to the four goals implicit in the Indian model with reference to which the achievements and failures of democratic polity can be discussed.

The very achievement and sustenance of procedural democracy partly realises the first goal of political democracy. A democracy provides dignity and liberty simply by being there. In the Indian model, democracy was also the key instrument, the necessary condition, for the realization of all its other goals. In that sense, taking into account the growing limitations mentioned above, Indian polity has achieved something worth defending. It has also met, at least until now in most parts of the territories that fall within its boundaries, the minimal substantive expectations of any regime, democratic or otherwise: protecting its own form and protecting its citizens from complete anarchy. The fact that India has kept at bay even the remote possibility of a military takeover; that it has successfully defended (at times through brutal and undemocratic means in the states of Nagaland and Mizoram in the north-east) the territorial borders it inherited; and that most of its citizens have been spared the experience of complete anarchy, is unlikely to enthuse a radical democrat. But it is useful to remember that democratic regimes usually collapse not because they fail to realise the higher ideals associated with democracy, but because they cannot be relied upon to meet the bare minimum expectations.

The achievements of democracy as a set of institutions or as a regime do not, of course, satisfy the deeper ethical impulse associated with the idea of democracy. As a political ideal, democracy gives rise to the promise of a community of equals, where ordinary citizens enjoy true liberty and are governed by none except themselves. The nationalist movement in India had translated this ideal as the goal of *swaraj*, of self-rule, in a deeper sense. It would indeed make impossible demands on one's credulity to suggest that Indian democracy has come anywhere close to meeting this ideal. Perhaps no democracy has, but this constitutes a poor consolation to those who accepted the ideal for its ethical appeal. Ever since the famous "tryst with destiny" speech given at midnight, 14 August 1947, the promise of a community of equals has been a false one. What has come about as a result of the working of democracy is neither a community nor equality. The political community, or rather politicised social communities, it brings into existence is no community, for its shared life is shallow, if not perverse. The liberty it offers, at least formally, is distributed in extremely unequal measure. The power it brings to the people as an abstraction is rarely, if ever, exercised by the real people. And there are still many people – full citizens of the Republic of India – who feel as powerless under this democracy as they did under British rule.

The performance of Indian democracy in achieving national integration has left much to be desired. But, as the examples of India's neighbours show, we could have done worse. There are areas (Kashmir and the hill states in the north-east) and periods (Indira Gandhi's second regime, for example) that constitute exceptions, but on balance the Indian elite has stuck to the "salad bowl" rather than the "melting pot" model of integration of diversities. That is to say, various communities and aspiring nationalities have not been forced to give up their identity as a precondition of joining the Indian enterprise. They have been accepted as distinct and different ingredients in the Indian mix of multiculturalism. And, again on balance, it has worked: legitimate political articulation of social and regional diversities and the mediation of competing claims through mechanisms of political accommodation have achieved what consociational arrangements for power sharing among different social groups do in other societies. There has been more than one instance of majoritarian excess (the anti-Sikh riots in 1984 and the demolition of the Babri mosque in 1992, to take two examples from recent history), but democratic politics seems to have evolved mechanisms of self-correction in this respect (as illustrated by the 1997 elections in the Punjab and the politics of Uttar Pradesh). In retrospect, effective political accommodation of visible diversities looks like one of the outstanding achievements of Indian democracy in the last fifty years. By its very nature, however, this is an inherently fragile achievement, ever contingent on the skills of the political actors in working out the power-sharing arrangements or in allowing the mechanisms of self-correction to work themselves out. This is a lesson well worth remembering as India confronts the most organised challenge to the politics of diversity in the form of the BJP government at the centre. The most serious challenge to the survival of diversity comes from forces that are less organised, less visible, and not even considered political in the ordinary sense: forces of cultural homogenisation, the monoculture of modernity, and the ideology of nation-state. While there is something to be said for the capacity of democratic politics to deal with the more obvious political challenges to diversity, it has proved a weak ally in the struggle against these deeper threats from within.

The promise of social revolution that the democratic invitation has always contained has been realised only in parts and in fragments. It is not that democratic politics has left society unaffected. In fact, these fifty years may be recorded in the history of Indian society as years of fundamental transformation triggered, above all, by the mechanism of competitive politics. At least in one respect, it did bring about something of a revolution: the role of ritual Hindu hierarchy as a predictor of secular power has diminished dramatically over the last fifty years. While this is a fundamental change, it does not in itself guarantee equality. Unsurprisingly, the functioning of democratic politics has contributed more to a vigorous circulation of the elite and to an expansion of the circle itself than to the establishment of social equality. Its contribution to social equality is mainly by way of the politicisation of castes and communities, which then struggle in the secular domain for equality of self-respect.

Since the gender divide does not lend itself to easy aggregation along party political lines, competitive politics has failed to bring about the kind of change in this aspect that it has on caste inequality. The representation of women in parliament and the state assemblies has stagnated at the abysmally low levels of 8 and 4 per cent, respectively, over the last fifty years. The national movement may not have had a greater proportion of women's participation, but it ensured that women had a stronger voice in public life. If women's issues are discussed much more in the political arena than their presence in legislatures or their voice in political parties would warrant, the principal reason is the politics of ideas to which the growing women's movement has contributed a great deal. Consequently, India has had fairly "progressive" legislation on gender justice, including the provision for reservation of one-third of the seats for women in the election of local democratic bodies. The resolute opposition to a similar bill for the Lok Sabha and state assemblies shows the lack of political will that underlies the symbolic progressivism on women's issues.

The single biggest failure of democratic politics lies in the nonfulfilment of the promise of material well-being. Far from ensuring a life of equal and reasonable comfort for everyone, it has not succeeded even in providing the minimum needs of the people, or in removing the worst indignities or the ugliest disparities in the material conditions of life experienced by its citizens. It is true that the conditions of life for most of the people have not deteriorated substantially, that India has achieved some reduction in the proportion of the poor in its population, and that the Indian economy is not caught in an impossible spiral of inflation or in a debt trap. That is perhaps an achievement, at least in comparative perspective. It is also true that the majority of the population feels that its economic condition has improved in the recent past and that an overwhelming majority of people think that their children have better opportunities in life than they did. But there is a significant minority – mainly artisan communities and Scheduled Tribes – that disagrees and has experienced an overall deterioration in quality of life. For others, too, there has been a visible decline in some of the crucial resources such as the availability of public health and the quality of public education.

Democratic politics only provides a potential formal mechanism for conversion of the majority of the poor into a political majority that can then take charge of state power to redistribute material resources and to augment them in such a way as to meet the needs of the most disadvantaged. The functioning of democracy in itself does nothing to ensure that the mechanism is actually used to this end. The other condition, that of the availability of a political agency that can transform the potential majority into a political majority by winning their political trust, has proved to be highly contingent. The Indian model expected politics to provide three crucial elements of what was then called economic development: politics was to provide the blueprint for economic development; it was to confer the political will to implement the design in the face of structures of economic interests; and it was to create popular support for egalitarian politics. In practice, it succeeded in providing only the third component – and that only in part. The most recent phase of globalisation and liberalisation marks a decisive retreat from what remained of the politics of egalitarianism. Not only is there no effective political will to do something, there is very little by way of a coherent intellectual design as to what needs to be done in the first place. This combination of political amnesia and cognitive paralysis poses the most important challenge to the ethical impulse underlying the Indian enterprise today.

Conclusion

Let me round off this story by asking a general question implicit in it: What happens when the idea of democracy travels downward? Fifty years ago, no one felt it necessary to ask this question. Fifty years ago, the decision to establish democracy in a poor, unequal, post-colonial society did not look as courageous as it does now in retrospect. The spirit of the time helped everyone overlook the fact that no other society had successfully taken this path before. Nor has anyone done so since then. India has failed to remove poverty or inequality or to shake off the cultural burden of colonialism, yet it has succeeded in remaining a democracy. Fifty years ago, hardly anyone had thought about this possibility: of democracy being the lone survivor in the family of ideals we set out with. Neither the historians nor the political theorists of democracy had prepared us for this possibility, nor have they done so since.

There was another reason for not thinking about this question. The founding fathers of our democracy, the original hosts of this game, entertained the illusion that the democratic idea would remain intact as it travelled downward. The Indian model assumed a pure diffusion of ideas; it was assumed that the grafted institutions and ideas of Western democracy would travel down in their pure form to the masses. The model was unspoiled by the suspicion that the recipients of these ideas were themselves thinking minds, that they could transform the received ideas just as the elite had done to the doctrine of liberalism. What this model did not have, to use the recent vocabulary of social science, was a theory of reception. This was a crucial blind spot, for the success of democracy depended in large measure on recreating the democratic dream in the popular imagination, in anchoring the universal ideal in the specifically Indian context. Some of the founding fathers may have entertained a different kind of illusion: that the idea of democracy would be automatically transformed by the people when it travelled downward. In this romantic version, the people would make democracy speak their language and devise the system best suited to their needs.

The experience of the last five decades confirms neither of these versions. The journey of the idea of democracy in India has not only changed the lives of the millions it has touched, but it has also changed the idea of democracy itself in more ways than one. Call it "creolisation" or "vernacularisation" of democracy, this transformation is at the heart of whatever success democracy has achieved in India. The serious attempt to marry the democratic idea to popular beliefs, to develop shared protocols with the preexisting language of the people, is what has distinguished India from other countries where the democratic enterprise never took off. And that is also what can continue to maintain this distinction in the future.

Creolisation in itself is no magic remedy. Indigenisation of democracy is a necessary condition of the working out of this idea, but it is not a sufficient condition. A large historical process like this one follows no single script and does not produce neat outcomes. It leaves gaps, it produces contradictions. And there is no hidden hand at work here that might straighten every wrinkle. There is, in other words, no shortcut to creating and sustaining the language of radical democracy beyond weaving every strand and tying every thread.

Acknowledgements

An early version of this paper was presented at a workshop, "India at Fifty", organised by the Institute of Commonwealth Studies, London, in May 1997. I would like to thank Professor James Manor for inviting me to this workshop and all the participants for their comments. The libraries of Queen Elizabeth House, the Social Sciences Faculty, and Nuffield College, all at Oxford, provided congenial settings and useful references. Rita and Donald Cruise O'Brien's "Gift to Indian Democracy" was an invaluable asset. Some fragments of this paper were carried in *The Hindu* and in *Seminar*. I owe special thanks to Rajni Kothari and Alfred Stepan for reading an earlier draft, Sudipta Kaviraj and Sunil Khilnani for their valuable comments on its presentation, and Philip Oldenburg for being amazingly meticulous, patient, generous, and demanding, all at the same time.

2

From Hegemony to Convergence

Party System and Electoral Politics in the Indian States 1952–2002

THE CHALLENGE OF theorising the party system in India at the state level has never been felt as acutely as it has in the last decade or so.* One reason for this is too obvious to miss. The 1990s have witnessed a sea change in the political arena in India. It may be a long time before professional students of Indian politics arrive at a shared "common sense" about what these changes signify. However, it is unlikely that anyone would doubt the extent and depth of the impact of these changes. Even to a casual observer the map of Indian politics today appears strikingly different from what it was in the late 1980s. Professional students of politics have begun to see this change from the late 1880s to the 1990s as signifying a "reconfiguration" of Indian politics: it is not just that the game has started yielding different and surprising results; in some ways the rules of the game have changed (Yadav, 1996). It is obvious that there is a need to better understand the changing nature of the party system in order to figure out these changing rules of the game.

More than the extent and depth of these changes, their nature constitutes a more compelling reason for a second look at the party system. For, these changes, big or small, do not fit into the dominant narratives of Indian politics. Hence the knee-jerk response to some

*This essay is co-authored with Suhas Palshikar.

of these changes. Typically, what catches the eye is the changing fortunes of individual political parties: the sudden decline of the Congress, the Bharatiya Janata Party's (BJP) dramatic rise to power, the Bahujan Samaj Party's (BSP) take-off, and so on. The underlying change in the structure of political competition itself is less noticed and inadequately analysed. Similarly, it is easy to note an increase in electoral volatility but its causes are not well understood. There is a lot of talk of politics being increasingly shaped on the basis of social cleavages like caste and community, but the change from the past is insufficiently mapped.

The 1990s have unleashed several independent yet simultaneous trajectories. The intensity of electoral competition has increased with the rise in electoral volatility. This has been accompanied by something of a participatory upsurge. The level of politics has shifted from "all-India" to the states. The "national" electoral verdict appears no more than an aggregation of state-level verdicts. These changes have been accompanied by a change in the idiom of politics. All this adds up to quite a messy picture. Messy not only because many of these dimensions are intertwined, but also because we do not understand many of them very well and lack a frame to see their interconnections. No wonder we are unclear about the durability of these changes. Are these changes here to stay? Or, are these only precursors to something else? A somewhat jumbled picture arising out of empirical complexity, future uncertainty, and under-theorisation marks any attempt to map Indian politics of the 1990s. The present essay seeks to address this messy picture. We treat this apparent mess as an intellectual puzzle. We aim at defining this puzzle and situating it in a historical and comparative perspective – historical in that we trace the trajectory through which India's party system evolved since democratic political competition was instituted after Independence; comparative in that we compare different patterns of political competition obtaining in the different states of India. Both these exercises, especially the latter, are badly in need of academic attention in India. There is little in the existing scholarly literature that compares to, say, the exercise undertaken by Lipset and Rokkan (1967) in their celebrated essay situating the present party competition in Europe in the comparative historical sociology of the formation and freezing of social cleavages in Europe. An enquiry that asks similar questions in the Indian context is waiting to be carried out. The present essay, though, does not undertake that ambitious task. Our limited ambition is to frame the terms of such an enquiry and sketch an outline of how the structure of party competition at the state level has come to be what it is.

A word about the perspective that informs this reading of the party system may not be out of place here. We are interested in the party system because we are interested in the possibilities of social transformation in and through democratic politics. We are interested in mechanisms through which competitive politics opens or closes possibilities of expanding meaningfully the available range of options or the probability of the more effective options being taken up. The party system is a critical mediating factor in this possible relationship between democratic politics and social transformation. It defines the structure of political competition that shapes and constrains the political choices that a citizen can exercise. The party system thus forms the menu of choice that determines the possibility of social transformation through democratic means. To believe in this is to share the conviction that democratic politics opens the possibility of electoral choice being turned into a radical instrument of social change, of rearranging the composition of the power elite, of renegotiating the political agenda, of redefining the relations of power in society. At the same time this reading is tempered by the knowledge that needed structures of social and economic inequality work systematically against the realisation of this possibility. Hence our insistence here on relating the party system to social and economic structures.

This essay begins with a brief review of the existing literature on state politics in India so as to trace the emergence of the discipline and its treatment of comparative study of party systems. In order to situate the present party competition in a historical perspective, Section II will undertake a reassessment of the famous "congress system" argument, first developed by Rajni Kothari. Section III takes a theoretical detour to develop a model of a party system that might help us categorise the various types of party systems that developed in India after the demise of the congress system. Our hope is that this model, that situates party systems along the two dimensions of competition and the intensity of socio-political divisions, does greater justice to the Indian context and to our objective than other received models. This exercise yields a typology of the party system, developed in Section IV, that covers what we describe as the "two lives" of the congress system and thereafter. In Section V, we discuss the "moment of differentation" – how different states, at different points of time, and through different routes broke away from the congress system. Various factors such as participatory upsurge, electoral volatility, etc. that contributed to electoral realignments and changes in the party system in the 1990s are outlined here. Section VI presents an overview of trends and patterns in state politics in the post-Congress polity. In Section VII we return to our starting point, namely, the link between the party system and transformative politics, by evaluating the social consequences of the various political routes taken in the post-Congress polity. The final section gathers together the various strands of the arguments and tries to ask the big question: how should we characterise the changes in the party system in the last decade or so? And what does it mean for the possibility of social transformation through democratic politics?

I: The Emergence of State Politics as a Frontier Discipline

One of the significant developments both in real politics and in the academic enterprise of making sense of politics has been the emergence of state politics as the centre of attention. Once upon a time, the study of Indian politics involved "national"-level politics alone. State politics was seen as a matter of detail and would be referred to only as an unavoidable appendage of "all-India" politics. Delhi, Nehru and the national level political competition used to constitute the fact of Indian politics and the subject matter of its study. A casual remark in Rajni Kothari's *Politics in India* sums up the "shudra" status of this discipline of state politics. While looking at the "Indian political system as a whole", Kothari says that he did not intend "to get lost in the esoteric details of its many constituents" and further explains this in a footnote saying that he was looking at state politics from a national perspective and those interested in state politics from the state perspective may consult Weiner or Narain, etc. (Kothari, 1970, p. 122). Two unstated assumptions inform this statement: one, that state politics was different from national politics, and second, that state politics from the perspective of state was a matter of interesting detail, but no more. For that generation of theorists of Indian politics this was perhaps a natural reaction in view of the background of the national movement and the task of "nation-building" in which the national-level political class was presumably engaged. In contrast, politics at the state level was about power, personal aggrandisement, parochial interests and their protection through lobbying, etc. Also, in the 1950s and the 1960s, one could understand a good deal of politics by looking exclusively at national-level politics, national-level-leadership, policymaking, and so on. Given the monotonous dominance of the Congress everywhere, state politics must have appeared a poor copy of national-level politics. As political developments unfolded through the 1960s, the discipline of state politics emerged gradually. The inadequacy of analyses of Indian politics focusing exclusively on the national-level became apparent as states actually started playing a crucial role in shaping the so-called national-level politics. Thus, studies on individual states started taking place. Soon this trend was strengthened by theorisations about state politics and collections where studies on state-level politics were put together.

One of the early such collections was Myron Weiner's *State Politics in India* (1968) where he tries to address the question of why state politics has been a neglected discipline (Weiner, 1968, pp. 5–6). But his justification for studying state politics is much more interesting. He argues that since states constitute the main centre of decisions regarding many developmental aspects, a student of the politics of development has to look at state-level politics. Besides, states provide an excellent platform for comparison. Interstate comparisons can actually tell us more about Indian politics than anything else (ibid., pp. 3–5). Broadly, his scheme has three grids on which to assess state politics: the federal structure of the polity, party competition with reference to participatory patterns and state party systems, and performance of state government (the last is important for his developmental approach) (pp. 18–58). Weiner makes a distinction between a national-level party system and state-level party systems. He argues that in the backdrop of the 1967 elections, state party systems had already started evolving in directions different from the national party system. At the theoretical level, Weiner's thrust is on the socio-economic bases of conflict and conditions for political stability. This was in keeping with the overall thrust of political science in those days. Weiner's volume was followed by a more comprehensive work, at least in terms of the number of states included, edited by Iqbal Narain (1976). While the essays in Narain's book are quite informative in themselves in terms of the details of state-level socio-economic processes, the book as a whole does not contribute to the discipline of state politics. This is mainly because it overemphasises the structural dimension of state politics and operates within the then dominant framework influenced by North American scholarship. However, Narain makes an interesting point towards the end regarding state politics being "sandwiched between inter-regional differences and intra-regional imbalances" (Narain, 1976, p. 592).

In fact many studies of state politics were a response to the felt unintelligibility of national politics in the absence of state-level analysis. The framework of national politics was supposed to be a given and whenever that "given" was not strictly followed, scholars turned to the study of state politics to find out what was wrong with Indian politics and how it was likely to restore the "natural" framework. As Indira Gandhi came to power and sought to redefine some aspects of the political game in India, observers were inclined to believe that it was the end of the "given" framework. This gave rise to the language of crises, deinstitutionalisation, and restoration. Rajni Kothari's analysis of the congress system was stretched by many observers to mean that it was the necessary state of equilibrium for democracy to survive in India.

Such sentiment gave rise to John Wood's theme of "Crisis or Continuity" in another significant collection on state politics. Yet, Wood was right when he mentioned that one major issue in Indian politics since the late 1970s was the centre's intervention in state politics.

He went on to suggest that the ability of the central leadership to control state politics and the responses of the states would constitute the main axis around which Indian politics would be shaped (Wood, 1984, p. 3). In the concluding essay of Wood's volume, Church pointed to two "crises" facing Indian politics: the issue of participation of new social forces and the future of the Congress party. He suggested a classification of states on the twin bases of lower-caste entry into positions of power at the state level and the ability of the Congress to accommmodate the claims of the lower castes (Church, 1984, pp. 236–41).

As Wood's volume was going into press, Indira Gandhi was assassinated and a new era in Indian politics emerged. This happened not so much because of the disappearance of a strong personalised leadership style, but because of the strengthening of some features that had emerged in her own time: the continuation of the shift in economic policies from a command economy to a more market-oriented economy, the continued shift towards competitive communalism, and the evolution of states as the main theatre of the enactment of many social conflicts. Interestingly, notwithstanding the initiatives taken by Narain and Weiner, studies of Indian politics did not respond to the emerging trend by further probing state politics. Since the late 1980s, although the states were occupying the centre stage of Indian politics, scholarly attention on state politics was largely missing. Many of the writings on Indian politics during the late 1980s and early 1990s in fact reverted to the tradition of "national-level" explanations although the empirical details were collected from state politics. Alternatively, in the absence of a comparative approach, narratives of state politics inevitably got entangled with what Church refers to as the uniqueness of the situation at the state level (Church, 1984, p. 230), resorting to reports of the "esoteric".

This is not to say that political process at the state level was not studied at all during this period. Many states were individually studied by state experts and collections of state politics also appeared. More importantly, a two-volume set, not strictly on state politics, edited by Francine Frankel and M.S.A. Rao, was published (Frankel and Rao, 1989 and 1990). This work went a long way in enriching our understanding of the dynamics of state politics. It opened up possibilities of linking the analysis of electoral and party politics to issues of resource control and domination. Departing from the practice of looking at electoral politics almost in isolation, Frankel and Rao sought to situate historical developments in the respective states in their political economy. The same point is made in the volume edited by Drèze and Sen (1996). What Frankel and Rao opened up for analysis is the possibility of looking at states as autonomous units in which systems of domination evolve, and therefore at which party competition will also have a state-specific trajectory. Thus, their work helped establish the state as the unit of analysis of Indian politics. However, this major enterprise stopped well short of providing a framework for comparing state politics or attempting a typology of states. It also did not go a long way in developing an analysis of India's party system. The essays in these volumes focus more on the social bases of politics than on the actual electoral competition. Yet, some essays, notably those on Bihar and Uttar Pradesh, dwell at length on the effect of caste mobilisation on the party competition in those states. Also, the essay on Maharashtra deals with the relationship between party factionalism and caste.

As Indian politics became more and more state specific during the 1990s, electoral outcomes were also studied state-wise. Thus, Roy and Wallace (1999) and Wallace and Roy (2003) seek to cull the meaning of two major Lok Sabha elections – the last in the twentieth century – on the basis of state-wise analysis of these elections. These two volumes indicate a range of issues that might be taken into consideration for constructing a meaningful framework for comprehending contemporary political process in India. These include regionalism, identity politics, and Hindutva. Wallace takes a look at the compulsions of coalition politics affecting the political process (Roy and Wallace, 1999, pp. 17–22). Both volumes implicitly underscore the fact that the state is the unit at which politics actually unfolds. Similarly, arguing that two-party competition is the main feature of India's party system in the 1990s, Chhibber and Nooruddin conclude that it is at the state level that "future analyses of Indian politics must concentrate" (Chhibber and Nooruddin, 1999). The developments in the 1990s and scholarly response to them have contributed to the emergence of state politics as the frontier discipline essential for a nuanced understanding of Indian politics.

However, this realisation is yet to change the face of the discipline. Many of the studies of state politics rarely adopt a comparative perspective or ask questions that would lead to the theorisation of Indian politics. The usual practice is to review the politics of different states and stop there. Yet there are signs of a fresh beginning being made in the 1990s in the direction of a truly comparative study of state politics that could lead to a reappraisal of Indian politics. The growing literature includes three kinds of works. First, there are some studies that focus on a single state, but use it to develop a larger argument about Indian politics. These include Jaffrelot on Madhya Pradesh (1999), Narendra Subramanian on Tamil Nadu (1999), Zoya Hasan on Uttar Pradesh (1998), D.L. Sheth (2002) and Ghanshyam Shah (2002) on Gujarat, Peter de Souza on Goa (1999), and some articles in the *Economic and Political Weekly* collection on electoral politics. Second, there are some studies that offer direct comparison of politics in more than one state (Kohli, 1987; Sinha [forthcoming]; the volume under preparation by Robert Jenkins). Third, some analyses have attempted to offer an overview of the trends and patterns of party politics across a number of states (Pradeep Kumar, 2000; Sridharan, 2002; Yadav, 1996, 1999; and most recently Jaffrelot, 2003). While Sridharan's detailed analysis ends by emphasising the structural aspect of political competition more than the social, Jaffrelot's study focuses on the strategic alternatives available to the Congress after the decline of the party had already begun. For instance, Sridharan argues that "systemic properties" explain most satisfactorily the changes in India's party system (Sridharan, 2002, pp. 495–6). On the other hand, Jaffrelot shows how the Congress party in Madhya Pradesh moved from a "catch-all party" to a more nuanced "coalition of extremes" during the 1990s and that this paid rich dividends (Jaffrelot, 2003, pp. 435–52). In other words, contemporary scholarship on the party system and electoral politics in India offer two entirely different approaches. A more ambitious and comprehensive framework for the study of state-level party politics is offered by Harris (1999). He pleads for differentiating among state-level party systems on the basis of caste and class balance in the respective states. This, he believes, has implications for the differences in the functioning of democracy in different states. Our attempt here is to draw upon this growing literature and contribute to it by looking back at the last half-century of Indian politics from the vantage point of the present moment in order to link the changes in the party system and electoral politics to developments in the field of state politics. While there is a considerable amount of literature on state-level electoral politics, this has not produced any new thinking on the party system in India. As a matter or fact, analyses of changes in India's party system often stop at declaring the decline of the Congress and the arrival of the post-Congress polity. That these developments were taking place at the state level and not just at the all-India level is somewhat ignored. It may also be said that analyses of Indian politics do not seriously take into consideration the issue of social change. The party system and social change are seldom seen as interrelated

II: "Congress System" Revisited

Any attempt to understand the changes in party system in contemporary India must begin by asking one elementary question: what is that original point with reference to which we seek to measure the change? An answer to this enables us to take the next logical step and ask: what has changed in respect of the party system? In current readings there is implicit a map of Indian politics which existed in the era prior to the contemporary cataclysmic changes. This map or picture informs the contrast that is often drawn. The party system is now said to be moving from a one-party-dominance system to multiparty competition, from social cohesion to fragmentation, from a stable pattern to fluidity, from order to chaos as the principle of party competition. In order to rethink this dominant picture of the party system as it exists today, it is necessary to revisit the point of departure itself.

From the 1960s a common sense had evolved about the nature of party political competition through the first decade and a half of India's democratic experience (Kothari, 1961; Krishna, 1967; Morris-Jones, 1964). The most powerful formulation of this common sense was, of course, captured by the term "congress system" (Kothari, 1964; Kothari, 1970, pp. 152–99). Developed in the mid-1960s, this formulation served to summarise India's competitive politics through the 1970s. It was a bold attempt to theorise the unique party system that India had developed that did not fit the straitjacket of one-party system or multiparty competition. Kothari himself "revisited" the idea of the congress system in the mid-1970s and concluded that though some modifications needed to be made to the original formulation, the basic idea could be deployed for understanding the structure of party political competition in the 1970s and perhaps beyond (Kothari, 1989).

The "congress system" formulation contained the argument that in spite of an apparent one-party dominance, interparty and intra-party competition did take place. This competition often took place within the confines of a consensus because the Congress party was occupying the "centre"; opposition was allowed within the margins of this centre both inside the Congress party and outside it. Apart from the structural features, Kothari's formulation involved an ideological component. The congress system was a system of legitimacy. The issue was establishment of a democratic authority. This was achieved in India on the basis of a historical consensus that was converted by the party system into "present consensus" (Kothari, 1989, p. 25). This was possible because, the congress system encompassed all major sections and interests of society (ibid., p. 27). Kothari believed that the congress system combined the efforts to gain legitimacy and the efforts towards social transformation. The system did so by neutralising all potential sources of disaffection. The Congress party's democratic background and the policies adopted by the Congress government were instrumental in achieving this objective. This model emphasised the role of government in social change. Also, in Kothari's initial formulation, Nehru's leadership played a very important part in shaping this aspect of the congress system.

The mid-1970s witnessed the initial challenge to the congress system. In the 1980s, the Congress party managed to return to power, though the congress system was considerably weakened. Cataclysmic events since the late 1980s changed both the discourse and the framework of Indian politics. Yet it is worth noting that analyses of these changes were often anchored in the framework of the congress system. This points to the obvious strength of the idea of the congress system argument. Instead of trying to fit India into the received images or models of party competition from the West, Kothari's formulation sought to capture the specificity of Indian politics. It recognised the fact of one-party dominance without accepting the image of the authoritarian nature of politics associated with it. Refuting that there was a closure in this form of political competition, the formulation drew attention to the oppositional role of the factions within the Congress, a feature that gave a competitive character to both inter- and intra-party politics. Kothari's path-breaking formulation sought to go beyond the structural aspects and looked at the more substantive aspect of the ideological dimension of party competition that actually sustained the system.

These merits and strengths of the congress system argument notwithstanding, with the benefit of hindsight it can be seen that this argument, or at least its popular versions, may have overlooked or underemphasised some aspects of the party system as it prevailed through the 1960s. In revisiting the congress system, we need to take a quick look at these aspects. First of all, the formulation drew our attention away from the simple fact that anything between a quarter to half of India was never covered by the congress system. West Bengal, Kerala, Tamil Nadu, and Punjab are examples of states where the congress system met with opposition early on or simply did not materialise. Besides, states like Orissa, Rajasthan, Madhya Pradesh, and Assam were states where the Congress continued in power but was far from exercising dominance. Kothari himself points out that in the ex-princely states the congress system was weak. But viewed in totality, these exceptions are just too many and too significant to ignore. The only conclusion we can draw from these exceptions is that the congress system was perhaps a description of the party system existing at the "national" level more than the description of an "Indian" party system. This fits well with Kothari's above-cited view that he was looking at politics from the national perspective. In the 1960s and later it was a commonly accepted view that national politics was the unit to be understood and politics in the states was to be seen as an expression of national politics.

Second, in Kothari's formulation, the congress system was presented as a "natural" outcome of an unequal and decentred society where a political centre was instituted. This invited the reader to think that the system had greater enduring capacity than it really did. Thanks to this formulation, the congress system appeared as a regular and long-term phenomenon whose absence or erosion required explanation. In retrospect, it appears that Kothari may have read too much into what was a temporary political form of the first phase of competitive political mobilisation. At a time when mobilisation was rather limited, political competition could be conducted only in a circumscribed manner. In the Indian context, the existence of the Congress as a movement, as a party, and as an instrument of government combined with a towering and popular leader produced a particular structure of competition. There was nothing in this situation that ensured the continuation of the congress system once the terms of popular mobilisation changed.

Thirdly, the congress system argument underlined the "catch-all" and consensual nature of politics. This description was factually correct. However, it does not probe the inner logic of this consensus. Nor does the argument take notice of the play of dominant interests. The "catch-all" character and the façade of consensus helped the congress system in two respects. In the first place, the congress system sought to make compromises with upper castes and allow their domination in the political realm. A consensus about procedural democracy coupled with welfare-oriented developmentalism helped in de-emphasising the claims of the lower castes. On the other hand, the catch-all character of the Congress party won elections for it, without forcing any change in its policies or leadership pattern. The Congress party was supported by the masses, which belonged to various social backgrounds. This gave the party the famous tag of a catch-all party. At the same time, the party and the congress system worked to keep the dalits, adivasis, peasants, and workers, at a distance from positions of power. The congress system was based on a trade-off: the Congress party would symbolically incorporate the various social sections, but the party's upper-class/upper-caste leadership should be recognised as legitimate and as representative of the masses. In other words, the congress system was not really as open as its theorists thought it was: it was as much about exclusion as inclusion. Under the cloak of consensus, a distance was always maintained between the supporters and the beneficiaries of the congress system. Perhaps, this could be possible because, as Kothari himself points out, the political class as a whole came from a common social background and was not sensitive to these sociological dimensions of democracy. This consensual nature of the political elite and their common perception about nation and development was the core of the consensus, rather than any socially agreed vision or consensus in the true sense of the term.

There is also a tendency in Kothari's argument to underplay the plebiscitary nature of politics right from the beginning of India's democratic politics in the post-Independence period. With hindsight, we can say that Kothari may have overstated the system dimension of the party competition. The Congress, in spite of being a well-knit organisation, depended quite happily on the charisma of Nehru for winning elections. It was a combination of state-level organisation and Nehru's plebiscitary leadership that ensured the dominance of the Congress. The organisation alone could not have brought the success, which the Congress enjoyed for a long time. In fact, Indian politics in general and the Congress movement in particular always had this plebiscitary character even in the pre-Independence period. In the post-Independence period, successive elections were turned into a plebiscite. Just as the organisational dimension helped the Congress marginalise the opposition parties, the plebiscitary leadership style ensured that issues would be framed in a fuzzy manner, that the focus would be more on personal charisma than on concrete programmes or performance. As we know, this characteristic continued and played an important part in politics in the 1970s. Much of the argument about the shift from Nehru to Indira Gandhi could really be saved if we are aware of this particular dimension of the congress system that became more prominent at the later stage.

This critique of the congress system does not render the formulation obsolete. In fact, the label, the congress system, needs to be retained since it reminds us of the principal character of Indian politics in a particular era. Our purpose in developing this critique is twofold.

Firstly, we wish to underline the point that the congress system was a necessarily short-term response of the early phase of democratic mobilisation following the opening up of the floodgates of universal franchise. This puts in perspective the oft-expressed nostalgia for the return of the congress system: this nostalgia hides a desire to go back to a stage of democracy when the masses were not politicised, when politics was still the game of the few. Secondly, the critique serves to remind us that the "consensus" of the congress system was a hegemonic construct: it did allow for the incubation of democratic politics and for a safe experiment with social change, yet it could not have been the political form for a full-fledged engagement of competitive politics with social transformation. Very early in its long life, the congress system had become a constraint on the possibility of transformative politics.

Thus, for the congress system to be an intelligible frame of analysis, it is necessary to trace two phases of it. Unless we do this, we are likely to adopt a static and singular image of politics in the period 1947–77. Kothari himself is not guilty of doing this, but the popular rendering of his argument has contributed to such an understanding. To revisit the congress system today, then, means being aware of the hegemonic dimension of Congress dominance and to try and construct a typology of the party system in India in a manner that will include the congress system but extend beyond it.

III: A Model for a Party System

It is very common to invoke "party system" in any discussion of Indian politics. But more often than not discussion of the party system tends to be a loose and generalised way of discussing the shared attributes of parties in a given political system. Or else it is a simple numeric description of the number of relevant parties in a given polity: one party systems, two-party or bipolar systems, and multiparty systems. Both these prevalent ways of discussing the party system lose sight of the basic point behind the idea of a party system: that it is a "system" that conditions and constrains all the parties that operate within it, that it is "more than the sum of the parts" (Mair, 1977, p. 51). Therefore we need to distinguish between the changing fortunes of parties and changes in the party system. For instance, what we are looking for is not so much an explanation of why Congress came to lose power, but how and why it found itself facing a radically different pattern of political competition, and the implication of this for the existing parties and popular mobilisations. Thus, the basic idea is to grasp that the configuration in which parties find themselves locked happens to be an independent factor that constrains what individual parties and voters can do. In this sense, this configuration provides a framework within which party competition and popular mobilisation take place. The nature and structure of the competition determine how open or closed a party system is in processing societal claims, in allowing in new entrants, in admitting unattended issues, etc.

At an epistemic plane, the conventional thinking about party systems tends to be passive in that it is assumed that there is a correct classification of the party system that cuts across time and space. In that understanding the task of a political analyst is to identify the "right" classification and place the polity under examination in the appropriate slot in a given typology. Epistemic common sense and political wisdom require us to move away from such a passive stance vis-à-vis the received classifications. For classifications and typologies are not "out there"; these are analytical constructs meant to put cognitive order on the material we seek to examine. Typologies are thus not "right" or "wrong'; they are more or less helpful depending on how well they allow us to order the experience that we seek to categorise and in answering the questions that led us to this typology. On this understanding, the exercise of classification is dependent on our vantage point, our location, our objectives. Therefore this attempt to understand the role of the party system in the democratic politics of social transformation cannot take up and simply deploy the received typologies of the party system. We must interrogate the received classifications from our vantage point, the experience of competitive politics in India in the second half of the twentieth century, and the search for democratic politics for social transformation.

Once we foreground these concerns, it is clear that there has been something of a regress in thinking about the specificity of the party system in India after the decline of the Congress. Notwithstanding the limitations in the theorisation of the congress system, no one can deny that a lot of thought went into the understanding of the party system that operated in the first phase of democratic politics in India. The uniqueness of the political situation forced Indian political scientists to look beyond mechanical replication of the party system models received from the West. The decline of the Congress has removed that constraint and produced a surface resemblance between the party system in India and its counterparts all over the world. This has led to a tendency to slip into the traditional classifications of the party system produced by old-style comparative politics. Unfortunately, most of these classifications tend to be one-dimensional, based as they are on the number of parties (Duverger, 1954; Blondel, 1968; Rokkan, 1968).

To be fair, it should be recognised that implicit in the numerical dimension of traditional classifications of party systems is another dimension. The two-party system is linked with the politics of moderation and governmental stability; the multiparty system is linked with the politics of antagonism, extremism, and governmental instability. But these remain at the level of universal assumptions that are built into this classification and do not lend themselves to empirical examination. Besides, the very labels invite one to think principally about numbers and nothing else. In that sense, in the last instance, this classification remains one-dimensional. It may still be of use to political analysts who share the normative assumptions built into this paradigm that place a premium on governmental stability and moderate choices. But it may not help students of the Indian party system who see democratic politics as a vehicle of social transformation.

Such analysts must turn to other ways of classifying party systems. The most obvious starting point would be attempts to introduce more than one dimension in the classification of party systems. Doing away with the numeric dimension, Dahl (1966) introduced a fourfold classification based on the nature of competitiveness obtaining in the party system. Sartori (1976) sought to understand party systems in a two-dimensional space. Apart from the numerical dimension (one party, two-party, and multiparty) he looked at the ideological distance among the parties (moderate and polarised) and suggested a fourfold classification based on that. There is an obvious attraction to this way of thinking about party systems along a two-dimensional space. Sartori's categorisation allows us to consider not only the format of political competition but also its substance. That relates to our objective in this essay.

At the same time, we cannot lift Sartori's classification and apply it in the Indian context. For one thing, while he talks of one dominant party system, it does not fit well with his classification since the pattern of one-party dominance could exist either in a two-party or multiparty format. And in this system ideological distance could also be "small" or "large" (Mair, 1997, p. 203). Secondly, Sartori's classification of the numerical dimension and "format" of competition was meant to accommodate the proportional representation systems. The operation of the first-past-the-post (FPTP) system and the attendant high threshold of electoral viability have tended to eliminate smaller political actors and formations. Its effect is that in India we have a more limited range of competitive formats to focus on. The third and principal difficulty with using Sartori's classification in the Indian context is his focus on ideological distance along the left–right continuum as the other dimension of the party system. The problem is not, contrary to what many political analysts in India assert, that ideology plays no role in Indian politics. It does, except that ideological differences are not to be found in the conventional language of "high" ideology; understanding ideological differences requires that we reconstruct these from day-to-day "operative" ideological positions. A focus on formal ideologies can be utterly deceptive in indicating the substance of politics. A much deeper difficulty arises because these ideological differences cannot be arranged very meaningfully along a single dimension like the left–right axis. Post-Independence India, particularly post-Congress polity, is characterised by the simultaneous operation of multiple and competing ideological axes. Besides, the whole idea of bringing in a second dimension in party system classification is to focus on the substance of politics from the vantage point of the possibility of meaningful choices. Even if we overlook the above-mentioned difficulties, it seems much better to focus directly on the nature of political choice rather than allow any factor like ideology to serve as its proxy. Ideological differences may and sometimes do indicate the nature of political choice, but they need not always do so. Thus, in order to map the changing party system in India's various states and different political phases we need to tailor the two dimensions according to the specificity of the Indian experience.

We propose that a classification suitable for India can be developed on two axes – format of party competition and the nature of political choices. Let us first look at these two dimensions separately before bringing them together to generate a typology of the nature of the party system.

The first dimension retains the conventional focus in the party system literature on the number of relevant political actors or the format of party competition. The underlying insight here is that political choices are deeply influenced and conditioned by the rules of the game set by a specific type of competition. The established format of political competition – straight, triangular, or multipolar or a version of these – determines not only what kind of political choices will be made but also what kind of choices will be offered. This dimension lends itself to robust quantification. The Taagepera-Shugart index for calculating the effective number of political parties (denoted by N in this essay; the suffix V or S indicates whether the calculation is for the proportion of votes or that of seats) is very precise in giving numeric expression to the commonsensical way of summarising party fractionalisation in the legislature and among voters. The differences on this dimension can be placed on a spectrum that ranges from the supreme dominance of one party all over the state to multi-cornered contests in each seat resulting in the complete fragmentation of political competition into a large number of small parties and independents. Keeping the Indian experience in mind, it is useful to divide this spectrum into four categories. (The calculated results are presented in the tables and charts at the end of this essay.)

One-party Dominance

In this format the dice is already loaded very heavily in favour of the biggest political party. It is not uncommon to find the NS to be below 2.0, indicating a more than three-fourths majority for the ruling party. The Congress victory in the first two general elections to Vidhan Sabhas in the states of Uttar Pradesh, Madhya Pradesh, and Maharashtra serve as apt illustrations of such dominance. However, in its Indian version, one-party dominance rarely translated into a similar dominance in terms of votes. Even in its heyday, the Congress rarely crossed the majority mark in terms of popular votes. Most of the overwhelming victories of the Congress were achieved not because the electorate voted overwhelmingly for the Congress, but because the opponents of the Congress were badly splintered. In such a situation, it is not unusual to see the NY to be as high, four or even five, under single-party dominance. The first general elections to the Vidhan Sabha in Uttar Pradesh returned a complete dominance of the Congress in the assembly (NS = 1.2) without any consolidation of votes in its favour (NV = 4.3).

Two-party/Bipolar Competition

This type of competition is most familiar to students of party competition. There are two principal rivals who contest against each other in almost all the seats and divide all but a few seats among themselves. In case one of them sweeps the election in a "wave" the NS can drop to less than two (e.g., Delhi 1993 and 1998, Gujarat 1995, Himachal Pradesh 1993, and Rajasthan 1998), but generally it stays between two and three. Given the consolidation of votes between the two parties, both the parties poll anything between 80 and 90 per cent of the valid votes. The NY averages around three, for the independents and rebels of the two parties tend to act as "spoilers". In the Indian context one has to include under this category the bipolar competition resulting from long-standing coalitions. The classic example under this category is that of the United Democratic Front (UDF) and the Left Democratic Front (LDF) in Kerala since 1980. A formal count would categorise Kerala as a case of extreme fragmentation with the NY being six or more. But the two coalitions now offer a neat bipolar choice to the electors in each constituency of the state and share around 90 per cent of the votes between them. If each coalition is treated as a party for the purposes of calculating the NY, the number of parties comes down to around three, as in classic two-party competition. The Dravida Munnetra Kazhagam (DMK) versus All India Anna Dravida Munnetra Kazhagam (AIADMK) competition in Tamil Nadu and the Left Front's competition with the Congress till the 1996 election also belong to the same category. It should be noted that a two-coalition competition is less restrictive in its options than a two-party competition. But often the short-term constraints of both these types are not very different.

"Two-plus" Competition

This type is less noticed though not entirely unknown in the literature on party systems. It involves a multiparty competition with two principal actors and one secondary actor. Punjab has been a classic instance of this competition. The Akali Dal and the Congress are the principal contenders for power and the Bharatiya Janata Party (BJP) has played a secondary role. This is not quite a triangular contest, for the third party cannot offer competition in all parts of the state or among all sections of society and may often enter into an alliance with one of the major parties. During the 1980s, the Congress performed a similar role in Tamil Nadu. The enduring presence of a party of the indigenous people has had a similar effect on political competition in Tripura. The 1990s have witnessed a proliferation in this form of competition with the entry of the BJP into new states like Karnataka, Andhra Pradesh, and Orissa. It is difficult to tell this competition type from a summary aggregate figure like the effective number of parties, for the summary indicators for two-plus competition often mimic those of two-party competition. By and large this category has sheltered party competition in times of transition, for our electoral system has built in disincentives for small parties. Often the third party tends to disappear. This category tends to persist only if there is an enduring regional or sectoral interest that is continuously ignored by the two leading formations.

Multiparty Competition

This omnibus category contains within itself various kinds of cases, all involving states where three or more political parties have entrenched themselves in electoral competition. This could involve three- or four-cornered contests in each of the constituencies (e.g., Uttar Pradesh since 1991) or different parties involved in bipolar or triangular competition in different parts of the state (e.g., Bihar in the 1990s before the creation of Jharkhand, or Assam since 1985) or a mix of the two (Kerala in the 1960s and 1970s). The NS being consistently above three, or sometimes above four, indicates the presence of multiparty competition. In this category, the NV is typically five or above. The last two assembly elections in Bihar held in 1995 and 2000 recorded the NS as 3.3 and 4.7 and NV as 7.5 and 7.7, respectively. These are levels of fragmentation one usually associates only with a proportional representation, not with our FPTP system. But the simultaneous activation of regional and social cleavages can sometimes make majoritarian elections into mimicking proportional contestations. This category also contains another group of cases where political and electoral competition has never been crystallised along party political lines. A large number of political parties come up and disappear at regular intervals, parties change their labels regularly, and a large number of these manage legislative presence along with unusual proportion of independents. This syndrome typically affects the smaller states like Goa, Haryana, or the states of the North East. There have been several instances (involving Mizoram, Manipur, and Pondicherry) in which the effective number of political parties in terms of votes (NV) went into double digits. Here party competition lacks a structure; in fact it is not party competition at all.

Having described the various categories of the first dimension of party system classification – the format of party competition – in some detail, it is time to turn to the second dimension that focuses on the substance rather than the form of choice. This dimension is critical to our basic purpose of judging party systems by how they affect social transformations. Ordinary citizens cannot choose to bring about social change through electoral politics unless this option is available to them. While they can, in principle and in the very last instance, shape the menu of choices that is offered to them, the resources, the skills, and the luck required to bring this about rules it out as an effective strategy for most ordinary citizens in their lifetime. For all practical purposes, ordinary citizens are conditioned by the menu they have to choose from. Sometime the voters get a wide range of substantial choices to choose from. But very often they have a rather narrow range of shallow options. Here "substantial" and "shallow" are not expressions of ideological judgement: citizens may and often do prefer to exercise their choices in politically incorrect ways. Here these terms are being used in a more open-minded manner. A substantial choice refers to the presence of options that could make a difference to the conditions of ordinary citizens and thus bring about social change. This definition does not privilege any one domain of ordinary life over others or prescribe any definite policy route to the realisation of citizens' preferences. The citizens may and often do choose privilege issues of collective/community dignity over those of material well-being. They might prefer the "populist" route to that of structural transformation. While we may hold strong positions on these issues, we do not mean to make these an essential element of our classification. Nor do we link the substantial choices to any particular origins: these may come about through ideological politics of social change (e.g., that of the Communists or those of the Socialists or Ambedkarites) or the mobilisation of a certain social group (the BSP and the Samajwadi Party in Uttar Pradesh, the Asom Gana Parishad in Assam).

These minimal considerations offer the following three-fold classification of the nature of political choices available to citizens through party political competition:

Substantial and/or Wide Range of Choices

This condition obtains when the different parties offer radically different policy packages that have perceived consequences for the lives of ordinary citizens. This often comes about at the time of the rise of a new political formation that challenges the existing political spectrum on issues of policy and practice (e.g., the rise of the Left Front to power in West Bengal through the 1960s and 1970s, the rise of the Dravida Munnetra Kazhagam in Tamil Nadu in the 1960s) or in conditions of deep social upheaval and ethnic strife (Uttar Pradesh and Bihar in the 1990s, Punjab in the 1980s, Assam during 1980–5) or in both (Kerala in the 1950s). Voters choose between very different options with long-term consequences. This tends to be a short-lived phase, for periods of wide options are soon followed by a narrowing range of options. Either the original challenger dilutes its agenda (e.g., the Asom Gana Parishad in Assam) or rivals adopt the new agenda (e.g., rise of the All India Anna Dravida Munnetra Kazhagam as a rival to the DMK in Tamil Nadu) or there is a mix of the two (e.g., West Bengal, since the establishment of Left Front dominance).

Moderate and/or Limited Range of Choices

This is the nodal category of bourgeois democracy, often celebrated as the basis of moderation and stability, and derided by its radical critics as offering fictitious choices. There are choices, but within defined limits. The main parties do not offer anything that is substantially different, except a certain brand image. Usually political competition takes place around rival claims of doing the same thing better than the other. Sharp ideological differences are avoided by the principal political parties. Much of the differences revolve around one or two highly publicised issues of symbolic significance or around major personalities. Kothari had pointed out that the congress system, despite being dominated by one party, offered a moderate choice as a result of factional disputes and contestations within the ruling party. In contemporary times, the choice available in states dominated by the Congress–BJP contestation (Rajasthan, Madhya Pradesh, Delhi, Himachal Pradesh, Gujarat) offers a classic instance of this category. Both the parties do not even pretend to offer any different economic or social policy. Even on the question of communalism that ostensibly divides them, both parties make sure they are not at a great distance from the operational position of the other. The same is true of Congress–TDP competition in Andhra Pradesh or the Congress–Janata Dal contest in Karnataka. This category also includes instances of states where the politics of radical choices is on the retreat. The difference between the UDF and the LDF in Kerala today or the choice available in West Bengal, Uttar Pradesh, or Bihar can only be described as a moderate choice.

Shallow and/or no Choice

This category includes two very different types of cases. On the one hand there are instances where political choices were forcibly denied by the use of undemocratic means (e.g., Jammu and Kashmir and Nagaland) and the imposition of regimes that lacked political legitimacy. On the other hand, there are cases where the absence of party structures means that there is virtually no systematic choice that the voters get to evaluate. Choice, if any, is at the local and personal level, and not at the party political level. Democratic theory would have us believe that such instances are exceptions, eliminated once competitive mobilisation passes the initial stages. But the Indian experience shows that such maladies can get institutionalised.

Having discussed the two dimensions separately, we can now discuss their interaction and the cumulative effect on the party system. Figure 1 summarises the interaction of the two dimensions and spells out the seven party system types that result from this. The interaction of three categories on each dimension (the "two-plus" category of competitive format has been merged with "bipolar" for reasons of convenience here) would yield nine cells in all. But the merging of two possible cells with their neighbours has reduced the number to seven. Each of these seven cells represents a certain combination of competitive form and the range of choice available within that system. Each cell mentions the dominant characteristic of the nature of political power in that category. The cell also contains some illustrations that capture the characteristics of that system.

Of the seven party system types that this classification yields, four can be said to belong to the "regular" types of party systems that are prevalent in post-Independence India. These are: (1) system of unipolar hegemony, (2) system of bi-polar convergence, (3) system of multipolar convergence, and (4) system of competitive divergence. Besides these, there are three "irregular" system types, each of which is the product of special and unusual circumstances. These are: (5) system of one-party domination, (6) closed one-party system, and (7) systemless competition. It cannot be overemphasised that each of these is an ideal type, illustrated by a few states and that too in a specific

Fig. 1: Structure of Political Competition and Nature of Political Power in Indian States

Nature of choices	Competitive format One-party (Single dominant party)	Two-party (Two-party or two coalition)	Multi-party ("Two plus" or "four or more")
(1)	(2)	(3)	(4)
		TRANSFORMATION	
Wide and/or Substantial options	**EXCLUSION** J&K 1987 Assam 1983 Punjab 1992 ***One-party domination***	Tamil Nadu 1960s West Bengal, 1969–82	Kerala, 1960s and 1970s Bihar, 1989–95 UP 1989–96
		Competitive divergence	
Moderate and/or limited options	**HEGEMONY** Congress system Maharashtra up to 1978 UP, Bihar up to 1967 AP, Karnataka up to 1983 West Bengal since 1982 ***Unipolar hegemony***	**CONVERGENCE** Kerala since 1980S Gujarat since 1991 HP since 1977 Rajasthan MP since 1989 (1977 ?) Orissa, 1990–9 Karnataka 1983–96 AP, 1983–99 Punjab since 1997 ***Bipolar convergence***	**FRAGMENTATION** UP since 1996 Bihar since 1995 Assam since 1985 Tamil Nadu since 1996 ***Multi-polar convergence***
Narrow and/or no options	**CLOSURE** J&K, 1953–77 ***Closed one-party system***		**FLUIDITY** Haryana 1967–72 Goa in 1990s Manipur Arunachal Pradesh Mizoram before 1985 ***Systemless competition***

period of history. It is not necessary that each state must fit into one of these categories neatly all the time. At any given time, a state may combine elements from different systems. A detailed analysis of these seven categories may help us appreciate this point better.

System of Unipolar Hegemony

The discussion of the congress system in the previous section captured the structural attributes of the system of unipolar hegemony specific to India. It was a unipolar system in that political competition revolved around and was defined with reference to the one dominant actor. The hegemony of the Congress was sustained through its "catch-all" character, through its capacity to forge a rainbow coalition of all kinds of social groups. The system depends on not allowing deep social or ideological cleavages to be politically activated. It is important to emphasise that unipolar hegemony of this kind does not depend on legal or actual elimination of rival political parties from the field of political competition. In that sense it is different from one-party systems that came up in many third world countries. More importantly, it differs from these one-party regimes in that the congress system allowed external critique and internal dissent. The various factions within the Congress performed the function of opposition. The options available to citizens were no doubt severely limited, but the range was not much narrower than the one offered by moderate two-party systems in advanced industrial countries. This category is so intertwined with the congress system that it is hardly surprising to find most of the classical illustrations coming from it.

In describing this system as "unipolar hegemony" we do not wish to invoke the vocabulary of international relations where unipolar hegemony of the US stands for the confluence of economic, political, and military power in the hands of one unaccountable actor. We use the word hegemony here by drawing upon the tradition of social scientific usage that distinguished "hegemony" from simple domination. While domination is exercised through the use of might, hegemony requires consent on the part of the ruled. In that sense the system of unipolar hegemony involved democratic legitimisation and acceptance of the moral authority of the largest political party. At the same time, "hegemony" reminds us that this system was not based on pure and spontaneous consensus as is sometimes made out. As Gramsci reminded us, a system of hegemony routinely involves the manufacturing of consent.

We have mentioned the Left Front regime in West Bengal as an illustration of this system in order to draw attention to the fact that this category does not necessarily belong to the Congress or to the past. In many ways, the hegemony of the Left Front since 1977 surpasses that of the Congress in any state of India. Notwithstanding the appearance of a coalition, it is in the last instance the hegemony of a single party, the Communist Party of India (Marxist) CPI(M). Notwithstanding the allegations, made often, of electoral fraud and strong-arm tactics, this regime does draw upon popular consent and legitimacy. It may well be that the Left Front regime offers a somewhat greater range of options than the Congress did, say, in Uttar Pradesh or Maharashtra. But even the supporters of the regime will not claim that it is currently involved in "revolutionary", transformative politics. On balance, it seems justified to view West Bengal under the Left Front as an instance of unipolar hegemony.

System of Bipolar Convergence

Duverger's famous formulation stipulated that the FPTP electoral system in single-member districts would yield a two-party system. Literature on the party system has emphasised that this type of political competition is bound to bring about political moderation and, in the long run, force both the actors to converge with each other. The Indian party system defied Duverger's expectations for nearly two decades of competitive electoral politics. With the partial exception of Madhya Pradesh and Delhi, it was difficult to find instances of two-party systems in India till as late as the 1980s. The sudden demise of the congress system has witnessed a proliferation of bipolar or "two-plus" competition. Either a straight two-party competition or a competition between two coalitions became the nodal category in the 1990s.

India may have delayed the operation of Duverger's law, but once bipolar competition arrived on the scene it was, as expected, a system of convergence. Bipolar convergence in the Indian context involves homogenisation and emptying the political space. In most cases involving bipolar convergence, it was the outcome of a rapid expansion of a non-Congress party (the BJP in Gujarat, Rajasthan and Himachal Pradesh, the Janata Dal (JD) in Karnataka, and the TDP in Andhra Pradesh), from some regions within the state, to becoming a statewide party. In most of these cases, the bipolar competition is sustained by the catch-all character of the leading parties. It is not that politics lacks social cleavages or that both the parties must gain equal proportion from all sections of society. Yet the system depends on avoiding social polarisation.

On policy issues and agenda of governance, the system is marked by the strong convergence of both formations. In this category, it is not very useful to draw a distinction between the moderate and the narrow options, for there is a seamless continuum between the two. The very existence of two parties keeps up an appearance of contestation and rules out a situation that may be formally described as that of no options. Yet the contest is often reduced to a friendly match. This applies not just to the Congress–BJP competition, where the two parties have to work hard to invent an issue that might differentiate them from the other in the eyes of the electorate. The LDF–UDF competition in Kerala is also marked by considerable reduction in policy differences between the two fronts. Bipolar convergence is characterised by a routine oscillation of governmental power between the two rivals, though it is not a necessary attribute of the system.

System of Multipolar Convergence

The received literature on party systems does associate multipolar competition with convergence. Multipolarity is associated with deep cleavages, social fragmentation, political antagonism, and governmental instability. The experience of the Indian state does not confirm this picture. It is true that the rise of multipolar competition was associated with social fragmentations and sharp antagonisms. Yet within a decade or so of its operation, the system seems to have settled for an unusual combination of social fragmentation and policy convergence. Uttar Pradesh and Bihar saw intense caste polarisation, while Assam experienced an enduring ethnicisation of politics. These polarisations have instituted social cleavages in the electoral arena that may continue for a very long period. Each of these witnessed sharp policy divergences for a brief period. But very soon all the differences were confined to the core "ethnic" issue (implementation of the Scheduled Castes/Scheduled Tribes Atrocities Act in Uttar Pradesh, Yadav dominance in Bihar, the Liberation Tigers of Tamil Eelam [LTTE] issue in Tamil Nadu and the foreigners' issue in Assam), thus clearing the ground for a convergence in economic and other policy matters.

Part of this convergence was induced by the electoral system. The compulsion of manufacturing a majority in our system forced political actors to realise the limits of the politics of polarisation. They were forced to seek support from those very sections that they had sought to exclude from political power (e.g., the BSP's and SP's overtures to upper castes, the AGP's attempt to court the Muslims and the migrants). But a good deal of this convergence was forced from outside by the diminishing space for politics in a globalising economy.

System of Competitive Divergence

We use this expression to describe a system where political competition, bipolar or multipolar, is used to offer substantial choices to voters and becomes the basis of bringing about a change in the life situations of ordinary citizens. The received literature on the party system looks at this category with suspicion, for it represents antagonism and instability. Looked at from our vantage point, this category represents the principle of transformation and the possibility that democratic politics may become the vehicle of social change.

The different instances listed under this category represent very diverse foci and political strategies of the politics of social change. While the mobilisation in Tamil Nadu was along the lines of language and caste, that in Kerala was along class and caste; Bihar and Uttar Pradesh used caste as the master cleavage, while it was class in the case of West Bengal. The format of political competition varied. While Tamil Nadu and West Bengal achieved this in the process of moving from unipolar hegemony to bipolarity, the remaining three states – Kerala, Uttar Pradesh, and Bihar – took advantage of the opportunities offered by multipolar competition that replaced the congress system. These different cases have had varying records of success of the change they attempted to bring about; none succeeded in sustaining the transformative impulse beyond a few years. With the possible exception of Bihar, all these states witnessed sharp radicalisation and polarisation when the party of change was still in opposition. Yet all these cases have one thing in common: the common voter in these states used the ballot to change regimes in order to upset the existing social order and its hierarchies.

One-party Domination

The "domination" here stands in contrast to "hegemony" in the first type of party system. This category is used to describe such deviant but theoretically significant cases where the polity did have groups and parties that could have offered substantial choices on the questions that deeply affected society (the Muslim United Front in Jammu and Kashmir, the ongoing Assam movement in Assam, and Badal's faction of the Akali Dal in Punjab), but the option was not made available to the people through the instrumentalities of the state. The result in each case was a deep sense of exclusion from the power that was handed over to a dominant party. The election lacked popular legitimacy and was perceived as a show of strength by the Indian state. Hence its description as "domination".

Closed One-party System

This category would house the one-party democracies established in many third world countries where citizens had no choice. They either did not have a vote, or if they did it was of no consequence. Fortunately, the operation of democracy in India still does not offer too many instances of that. But the one-party rule thrust by the central government on Jammu and Kashmir between 1953 and 1977, a rule sustained by regular electoral fraud, could serve as an illustration of this possibility.

Systemless Competition

The discussion of the party system assumes the existence of a system in the first place. This involves the somewhat regular existence of the same or similar political parties across a span of time, at least a rudimentary organisational structure of the parties, an established pattern of partisanship, and party identification among voters and social groups. But several states in India defy this minimal expectation and thus require a new category where electoral competition is not bound by party political conventions. It is either pure individual entrepreneurship or loose and very short-term groupings that control the situation. It needs to be underlined that "systemlessness" as defined here is not confined only to the states mentioned under this category. The malady is much more widespread and invites a separate inquiry into the systemic and external factors that bring it about and then sustain it.

IV: Two Lives of the "Congress System"

After this long but necessary detour, we can now resume our journey of the evolution of the party system in the Indian states and to evaluate the usefulness of the revised typology of the party system offered above. We have already noted that the congress system was a product of the specific context in which democratic politics unfolded and became institutionalised in post-Independence India. In order to appreciate this point one needs to be sensitive to the historical contrast between the path of bourgeois democracy in the West and the trajectory of democratic politics in post-colonial societies. In the West, enfranchisement was a gradual process. As this process was in progress, social divisions were also taking shape. Thus, the final moment of enfranchisement was also the moment of freezing of party political divisions. This happened because mobilisation along various social divisions and the evolution of political organisations around these divisions had already taken place (Lipset and Rokkan, 1967). Broadly, the national revolution and the industrial revolution created structures of cleavages that formed political divisions.

In India, the anti-colonial struggle that provided a platform for powerful and mass mobilisation also foreclosed the entry of many social cleavages into competitive politics. Thus, the introduction of universal adult franchise took place in a situation where structures of cleavages had not evolved and thus a large part of society was yet to be mobilised. This provided an extraordinary autonomy to politics in twentieth-century India, for it could activate, institute, or mask various kinds of potential cleavages. The national movement played a crucial role in this regard. It was not that various competing cleavages dictated the terms to this political movement; it was rather that the national movement played a decisive role in upholding certain cleavages and pushing to the background some others.

At the time of Independence, quite a few social divisions were available for political mobilisation. Even a cursory look at these would invite a question as to why many of these were never actualised in politics. At the micro level, the village community, the jail, the locality, were the possible platforms of mobilisation. At the macro level, caste blocs, communal divisions, and regional divisions within and among states could become some of the political cleavages. Also, the division between rural and urban interests, and the division between the agricultural and modern economic sector could have become the bases of political contestations. Or, ideological divisions on the basis of modern versus traditional and Left versus Right were also the potential platforms for political mobilisation. Mobilisation could also take place along issue-based or class-based divisions.

These potential cleavages were mediated by the imperatives of the design of modern democracy. The institutional arrangements adopted by modern democracy coupled with the background of the nationalist movement made it necessary to mobilise people on a macro scale. Political competition, too, came to be conducted on an all-India basis. This meant that localised, micro-level divisions would not gain relevance. The aggregative compulsions of the FPTP electoral system did not encourage the formation of cleavage-based politics. Some social categories were recognised constitutionally, thus providing space for mobilisation of these groups. Scheduled Castes, Other Backward Classes and some others, though not recognised, already existed (Muslims, for instance). The system of reserved seats in joint or single electorates, however, limited the potential of these categories for exclusivist mobilisation.

The partition of the country foreclosed the possibility of mobilisation on the basis of minority status (particularly in the case of the Muslim community). The minority category was accommodated by including minority rights in the constitution and postponing the issue of reform in the personal laws of the minorities. Ironically, these very features were to later become the basis of mobilisation both among the majority community and the Muslim minority. In the course of the freedom movement under the leadership of Mahatma Gandhi, two other social divisions were accepted as more or less authentic. One was the rural–urban divide. The other was regional identity based on linguistic states. In the post-Independence period, the rural–urban divide could not develop as a basis of political mobilisation, for the Congress began with a support base that cut across this divide. Language did become a platform for mobilisation but once again the Congress was well placed to tackle it. By accepting the demand of reorganisation of states on the basis of language the Congress rendered the language divide politically harmless.

In the period immediately following Independence, political parties attempted to cultivate social support by appropriating the different potential divisions. The map of the party system of this period reflected the different spaces available for mobilisation during that period. It also reflected the map of political movements of the first half of the twentieth century. The depth of support enjoyed by different parties corresponded to the way in which the Congress in the pre-Independence period related to the various divisions in Indian society. Thus, during the first decade of Independence, Congress was quite strong in parts of North India where it had accommodated the upper-caste landed interests within the scope of nationalist rhetoric. It was also strong in the areas where, as in Maharashtra, it had amalgamated the middle peasantry castes with a moderate reformist appeal. In other words, the Congress cultivated different social sections in different parts of the country and put them together on the basis of the nationalist ideology. The nationalist ideology thus performed an aggregative function.

This master cleavage put other more specific cleavage-based mobilisations in a position of disadvantage. The socialists were looking forward to an ideology-based political division and sought to take advantage of the legacy of the 1942 Quit India movement. The communists were quite strong in West Bengal and the Telangana region as also in Kerala. They pushed to the forefront the class divisions, particularly in the context of landlordism. The legacy of the self-respect movement and land reform movement along with trade unions in industrial centres formed the bases of the communist mobilisations. The Swatantra Party made initial inroads in the ex-princely states while the Bharatiya Jan Sangh, an offshoot of the Rashtriya Swayamsevak Sangh (RSS), sought to construct a Hindu constituency by capitalising upon the anti-Muslim sentiment among the upper castes. The social justice movement formed the basis of the Dravida Kazhagam in South India, while the Akali movement gave birth to the Akali party in Punjab. This brief summary is indicative of the nature of most of the non-Congress parties that operated in the period immediately following Independence. While these parties corresponded to the different potential divisions in society, they stood in contrast to the aggregative character of the Congress party. Also, the support base of these parties depended upon the extent to which these divisions were actually explored for mobilisation in the course of the nationalist movement. Mobilisations which were either explored by the Congress itself, or which evolved in spite of the Congress (as in the case of the Social Justice movement), or had sympathisers within the Congress (as in case of the supporters of Hindu nationalism), stood some chance of being relevant in the post-Independence period as independent political formations or as viable political issues within the Congress party.

The "congress system" was the inevitable product of this period and this historical backdrop. The central cleavage instituted by the nationalist movement (colonial rule versus the Indian nation) was aggregative in nature and strong enough to override almost all other divisions. The Congress project was the creation of a national political community that cut across all divisions. This engagement with the "imaginary institution of India" (Kaviraj) continued after Independence. Congress became a rainbow coalition precluding other cleavages from any significant space in the political arena. It must be noted, however, that other cleavages were not, at least on the whole, denied legitimate existence; they were, instead, accommodated. We have already noted the accommodation of regional linguistic cleavages. By a series of micro designs and localised coalitions, the Congress managed to hold together the macro design called the national political community. This gave the Congress a "catchall" character constituting cross-cutting cleavages. To go back to our typology, the congress system had the political form of a hegemonic party that allowed competition, dissent, and opposition. Its hegemony never allowed political divisions to be intense, either in terms of exclusiveness of party structure or in terms of ideological persuasions.

This did not mean that no section or state gave rise to a more intense division that the congress system cared to allow. In the first "life" of the congress system itself, one can come across states and social forces over which the hold of the congress system was at best moderate. We have already mentioned that many areas escaped the congress system. These were undermobilised areas such as the ex-princely areas in Rajasthan, Orissa, and Madhya Pradesh, as also the states in the north-east. Interestingly, the states that had a comparatively overmobilised background (Kerala, West Bengal, Tamil Nadu, Punjab) also remained outside the congress system. Similarly, challenges to the congress system came both from the socially excluded (tribals, peasantry castes) and those who were firmly "included" (such as the urban, educated, upper castes). As we shall see later, the map of these challenges almost anticipates the two different directions in which the party systems would develop once the congress system gives way. During this first life of the congress system, there were two failed efforts to challenge the congress system, one by Lohia through a social coalition of lower and peasantry castes and the other by the communists through class divisions (Figure 2).

The first serious challenge to the congress system came in 1967

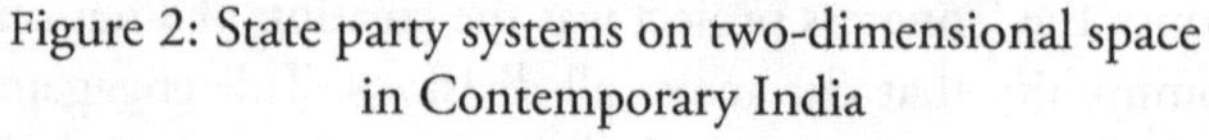

Figure 2: State party systems on two-dimensional space in Contemporary India

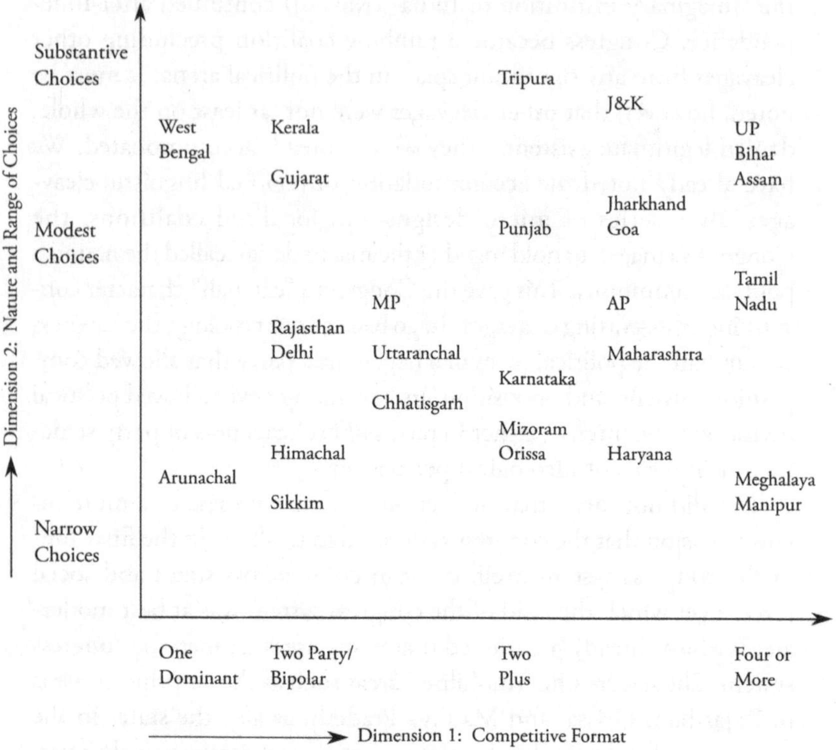

Dimension 2: Nature and Range of Choices

Substantive Choices
Tripura
J&K
West Bengal
Kerala
UP
Bihar
Gujarat
Assam
Jharkhand
Modest Choices
Punjab
Goa
Tamil Nadu
MP
AP
Rajasthan
Delhi
Uttaranchal
Maharashrra
Karnataka
Chhatisgarh
Mizoram
Himachal
Orissa
Haryana
Arunachal
Meghalaya
Sikkim
Manipur
Narrow Choices

One Dominant
Two Party/ Bipolar
Two Plus
Four or More

Dimension 1: Competitive Format

when a reconfiguration of party competition took place across the states. The hegemonic party competition weakened and short-lived coalitions were formed in many states. It was a challenge to the congress system also in the sense that the ability of the Congress party to accommodate dissent within itself eroded considerably, forcing many groups to break away and form various Congress parties in the states. The national political community drawing its sustenance from the nationalist movement and Nehruvian developmental dream was threatened by the aspirations of the disparate social forces.

The second attempt to construct a national political community cutting across regional and social divisions marks the second "life" of the congress system. Indira Gandhi sought to explore the mobilisational potential of the issue of poverty in such a manner that cleavage-based politics produced a nationwide sensibility in support of the new national political community. Thus, a clear class appeal was employed to neutralise other competing cleavages. Another national political community was born. Indira Gandhi's victory both over her intra-party opponents and competitors outside the Congress in 1971 and her quick comeback in 1979–80 had the signature of a reborn congress system.

Underlying this macro-level issue-based cleavage was a careful reconstruction of the social coalition led by the Congress party. It was still a rainbow all right, but thick at its edges. There were state-specific aspects to this reconstruction. In Karnataka, Devraj Urs brought to the forefront the lower Other Backward Classes (OBCs), Gujarat witnessed the Kshatriya, Harijan, Adivasi and Muslim (KHAM) coalition sidelining the Patidars, while in Uttar Pradesh, a brahmin–dalit alliance was put in place. The new social coalition of the Congress had spectacular success. It cut across all other cleavages and resulted in the masking of all interstate differences. And yet, it is possible to see in retrospect that the state-specific reconstruction undertaken by Indira Gandhi's Congress indirectly allowed consolidation of the state as the main theatre for carving out social coalitions. This hidden aspect of the second "life" of the congress system was to play a crucial role in the formation of the "third electoral system" later in the 1990s. Indira Gandhi's political success hinged on the political architecture that was based on state-specific strategies but one which could hide these specificities in order for the macro cleavage to occupy the centre stage. In the 1970s and early 1980s, Indira Gandhi's macro mobilisational strategy was challenged mainly from two quarters. Charan Singh continued to press for the rural–urban cleavage as the principal division of India and uphold agrarian interests throughout the 1970s and the 1980s. The Jan Sangh and later the BJP sought to shape a counter-cleavage around the issue of Hindu nationalism (initially a narrow version, followed by the "integrated humanism" of Deen Dayal Upadhyaya and Gandhan socialism). These challenges, however, remained on the periphery. Indira Gandhi's defeat in 1977 came about from an entirely different route. Non-Congressism was turned into an electoral platform producing the momentary displacement of the Congress party. But this moment could not produce an alternative master cleavage for politics to stabilise around it. As a result, the Congress could reassert itself electorally in 1980.

In spite of the comeback of the Congress, the national community, artificially constructed during the second life of the congress system, was developing cracks. Already, the states of Tamil Nadu, Kerala, and West Bengal had evolved their separate political rhythm independent of the national political waves. Haryana, Karnataka, and Andhra Pradesh also redefined their respective state-specific patterns through the seventies and early eighties. This same period also witnessed major challenges to the national political community emanating from the states of Assam and Punjab. Thus, a large part of the nation was drifting away from the congress system. The congress system was being redefined during the leadership of Rajiv Gandhi, both ideologically and in terms of the social basis of politics. Rajiv Gandhi extricated Congress politics from its vacuous rhetoric of socialism and instead brought issues of technology and globalisation on to the centre stage of political discussions. The 1980s also witnessed the entry of new sections of Indian society into the political process. Rajiv Gandhi was successful in attracting the urban middle-class sections into the process of shaping the political agenda. These sections now started dominating and legitimising the agenda of politics and influenced the thrust of the decisions of the government. For all practical purposes, this redefinition of the congress system anticipated the momentous changes in economic policy that were to take place later. Rajiv Gandhi's efforts to resolve the Punjab, Assam, and Mizo disputes also forced him to redefine the terms of political competition between the Congress and the regional political parties. In retrospect, his attempt at redefinition of the Congress contained within itself the seeds of the erosion and decline of the congress system. But no one thought so at that moment.

V: The Moment of Reconfiguration and Differentiation

The second life of the congress system came to an abrupt end, an abruptness that could only be seen retrospectively. The last years of

Rajiv Gandhi's regime provided ample signs that the congress system was becoming a closed system, devoid of any meaningful choices. The huge majorities enjoyed by the Congress in most of the states of north and west India in the wake of Indira Gandhi's assassination became a stone around its neck. By insulating the party against any pressure from within or outside, these massive majorities served to block the few remaining avenues of political learning and feedback. While on paper most of these states fell under the system of one-party hegemony, the reality was somewhat different.

The congress system was developing elements of both the other possibilities inherent in situations of one-party dominance: those of exclusion and closure. The legacy of the last phase of Gandhi's regime had turned it into a system of domination over the various minorities and ethnic nationalities. Rajiv Gandhi's regime had the effect of making the regime appear a closed one-party system that left little for citizens to choose from. Towards the end of its second life, the congress system desperately needed an overhaul; it needed nothing short of a third attempt to reinvent a national political community and in the process reinvent the Congress the way Mahatma Gandhi did. Rajiv Gandhi was simply not up to this historic task.

The hold of Rajiv Gandhi over the imagination of India's middle classes began to slip after the Bofors' exposure of 1987–8. The run-up to the 1989 Lok Sabha elections indicated a stiff challenge to the Congress and the result was worse than the Congress feared. But even the defeat of the Congress in the 1989 Lok Sabha elections did not suggest a collapse of the congress system. On the face of it, the election results of 1989 seemed to be a repetition of the familiar pattern of 1977: opposition unity, popular wave in North India against the Congress party, a repetition of the Lok Sabha results in the round of assembly elections held in 1990, disintegration of the JD–BJP alliance reminiscent of the break-up of the Janata party, formation of a minority government by Chandrashekhar on the lines of the Charan Singh regime. All the details seemed to fit the model of 1977–9. It was, therefore, natural to expect the return of the Congress in the 1991 election to the Lok Sabha. That did not happen, not even with the support of a sympathy swing after Rajiv Gandhi's assassination during the campaign. This, perhaps, was the moment of demise of the congress system. Ironically, the first government to be formed in the post-Congress polity was a Congress government. But the rules of the game had now changed. This was demonstrated by a string of Congress defeats in the series of assembly elections between 1993 and 1995.

The transition from the congress system to the post-Congress polity was neither gradual nor smooth. It was the product of a systemic shock, a cataclysmic transformation. It was not merely the change in the ruling party or a change in the political actors engaged in competition for power. The terms of political competition and the issues involved in this competition changed dramatically around this time. This period was marked by a fundamental reconfiguration of the party political space. While the decline of the Congress seemed like a crisis initially, it was also an opportunity to revitalise the democratic political competition and introduce greater substance in this.

This reconfiguration of the structure of political competition was marked by the arrival of the three "Ms" on to the national political stage: Mandir, Mandal, and Market. This moment of sudden transformation deserves careful recall and scrutiny, if only to understand better the momentous consequences of some of the changes that happened almost overnight. The controversy over the disputed site at Ayodhya was revived by the Vishwa Hindu Parishad (VHP) and later picked up by the RSS and the BJP. This resulted in the Ramjanmabhoomi agitation, which witnessed high emotional mobilisation among the Hindus and attempts at constructing a homogenised Hindu constituency across caste and region. The politics of Mandir, however, also brought into sharp focus questions about the plural character of Indian society and the resilience of the democratic political process. The Mandir controversy was associated with the division of society between majority and minority religious communities, communal violence, and challenges to the institutional set-up. With Advani and Govindacharya as the chief architects, the Mandir issue sought to shift the terms of political discourse from plural democracy to majoritarian politics. What began in the 1980s as an agitation by a small section of fanatics turned into a major framework for conducting politics during the 1990s. Even before the actual demolition of the Babri Masjid in December 1992, the politics of Mandir had already occupied a central position in national politics. The BJP was catapulted to the centre stage by the events of 1989–91. First, the BJP propped up the V.P. Singh government so long as it suited the interests of the BJP. Then, the BJP came to power in the most crucial state, Uttar Pradesh. This was followed by the party's spectacular performance in the Lok Sabha elections of 1991 that saw it emerge as the main national opposition party.

But, alongside these developments this period also witnessed the unfolding of another process, the rise of dalits and OBCs in Indian politics. The politics of the backward classes has a long history. In the states of South India, the rise of the backward classes happened in the 1960s. But both in North India and at the national level, the entry of the backward classes was stoutly resisted. The failure of the Congress to adapt to the ambitions of these sections in most parts of the country and especially in North India had cost it dearly in 1977–8. Yet the party chose to ignore the recommendations of the Mandal Commission and let the commission's report become the symbol around which the politics of the OBCs was built in North India. When the recommendations were actually accepted by the V.P. Singh government, there were clashes between the forward castes and the backward castes. Both the Congress and the BJP sought to ride piggyback on this upper-caste backlash. The politics of OBCs had already been inaugurated. Sweeping the states of Uttar Pradesh and Bihar, the Mandal issue brought into focus questions about not only the reservations and backwardness of the "lower" castes, but also the question of share in political power.

The Mandal factor instituted caste cleavage into the heart of North Indian politics. It set the tone for the discussions of social justice and symbolised the upsurge of the subalterns. The upsurge was not limited to the OBCs. The BSP, under Kanshi Ram's leadership, had shifted its emphasis from Punjab and Haryana to Uttar Pradesh and started scoring upsets quietly under the din of Mandir and Mandal. The BSP was to make deft use of the sudden opening in Uttar Pradesh politics and surprise everyone by striking an alliance with the Samajwadi Party and winning the 1993 assembly elections in the state. Uttar Pradesh has never been the same again. Although V.P. Singh may be seen as the chief architect of the Mandal strategy, "Mandalisation" of the politics of North India could not have happened without Kanshi Ram, Mayawati, Lalu Prasad, and Mulayam Singh. Soon, no party could afford to take this issue lightly.

If Mandir and Mandal had their rise in the late 1980s, the third "M" surfaced as the new decade unfolded. Yet, it may be noted that the beginnings had been made in the 1980s. Throughout the 1980s, the Indian state was following, somewhat surreptitiously, the programme of restructuring the economy. However, it was only in 1991–2 that bold justifications of the "market economy" started emanating from the official discourse of the Indian state. Narasimha Rao and Manmohan Singh were its architects. Once it emerged, it went almost unchallenged by the political establishment amid the din over Mandir and Mandal. In any case, V.P. Singh was the finance minister in 1985–6 when Rajiv Gandhi took bold initiatives in this direction and the BJP said that the new initiatives were what it had always wanted. Thus, there was little political resistance to the adoption of new ideological positions on the economic policy. But more than a state ideology, "market" ascended to become the ideology of the intelligentsia, the bureaucracy, civil society, as it were. A false or misplaced debate over "socialism" quickly gave way to a more fashionable Nehru baiting. By the time the United Front government came to power at the centre, all this was history. The new government quietly and willingly set about the task of continuing the economic policies initiated by its Congress predecessors. When the BJP finally came to power, it sped up the pace of changes, perhaps somewhat brazenly. The market design of politics did not aim at producing a class cleavage. However, the project of letting loose the "middle-class" consumerist ambition and developing unbridled capitalism ended up instituting class cleavage. At a more subtle level, the market design redefined the political discourse by replacing the nationalism–colonialism contrast that had sustained the national political community since the freedom movement. Such a reworking of the political discourse could have taken place only after the collapse of the USSR.

In retrospect, these three "Ms" look like three projects: three new frameworks of politics trying to replace the old and tattered framework left by the congress system. It is worthwhile to pause and note what they were actually trying to replace. In its first life, the congress system drew strength from projecting a master cleavage: the nation versus the colonial power. This construction helped the congress system build a "national" or "all-India" political community. This was to be the node around which Congress domination was carved out. In its second life, when the relevance of the earlier cleavage had declined considerably, Indira Gandhi sought to construct the "all-India community" by exploiting the cleavage between the poor masses and the rich.

Mandir, Mandal, and Market should be seen as three projects to recreate the "national community". The Mandir design aimed at establishing the national community with the Hindu community as its central pillar, while the Mandal design privileged the OBCs as the core of the national community. The third design saw the middle class as the anchor of the reinvented national community. In doing so, these designs also tried to project a meta-cleavage around which competitive politics would be conducted. The congress system collapsed both under the weight of its own weaknesses and the pressure of these new designs.

The history of Indian politics since 1989 is the history of these three competing frameworks colliding at different points with unequal force and producing consequences no one intended or anticipated. In the period of electoral volatility and governmental instability, collision and competition among these three powerful designs created unprecedented space for the reconfiguration of the party system. The complexities involved in the competition between the new forces emerging out of these new designs and the competition among these designs themselves define the moment of differentiation, the moment of the shift away from the congress system in the 1990s. Many states, through their separate trajectories, saw the break of the Congress party in assembly elections in the 1990s and, by the mid-1990s, this trend appeared on the national political scene.

Looking back at that moment after more than a decade, it is clear that none of these three frameworks have fully realised their own designs. In fact, the main architects of these frameworks, except Advani, are all on the political margins or in the wilderness. And yet, all three have transformed the conditions of political competition as well as the content of politics. The Mandal framework did not succeed in instituting an all-India backward–forward cleavage to serve as the basis of a new political formation or coalition. The rise of dalit and OBC parties did achieve localised success in instituting caste cleavage in some states, like Uttar Pradesh and Bihar. Even there, the Mandal framework could not realise the unity of all backward castes, let alone a broader dalit–OBC unity. Instead, it intensified caste awareness and political ambitions among the various backward and dalit castes.

The main success of the Mandal framework, however, lies in changing the social composition of the political elites within different parties. Post-Mandal, all major parties accommodated the ambitions of the backward classes and facilitated the entry of leaders belonging to the backward castes both at the state and central levels. Ironically, this success of the Mandal framework has meant that the aspiration of its chief protagonists to emerge as the leaders of all backward castes has not been fulfilled and they (particularly Lalu and Mulayam) have been mostly confined to their respective states. The Dalit upsurge has more substantive achievements to its credit than has the rise of the OBCs. At least in Uttar Pradesh the entry of the BSP into high politics has changed the texture of daily life and contributed to the dignity of the ordinary dalit citizen. Notwithstanding all these achievements, the fact remains that the Mandal framework failed to realise its principal ambition of instituting an enduring all-India cleavage and in aggregating the gains of the dalit and OBC upsurge. Mandal was fragmented, localised, and thus contained.

The success and visibility of the Mandir framework has been a little more pronounced than the Mandal framework. Its objective of instituting an all-India issue cleavage along Hindutva versus non-Hindutva lines that would render other divisions obsolete did not succeed, at least not in the way the RSS family wanted. The attempt to create an all-India Hindutva community soon came up against regional and caste divisions. These limitations notwithstanding, the

Mandir framework has been successful in three respects. First, it has caught the imagination of the educated middle classes. Second, the communal cleavage has made its presence felt across the country in areas where the BJP or Jan Sangh did not have any space earlier. Third, and perhaps most importantly, the Mandir framework has altered the terms of political discourse. It has pushed the secular democratic character of the nation-state into the arena of contestation. Though its immediate objective of constructing a temple at Ayodhya has not been fulfilled and its dream of becoming a natural party of governance in Uttar Pradesh on this basis lies in tatters, the Mandir framework has exploited its failures to shift the terms of political discourse about the nature of the Indian nation. In that sense the fate of Mandir has been quite the opposite of Mandal: it has met with local failure but has succeeded in creating something of an issue cleavage at the national level.

Market has been the least voluble or visible of the three projects, but it is perhaps the most successful of the three in realising its objectives. As mentioned earlier, its success hinged mainly on creating a subterranean convergence involving all the major political parties and thus insulating economic policies from the logic of democratic politics. Successive finance ministers shared the common policy space in the 1990s, making it possible for the Market project to be realised. The liberalisation of the economy and its integration with global capitalism replaced the national versus colonial cleavage from the cognitive map of the politician and the middle class alike. The Market project facilitated not only the integration of Indian capitalist classes with their global counterparts, it also provided the ground for an alliance between India's capitalist class and the burgeoning middle classes. This alliance ensured that the economy would be insulated from the volatility of electoral verdicts. Thus, the Market project succeeded in de-linking itself and economic policy decisions from party political competition. While politics would contest the social character of power and the ideological content of the nation, economic policy-making was "depoliticised". Thus, Market succeeded in emptying democratic decision-making of a significant range of choices. The choices were not available to the citizen, for the subject matter had been taken away from the arena of democratic politics. This is how, despite governmental instability, India witnessed remarkable continuity in economic policy. Hidden in these successes of the Market project, however, have been many unintended consequences. As observed earlier, class cleavages have become sharper, the normalisation of the workforce has been under way and this has been altering the patterns of mobilisation, the social location of the middle classes has moved farther from the poor and the disprivileged, civil societal sensitivity to poverty and suffering has declined, and so on. These developments have changed the ground for politics in the long run. The consensus on the new economic policy cutting across the political spectrum has brought about a subtle shift in the party system. Whatever the format of electoral competition, and wherever their prior location on the two-dimensional map of the party system space, all the states have moved downwards on the dimension of the nature of political choice.

This collision of attempts at creating caste, communal, and class cleavages may or may not have succeeded in creating any of its intended divisions, but it did certainly produce a lasting effect on the nature of party political competition that no one designed: the rise of regional or state-based politics. Suddenly, in the 1990s, state boundaries became the real boundaries of the political universe. The state became the relevant unit at which politics was conducted and was intelligible as well. This takes us to one of the central puzzles of Indian politics at the turn of the century: how did three competing attempts to homogenise politics and to create a national political community end up creating quite the opposite: a political community differentiated at the state or regional level?

To begin with, the existing party system constrained the extent to which these homogenisation projects could be realised. Given the unevenness that had developed towards the end of the congress system, the existing structure of political competition offered uneven opportunities to different projects in different parts of the country, creating an impression that the state was the theatre where this drama was being unfolded. There was, for instance, little space outside the congress system for the caste or communal project to spread. This excluded West Bengal, Andhra Pradesh, Tamil Nadu, and Kerala from the location likely to be affected by the Mandal or Mandir projects. In many parts of South India, the caste issue had already been routinised and the Mandal project only effected an additional closure as far as the terms of political competition were concerned. It was mainly in Uttar Pradesh and Bihar where the Mandal project redefined the terms of political competition. In the rest of the North Indian states it was not as successful, mainly because of the lack of a political carrier. In states like Maharashtra and Gujarat, issue space was fuzzy and a political carrier was lacking. For the Mandir project too, North India provided the main theatre because of the availability of both issue space and political carrier. Gradually, the Mandir project penetrated those states where the congress system was declining (for instance, Maharashtra and Gujarat). This led to a differentiated structure of opportunities and political competition. Initially, the occasion for differentiation arose out of the desire of the political actors to take advantage of uneven opportunities in different states. Later, the Mandal and Mandir projects attempted to restructure the opportunity space and the party competition itself.

Second, a long-term change in political geography had prepared the ground for effective utilisation of this unevenness. The politico-administrative structure had produced internal political homogenisation of most of the states. The struggles for formation of a separate state (as in case of Andhra Pradesh, Punjab, Maharashtra, etc.), occasional rhetoric of regionalism or backwardness and discrimination (for instance in Tamil Nadu, or, say, Bihar), separate political trajectories different from the congress system (West Bengal, Kerala) were some of the factors responsible for creating opportunities of internal homogenisation within the state. Besides, the existence of the state as a unit of federal governance had created the salience of the state as a political unit. People of various states got used to the state as the scale of political choices. This had two implications. While people understood national politics through the prism of the state, there was an unwillingness to recognise any other scale or unit of politics between the state and the central government. This contributed to the homogenisation of the state. On the other hand, the emphasis on the state also means that any alternatives smaller than the state disappeared from the political consciousness of the people. Regions within states or districts, etc., became only administrative categories and lost much of their political salience.

The cumulative effect of all these factors was the process of intra-state homogenisation that has been slowly and gradually taking place almost since the 1950s. It has had an inverse relationship with the level of interstate variation. Three patterns may be observed in this respect. Initially, just after the constitution of the Indian union, when interstate variation was moderate, intra-state variation was very high. This was followed by a period, during the second life of the Congress, of low interstate variation coupled with moderate intra-state variation. Finally, we are now witnessing a phase when interstate variation has increased, but intra-state variation has become insignificant. This sums up the story of the rise of states as the authentic node around which political competition becomes intelligible.

Third, the political and economic experience of the last five decades promoted the growth of states as the principal political unit. During India's journey on the road of development, state governments became the loci of all the day-to-day concerns and aspirations of the citizen. Simultaneously, the formation of states on a linguistic basis provided a common cultural platform. Now what Anderson calls the "print cultures" of the regions coincided with the boundaries of the states. This strengthened the separateness and identity of the state. These factors ensured that the three M's discussed above were institutionalised in the party political space in a state-specific manner. This explains the paradox of the drive for homogenisation producing differentiation.

Let us briefly sum up the nature and consequences of this differentiation for party political competition. It must be emphasised that what we are witnessing is not "regionalism". Paradoxical though it may seem, the ascendance of region or state to the centre stage of Indian politics is not an outcome of any conscious ideological mobilisation or movement based on regional outlook or sentiment. Instead, it is a structural consequence that was largely unintended. Moreover, this ascendance of the states is not accompanied by the regionalist tendency. It is a shift of the "locate" of politics and, as a consequence, the filtering of the three frameworks of politics through state-specific configurations. Further, it will be a mistake to describe this development as the rise of a centrifugal tendency or mere "de-centring" of the nation, for the process has given rise to intra-state homogenisation and in the process turned the state into a strong locus of power.

This process of differentiation has already had three long-term consequences for shaping the structure of political competition and filtering the range of effective choices available to ordinary citizens. First, we witness the emergence of the state as the effective level of exercising political choice. Contemporary politics in India has rendered lower levels as unviable and anything higher than the state is perceived as unconnected or remote. This means that national-level electoral verdicts are mere aggregations of state-level verdicts. It has also meant that national-level verdicts become intelligible only when understood in their state-specific context. Second, there is now greater space and incentive for state-level political formations to emerge. In the period of decline of the congress system, a number of "state-level" parties have come to the forefront. Parties like the SP, Rashtriya Janata Dal (RJD), Indian National Lok Dal (INLD), Trinamool Congress (TMC), and Biju Janata Dal (BJD) are some examples of this. Finally, the process of formation of new states has also become less contested than before. The relative ease with which Uttaranchal, Chhattisgarh, and Jharkhand were added to the Indian Union in November 2001 is a case in point. Wherever the project of intra-state homogenisation encountered variations that resisted streamrolling, new states could be formed without the anxieties previously associated with such decisions.

VI: From Hegemony to Convergence in the Post-Congress Polity

The period of transition from the "second life" of the congress system to the "post-Congress polity" was marked by a very unusual historic moment around the beginning of the 1990s, a moment of the reconfiguration of the party system and differentiation of state-level political trends and patterns from the national level. As noted above, this moment was characterised by a confluence of long-term forces, cataclysmic events, and historic personalities. The moment of reconfiguration and differentiation thus created different opportunity spaces in different states and for different social groups. The political story of the 1990s is the story of how different political actors – parties, leaders, and social groups – came to utilise this differential and differentiated opportunity space depending on their skills, resources, vision, mobilisational capacity and, of course, sheer luck. The focus of social science reasoning on structures often leads us to underestimate the role of agency in such critical and fluid moments of "structuration". Could, for instance, Congress have had a "third life" if Rajiv Gandhi have not been assassinated, or if he had been succeeded by a mass leader capable of transforming the party? More realistically, was Gujarat likely to develop a two-party system if Chimanbhai Patel had not led the suicide of the JD? Would Bihar have witnessed the regime transition without the presence of Lalu Prasad? What if, for instance, Mulayam Singh had pre-empted Kanshi Ram in mobilising dalit voters and thus forging a dalit–OBC unity from below?

In particular, the story of the 1990s is the story of a radical opportunity opening up due to the end of Congress hegemony. There was a historic opportunity of freeing democratic politics of the closures and exclusions that the congress system had come to apply and to open up political space for the articulation and aggregation of interests and aspirations of the various social groups and regions that the congress system found itself increasingly incapable of addressing. At a more general plane, the end of the congress system opened up the possibility of competitive politics providing greater room for substantive choices for ordinary citizens. The story of the last fifteen years is the story of how this historic opportunity was missed and negated in and through the arena of competitive politics. At the level of the party system, it is a story of the transition from a system of one-party hegemony to a system of bipolar and multipolar convergence. While the format of political competition underwent a radical change, there was little corresponding change in the nature and range of choices available to citizens. If anything, at the state level there has been a rolling back of the temporary expansion of the range of effective choices available to citizens. In that sense, the story of the 1990s is the story of how the logic of structures of socio-economic inequalities worked as a constant "drag" and finally overpowered and contained the democratic upsurge in the post-Congress polity.

The opportunity opened up by the end of the congress system was not available in equal measure or in a similar measure in all the states. Many states had already broken away decisively from the congress system before the critical moment of reconfiguration of differentiation. Karnataka and Andhra Pradesh had their "critical" elections in 1983, reinforced by mid-term polls to the assembly in both the states, where the long-established patterns of Congress partisanship were decisively broken to give way to what appeared like a two-party system. The Congress hegemony in Assam came to an end with the 1985 elections. The Congress hegemony in Haryana was always suspect; for, ever since the formation of the new state the party could never develop enduring support among the dominant Jat community. Whatever remained of its hegemony was washed away in the 1987 electoral wave by Devi Lal. And then there were states like West Bengal, Kerala, and Tamil Nadu that had broken free of the Congress hegemony way back in the 1960s. The reconfiguration of the party system, especially at the national level, was to have some effect on these states too. In particular the logic of differentiation applied to these states with equal measure. But these states were not the principal sites of the effect of the end of the Congress hegemony.

The principal sites open to radical reconfiguration were of course the states, mainly of North and West India, that were still under the system of Congress hegemony till 1989 or so: Uttar Pradesh, Bihar, Madhya Pradesh, Rajasthan, Gujarat, Maharashtra, Orissa, and, in lesser measure, Himachal Pradesh and Delhi. The sudden demise of the congress system created room in these states for the entry of new political forces or for rearranging the format of party competition. It created an opportunity for new issues and demands to be articulated effectively within the party political arena. It released, even if momentarily, the various subaltern communities and groups that were traditionally affiliated to the Congress and opened up for them the opportunity of political bargaining. In particular, it left Congress vulnerable to aggressive sectional mobilisation of these groups. This had implications for the political strategy of the Congress and its rivals. As opponents of the Congress pursued successfully the path of sectional mobilisation, the Congress found that its catch-all strategy was increasingly not viable. In response to the sectional mobilisation by its rivals, the Congress too became more of a sectional party than it had even been before (Yadav, 2003).

The states that broke away from Congress hegemony around or after 1990 followed three broad trajectories. In the first group are the states of North and West India – Rajasthan, Gujarat, Madhya Pradesh, Delhi, Himachal Pradesh, and possibly the new states of Uttaranchal and Chhattisgarh – that shifted from Congress hegemony to a neat bipolar convergence involving the Congress and the BJP. The second group of states include Uttar Pradesh and Bihar – and now Jharkhand – that utilised this opportunity in a more radical way by moving from Congress hegemony to a system of competitive divergence of a multipolar variety. However, these states did not stay here for very long and have moved towards a system of multipolar convergence. The third group of states – Maharashtra and Orissa – took a more ambiguous route involving a transition from Congress hegemony to multipolar convergence of sorts. Let us look at each of these routes closely.

In terms of democratic possibilities of social transformation, the transition from Congress hegemony to Congress–BJP oscillation is the least promising. The transition involved merely a reshuffling of the political furniture with little or no change in the range and nature of choices available to citizens. The principal change in the format of political competition here was the elimination of the third force from the menu of political options. It needs reminding that all these states had a significant presence of some version of JD till as late as 1990: the JD of Rajasthan was well entrenched in the eastern and northern regions, especially among the Jats; the JD of Gujarat was in fact electorally stronger than the BJP; the JD and the communists were weaker in Madhya Pradesh and Himachal Pradesh, but not extinct; the rural outskirts of outer Delhi had a strong presence of the JD. In all these states, the third force suddenly disappeared in the Lok Sabha elections in 1991 and the assembly elections held subsequently. The BJP used its Ram wave votes to become a statewide rival to the Congress in all these states. Ever since the emergence of a neat two-party system in this group of states, there has been a distinct "dumbing down" of the political discourse. While the Congress has a distinctly lower-caste, lower-class profile in terms of its support, this is not reflected in its policy postures or actions. Power oscillates between the two parties – regularly in Himachal Pradesh, Rajasthan, and Delhi and less regularly in Gujarat and Madhya Pradesh – but without much change in the agenda of politics. The high entry barrier set by the bipolar system enables both the parties to push any serious challenger – the BSP in Madhya Pradesh, the Himachal Vikas Congress (HVC) in Himachal Pradesh, and the various Uttarakhand groups in Uttaranchal – below the threshold of electoral viability. In many ways the choices and bargaining opportunities available to citizens have reduced since the emergence of the two-party system. Arguably, Gujarat may not have gone the way it did in 2002, but for the elimination of the third force and the neat bipolar choice.

In Uttar Pradesh and Bihar the demise of the congress system was accompanied by the sharp decline of the Congress party. In Bihar the Congress never fully recovered from the socialist challenge in the 1960s and continued to lurch in the state while it had a vibrant second life all over the country. In Uttar Pradesh, it was less a case of inherited weaknesses than of an inability to respond to the multipronged onslaught from the BJP, the BSP and the JD (later SP) between 1989 and 1991. The very sharp decline of the Congress party in both these states opened up a huge opportunity for its rivals, unlike the states in the first group where the space released was very limited. The BJP's famous victory in the 1991 Lok Sabha and assembly elections in Uttar Pradesh barely concealed a fundamental change in the rules of the game: electoral contests all over the state had become triangular, if not quadrangular. The BJP took away a slice of the upper-caste and lower-OBC vote of the Congress, but created a new constituency for itself. The SP consolidated the traditional peasant base of socialist parties and combined it with the Muslim vote snatched from the Congress. The BSP's dalit vote came principally at the cost of the Congress.

Attacked from all sides, the Congress was left with no section of its own and was reduced to a rump. The fragmentation of party political space and the competitive politics of caste/community polarisation opened up spaces for regions, issues, and groups that had no voice during Congress hegemony. The issues of dalit dignity and atrocities against dalits have forced themselves on to the political agenda. The Muslim vote cannot be taken for granted. Demand for regions like Uttarakhand, Harit Pradesh, and Poorvanchal have been placed on the political agenda. And, the competition for the lower-OBC vote has improved their bargaining capacity.

Uttar Pradesh did not stay in the system of competitive divergence for very long. Once the three big players had reached a point of saturation of their respective caste–community support, they started looking for strategies to go beyond their "natural" constituency. This imperative of manufacturing a stable majority in this electoral system combined with a lack of economic agenda of the SP and BSP and their inability to come together has meant that the major players are involved in an unfinished search for points of convergence. Their antagonism has turned more personal than political, more episodic than policy driven. It seems that the possibility of the system of competitive divergence producing transformative social and economic policies has receded in Uttar Pradesh. Bihar has reached a similar state through a different route. Here the space vacated by the Congress and the absence of a strong Ram *lehar* or a dalit formation around 1990 was ably utilised by Lalu Prasad to create an enduring social bloc that has ensured a continuous rule of this party. Here again, the fracturing of party political space has opened up many democratic possibilities: the stranglehold of the upper castes over positions of power has been eased, the demand for Jharkhand state was conceded, the voice of backward communities within Muslims is being recognised. But the continuous electoral dominance of the RJD despite a dismal track record on development has meant the disappearance of developmental issues from the political agenda. The citizens of Bihar do have a wider range to choose from, but may not have any substantial choice on the menu. The party system in the newly formed state of Jharkhand is yet to crystallise. As of now, the competitive format lies somewhere between the "two plus" and the multipolar types of contestation. It is more likely that it will move straight into multipolar convergence, with the crucial issue of the control of adivasis on natural resources being kept outside the political domain. But there is an outside chance of a bipolar convergence between the Congress and the BJP at the cost of the Jharkhand Mukti Morcha.

The third route is more varied but the destination is not very different from that of the first two. It involves moving from Congress hegemony to multipolar convergence with a brief halt at bipolar competition. The longest-lasting and perhaps the most intricately worked-out system of Congress hegemony came to an end in Maharashtra in 1995. Since then the competitive structure is basically bipolar, though the presence of the BJP as the Shiv Sena's smaller partner and the split in the Congress gives political competition a quadrangular appearance. Since the Congress hegemony in this state had not become a system of exclusion and closure as it did in many others, it is not clear if the bipolar or quadrangular competition has added much to the menu of choice. In Orissa, the institution of first a bipolar (Congress–JD) and then a triangular (Congress–BJD–BJP) competition has added little to the political agenda except the question of regional discrimination. In this state, untouched by Mandal, dalit upsurge, or class mobilisation, the choices available to the electors are perhaps among the narrowest in the country.

A similar pattern of change in the competitive format characterises Andhra Pradesh, Karnataka, and Assam, though this has been accompanied by a marginal expansion of the range of choices available. In all these states, the entry of the BJP has changed the competitive format. In Karnataka it happened first in the 1991 Lok Sabha elections, but the BJP has stagnated since then. Despite its many splits and unities, the JD has maintained a significant presence especially among rural agrarian classes. The TDP, especially under the leadership of Chandrababu Naidu, built on the opportunity it gained in 1983 in a way in which the JD of Karnataka failed to. The TDP replicated the "catch-all" character of the Congress in social terms and was in fact one of the few non-Congress parties to develop an enduring support among the poor and the very poor. Naidu also deftly used the opportunity provided by coalition politics to prevent third-party inroads into an essentially two-party system. With a strong challenge to the established parties from the Telangana Rajya Samiti, the state may be headed for a "two plus" or even multipolar competition. Despite one-party rule currently, Assam is more multipolar than any other major state of India. The AGP's inability to hold on to its social constituency or build enduring social coalitions has opened the space for the BJP's entry into the state. More than the BJP's entry, it is the fractionalisation of the party political space along ethnic lines that may be the defining characteristic of Assam's party system for some time to come. This fragmentation has created room for the articulation of the demands of smaller groups and ethnicities, but it is not clear if this expansion has any transformative implications.

The states that had broken away from the congress system in the 1960s have not been affected by the demise of the system, though some changes have come about in these due to other factors. Kerala is the one state that has seen virtually no change in its party system in the last twenty years. In the period since 1990, the bipolar competition between the UDF and the LDF has continued as in the past with some minor adjustment among the UDF partners. This tight bipolar competition has left no space for the BJP or any outsider to gain a toehold. The end of the congress system has not meant a decline of the Congress party in Kerala. The overall tendency is for the two alliances to come closer to each other on the issue space in Kerala politics, though it is not quite a case of full convergence. In West Bengal, the dominance of the Left Front and within it the growing dominance of the CPI(M) continued uninterrupted in the 1990s. But the party system was influenced by the logic of differentiation and reconfiguration. In the period of the Left's rise to power, West Bengal was a clear instance of competitive divergence leading to transformative politics. In the last decade, two developments have changed the categorisation. The continued and overwhelming dominance of the CPI(M) and the splintering of the opposition makes West Bengal the only case of one-party hegemony in contemporary India. Over the years the Left has diluted its original agenda, its opponents have taken up some of its issues and thus the divergence has come down. In the case of Tamil Nadu, it was not so much the demise of the congress system as the decline and split of the Congress party in the state that triggered party system reconfigurations. The last decade has seen the rise of many region- and community-based parties in Tamil Nadu, as has been the case in Uttar Pradesh and Assam. In that sense there has been a move towards multipolarity that has ensured more space for smaller formations and interests. The recent practice of creating two grand alliances, on the lines of Kerala, under the leadership of the DMK and the AIADMK would institutionalise the role of smaller parties. This would also bring the system one more step in the direction of convergence, now that the DMK has given up its old ideological positions.

That leaves the last category of states that have seen systemless competition in conditions of continued political fluidity. Haryana stands on the fringe of this category and its position seems to move from election to election. At the moment it appears less unstructured than before, but in the absence of any stable voter–party and leader–party relationship, it could change. The entry of the BJP in Goa seems to have reduced the level of fluidity and introduced an element of competitive divergence in the state. But if the state settles for a Congress–BJP bipolarity, the long-term trend may be for a convergence. The BJP's entry in some hill states of the north-east may have increased the role of national parties in the region, but has done little to change the conditions of fluidity. Manipur and Arunachal Pradesh continue to be the most fluid states in terms of their party system, while structures of competitive politics are emerging in Meghalaya and Mizoram. Tripura has had a stable "two-plus" system of competitive divergence that does not show signs of convergence on the ethnic question. Holding a fair and largely free election in Jammu and Kashmir and then in Nagaland may allow a system to develop in these places, but it is too early to comment on these states.

Conclusions

This preliminary overview of the evolution of the party system at the state level brings to our attention a paradox. Our insistence on classifying the party system in the Indian context along the two dimensions of the competitive format and the nature of choice set helps us define this paradox. On the one hand there is a trend towards opening of the competitive format: single-party dominance is now an exception rather than the rule, a large number of states have shifted to a two-party or two-plus party competition and there are many more multipolar systems than before. On the other hand, there is no clear trend of a corresponding expansion in the range and deepening of the nature of the choice set available to citizens. If anything, the overall impression is that of stagnation or shrinkage in the choice set. Electoral politics does provide occasions for radical choices to be placed on the political menu. But such choices do not stay there for very long. The analysis offered above suggests something of a systemic "drag" towards what we have called "convergence", the tendency for the major players in the party political arena to become like one another and the gradual disappearance from the political agenda of issues with transformative potential.

A tension between these two dimensions of democratic politics has existed for quite some time. But the developments of the last decade in Indian politics have sharpened this contrast. The sudden collapse of the Congress hegemony opened a radical possibility of electoral political competition becoming an instrument of social transformation through effective use of the expanded choices that it was expected to offer. The experience has not borne out this expectation. The emergence of the state as the effective unit of political choice and the development of trends and patterns of state politics independent of one another did open up the stagnant party system for a reconfiguration. As a result of this reconfiguration, party political competition has become more intense. In some cases this new competitiveness has helped marginalised social groups get access to a voice or register their presence. On balance, however, it looks like a case of more and more competition about less and less. Attempts at transformative politics either do not get to cross the entry barriers or are contained in a short span of time through various mechanisms of "emptying" the party political space of its content.

Are we dealing here with a practical failure or is it a systemic outcome, something that is written in the logic of our kind of democracy? If it is a failure of political practice, what is the mechanism of incentives and disincentives that produces such a collective outcome? If, on the other hand, we are talking about a systemic phenomenon, which system are we talking about – the electoral system or the socio-economic system? What are the institutional constraints that account for the systemic "drag"? We leave these questions for students of comparative democratic experience.

References

Anderson, Benedict, 1991. *Reflections on the Origin and Spread of Nationalism*, revised edition. London and New York: Verso.

Blondel, Jean, 1968. "Party System and Patterns of Government in Western Democracies", *Canadian Journal of Political Science*, vol. 1, no. 2.

Chatterjee, Partha, and Gyanendra Pandey (eds), 1993. *Subaltern Studies*, vol. VII, Delhi: Oxford University Press.

Chhibber, Pradeep, and Irfan Irfan Nooruddin, 1999. "Party Competition and Fragmentation in Indian National Elections, 1957–1998", in Roy and Wallace, 1999, *vide infra*.

Church, Roderick, 1984. "Conclusion: The Pattern of State Politics in Indira Gandhi's India", in Wood, 1984, *vide infra*.

Dahl, Robert A. (ed.), 1966. *Political Oppositions in Western Democracies*. New Haven: Yale University Press.

De Souza Peter Ronald, 1999. "Pragmatic Politics in Goa: 1987–99", *Economic and Political Weekly*, vol. 34, nos 34–5.

Drèze, Jean, and Amartya Sen (eds), 1998. *India: Economic Development and Social Opportunity*, New Delhi: Oxford University Press.

Duverger, Maurice, 1954. *Political Parties*. New York: Wiley.

Frankel, Francine and M.S.A. Rao (eds), 1989 and 1990. *Dominance and State Power in India: Decline of a Social Order*, vols I & II. New Delhi: Oxford University Press.

Harris, John, 1999. "Comparing Political Regimes across Indian States: A Preliminary Essay", *Economic and Political Weekly*, vol. 34, no. 48.

Hasan, Zoya (ed.), 1998. *Quest for Power: Oppositional Movements and Post-Congress Politics in Uttar Pradesh*. New Delhi: Oxford University Press.

——— (ed.), 2002. *Parties and Party Politics in India*. New Delhi: Oxford University Press.

Jaffrelot, Christophe, 1993. *The Hindu Nationalist Movement and Indian Politics: 1925 in the 1990s*, New Delhi: Viking.

———, 2003. *India's Silent Revolution: The Rise of the Lower Castes in North India.* New York: Columbia University Press.

Kaviraj, Sudipta, 1993. "The Imaginary Institution of India", in Chatterjee and Pandey, 1993, *vide supra.*

Kohli, Atul, 1987. *The State and Poverty in India.* Bombay: Cambridge University Press, in association with Orient Longman.

Kothari, Rajni, 1961. "Form and Substance in Indian Politics", *The Economic Weekly*, 3 June.

———, 1964. "The Congress System in India", *Asian Survey*, vol. 4, no. 12, December.

———, 1970. *Politics in India.* Boston: Little, Brown.

———, 1989. "Politics and the People", in *Search of a Humane India*, vol. 1, Delhi: Ajanta.

———, Gopal Krishna, Ramashray Roy, Tarun Sheth, Ghanshyam Shah, Bashiruddin Ahmad, and Rushikesh Maru, 1967. *Party System and Election Studies.* Bombay: Allied Publisher.

Krishna, Gopal, 1967. "One Party Dominance: Development and Trends", in Kothari *et al.*, 1967, pp. 19–98.

Kumar, Pradeep, 2000. *The Uttarakhand Movement: Construction of a Regional Identity.* New Delhi: Kanishka Publishers.

Lipset, Seymour Martin, and Stein Rokkan, 1967. "Party Systems and Voter Alignments", *Cross-National Perspectives.* New York: Free Press.

Mair, Peter, 1997. *Party System Change: Approaches and Interpretations.* New Delhi: Oxford University Press.

Morris-Jones, W.H., 1964. *The Government and Politics of India.* London: Hutchinson University Library.

Narain, Iqbal (ed.), 1976. *State Politics in India.* Meerut: Meenakshi Prakashan.

Rokkan, Stein, 1968. "The Growth and Structuring of Mass Politics in Smaller European Democracies", *Comparative Studies in Society and History*, vol. 10, no. 2,

Roy, Ramashray, and Paul Wallace (eds), 1999. "Indian Politics and the 1998 Elections", in *Regionalism, Hindutva and State Politics.* New Delhi: Sage Publications.

Sartori, Giovanni, 1976. *Parties and Party System: A Framework for Analysis.* New York: Cambridge University Press.

Shah, Ghanshyam, 2002. "Contestation and Negotiation: Hindu Sentiments and Temporal Interests in Gujarat Elections", *Economic and Political Weekly*, vol. 37, no. 48.

Sheth, D.L., 2002. "Politics of Communal Polarisation: Precursor to Gujarat Carnage", *Manushi*, 129.

Sinha, Aseema, forthcoming, *Divided Leviathan: Comparing Sub-national States in India.*

Subramanian, Narendra, 1999. "Ethnicity and Popular Mobilisation: Political Parties", in *Citizens and Democracy in South India.* New Delhi: Oxford University Press.

Sridharan, E., 2002. "The Fragmentation of Indian Party System, 1952–1999", in Zoya Hasan, 2002, *vide supra*, pp. 475–503.

Weiner, Myron (ed.), 1968. *State Politics in India.* Princeton: Princeton University Press.

Wallace, Paul, and Ramashray Roy (eds), 2003. *India's 1999 Elections and 20th Century Politics.* New Delhi: Sage Publications.

Wood, John R. (ed.), 1984. *State Politics in India: Crisis or Continuity.* Boulder: Westview Press.

Yadav, Yogendra, 1996. "Reconfiguration in Indian Politics: State Assembly Elections, 1993–95", *Economic and Political Weekly*, vol. 31, nos 2–3.

———, 1999. "Electoral Politics in the Time of Change: India's Third Electoral System, 1989–99", *Economic and Political Weekly*, vol. 34, nos 34–5.

———, 2003. "The New Congress Voter", *Seminar*, no. 526.

Table A1: Effective Number of Parties by Votes: State Assembly Elections, 1952–2003[1]

States	1952–6	1957–61	1962–6	1967–70	1971–7	1977–9	1980–4	1985–8	1989–92	1993–7	1998–2003	State average
Andhra Pradesh[2]	4.5	4.7	3.8	5.0	3.7	4.0	3.1	2.8	2.7	3.1	2.7	3.6
Assam	5.2	3.5	4.1	5.2	3.5	9.0	3.7	5.1	7.6	5.0	4.8	5.2
Bihar	5.0	5.2	4.7	7.3	6.6	4.3	7.6	5.1	6.7	7.5	7.7	6.2
Delhi	3.2	–	–	–	2.7	2.5	2.8	–	–	3.1	2.8	2.9
Gujarat	–	–	3.3	4.0	3.9	–	3.1	2.7	3.9	3.4	2.9	3.4
Haryana	–	–	–	4.8	4.5	4.3	4.7	4.0	5.2	6.7	5.0	4.9
Himachal Pradesh	4.1	–	–	5.5	3.5	3.2	3.3	2.4	3.1	2.6	2.8	3.4
Jammu and Kashmir	–	–	2.1	3.3	3.3	3.5	3.2	6.4	–	5.1	6.3	4.2
Karnataka[3]	3.8	3.7	3.8	2.3	3.0	3.0	3.8	2.7	3.5	4.5	4.2	3.5
Kerala[4]	5.6	3.7	6.6	9.1	–	12.5	19.6	7.4	5.7	6.3	6	8.3
Madhya Pradesh[5]	4.2	4.0	5.8	4.1	3.5	2.9	3.2	2.8	3.6	3.0	3	3.6
Maharashtra	3.8	4.3	3.8	4.5	3.2	6.2	4.3	4.3	5	6.9	5.6	4.7
Orissa	5.2	4.3	4.3	6.2	5.8	3.0	4.0	2.8	2.6	3.5	4.2	4.2
Punjab[6]	6.5	4.3	5.0	4.9	4.0	5.0	3.7	3.4	3.9	4.4	4.3	4.5
Rajasthan[7]	5.6	5	5.5	4.5	3.5	2.9	4.7	3.5	4.4	3.3	3.1	4.2
Tamil Nadu	8.3	5.0	5.0	3.1	2.8	5.0	4.1	–	4.2	4.1	5.5	4.7
Uttar Pradesh	4.3	4.3	6.2	6.0	6.2	3.1	5.2	4.6	5.2	5.0	6.1	5.1
West Bengal	6.2	4.1	3.5	4,.8	4.3	4.7	3.8	2.9	3.6	3.2	4.5	4.1
Average (excluding smaller states)	5.0	4.3	4.5	5.0	4.0	4.7	4.9	3.9	4.4	4.5	4.5	4.5

Tablet A1 (*Contd.*)

Tablet A1 (*Contd.*)

States	1952–6	1957–61	1962–6	1967–70	1971–7	1977–9	1980–4	1985–8	1989–92	1993–7	1998–2003	State average
Arunachal Pradesh	–	–	–	–	–	3.8	3.7	–	3.2	3.7	3.1	3.5
Goa	–	–	–	3.3	4.0	3.7	4.3	–	3.1	4.8	4.2	3.9
Manipur	–	–	–	9.0	7.3	–	11.7	–	3.7	6.0	6.8	7.4
Meghalaya	–	–	–	–	8.3	5.8	6.2	5.0	–	5.6	4.9	6
Mizoram	–	–	–	–	11.1	6.6	3.5	6.0	3.5	3.6	4.9	5.6
Nagaland	–	–	–	5.5	4.7	5.0	5.0	3.8	2.2	3.1	3.8	4.1
Pondicherry	–	–	3.1	3.3	6.2	5.0	6.6	4.4	5.4	6.7	10	5.6
Sikkim	–	–	–	–	–	6.2	–	2.2	1.8	3.0	2.2	3.1
Tripura	–	–	–	2.7	2.9	3.8	3.2	2.7	–	3.1	3.0	3.1
Overall average	5.0	4.3	4.4	4.9	4.7	4.8	5.1	4.0	4.1	4.5	4.6	4.5
Lok Sabha Elections	4.5	3.9	4.4	5.1	4.6	3.3	4.0	–	4.9	7.1	6.8	4.9

Notes: 1. The effective number of parties by votes is calculated by the formula

$N = 1/\Sigma P_i^2$

where p, is the fractional share of the i-th component and Σ (sigma) stands for the summation over all components. For more details on this, refer to the introduction to the statistical appendix.

2. Hyderabad has been included in Andhra Pradesh.
3. Coorg has been included in Karnataka.
4. Travancore-Cochin has been included in Kerala.
5. The former states of Bhopal, Madhya Bharat, and Vindhya Pradesh have been included in Madhya Pradesh.
6. PEPSU has been included in Punjab.
7. Ajmer has been included in Rajasthan.

The figures have been rounded off to the first decimals in calculating the effective number of parties in each state as also to calculate the averages. The effective number of parties by votes for Saurashtra is 2.3, but has not been included in this table.

Table A2: Effective Number of Parties by Seats: State Assembly Elections 1952–2003[1]

States	1952–6	1957–61	1962–6	1967–70	1971–6	1977–9	1980–4	1985–8	1989–92	1993–7	1998–2003	State average
Andhra Pradesh[2]	3.0	2.6	2.7	3.1	1.7	2.5	1.9	1.9	2.2	1.8	2.1	2.3
Assam	2.0	2.3	1.7	3.9	1.4	4.7	1.4	3.0	3.2	3.1	2.8	2.6
Bihar	1.9	2.3	2.8	6.0	3.4	2.2	3.5	2.5	4.6	3.3	4.7	3.4
Delhi	1.5	–	–	–	1.6	1.4	2.1	–	–	1.8	1.6	1.7
Gujarat	–	–	1.8	2.2	2.7	–	1.6	1.4	3.1	1.9	2	2.1
Haryana	–	–	–	2.7	2.4	1.4	3.7	2.0	2.6	4.3	3	2.8
Himachal Pradesh	2.7	–	–	3.1	1.6	1.6	2.7	1.3	1.9	1.6	2.3	2.1
Jammu and Kashmir	–	–	1.1	1.5	1.6	2.5	2.0	2.5	–	2.2	5.1	2.3
Karnataka[3]	2.2	2.0	2.3	3.0	1.7	1.8	3.4	2.1	1.5	3.1	2.5	2.3
Kerala[4]	5.4	3.1	11.1	8.3	–	9	14.5	6.2	4.3	5.4	4.0	7.1
Madhya Pradesh[5]	1.7	1.5	3.8	2.7	1.7	1.7	1.6	1.5	1.9	2.3	2.3	2.1
Maharashtra	1.3	2.9	1.5	1.7	1.4	5	2.3	2.7	3.3	5.1	4.7	2.9
Orissa	3.8	3.5	2.5	4.7	3.9	1.7	1.5	1.5	1.4	2.5	3.1	2.7
Punjab[6]	2.4	1.6	2,9	3,6	2,2	2,7	2,7	2.1	1.7	2.2	2.1	2.4
Rajasthan[7]	2.8	2.2	3.4	3.3	1.6	1.6	2.2	2.6	3.1	2.6	1.6	2.5
Tamil Nadu	5.5	1.8	2.0	2.6	1.6	2.8	2.7	–	1.9	1.7	3.1	2.6
Uttar Pradesh	1.2	2.2	3.0	3.5	3.1	1.4	1.9	2.2	3	3.6	4.1	2.7
West Bengal	2.5	2.5	2.4	6.34	2.5	2.7	2.7	2.2	2.2	2.6	3.7	2.9
Average (excluding smaller states)	2.7	2.3	3.0	3.6	2.1	2.7	3.0	2.4	2.6	2.8	3	2.7

Tablet A2 (*Contd.*)

Tablet A2 (*Contd.*)

States	1952–6	1957–61	1962–6	1967–70	1971–6	1977–9	1980–4	1985–8	1989–92	1993–7	1998–2003	State average
Arunachal Pradesh	–	–	–	–	–	2.7	2.3	–	2.4	2.0	1.2	2.1
Goa	–	–	–	–	2.1	3.7	3.0	–	2.2	3.2	2.9	2.9
Manipur	–	–	–	3.4	6.2	–	9.0	–	3.7	4.1	4.9	5.2
Meghalaya	–	–	–	–	3.3	5.8	3.5	4.0	–	4.7	3.4	4.1
Mizoram	–	–	–	–	25.0	2.2	2.0	8.9	2.2	3.5	2.5	6.6
Nagaland	–	–	–	2.7	3.3	2.5	3.1	2.4	1.9	2.3	1.2	2.4
Pondicherry	–	–	2.0	2.8	4.3	3.7	3.1	3.1	3.5	5.2	5.5	3.7
Sikkim	–	–	–	–	–	2.7	–	1.3	1	2.2	1.6	1.8
Tripura	–	–	–	1.2	1.9	1.3	2.3	2.6	–	1.7	2.2	1.9
Overall Average	2.7	2.3	2.9	3.4	3.4	2.9	3.2	2.7	2.6	3.0	3.0	3.0
Lok Sabha Elections	1.7	1.7	1.8	3.1	2.1	2.6	1.9	–	4.0	5.8	5.5	3.0

Notes: 1. The effective number of parties by votes is calculated by the formula.

$N = 1/\Sigma P_1^2$

where p, is the fractional share of the i-th component and Σ (sigma) stands for the summation over all components. For more details on this, refer to the introduction to to the statistical appendix.

2. Hyderabad has been included in Andhra Pradesh.
3. Coorg has been included in Karnataka.
4. Travancore-Cochin has been included in Kerala.
5. The former states of Bhopal, Madhya Bharat, and Vindhya Pradesh have been included in Madhya Pradesh.
6. PEPSU has been included in Punjab.
7. Ajmer has been included in Rajasthan.

The figures have been rounded off to the first decimals in calculating the effective number of parties in each state as also to calculate the averages. The effective number of parties by votes for Saurashtra is 2.3, but has not been included in this table.

Chart A1: Effective Number of Parties by Votes: State Assembly Elections, 1952–2003

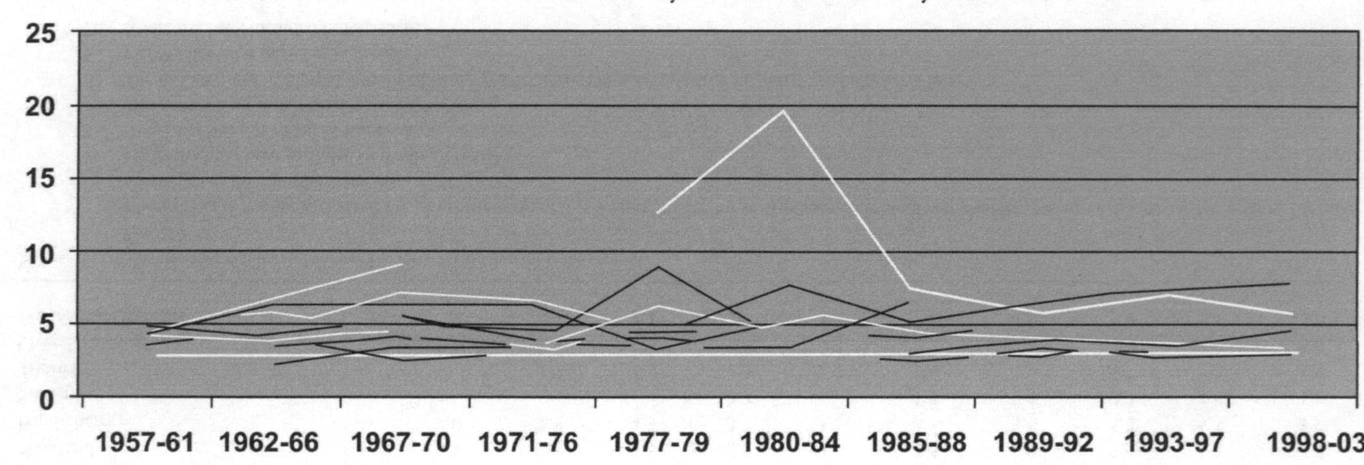

Chart A2: Effective Number of Parties by Seats: State Assembly Elections, 1952–2003

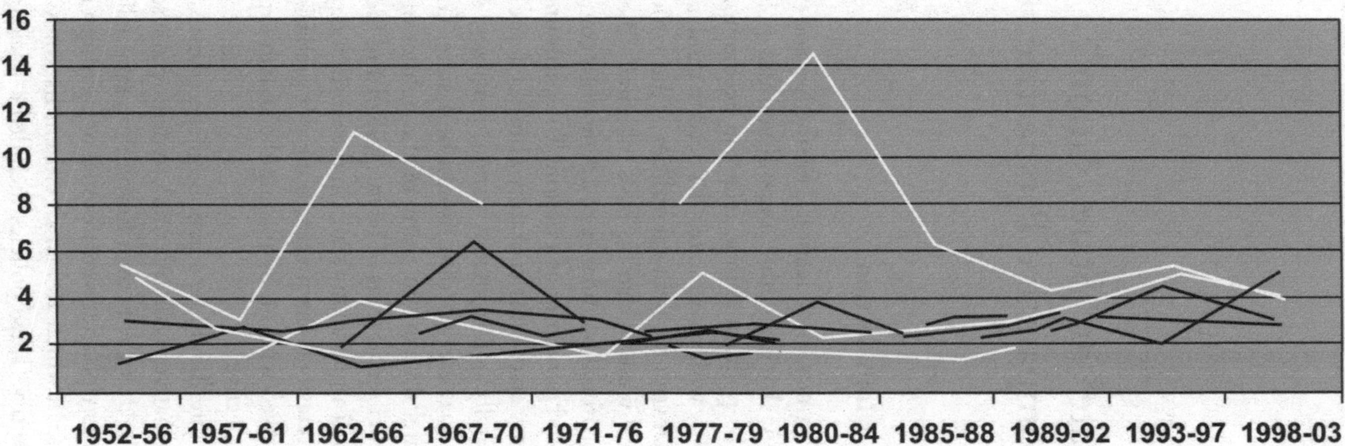

3

"Nation State" or "State Nation"? India in Comparative Perspective

Introduction

ONE OF THE MOST URGENT conceptual, normative, and political tasks of our day is to think anew about how polities that aspire to be political democracies can accommodate great socio-cultural diversity within one state. The need to think anew arises from a mismatch between the political realities of the world we live in and an old political wisdom that we have inherited. The old wisdom holds that the territorial boundaries of a state must coincide with the perceived cultural boundaries of a nation. Thus, this understanding requires that every state must contain within itself one and not more than one culturally homogeneous nation, that *every* state should be a nation, and that *every* nation should be a stare. Given the reality of socio-cultural diversity in many of the polities of the world this widespread belief seems to us to be misguided and indeed dangerous since, as we shall argue, many states in the world today do not conform to this expectation. The present essay is a preliminary attempt to revise the received wisdom by placing the Indian experience in comparative perspective.

The belief that every state should be a nation reflects perhaps the most widely accepted normative vision of a modern democratic state, that is, the "nation state". After the French Revolution, especially in the nineteenth century, many policies were devoted to creating a unitary nation state in France in which all French citizens had only one cultural and political identity. These policies included a package of incentives and disincentives to ensure that French increasingly became the only acceptable language in the state. Political mechanisms to allow the recognition and expression of regional cultural differences were so unacceptable to the French nation state builders that the advocacy of federalism was at times a capital offence. Throughout France, state schools at any given hour were famously teaching the same curriculum with identical syllabi by teachers who had been trained and certified by the same Ministry of Education rules and tests. Numerous other state institutions, such as universal conscription, were designed to create a common French identity and to be robustly assimilative.[1]

Some very successful democracies, such as contemporary Sweden, the Netherlands, Japan, and Portugal are close to the ideal type of a unitary nation state. Some federal states such as Germany and Australia have also become nation states. In our view, if in a polity (at the historical moment when a state-directed political programme of "nation state" building begins) socio-cultural differences have not acquired political salience, and most of its politicised citizens have a strong sense of shared history, the aspiration to create a nation state should not create problems for the achievement of an inclusive democracy. In fact, the creation of such a national identity and relative homogeneity in the nineteenth century was identified with democratisation and was possible in consolidated states. In the twentieth century, however, attempts to create a nation state by state policies encountered growing difficulties, even in an old state like Spain. In our judgement, in the last century virtually no new nation states have been created except as the result of wars, violence, international decisions, oppression, and secession.[2] However, if a polity has significant politically salient cultural and/or linguistic diversity (and a large number of polities do) we will argue that political leaders in such a polity need to think about, and normatively legitimate, a type of polity with characteristics of a "state nation".

Linz and Stepan first introduced this concept in 1996, but only in a paragraph (and one figure):

> We . . . believe some conceptual, political, and normative attention should be given to the possibility of state nations. The states we would like to call state nations are multicultural, and sometimes even have significant

> multinational components, which nonetheless still manage to engender strong identification and loyalty from their citizens, an identification and loyalty that proponents of homogeneous nation states perceive that only nation states can engender.

They went on to say that neither Switzerland nor India were (in the French sense) strictly speaking a nation state, but we believe both can now be called state nations. Under Jawaharlal Nehru, India made significant gains in managing multinational tensions by a skilful and consensual usage of numerous consociation practices. Through this process India became in the 1950s and the early 1960s a democratic state nation.[3]

In order to develop the concept of "state nation" we think it necessary to clear some conceptual ground. In thinking about how "socio-cultural diversities" are politically managed, there are two axes that need to be mapped, with the help of analytical distinctions. The first axis pertains to the nature of socio-cultural diversities that present themselves to political actors. Such diversities are of course a product of developments over a long historical period, but they appear as "givens" to political actors. Hence the temptation to see these diversities as essential, natural, or primordial. Nevertheless, what appear as essential divisions in any given society are no more than social cleavages that happen to be politically activated and mobilised at that moment. There is always a gap between the map of potential cleavages that underlie every society and the actual map of politically salient divisions.

All too often this axis is seen as ranging from "homogeneous societies" to "diverse societies", as if homogeneity or its absence were a "natural" condition or starting point. However, the division between so-called "homogeneous" and so-called "diverse" societies is better captured as a distinction between societies in which socio-cultural divisions have not acquired political salience, on the one hand, and societies in which they have, on the other. A historical context is built into this distinction; and in our assessment, the crucial question is whether such potential cleavages have become activated by the time competitive politics is instituted.

Furthermore, we need to distinguish among societies with different types of politically activated socio-cultural divisions. At one extreme are societies where social divisions have a geographical concentration and are articulated in more than one "nationalist" vocabulary throughout the territory of the state. Such a society may be called a "multinational society". At the other extreme are societies where socio-cultural divisions exist but are not geographically concentrated and are not articulated in a "nationalist" vocabulary. Following the recent literature, we would call such a society a "multicultural" society.

Between these two extremes are a range of societies in which politically salient social divisions do permit varying degrees of geographical concentrations yet are not articulated in a "national" vocabulary but of some other identity, such as class. We stress that the distinctions we are making here are between "ideal types". In reality, a society can be both "multinational" and "multicultural" at once, as well as class divided.

The second axis that invites theoretical clarification is the one we will be principally concerned with in this essay. It relates not to the nature and articulation of socio-cultural diversities, but to the models of *political strategies* and some *specific institutional responses* for dealing with such diversities. Two ideal types can be delineated along this axis, which we shall call (1) "nation state" or (2) "state nation".

"Nation state" policies stand for a political-institutional approach that attempts to match the political boundaries of the state with the presumed cultural boundaries of the nation. Needless to say, the cultural boundaries are far from obvious in most cases; thus the creation of a nation state involves privileging *one* socio-cultural identity over other potential or actual socio-cultural cleavages that can be politically mobilised. "Nation state" policies have been pursued historically by following a variety of routes from relatively soft to downright brutal: (1) by creating or arousing a special kind of allegiance or common cultural identity among those living in a state; (2) by encouraging the voluntary assimilation of those who do not share that initial allegiance or cultural identity into the nation state's identity; (3) by various forms of social pressure and coercion to achieve this and to prevent or destroy alternative cultural identities; and (4) by coercion that might, in the extreme, even involve ethnic cleansing.

By contrast, "state nation" policies stand for a political institutional approach that respects and protects *multiple but complementary* sociocultural identities. "State nation" policies recognise the legitimate public and even political expression of active socio-cultural cleavages, and they evolve mechanisms to accommodate competing or conflicting claims made on behalf of those divisions without privileging or imposing any one claim. "State nation" policies involve creating a sense of belonging (or "we-feeling") with respect to the statewide political community, while simultaneously creating institutional safeguards for respecting and protecting politically salient socio-cultural diversities. The "we-feeling" may take the form of defining a tradition, history, and shared culture in an inclusive manner, with attachment to common symbols of the state and/or inculcating some form of "constitutional patriotism".

In democratic societies, the institutional safeguards constitutive of "state nation" policies most likely take the form of federalism, and often specifically *asymmetrical* federalism, and/or consociational practices.[4] Virtually every long-standing and relatively peaceful contemporary democracy in the world whose polity has more than one territorially concentrated, politically mobilised, linguistic-cultural group that is a majority in some significant part of the territory is not only federal, but "asymmetrically federal" (Belgium, Spain, Canada, and India).[5] This means that, by a certain point, these polities, in order to "hold together" their great diversity in one democratic system, had to constitutionally embed special cultural and historical prerogatives for some of the member units, prerogatives that respond to their somewhat different linguistic/cultural aspirations, demands, and/or historical identities.[6] We believe that had political leaders in India, Belgium, Spain, and Canada insisted upon attempting to impose one language and culture on the country and insisted upon a homogenising nineteenth-century French-style unitary nation state, the cause of social peace, inclusionary democracy, and individual rights would not have been served in any of these four long-standing democratic states. This was so because more than one territorially based linguistic cultural cleavage had already been activated in each of these four countries. The strategic question therefore was whether to attempt to *reject* or *accommodate* this pre-existing, politically activated diversity.

Asymmetrical federalism historically emerged in Belgium, Spain, Canada, and India as a policy response aimed at accommodation. We therefore think that, as a normative concept, an institutional framework, and a set of historical experiences, "asymmetrical federalism" should be strongly considered, by theoreticians and political leaders alike, as a possible approach to democracy in polities such as Sri Lanka and Myanmar that have at least one territorially based, already politically activated, linguistic-cultural cleavage within the existing state.[7] At the same time it needs to he clarified that federalism is neither sufficient nor necessary for the establishment of a state nation.[8] The creation and maintenance of a state nation requires a number of diversity sustaining measures that are not exhausted by federal instruments. For the same reason, it is possible for a unitary state, where diversities are not geographically concentrated, to institute many multicultural practices towards establishing a state nation.

In sum, then, the idea of the nation associated with the "nation state" approach implies creating one common culture within the state, while the idea of the nation associated with the "state nation" approach can contain more than one politically salient culture, but nonetheless encourages and requires respect for the common institutions of the state, as well as respecting existing socio-cultural diversities.[9]

Thus, "state nation" is a term introduced to distinguish democratic states that do not, and cannot, fit well into the classic French-style "nation state" model based on a "we feeling" resulting from an existing or forged homogeneity. For the difference between "nation state" and "state nation" as ideal types see Table 1. Our conception of "state nation" derives from our belief, based on historical case studies and analyses, that democracy is possible in polities that are sociologically and politically multicultural and even partly (but not exclusively) multinational, *if* an effort is made to legitimate the state by those minorities and majorities who could conceivably aim at its delegitimation. Our advocacy of the term "state nation" is also based on our recognition that in some countries cultural groups are not territorially concentrated but

Table 1: Two Contrasting Ideal Types of Democratic States and Cultural Nation(s), "Nation State" and "State Nation"

	Nation state	*State nation*
Pre-existing conditions		
Sense of belonging we-ness	Awareness of, and attachment to, one major cultural civilisational tradition. This cultural identity corresponds to existing state boundaries with minor exceptions	Awareness of, and attachment to, more than one cultural civilisational tradition within the existing boundaries. These attachments do not preclude identification with a common state
State policy		
Cultural policies	Homogenising attempts to foster one core cultural identity, non-recognition of multiplicity of cultures. Unity in oneness	Recognition of, and support to, more than one cultural identity, even more than one cultural nation. All within a frame of some common polity-wise symbols. Unity in diversity
Institutions		
Territorial division of power	Unitary states or mono-national federations. Federacies possible	Federal system. Often de jure, or de facto, asymmetrical. Can even be a unitary state if aggressive nation state policies not pursued. Federacies possible
Politics		
Ethno-cultural-territorial cleavages	Not too salient	Salient and are recognized and democratically managed
Autonomist and/or secessionist parties	Autonomist parties are normally not "coalitionable', Secessionist parties are outlawed or marginalised in democratic electoral politics	Autonomist parties can govern in federal units and are "coalitionable' at the centre. Non-violent secessionist parties can

Table 1 (*Contd.*)

Table 1 (*Contd.*)

	Nation state	*State nation*
		sometimes participate in democratic politics
Citizen orientation		
Political identity	Single identity as citizens of the state and overwhelmingly as members of the nation	Multiple but complementary identities
Obedience/loyalty	Obedience to the state and loyalty to the nation	Obedience to the state and identification with institutions, neither based on a single national identity

instead are so difusely located that even "asymmetrical federalism" is not an option. However, given the robustness of these different politically salient cultural groups, a classic French-style "nation state" may also not be an option for a peaceful democracy without a costly, and most likely non-democratic, period of state-imposed assimilation efforts, and possibly even ethnic cleansing. Nonetheless, in the same cultural context, a state nation may be a possibility, and probably the most possible democratic model to pursue.

Our introduction of the term "state nation" is intended both to introduce a normative standard to which democracies in politics that appear highly diverse can aspire to, and to introduce a set of at least four observable empirical socio-political realities that a polity, if it is a state nation, will manifest.

Although "nation state" and "state nation" at one level are analytic ideal type distinctions, they can be operationalised using a range of indicators. "State nations" can, and have, managed to create powerful and positive citizens' identification with the institutions and symbols of the state, such as the constitution, inclusive democratic institutions and procedures, and guarantees of basic freedoms. A diverse polity, if it has become a state nation, will have the four following empirically demonstrable patterns: (1) Despite multiple cultural identities among the citizens of the polity there will be at the same time a high degree of *positive identification* with the state, and pride in being citizens of that state. (2) Citizens of the state will have *multiple but complementary* political identities and loyalties. (3) There will be a high degree of *trust* in the most important constitutional, legal, and administrative components of the state. (4) By world democratic standards, there will be a comparatively high degree of positive *support for democracy*, among all the diverse groups of citizens in the country, for the specific state-wide democratic institutions through which the multicultural and possibly multinational polity is governed.

At this point, we need to address a potentially powerful but in our view misguided argument about socio-cultural diversity. After the bloody disintegration of Yugoslavia and parts of the Soviet Union, many analysts have begun to reject wholesale all political and institutional frameworks that grant any form of prerogatives to territorially concentrated socio-cultural groups – arrangements which they refer to as "ethno-federal" and/or "national federal". These scholars criticise "ethno-federal" arrangements because they believe that such arrangements privilege "sub-national" socio-cultural identities at the expense of identification with common symbols, institutions, and individual rights. This privileging, they claim, is likely to foster, at least, the activation of conflictual, *as opposed to complementary*, identities, and perhaps violence and fragmentation.[10]

These critics ignore, however, the fact that nearly all successful democratic states with at least one politically activated, territorially concentrated, linguistic-cultural cleavage have institutional frameworks that include a substantial (but absolutely *not*, as in Yugoslavia by the late 1980s, a virtually exclusive) "ethno-federal" dimension. In successful state nations, group rights do not, and should not ever violate the individual's rights that come to them as individual members of the state. Witness the institutional frameworks of the states that we consider to be exemplary state nations – namely, Switzerland, Belgium, Canada, Spain, and India. The institutional frameworks of all of these contain an element of "ethno-federalism". Nevertheless, none of these states can be classified as purely "ethno-federal" either, since in these states recognition of the legitimate public and political expression of active socio-cultural "national" cleavages is balanced with constitutionally sanctioned respect for common symbols, institutions, and individual rights, thus facilitating the maintenance and nurturing of *multiple and complementary*, as opposed to *exclusive and conflictual*, identities.

We believe that it would be a grave error to discard the state-nation approach simply because the institutional framework associated with it tends to contain a significant ethno-federal dimension. In our analysis for a variety of states (such as Sri Lanka or Myanmar) that are not now peaceful and/or democratic to achieve a consolidated democracy, they would have to strive to become state nations. This means, quite simply, that for consolidated democracy to be possible, these states would have to craft institutional frameworks that contain both a substantial "ethno-federal dimension" and (2) mechanisms facilitating identification with common symbols and institutions. If, in the process of democratisation, leaders of these states were to pursue either a pure nation-state model, or a pure ethno-federal model, the result would almost certainly be continued armed struggle and failure to achieve democratic consolidation (see Figure 1).

Let us now attempt to develop our analytic argument in more empirical detail to see if, and if so how, culturally diverse countries such as Spain, Belgium, and, especially India, approximate our ideal-typical model of "state nations". We shall first examine the key role of the *origins* of federalism in state nations (which tend to grow out of an effort to "hold together", rather than an effort to "come together"). The traditional theory of federalism relies heavily on the US experience in which a group of political entities with great political autonomy make a decision to pool some of their sovereignty to create a new state which is federal in form. We call this process "coming together" federalism. Many observers think this is the only model of federation formation.

However, federations can also be formed by political groups in existing unitary states that come to the conclusion that, in order to hold together peacefully and democratically, it is necessary to devolve substantial power to territorially based cultural groups, and in the process shift from being a unitary state to becoming a federal state. Two major examples are Spain after Franco and Belgium from the mid-1970s to 1993. We call the origins of this type of polity "holding

Fig. 1: Democratically Probable and Improbable Relationships between Activated, Territorially Concentrated, Socio-Cultural Identities and Political-Institutional Strategies

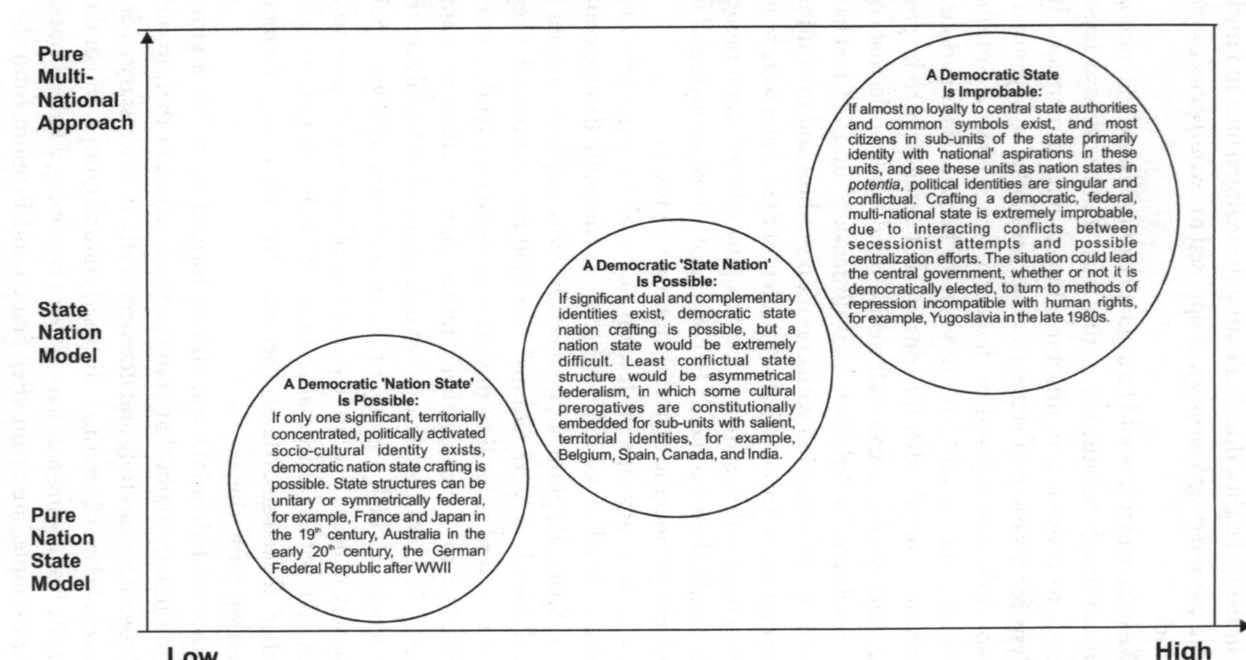

together" federalism. Because of their quite dissimilar origins, the prerogatives and powers of the member units of these two types of federations also tend to differ. Coming together federations tend to arrive at constitutional agreements whereby all full constituent members have exactly the same rights and obligations. They are thus called "symmetrical" federations. However, holding together federations, in order to accommodate some of the most politically salient cultural differences (such as language or religion) that were threatening the unitary state, might constitutionally embed somewhat different prerogatives for different constituent members, such as the status of the French language, Napoleonic Code, and the Catholic Church in Quebec when the Canadian Federation was first formed in 1867, or the status of non-Spanish languages in Spain in Catalonia and the Basque Country when the Spanish federation was created after the death of Franco. Such federations are called "asymmetrical" federations.[11]

Some federal states are based on a strong national identity shared by practically all its citizens. They are relatively homogeneous in their culture, language, and sense of history and can be seen as nation states as the state and the nation are one. Germany, after giving up claims to Alsace-Lorraine and losing the eastern territories inhabited by large numbers of Poles, is now a nation state with tiny minorities enjoying a special status like the Danes on the northern border and the Sorbs. However, with the Cold War division between the *Bundesrepublic* and the German Democratic Republic, there were two states and one nation. The two states each sought to legitimise their rule, in West Germany by what was called the *Verfassungspatriotismus* (constitutional patriotism), the loyalty to the democratic liberal state and its market institutions, and in East Germany by the construction of a socialist state.[12]

The first Austrian republic was founded in 1918 and in its constitution defined itself as part of the German nation and was committed to joining the German Federal Republic. Only after the Second World War did Austria acquire an identity of its own as a state, though not for a long time as a nation.[13]

Most of those writing about Switzerland do not see it as a nation state, but as a voluntary state that we would characterise as a state nation. With its linguistic heterogeneity of largely monolingual German-, French-, Italian-, and Raeto-romansch speaking cantons, Switzerland is a unique federation. Given the fact that none of its linguistic regions, nor its religious communities, or its cantons consider themselves nations, as many Basques and Catalans consider their Autonomous Communities in Spain, it would be wrong to consider Switzerland a multinational state. The Swiss confederation enjoys a legitimacy, felt by all its multicultural and largely cantonal-focused citizens, which is unique, and provides the ideal type of what we call a state nation, where the institutions of the state with its distinctive political culture is the basis of a particular type of identification of its citizens.[14]

In contrast to the ideal-typical state nation of Switzerland, in state nations with important multinational components, such as Spain, Belgium, or Canada, many citizens, who may constitute a significant proportion of the population of federal units, identify with a distinctive nation with its own language, culture, history, rights, and grievances against the state in which they live. The federal state nation is a nightmare to those who originally conceived of the state as a nation state, a nightmare to those who want to nationalise the whole population in the process of nation-building, of which the French Republic would be historically the most successful model, a nightmare for those nation-builders for whom federalism would be conceived, at the most, as a form of decentralisation for the purposes of administrative efficiency.

Multinational Societies: Multiple and Complementary Identities? Possible State Nations? Spain and Belgium

There are those who think that the multinational federal state is inevitably condemned to break up, who see federalism in those states as only a step towards disintegration, and who therefore want to limit the federal constitution and engage in a process of more or less aggressive nation-building. For complex reasons into which we cannot enter here, such efforts are likely to fail, producing a backlash that will lead to the opposite result from the one that their proponents pursue.[15] However, intelligent political engineering, constructive political leadership, and some favourable contextual factors can help overcome some, but of course not all, the tension inherent in multinational societies. A federal state in a multinational society can become a successful state nation. Unfortunately, we have few systematic studies of how this has been achieved.

A study of the Indian Republic and its history and institutions could make an important contribution to this important task for social scientists and policymakers – as can a closer study of Spain and Belgium. Unfortunately, some of the brilliant theorising about multiculturalism, particularly in the US and, to a lesser extent, in Europe, in recent years, is only in part relevant to this task. Multiculturalism in the way that we find it discussed in that literature is not distinctive to federal states. The literature is equally relevant to unitary states like France, with its increasingly important Muslim immigrant population. The literature on multiculturalism is especially relevant to cultural minorities, particularly immigrants claiming a range of rights as individuals and communities, but who are not the same as territorially based autochthonous communities with an articulated or latent national identity.

Most of the literature on nationalism treats national identities as if they were mutually exclusive. The literature is plagued with the use of expressions like "the Catalans", or "the Flemish", and their opposites, "the Spanish", or "the Belgians". However, such expressions represent a gross oversimplification. Though nationalists on both sides reject the idea of dual identities as a form of bigamy, in fact, in all more or less multinational societies, most citizens tend to have dual, and often complementary, or at least not exclusive, identities.

Spain provides a case in point. Since the late nineteenth century and particularly in the twentieth century, there has been a growing sense of cultural and, increasingly, *national* identities among people in bilingual regions in certain parts of Spain – most acutely, in Catalonia and the Basque Country.[16] At the turn of the century, nationalist parties emerged in both of these regions and began to articulate these identities. With the transition to democracy, such identities gained additional strength as a reaction to the Franco regime, since that regime had pursued an aggressive policy against peripheral nationalist movements, including discriminatory language policies. By the end of the Franco era, the democratic opposition had come to sympathise with the peripheral nationalist movements and to demand that their aspirations be at least partly recognised. In the transition to democracy the drafters of the 1978 constitution did just that; they agreed to accommodate linguistic, cultural, and national differences by organising the state as an "*Estado de autonomous*", a type of federal political system.[17]

Since the transition to democracy in Spain, a number of questions about national identity have been asked in opinion polls – all of which reveal the predominance of multiple and complementary identities. Exclusive and competing identities turn out to be the exception, not the rule. For example, when asked, "Which of the following sentences would you identify with most: 'I feel only Spanish', 'I feel more Spanish than Basque/Catalan/etc.', 'I feel as Spanish as Basque/Catalan/etc.'", only a small minority of the population registers an exclusive identity.[18] To be exact, in Catalonia a mere 16 per cent of the population identify themselves as exclusively Catalan, while another 9 per cent identify themselves as exclusively Spanish. The rest – approximately three-quarters of the population there – report some kind of dual identification. They feel as Catalan as Spanish (41 per cent), or more Spanish than Catalan (4 per cent), or more Catalan than Spanish (27 per cent); but they do not exclude one or the other identity. The same can be said for the Basque Country, the region in which identification with the Spanish nation is weakest: even there, those who identify themselves as exclusively Basque barely reach one-quarter of the population (see Table 2).

Nor is Spain an exception in this regard, for the same is true in the case of Belgium. Belgium was founded in 1830, as an independent unitary parliamentary monarchy. In the course of a complex process marked by considerable conflict, it evolved in the twentieth century into a basically binational and bilingual federal democracy.[19]

In Belgium, a number of relevant questions about national identity have been asked in opinion polls too, distinguishing between those who speak Dutch, those who speak French, and the inhabitants of Brussels. All of these again reveal the predominance of multiple and

Table 2: Subjective National Identity in Spain

	Basque Country	*Catalonia*	*Galicia*	*Rest of Spain*	*All of Spain*
Only Spanish	6	9	3	14	13
More Spanish than Cat/Basque/Gal	6	4	6	9	8
As Spanish as Cat/Basque/Gal	34	41	58	59	56
More Cat/Basque/ Gal than Spanish	23	27	27	12	14
Only Cat/Basque/Gal	27	16	5	3	6
Don't know/ Don't answer	4	3	1	4	4
	100	100	100	101	101
N	1,800	1,200	1,200	7,874	10,476

Note: All figures except N are in percentages rounded off to the nearest integral.

Source: For the Basque Country, Catalonia, and Galicia, *Sondeo de opinion del Observatorio Politico Autonomico 2003,* Barcelona: ICPS, 2004; for the rest of Spain and all of Spain, *CIS study* #2455–2002.

complementary identities. For example, when asked "Which of the following statements applies most to you: 'I consider myself only as a Belgian', 'I feel more Belgian than Flemish or Walloon', 'I feel as Belgian as Flemish or Walloon', 'I feel more Flemish or Walloon than Belgian', or 'I feel only Flemish or Walloon?,'" only 3 per cent of the Belgian population choose an exclusive Flemish or Walloon identity. Thus, despite all the talk about the polarisation of identities in Belgium, only a tiny fraction of Belgian citizens reject outright any kind of affective identification with the state. Though another 14 per cent choose an exclusive Belgian identity, the overwhelming majority choose a dual identity of one kind or another – in descending order, "as Belgian as Flemish or Walloon" (43 per cent); then "more Flemish or Walloon than Belgian" (21 per cent); and finally "more Flemish or Walloon than Belgian" (17 per cent).[20]

Among the French-speaking Walloons, who at the time of the founding of the state lived in the more prosperous and state-building communities, identification with the Belgian nation is somewhat stronger than it is for the whole of the population: 18 per cent of them identify themselves as only Belgian and a minuscule 2 per cent feel only Walloon. In the capital city of Brussels, the only place in the country where significant numbers of French speakers and Dutch speakers live side by side, 24 per cent identify themselves as only Belgian; and only 3 per cent fail to mention the Belgian identity. But despite the fact that identification with the region is stronger in Flanders than for the population as a whole, perhaps what is most surprising about the Belgian case is the strength of the Belgian among the Flemish people. In Flanders, which some analysts see as moving towards separation, those who identify themselves as exclusively Flemish amount to a mere 4 per cent of the population. Over 95 per cent of "the Flemish" identify to some degree with the Belgian state (see Table 3).

What's more, not only do the overwhelming majority of citizens in Belgium, regardless of the territory from which they hail, identify themselves at least sometimes as Belgians, but also register a very high degree of affective attachment to an important common state institution – specifically, the monarchy. Such attachment is evident in

Table 3: Subjective National Identity in Belgium, 1995

	All of Belgium	*Flanders*	*Wallonia*	*Brussels*
Only Belgian	14	11	18	24
More Belgian than Flemish/Walloon	21	17	25	27
As Belgian as Flemish/Walloon	43	45	44	32
More Flemish/ Walloon than Belgian	17	23	10	11
Only Flemish/Walloon	3	4	2	3
Don't know/Don't answer	2	1	25	
	100	101	101	101
N	3,651	2,099	1,258	311

Note: All figures except N are in percentages rounded off to the nearest integral.

Source: *1995 Belgian General Election Study*; see footnote 20.

the responses of Belgian citizens to a question about how much they trust their king. As many as 54 per cent of them claim to trust him either very much or a lot (13 per cent and 41 per cent, respectively); while a mere 11 per cent claim to trust him only a little or very little (6 per cent and 5 per cent, respectively). Now, it needs to be noted that among Walloons the level of trust in the king is moderately higher than it is among the Flemish. Whereas 59 per cent of the former claim to trust their king at least a lot, 51 per cent of the latter do so. Nevertheless, despite this difference, the fact remains that *both* communities share a very strong sense of attachment to the king, and by extension to the institution of the monarchy (see Table 4).

We understand this kind of affective attachment to a set of common institutions and symbols to be indispensable for the legitimacy, and therefore stability, of any state in contexts with a high level of cultural, linguistic, and even national heterogeneity. This is why we stress the importance of not only *multiple* but also *complementary* identities within a multinational, federal, democratic framework. Of course, as we have already suggested, there are two intimately related difficulties with this framework: one, that centralists often dream of doing away with the fact of *multiple* identities; and two, that peripheral nationalists often seek to undermine the fact of *complementary* identities. But, at least in the Belgian case, neither of these difficulties seem to be unmanageable. We do not share the scepticism of some other commentators, who feel that Belgium is falling apart. Both the

Table 4: Trust in the King in Belgium, 1995

	Trust very much	*Trust a lot*	*No trust, no distrust*	*Little trust*	*Very little trust*	*Don't know/ Don't answer*	*N*
All of Belgium	13	41	33	6	5	3	3,668
Flanders	11	40	35	7	4	3	2,099
Wallonia	16	43	30	3	5	2	1,258
Brussels	19	41	27	6	6	1	311

Note: All figures except N are in percentages rounded off to the nearest integral.

Source: *1995 Belgian General Election Study.*

overwhelming preponderance of dual identities and, especially, the high level of affective attachment to common symbols and institutions there justify our sense of optimism. Were such affective attachment to common symbols and institutions lacking, there would be reason for pessimism. In Yugoslavia, for example, it is highly doubtful that any Yugoslavian institution commanded a high level of trust by all the citizens of the country. Fortunately, however, the Belgian case is quite different from that of Yugoslavia.

By all means, nationalists would like the question formulated not as "Are you *more* Flemish *than* Belgian?" or "Are you *more* Catalan *than* Spanish?" but rather as "Are you *either* Flemish *or* Belgian?" or "Are you *either* Catalan *or* Spanish?" – despite the ubiquity of multiple and complementary identities in settings that are more or less multinational. And inevitably, both those who speak of self-determination, that is, the right of every nation to become an independent state, and those who favour a total national integration into a single cultural or linguistic community, reject the very idea of dual identities.

This is the main reason (and there are many) why democratic plebiscites are normally such an undesirable solution. People have to make one or another choice, like the one of defining the territorial units for which the decision should be binding. The quorum necessary to reverse such a decision is totally different from a normal election since it cannot be reversed four years hence. A plebiscite might be the only solution in certain extreme situations where the polarisation created by violent conflict has destroyed any dual identity. But in those cases it will mean a loss of rights and equal citizenship for those not supporting the majoritarian choice.

India as a State Nation: Where Does the Indian Polity Fit Comparatively?

For the rest of this essay, we will focus largely on the world's most diverse democracy, India, which we argue has created a state nation but cannot, in the foreseeable future, create a nation state in the French sense of the term. India, perhaps more than any country in the world, has rich lessons to offer about democracy and diversity.

Before we turn to some of these lessons, it is necessary to delimit the scope of this analysis. We are very aware of India's continuing problems with poverty and with low levels of literacy, nutrition, basic sanitation, as well as periodic communal riots. Some of these comparative problems are made abundantly clear in Table 5.

However, the focus of this essay is not on democracy and its linkage to development; we focus here only on how democratic political arrangements of the kind that we analyse below serve as mechanisms for handling societal diversity and potential conflict. It is quite clear to any student of democracy and democratisation in the world, or of nationalism, multinationalism, and diversity and extreme crises of "stateness" such as in the former USSR and Yugoslavia, that India began its democratic experiment with greater politicised diversity than any other long-standing democracy in the world. It is also evident to any analyst of survey data about contemporary India that democracy

Table 5: Comparative Indicators of India's Human and Income Poverty

Average GDP per capita in Purchasing Power Parity (PPP) in 2000 (US dollars) among Arend Lijphart's universe of the thirty-six continuous democracies of the world from 1977 to 1996	$20,252
India's GDP per capita in PPP in 2000 (US dollars)	$2,358
India's Human Development Index (HDI) Ranking among the 173 countries of the world ranked by the United Nations Development Programme (UNDP)	124/173
India's HDI ranking among Arend Lijphart's thirty-six continuous democracies	34/36
India's Human Poverty index (HPI-1) among the 88 developing countries ranked by the UNDP	55/88
Adult female literacy rate in India	45.4%
Percentage of underweight children in India at age 5	47.0%

Sources: UNDP, *Human Development Report 2002: Deepening Democracy in a Fragmented World*, New York and Oxford: Oxford University Press, 2002, pp. 149–52, 157–9, 172, 190–3, 224. Arend Lijphart, *Patterns of Democracy: Government Forms and Performance in Thirty-Six Countries*, New Haven and London: Yale University Press, 1999.

is increasingly supported by the overwhelming majority of these diverse groups in India. This pattern is not sufficiently recognised, or analysed, by general readers or even by most specialist scholars, so one of our major tasks in this essay is to attempt to document, and explain, these phenomena.

We believe that this task requires placing India's experience in comparative perspective. However, this does not mean a simple-minded comparison between India and the US; we believe that the terms of comparison need to be expanded for us to gain insights into the Indian experience of dealing with diversity. Since some basic characteristics of Indian society and polity are clearly distinct from the US, the experience of American democracy is not always relevant; indeed at times it can be quite misleading, for our understanding of India. Comparisons should not be limited to the federalism of the US (or, for that matter, to the party system of the UK, as is often done), but should extend to other long-standing democracies as well. India shares some institutional characteristics with a number of other federal democracies, which should allow us to understand better its problems, successes, and failures. This facilitates some comparisons with the US but also makes it necessary to think of India in the wider context of federal democracies. The US and India are both among the eleven long-standing federal democracies of the world but their federal structures have different historical origins and different functions.[21]

India houses substantially greater and more intense politicised diversity involving culture, language, and religion than the US. There is no numerically preponderant "ethnos" that might dominate democratic politics to the exclusion of the rest. Looked at in purely religious terms, it might appear that there is a dominant community, for the Hindus constituted 82.4 per cent of the population according to the 1991 census. But this apparent homogeneity breaks down if one looks at the regional and linguistic diversity. According to the same 1991 census, the speakers of the largest language, Hindi, comprised only 40.2 per cent of India's total population. Even this 40.2 per cent included a large proportion of persons who speak the various "dialects" of Hindi that are often mutually incomprehensible. In regional terms, the dominant "Hindi heartland", a broad strip comprising nine states of the union and two "union territories" from west to east of north India, had 43.8 per cent of the country's population. But if one looks for the signs of a dominant "ethnos" that shares religion, language, and region – those who are Hindus, Hindi speakers, and reside in the Hindi heartland states – the proportion is only a little over one-third, 34.7 per cent to be precise.[22] A group of this size is not in a position to dominate the country's politics, Besides, these 34.7 per cent of the Indian population articulate their political identities in many other ways, such as caste differences, that serve to fragment this group.

Furthermore, long-standing "separatist" struggles for national independence in some parts of the Indian republic, particularly in Kashmir and in Nagaland, introduce a multinational dimension into the Indian polity. India's federal structures, to a certain extent, reflect a territorially based pluralism. In contrast, the US, in spite of its multicultural society, is more homogeneous than India, its pluralism has little territorial basis, and federalism does not reflect that pluralism directly partly because, unlike India, Canada, Spain, and Belgium, the US does not have a politically salient multinational dimension. The distinct nature of India's diversity also means that the large body of theorising and analysis of multiculturalism in the US and in Europe as the result of large-scale immigration from other societies in recent decades is only in part relevant to India. This is so because in India the multicultural characteristics are the results of a long history and have a distinctive territorial basis to which Indian federalism has been a response. Witness the creation of the new linguistic states in the 1950s and the process of the creation of new states that continues to this day. It should be noted that although the latest creation of three states (Uttaranchal, Jharkhand, and Chhattisgarh) in 2000 was not on the basis of languages, it did reflect the logic of political representation of diversities, for these states gave better representation to tribal populations (as in Jharkhand and Chhattisgarh) or otherwise socio-culturally different groups (as in Uttaranchal).

Before turning to the Indian experience of dealing with diversities, it is worth noting some of the institutional features of the Indian state. India, in contrast to many countries in the developing world, has a relatively strong and usable state with a government, a bureaucracy, an army, a judiciary, and above all democratic institutions which enjoy considerable legitimacy and are able to exercise their authority over most of its population and territory. As we shall document, the overwhelming majority of Indian citizens respect the Indian state and generally expect it to serve the collective interests of its citizens.

In analysing the Indian experience, one cannot overlook the external aspects, specifically the fact that the exit options were effectively closed. It is true that the struggle for independence and the democratic institutions created at that time legitimated a sense of Indian nationhood and a conception of the nation open to its pluralism. This makes it unlikely that major political forces, parties, and intellectuals would favour whatever secessionist demands may appear in the periphery (with perhaps the exception of Kashmir). Even the two main communist parties, the Communist Party of India (CPI) and the Communist Party of India (Marxist) (CPI[M]), have on balance sided with the project of preserving the boundaries of the Indian state, even if by a selective use of coercive state apparatus.[23] This consensus on the importance of the Indian nation, *and* on the Indian state nation, gives support to the institutional rules in the constitution that allow the government to act in defence of the Indian Republic. At the same time, we must remember that, as in many other federal constitutions, there are provisions to defend the Constitution and the unity of the state, if necessary by coercive means. The awareness of that possibility, and the actual record of using those resources in Nagaland, Mizoram, and the Punjab has left those who might question the state in a "no-exit" position, one that forces the search for negotiated compromise within the context of the federal institutions of the state.[24]

Besides, India is not very vulnerable to "international" opinion when confronting secessionist threats, due to its long-standing democracy, its demonstrated atomic capability and large mobile ground forces, and its geopolitical location in the world. Also, it so happens that most of the states (with the exception of Punjab) where secessionist tendencies have been strong, or might arise, are numerically too small, geographically peripheral, and weak in terms of resources to sustain aspirations to independent statehood without external support.[25]

This again is not the case in some other federal multinational states, like Spain, or in the case of Quebec in Canada. Geography is also a favourable factor since there is a continuity of territory that, for example, does not exist in an island state such as Indonesia. The fact that India has a strong state with, as we shall show, long-standing and legitimate democratic institutions, a functioning legal system, and loyal armed forces makes it very different from other federal states in the developing world. Federalism and the processing of new member states, the asymmetrical status of different states, and the multi-tier federalism in some of the states are essential elements of the building of India as a state nation.

In India, as in other federal democracies like Spain or Canada, the institutionalisation of an asymmetrical federalism creates tension and hostility. Many think that only a constitutionally symmetrical federalism, like the one we find in the US, Australia, Switzerland, and Germany, is the ideal form of federalism. However, we want to argue, again, that a comparison of Indian institutions with those of the US, or for that matter Germany, is not the most fruitful approach. Once we enlarge our scope of analysis, we will see that many of the problems that scholars working on India see as unique and threatening may be found in one way or another in other federal multicultural multilingual and/or multinational societies in which there is no shared conception of the nation or a nation state. At the same time, the comparison will show that India and its democratic institutions enjoy legitimacy among the citizens equal to, if not greater than, the institutions in other long-standing democratic federal pluralistic societies. It should be noted that in no political system do all the citizens grant to the state, its institutions, and democratic processes a unanimous legitimacy or allegiance. It is only the size of India and the number of its people that makes these problems somewhat more significant than in some other countries, once we translate the proportions into absolute numbers of citizens.

The building of a state nation in India was not an accident. The idea of India, closer to state nation than to nation state, was nurtured by the national independence movement and would eventually be enshrined in the Indian constitution, sustained by the first generation of post-Independence leadership and institutionalised in competitive politics thereafter. Right from its early stages, much before it became a mass movement in the 1920s, the leaders of the nationalist movement were keen to present themselves as representing different regional identities while representing the Indian nation. The mass phase of the national movement under the leadership of Mahatma Gandhi took this one step further. Rather than deny linguistic and cultural heterogeneity within India, the national movement took pains to recognise and protect it. As early as 1921, the Indian National Congress reorganised its provincial units on the basis of the language spoken in that region and thus laid down the basis of regional autonomy based on language.

Recognition of and respect for diversity was at the heart of the various proposals for the constitution for independent India. Thus, when the Constituent Assembly formally set about its task in 1946, there was little doubt about the provisions for protection of linguistic cultural, and religious diversity. The makers of the Indian constitution did not use a phrase like "state nation". After the partition of India took effect in the middle of the deliberations of the Constituent Assembly, the constitution makers were reluctant to use an expression like "federalism", opting to use "union of states" instead. Yet the institutional structures they set up provided for a robust state nation. In this sense the Constitution of India inherited the intellectual legacy of modern Indian political thought.

The first generation of leaders of independent India, most notably Nehru, were very conscious of the need to accommodate diversity in what they saw as the uniquely Indian model of "nation-building". One of the most oft-repeated cliches of independent India, "unity in diversity", expresses the spirit of the Indian acceptance of what we call state nation. This ensured that the demand for reorganisation of all the remaining states on the basis of language was conceded, even though Nehru was personally disinclined to do so. It is this spirit that has made for a smooth transition from the national dominance of one-dominant party in the 1980s to a regionalised polity in the 1990s. The acceptance of this model is not confined to centrist parties like the Bharatiya Janata Party (BJP), which has questioned the consensus on the secular character of the Indian state, and has accepted the regional and linguistic diversity as one of the basics of Indian nationhood.

Some Indicators Characterising the Indian Polity as a State Nation: Pride in India and Multiple but Complementary Identities

After this broad comparative introduction we can turn to some of the relevant empirical evidence in the hope that it will stimulate Indian and foreign scholars to further research using broader and even better sets of indicators than the ones we now have.

One important indicator of identification of a citizen with the society and the state is the sense of pride, in this case the pride of being Indian. Fortunately, a similar question has been asked in the federal democracies we are comparing and is continuously asked in the member states of the European Union by the Eurobarometer surveys.

The question of pride has been asked in the widely used comparative public opinion survey World Values Survey (WVS) under the direction of Ronald Inglehart, *et al.*, based at the University of Michigan. To date there are four rounds of these surveys available for our comparative analysis, 1981–4, 1990–3, 1995–7, and 1999–2001. The first round covered twenty-two independent countries, the second forty-two, the third fifty-three, and the fourth seventy-five. India has been included in all four rounds. This set of surveys is particularly interesting for comparativists, because each country asks mostly the same questions and many of the questions have been used in all the rounds. We have from the WVS three fairly similar readings on the pride question. In all the three waves about two-thirds of the respondents said they were "very proud" to be Indian. Twenty to 25 per cent said they were "proud", thus pushing the proportion of "very proud" and "proud" to between 85 and 90 per cent. In each of these waves, the proportion of those who said they were "not proud" or "not at all proud" was recorded as less than 10 per cent. This can be confirmed with the State of Democracy in South Asia (SDSA) survey of the Centre for the Study of Developing Societies (CSDS) that has a larger and more representative sample. Better representation of rural and uneducated voters in the CSDS survey has led to a little higher proportion of "don't know" responses, but the basic pattern is the same as that reported by the WVS (see Table 6).

A sense of pride can be based on many different things – from political institutions, the cultural and artistic heritage, the landscape, and last but not least, cuisine. Indians, more than people in many countries of the world, have reasons to be proud of many aspects of Indian society, culture, and history, while the more recent history of some other countries makes it more difficult for its citizens to feel fully proud of their nation. One such case is Germany, for which the Nazi period and the holocaust legacy represent a heavy burden.[26] Those who feel an exclusive identity with another nation and reject the state in which they live are also not likely to feel proud of the state or the nation and its heritage. Some of the variations between countries reflect these different attitudes.

When asked "How proud are you to be an Indian?," 67 per cent say "very proud". Among the world's eleven long-standing federal democracies, only in the US (71 per cent) and Australia (70 per cent) was the number larger, but the percentage was less in Argentina (65 per cent) and Brazil (64 per cent), lower still in Spain (51 per cent), surprisingly low in Switzerland (23 per cent), and lower yet in Germany (14 per cent).[27] Those saying "not very" or "not at all" add

Table 6: Price in India, 1990–2005

	WVS 1990	*WVS 1995*	*WVS 2001*	*WVS 2005*
Very proud	67	66`	67	61
Quite proud	25	19	21	28
Not proud	5	8	5	2
Not at all proud	3	1	2	1
Don't know/ No answer	0	6	5	8
N	2,466	2,040	2,002	5,387

Note: All figures except N are in percentages rounded off to the nearest integral.

Source: WVS stands for different waves of the *World Values Survey*, while the SDSA stands for the SDSA survey conducted by the CSDS.

up to 8.3 per cent in India, certainly more than the US (1.8 per cent) and Australia (2.5 per cent), but less than in the other federal democracies, particularly Germany (31.6 per cent), and, surprisingly again, Switzerland. Perhaps these figures would be different with a more representative sample of the Indian population than the WVS, 1995–7, but they are certainly impressive (see Table 7).

The findings of the WVS can be largely confirmed with the SDSA study 2005. When asked this question in the SDSA 2005, as many as 61 per cent of Indians said they were very proud of being Indian. Surprisingly, citizens from the once-conflictual context of Tamil Nadu register a slightly higher percentage of "very proud" responses (68 per cent) than India as a whole, and in the once-secession-torn Punjab, the total percentage of "very proud" and "quite proud" response (92 per cent) is three points higher than the all-India average. However, citizens belonging to some of the country's other significant marginal groups do register "very proud" responses in lower proportions: even

Table 7: Pride in Nationality in the Eleven Long-standing Federal Democracies

	Very proud	*Quite proud*	*Not very*	*Not at all*	*Don't know/Not applicable*	*Total*
United States	71	23	4	0	2	99
Australia	70	23	2	0	5	100
India	67	21	5	2	5	100
Canada	65	28	3	2	2	100
Argentina	65	24	4	3	5	101
Brazil	64	19	14	2	1	100
Spain	51	36	6	3	1	100
Austria	50	37	6	2	5	100
Belgium	20	46	15	7	11	99
Switzerland	23	47	16	7	7	100
Germany	15	46	22	7	9	99

Note: All figures are in percentage, rounded off to the nearest integral.

Source: The data for all countries is from responses to the question "How proud are you to be (nationality)?' *Human Beliefs and Values: A Cross-Cultural Sourcebook Based on the 1999–2002 Values Survey*, eds Ronald Inglehart, *et al.*, Mexico, DF: Siglo XXI Editores, 2004.

so, among the seven marginal groups or states listed in Table 8, only in Mizoram does the proportion of those who feel very proud or proud dip below three-quarters of the population (see Table 8).

There are certainly citizens of India who do not question the Indian state but feel very strongly a part of another identity, which potentially can serve as a basis for a nationalist sentiment and political movement, as has been the case with a minority among Sikhs identifying with the project of Khalistan as an independent Sikh state. There are finally some groups in the North-East who share very little in Indian national identity, who feel a distinctive national, or at least tribal, identity, and who at one point or another have questioned the authority of the Indian state and fought for an independent status. Some of these, most notably in Mizoram, have been reintegrated into the Indian state and participate, thanks to federalism, in the Indian political process.[28] However, for some people, India is just a state nation, and for a few of them probably something like a multinational state from whose authority they cannot escape under normal circumstances. Fortunately for India's federal democracy there are not many such states and most can be found in the periphery in the North-East. The Nagas (inside Nagaland and to a lesser extent in surrounding states such as Manipur) are the prime example,[29] as are the people of the Kashmir Valley.[30]

Table 8: Pride in India for all Citizens and for Marginal Groups and States, 2005

	All India	*Tamil Nadu*	*Muslim*	*Scheduled Caste*	*Punjab*	*Scheduled Tribe*	*Non literate*	*Mizoram*
Very proud	61	68	58	57	55	44	44	36
Quite proud	28	24	31	31	37	38	34	38
Not proud	2	1	1	3	3	2	3	11
Not at all proud	1	0	2	2	1	1	2	2
Don't know/ No answer	8	7	8	7	4	15	17	13
Total	100	100	100	100	100	100	100	100
N	5,387	345	635	1,023	73	443	1,964	121

Note: All figures except N are in percentage, rounded off to the nearest integral.

Source: *SDSA, 2005*, CSDS, provisional figures.

Survey evidence gathered by the CSDS allows us to examine the question of political identities in contemporary India in an empirical manner. A question about subjective national identity was asked in two of its recent surveys based on a probability sample of the national electorate. The first survey, the NES, 1998, provided for three answer categories, while the most recent survey, the Indian component of the SDSA, 2005, also provided for the two in-between categories ("more Indian than state identity" and "more state identity than Indian"). Notwithstanding the minor differences in question wording, the pattern of responses is quite similar. Unlike both Spain and Belgium, the modal response category in India is "only Indian". Nearly half the respondents privilege their Indian identity over identities of their respective states, which also happen to be linguistic identities in most cases.[31] Even when the in-between category of "more Indian than state identity" was introduced in the 2005 survey, as many as 35 per cent of all respondents chose "only Indian" to describe their identity with 12 per cent opting for the new category. To recall, only 13 per cent Belgians and 14 per cent Spanish respondents opted for only national identity in response to the same question. This reflects the depth of nationalist sentiments in a country where nationalism emerged from an intense anti-colonial struggle. At the same time this response does not rule out significant reservations: about a fifth of the respondents privileged their state identity over their Indian identity. Even after providing the in-between option of "more state identity than Indian" the proportion of those who opted for "only state identity" was a little higher than in Belgium or Spain. Less than one-fifth Indians opted for the middle category of equally Indian and state identity, compared to about half of the respondents in Spain and Belgium (see Table 9).

Democratic State Nations: Who Supports Democracy in India?

We argue that democratic political institutions and processes are essential components of the viability and stability of multicultural, multilingual, multinational state nations. Democracy makes possible the identification with the state of many of its citizens who might have different identities, who might question their nation state, but

Table 9: Subjective National Identity in India, 1998–2005

	NES 1998	*SDSA 2005*
Only Indian	50	15
More Indian than state identity	NA	12
As Indian as state identity	16	19
More state identity than Indian	NA	10
Only state identity	20	12
Don't know/Don't answer	14	12
	100	100
N	8,140	5,385

Note: All figures except N are in percentage, rounded off to the nearest integral.
Source: *NES, 1998* and *SOSA, 2005*.

are ready to be loyal citizens of the state. Authoritarianism might serve to impose a nation state model on the society, as was the case of Spain under the authoritarian regime of Franco. But, as the data for Spain show, the result ultimately was a backlash of resurgence and, in the Basque country, violent extreme nationalism.

Democracy, and more concretely federal democracy, can serve to integrate such a society. The *Verfassungspatriotismus* of Dolf Sternberger, developed by Jurgen Habermas in the German Federal Republic, might not have been important in Germany after the unification of the Bundesrepublik Deutschland (BDR or West Germany) and the Deutsche Demokratische Republic (DDR or East Germany), but it certainly is an important component for more heterogeneous societies. It is not the only component of support for a state nation but is certainly one of the most important ones. It is for that reason that a more detailed discussion of the attitude of Indians and of different groups in Indian society towards democracy and democratic institutions is so vital to our interpretation of the politics of diversity.

In analysing the attitudes of citizens towards democracy and democratic institutions, there are some necessary distinctions that are not always made. For example, there is strong evidence from many countries that we need to distinguish the belief in the need for certain institutions and their desirability and legitimacy from the attitudes about the way those institutions actually perform. People in principle might support democracy, but they may often have serious misgivings about how their particular democracy is actually functioning. A distinction between the "legitimacy of institutions" and the "efficacy of institutions" is therefore crucial.[32] Citizens may believe that democracy is the best form of government for a country like theirs, but when asked if democracy is able to solve the problems of their society, they might be less enthusiastic. When that question is followed by "How is democracy working in our country?" the answers might be quite negative in many circumstances. The negative response to the actual performance of democratic institutions in the long run is likely to erode the belief in the need for those institutions, but there is also evidence from many studies that these are different dimensions. The same is true, even more so, with political parties. In many democratic countries people agree on the need for parties to articulate their interests and demands but, at the same time, a large number of people have little trust in actual political parties. There are many and complex reasons for this distrust in practically all democracies, a distrust which is not translated into rejection of political parties in principle as necessary institutions in a democracy, and even less of democracy itself.[33] Nor does it necessarily translate in declining levels of identification with actual political parties. The same is true to an even greater extent in attitudes towards the incumbents of many offices in democratic systems. The use of one or other indicator alone may capture different dimensions and sometimes lead to pessimistic perceptions about the stability of democracy.

A classic question that has been asked in many countries that we find quite useful because it gives the respondent four alternatives is: "With which of the following phrases are you most in agreement?" (1) "Democracy is preferable to any other form of government". (2) "In some circumstances an authoritarian government can be preferable to a democratic government." (3) "For someone like me a democratic or non-democratic regime makes no difference." (4) "Do not know" or no answer. Our studies document that in India the "do not know" response is more likely among poor and uneducated segments of the population and thereafter it should not be surprising that in the NES, 1999, this is 27 per cent, the largest proportion ever recorded in the list of countries where this question has been asked (though it had dropped to 20 per cent by 2004).

When we turn to the first alternative, agreement with the statement that democracy is better than any other form of government, the results vary considerably between countries, but nowhere is the proportion unanimous. In India, according to the NES, 2004, it is 70 per cent of all those interviewed, which means that 88 per cent of those expressing an opinion agree that democracy is preferable. The second alternative, that in some circumstance an authoritarian government may be preferable, is the choice of 4 per cent of the population. Those who say that for someone like themselves a democratic or non-democratic regime makes no difference are only 6 per cent of the population.

Let us look at the answers in a few other countries. In Brazil, the number with no opinion is 15 per cent, a large one in comparison to other democracies, but those clearly preferring democracy are only 41 per cent, those expressing the potential support for an authoritarian alternative 21 per cent, and those indifferent 23 per cent, a much less favourable response than we find in India. If we turn to a relatively new democracy, Spain, the number of "no answer" is quite small, 6 per cent, and those preferring democracy 78 per cent, those potentially supporting an authoritarian alternative 9 per cent, and those indifferent 7 per cent – figures that are very similar to those we find in India. The Spanish data have been consistently within this range over a long period of time. In Latin America, only Uruguay, with 80 per cent democratic, 8 per cent authoritarian, and 6 per cent indifferent, is regularly more supportive of democracy than India.[34] Even in Chile after the painful experience of authoritarianism, democracy is endorsed by only 52 per cent, 19 per cent do not exclude the authoritarian alternative, and 25 per cent are indifferent, though those without opinion are only 4 per cent. In summary, in an international comparative perspective the support for democracy in India is very high (see Table 10).

Despite India's high approval of democracy at the aggregate level, we immediately have to ask ourselves whether in the heterogeneous

Table 10: Attitudes towards Democracy and Authoritarianism in India and Five Important "Third Wave" Democracies

	India 2004	*Uruguay*	*Spain*	*India 1999*	*Korea*	*Chile*	*Brazil*
Democracy is preferable to any other form of government	70	80	78	60	58	52	41
(Per cent of valid responses excluding DK)	(88)	(85)	(83)	(82)	(62)	(54)	(48)
In some circumstances an authoritarian government can be preferable to a democratic government	4	8	9	6	27	18	21
For someone like me, a democratic or a non-democrate regime makes no difference	6	6	7	7	8	25	23
Don't know/ No answer	20	6	6	27	7	4	15
N	27,148	1,213	1.000	8,133	10,37	12,00	1240

Note: All figures except N are in column percentage, rounded off to the nearest integral. Figures in parentheses in the second row are for percentage of valid responses if the don't know, and no answer, are treated as missing data.

Source: The data for India are from the *NES, 1999 and 2004*, of the CSDS, Delhi. Data for Uruguay, Brazil, and Chile are from the *Latino Barometer 1996*, directed by Marta Lagos. The Spanish data are from the *Eurobarometer 37*, 1992. The Korean data is from the *Korea Democracy Barometer*, 2004, directed by Doh Chull Shin.

Indian population there are some segments of society that are much less supportive of democracy than the all-India average. A very important finding is that in India *all* religious groups are strongly supportive of democracy. Indeed, statistically, the responses are virtually identical across all religious groups. From a comparative perspective, it is also interesting to note that the 71 per cent of Indian Muslims saying "democracy is always preferable" is a higher figure than that recorded by any Latin American country ever, with the exceptions of Costa Rica and Uruguay (in some years). Evidently, whatever deep cleavages and differences might exist along religious or communal lines, they are not reflected in the attitude towards democracy. Democracy can be a key unifying element among all Indians (see Table 11).

Not unexpectedly, among the "very poor" the number of those who do not know or have no answer is particularly large. Even so, the majority of them, 61 per cent, opt for democracy, and 9 per cent opt for a non-democratic alternative. Among the "poor" the proportions are 71 per cent and 10 per cent respectively. Indeed, among those who expressed their opinions, the proportions were virtually identi-

Table 11: Support for Democracy in India as a Whole and for Marginal Groups and Minorities

	All India	*Muslim*	*Christian*	*Sikh*	*Scheduled Caste*	*Scheduled Tribe*	*Very poor*	*Poor*
Democracy is always preferable	70	71	74	71	65	61	61	71
(Percentage of valid responses)	(88)	(87)	(911	(88)	(87)	(81)	(87)	(88)
Sometimes authoritarianism is preferable	4	4	3	4	3	5	3	4
No difference	6	7	5	6	6	8	6	6
Don't know No answer	20	18	19	19	25	26	30	19
Total	100	100	101	100	100	100	100	100
N	27,145	3,103	838	687	4,967	2,356	8,117	9,409

Note: All figures except N are in column percentage, rounded off to the nearest integral. Figures in parentheses in the second row are for percentage of valid responses if the don't know and no answer are treated as missing data.

Source: *NES, India, 2004.*

cal across all income groups. What's more, a very similar pattern of convergence is apparent across the different castes. As such, it is clear that democracy is not the preference of either the more privileged or the more underprivileged, or of any given caste among Indians but is a shared preference.

In view of the historic tensions between Tamil Nadu and the Republic in the early years, and the more recent conflict in Punjab, it is noteworthy that a commitment to democracy is above the Indian average in both states. In Tamil Nadu, 81 per cent prefer democracy, 4 per cent authoritarianism, 5 per cent see no difference, and 11 per cent have no opinion. In Punjab, 70 per cent prefer democracy, 4 per cent prefer an authoritarian alternative, and 7 per cent see no difference for themselves. Similar patterns can be observed in two other conflictual contexts, namely, Gujarat and Mizoram. In Gujarat, 82 per cent prefer democracy, 6 per cent authoritarianism, 5 per cent see no difference, and 7 per cent have no opinion; while in Mizoram 89 per cent prefer democracy, 3 per cent authoritarianism, 3 per cent see no difference, and 5 per cent have no opinion (see Table 12).

In summary, whatever deep cleavages and differences might exist along religious, social, or regional lines, these are not reflected in the attitude towards democracy.

Although we will turn later to the problem of the distrust of different institutions and particularly political parties, it is important to note how much Indians agree with the need for parties in answering the question: "Suppose there were no parties or assemblies, and elections were not held, do you think that the government in this country can be run better?" Only 19.8 per cent of the population has no opinion, and 68.8 per cent reject a system of government without parties, assemblies, and elections, and only 11.4 per cent agree with that possibility. These answers are obviously quite consistent with the commitment to democracy we have just noted.

India as a State Nation: Assessing Trust in Institutions

Let us try to go beyond the overall question of support for democracy to trust in the major institutions of the Indian state. The study of trust

Table 12: Support for Democracy in India as a Whole and in Some States

	All India	*Tamil Nadu*	*Punjab*	*Gujarat*	*Mizoram*
Democracy is preferable (percentage of valid responses)	70 (88)	81 (91)	70 (88)	82 (88)	89 (94)
Sometimes authoritarianism is preferable	4	4	4	6	3
No difference	6	5	7	5	3
Don't know/ No answer	20	11	20	7	5
Total	100	100	100	100	100
N	27,145	843	814	1,106	505

Note: All figures except N are in column percentage, rounded off to the nearest integral. Figures in parentheses in the second row are for percentage of valid responses if the don't know and no answer are treated as missing data.

Source: *NES, 2004.*

has been a major research area in policy analysis and social science research for the last three decades or so. Recently, Pippa Norris from Harvard attempted to bring this research together so as to be able to make comparative judgements about trust in institutions.[35] Using the WVS, 1990–3, she constructed a composite index of trust by measuring expressed trust in five major institutions she felt were important for a democratic state: parliament, civil service, the judiciary, police, and the military. She did this for twenty-three democracies, one of which was India. India's composite score for citizens' institutional trust was the highest among these twenty-three democracies, clearly ahead of its closest competitor, Norway (see Table 13).

In order to see if India's very high comparative standing concerning trust in institutions held up in a later survey, we ran the data on trust in institutions for the eleven long-standing federal democracies

Table 13: Institutions and Political Trust in India and Twenty Other Democracies, 1990–1993

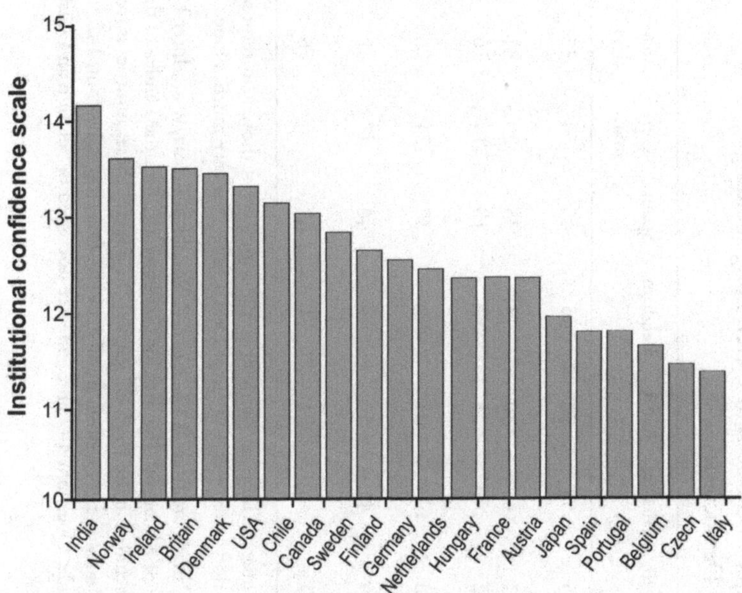

Source: Pippa Norris, *Critical Citizens: Global Support for Democratic Governance*, Oxford: Oxford University Press, 1999, Figure 11.2, p. 229.

based on the 1995–7 round of the WVS. If we combine the total percentages of respondents who answered that they had a "great deal of trust" or "quite a lot of trust" in an institution, India ranks first or second out of the eleven long-standing federal democracies in five of the six categories. No other country scores in the top two more than twice. At the opposite end of the scale Argentina ranks last in four of the six categories (see Table 14).

What's more, when we calculate the average ranking in trust for all of the major institutions indicated above, we find that of the eleven long-standing federal democracies, India is the country that ranks the highest on trust, followed by Switzerland, and then Canada. This finding is of major theoretical import, because none of these countries approximate the "nation state" model. Rather, they are all closer to the ideal type of the "state nation". Nor does such a finding appear

Table 14: Citizen Trust in Six Major Institutions in Eleven Long-standing Federal Democracies

Institution	India	India's rank	Switzer-land	Canada	Brazil	Austria	USA	Belgium	Spain	Ger-many	Aust-ralia	Argen-tina
Legal system	67	1st	65	54	55	58	36	45	45	54	35	27
Parliament	53	1st	41	38	33	41	30	43	35	28	31	16
Political parties	39	1st	25	NA	32	NA	21	NA	18	14	16	8
Central government	48	2nd	50	38	48	NA	31	NA	30	24	26	27
Civil service	53	2nd	43	50	59	42	52	43	40	47	38	8
Police	36	10th	67	84	45		71	51	61	70	76	23

Note: All figures are in percentage, rounded off to the nearest integral. Table entries refer to the sum total of those who respond "Great deal" or "Quite" to the question "How much confidence do you have in . . .? Great Deal, Quite, Not very much, None".

Source: The data for all countries except Austria, Belgium, and Canada are from *WVS, 1995–7*, Ronald Inglehart, *et al.*, Inter University Consortium for Political and Social Research, University of Michigan. The data for Germany are from the Lander of the former West Germany, Canada, Belgium, and Austria were not included in the 1995–97 survey. The data for these countries is from *World Values Survey: 1990–3*. For both the 1990–3 and 1995–7 surveys the question numbers were, from top to bottom, 142, 144, 137, 141, 143, and 145. Question 143, was not asked in Canada. Questions 142 and 143 were not asked in Belgium and Austria.

to be a fluke; for when we examine the entire universe of the eleven long-standing federal democracies and calculate and compare the mean trust score and average ranking of the five federal states closest to the "state nation" model with that of the six states closest to the "nation state" model, we find that on the whole the state nation set scores significantly better than the nation state set. The mean trust score for all the five state nations in this set is 46.8, while the score for the nation states is only 38.2. In terms of the rank, the average rank of state nations is 4.8, compared to 7 for the state nation. Prima facie, thus, it does not appear that the "state nation" model produces any deficit in political trust, as many analysts fear. To the contrary, there is strong evidence that shows a higher level of citizen trust in long-standing federal democracies approximating the model of the "state nation", than in the long-standing federal democracies that approximate the model of the "nation state" (see Table 15).

While very impressive, Tables 14 and 15 are based, as we discussed previously, on a sample in India that under-represents illiterates and rural dwellers and was only given in eight of the country's fifteen official languages, so we must look at other surveys to measure trust with greater confidence. Table 16 presents a comparison of the responses on trust in institutions from the latest round of the WVS of 2001 with the SDSA survey carried out by the CSDS in 2005. While the level of trust recorded in the latter is a little higher than the WVS, the internal order of the five institutions is more or less the same: the police and political parties finish at the bottom of the heap. The data from the survey carried out by the CSDS have the advantage of expanding the range of institutions about which we have information. The data show that two of the most trusted institutions in India are the judiciary and the Election Commission. An independent and powerful federal institution, the Election Commission of India is responsible for supervising the fairness and efficiency of the entire electoral process.[36] The fact that the Election Commission of India is a highly trusted institution helps give the democratic electoral process itself an enhanced legitimacy. In comparative terms, even when we substitute the CSDS survey for rhe WVS sample, India's relatively high trust ranking holds up (see Table 16).

Table 15: Citizen Trust in Major Institutions in the World's Eleven Longstanding Federal Democracies "State Nations' versus "Nation States'

Country and type	*Mean rank among 11 countries*	*Mean trust score for 6 institutions*
State Nations	4.8	46.8
India	3.0	49.3
Switzerland	3.7	48.5
Canada	4.0	52.5
Belgium	6.3	45.5
Spain	7.2	38.2
Nation states	7.0	38.2
Brazil	4.6	45.3
Austria	5.0	52.3
USA	5.9	40.2
Germany	7.6	35.9
Australia	8.0	37.0
Argentina	10.6	18.2

Note: See Table 12. For the two questions on which we do not have data for all eleven countries, we adjusted the rankings of the rest by multiplying the actual ranking by eleven, then dividing by the number of countries for which data exist.

Source: The data for all countries except Austria, Belgium, and Canada are from *WVS, 1995–7*, Ronald Inglehart, *et al.*, Inter University Consortium for Political and Social Research, University of Michigan. The data for Germany are from the Lander of the former West Germany. Canada, Belgium, and Austria were not included in the 1995–7 survey. The data for these countries is from *World Values Survey: 1990–3*. For both the 1990–3 and 1995–7 surveys the question numbers were, from top to bottom, 142, 144, 137, 141, 143, and 145. Question 143, was not asked in Canada. Questions 142 and 143 were not asked in Belgium and Austria.

What do our survey data, linked to our knowledge of voting and governing practices, indicate about India's overall political development in the last three decades? Contrary to observers who see growing signs of political disintegration in India, there are signs that in fact there is growing participation, a growing sense of efficacy and, despite the proliferation of parties, especially state parties, a growing commitment to Indian democracy as a way of managing diversity among previously marginalised groups.

Table 16: Trust in Institutions in India, World Values Survey, and State of Democracy in South Asia Survey

	WVS 2001	*SDSA 2005*
Legal system	NA	59
Parliament	41	43
Political parties	28	36
Central government	49	62
Civil service	38	47
Police	34	42
Election Commission	NA	51
N	2,002	5,385

Note: Table entries except N are for the percentage, rounded off to the nearest integral of respondents who said a "great deal" or "quite a lot" to a question about their trust in different institutions of India.

Source: *WVS, 2001, SDSA, 2005.*

There is a general presumption, especially in American sociological literature, that the lower the education level and income level, the lower the voting participation rates and the sense of personal political efficacy.[37] This is coupled with the belief that in the modern world political trust in institutions has been declining for over three decades. Finally, there is Samuel Huntington's famous axiom that if participation increases faster than institutionalisation, there can be a crisis of governability. Most of these assumptions and/or worries are true for the US, some are true for Western Europe, but none are true for India.

Let us first examine the widely held hypothesis that the lower the socio-economic status, the lower the voting turnout. In the US, this assertion holds true with brutal regularity. If we divide levels of income into the quintiles, for each quintile that income decreases in the US there is a monotonic decline in voter turnout, 77 per cent, 67 per cent, 59 per cent, 52 per cent, 43 per cent. The same holds true, even more sharply, for the six levels of education in the US. If the percentage of postgraduate voters is 84, then for each descending level of education the percentages are 79, 66, 57, 43, and 38. Also, Blacks and Latinos vote less than Whites. In the non-presidential year of 1994, for example, 47 per cent of Whites voted, 37 per cent of Blacks voted, and 20 per cent of Latinos voted.

In sharp contrast to the US, in India voting rates are not monotonic. Illiterates have a higher turnout than do postgraduates, who in fact have the lowest turnout rate. In terms of income, quintiles 3 and 4 vote at *higher* rates than do the two wealthiest quintiles, 1 and 2. In terms of ethnic/cultural community, in 1998 the Muslims, Sikhs, and Scheduled Castes (SCs) *all* voted at higher rates than did upper-caste Hindus. As Table 17 makes clear, the thesis linking lower socio-economic status with lower voting rate is confirmed for the US, but does not hold for India.[38] This has not happened in every election, as the Muslim turnout dropped in the Lok Sabha elections held in 2004. But the basic pattern holds: those at the top of the socio-economic hierarchy are not at the top of the voting turnout tables.[39]

Another major thesis in US political sociology literature is that there is a general decline in voting rates in the democratic world and some believe that this decline is due to a decrease in what is called a sense of "efficacy" on the part of voters. In the US, the NES based at the University of Michigan has shown a general decline in voters' sense of personal efficacy from the mid-1960s to the present. From 1952 to 1964, the average of four observations was 69.7 per cent. By contrast, the average of four observations between 1994 and 2000 was only 39.7 per cent.

The NES series in India uses the following question for measuring political efficacy: "Do you think your vote has an effect on how things are run in this country or do you think your vote has no effect?" Unlike the data from the US, we do not have a large number of points to plot the time series for efficacy for India. But the Indian NES offers three observation points – 1971, 1996, and 2004 – that allow us to read a trend. The trend in India is quite the opposite of the US: 48 per cent of the respondents felt efficacious in India in 1971, 59 per cent felt efficacious in 1996, and 68 per cent felt efficacious in 2004. To be sure, efficacy is being measured here with reference to the worth of votes and the significant changes in this respect partly reflect the growing competitiveness in India's electoral politics in the last two decades. Yet, if significantly greater proportions

Table 17: Socio-economic Status and Voting Turnout in USA and India

USA (1988)			India (1998)		
1998 Turnout 49%	1988 Turnout 60%		Turnout 62%		
(Turnout below expressed as percentage of voting age citizens)			(Turn of below expressed as percentage of electorate)		
Income			*Income*		
1) Lowest quintile	43%		1) Lowest quintile		57%
2)	52		2)		65
3)	59		3)		73
4)	67		4)		60
5) Highest quintile	77		5) Highest quintile		47
Education			*Education*		
No High School	38%		Illiterate		57%
Some High School	43		Up to Middle		83
High School graduate	57		College		57
Some College	66		Post-graduate		41
College Grad	79				
Post-graduate	84				
Community	% Voted		*Community*		
	1994 (Non-(Presidential Year)	1996 (Presidential Year)		1971	1998
White	47%	56%	Hindu (Upper)	61%	60%
Black	37	50	Hindu (OBC)	45	58
Latino	20	27	SC	58	75
			ST	36	59
			Muslim	88	70
			Sikh	85	89

Sources: For India, Yogendra Yadav, "Electoral Politics in Time of Change: India's Third Electoral System, 1989–99', *Economic and Political Weekly*, vol. XXXIV, 21–28 August 1999, pp. 2393–9. For the US, Jan E. Leighley and Jonathan Nagler, "Socioeconomic Bias in Turnout, 1964–1988: The Voters Remain the Same', *American Political Science Review*, vol. 86, September 1992, pp. 725–6.

of citizens feel that their vote makes a difference, this is undeniably positive for democracy and resonates well with the data on trust that we have examined.

Table 18 presents the data on changing levels of citizens' efficacy and legitimacy regarding the democratic system for some of the marginalised groups between 1971 and 2004. The most interesting thing about the Indian data is that if we select the groups that felt most marginal concerning their effective participation in 1971, virtually all of them express a growing belief that their "vote has an effect on how things are run in this country", that is, in their efficacy as a voting citizen. Out of sixteen groups whose sense of efficacy was recorded in 1971, the seven groups which expressed the lowest efficacy, in ascending order from the bottom were the Scheduled Tribes (STs), illiterates, women, the lowest economic quintile (the "very poor"), the SCs, the second lowest economic quintile (the "poor"), and the rural population. However, in 1996, *all* of those seven groups expressed significant increases in their sense of efficacy compared to 1971. Again in 2004, almost all of them expressed increased efficacy over 1996. This growing sense of efficacy could have expressed itself in a growing desire to be anti-system, and since India is a long-standing democracy this might have meant an increasing dissatisfaction with democracy. In India, however, what we see between 1971 and 2004 is a high correlation between the previously most marginal groups feeling more efficacious, and being more supporting of democracy (see Table 18).

Thus we can conclude that there is growing participation, a growing sense of efficacy and, despite the proliferation of parties, especially state parties, a growing commitment to Indian democracy as a way of managing diversity among previously marginalised groups.

Conclusion: India as a "State Nation": Past Accomplishments and Potential Threats

In our introduction to this essay we argued that being a "state nation" is an extremely important normative goal for culturally diverse, democratic federations, especially those with a multinational dimension to

Table 18: Growing Sense of Political Efficacy and Legitimacy of Democracy among Marginalised Groups in India, 1971–2004

	Political efficacy			*Support for democracy*		
Year	*1971*	*1996*	*2004*	*1971*	*1996*	*2004*
National average	48	59	68	43	69	72
Group						
ST	31	48	59	41	66	68
SC	42	60	65	38	67	69
Illiterate	36	47	55	31	62	61
Women	36	51	6t	32	64	67
Very poor	38	51	60	32	64	66
Poor	43	55	68	37	68	71
Muslims	50	60	66	40	72	73
Rural	44	57	66	39	69	70

Notes: All figures in row in percentage, rounded off to the nearest integral.

Sources: India, NES, 1971, 1996, and 2004. The efficacy question was: "Do you think your vote has an effect on how things are run in this country or do you think your vote makes no difference?" The support for democracy question was: "Do you think that the government in this country can be run better if there are no parties or assemblies or elections?"

their diversity. We also argued that the relative presence or absence of a polity's state nation characteristics could be empirically observed by focusing on three of the most politically important attributes: (1) the degree of pride in citizens' *identification* with being members of the polity, (2) the degree of citizens' *trust* in the most important state institutions such as electoral procedures, the judiciary, and the civil service, and (3) the degree of citizens' *support* for the democratic political system.

Notwithstanding the great linguistic, religious, ethnic, and caste differences within its diverse polity, India, as we have documented, is one of the world's democracies that scores most highly on those three state nation indicators of identification, trust, and support. We have seen that the evidence in this respect is quite strong. India also has extensive and rich patterns of *multiple and complementary* identities, which was our fourth indicator of a well-functioning democratic state nation. However, in a diverse polity, even if the average is fairly high, if within a major minority group support for democracy is low, this can present a problem. Yet this is not the case in India concerning religious minorities because the major religious minority group, the Muslims, support democracy at a slightly higher level than the Hindus. Of the major long-standing democracies in the world, India has by far the lowest per capita income. If the poorest segment of the population had a very low support for democracy, in contrast to the rest of the population, this could also present a problem, but the very poor in India prefer democracy in about the same measure as anyone else. Finally, given India's caste system, it is important to note that even even among the SCs (formerly called "untouchables"), support for democracy is no different from other groups once we focus on valid responses. In comparative terms, therefore, the percentage of India's Muslims, of India's former "untouchables", and of India's poorest strata, who answer that "democracy is preferable to any other form of government", is about 10 percentage points higher (for each of these potentially alienated anti-democratic groups) than the overall average of Latin American countries for 2001. More importantly, the proportion of those who may prefer authoritarianism, or are indifferent to the choice between democracy or non-democracy, is negligible in all the marginal social groups.

We would like to end this essay, however, with a cautionary note. There is a significant element of "social construction" in politics. What has been socially constructed can under some circumstances be socially destroyed. More than a quarter of a century ago Linz and Stepan edited a volume on the breakdown of democracy in twelve West European and Latin American countries. One of their major conclusions was that "the independent contributions made to the breakdowns by political incumbents is a theme that emerges in almost all cases."[40] Linz and Stepan also concluded that virtually none of the breakdowns were inevitable.

The authors of this essay have two major conclusions concerning India's political engagement with its socio-cultural diversity: (1) India is not a classic "nation state", (2) India has managed to create a functioning, democratic "state nation". In our judgement, the effort to attempt to forge a classic nineteenth-century French-style "nation state" in India would destroy the present functioning "state nation", and not assure the creation of a democratic nation state. Worse, the attempt to forge a nation state in India would be extremely dangerous and ultimately unsuccessful: it would almost certainly produce, at best, a lower quality democracy, an eroded state nation, and weaker attachments to the state. To the extent that the Indian state is not a classic nation state, and that India's federalism has historically recognised the diversity of people within the union, a nation-building campaign on the basis of a cultural, linguistic, or religious homogeneity, and the marginalisation of those not sharing in this sought-after homogeneity, is a potential threat to the Indian state. Many loyal segments of the population in India, many groups, and many political administrative units can be part of a state nation, but not part of a classical nation state.

However, some militant groups often referred to as "Hindu fundamentalists" (such as the Rashtriya Swayamsevak Sangh [RSS], the Vishwa Hindu Parishad [VHP], and the Bajrang Dal), all of which are frequenrly – but not always – supported by the BJP, often use a discourse, and carry out actions whose socio-political consequences, were their project for India ever implemented, would make India sharply less inclusive. In the Gujarat massacres of 2002, in which approximately 1500 Muslims were killed, many of the "Hindu fundamentalist" groups supported, indeed helped coordinate, the anti-Muslim attacks with the complicity of the BJP's government of Gujarat. In the wake of the massacre, the BJP swept elections in Gujarat and discussion of the "Gujarat model" as the future electoral strategy of the BJP was frequently referred to in Indian political discussions. After the Gujarati elections, Ashutosh Varshney wrote the following, which we will quote at length to give an indication of the worries that some important observers had about the threats to pluralism and inclusiveness in India.

> In effect, Gujarat's electorate has legitimized independent India's first unambiguous pogrom, a pogrom much more vicious than the killings of the Sikhs in Delhi in 1984, a pogrom that came closest to the classic, anti-Jewish pogroms of Russia and Europe in the late nineteenth and the first half of the twentieth century. The Congress Party, though deplorably

involved in anti-Sikh violence in 1984, never had an anti-Sikh ideology. For purely electoral reasons, the Congress became contingently anti-Sikh for a while. In contrast, the VHP, the RSS and their stormtroopers, the Bajrang Dal, have an anti-Muslim ideological core.

Therefore, the victory of Rajiv Gandhi's Congress in 1985 was basically a strategic phenomenon, cynically parasitic as the Congress campaign was on Mrs Gandhi's assassination by her Sikh bodyguards. The BJP's victory in Gujarat, on the contrary, is ideological. It is about a larger vision of the polity, in which minorities, as the RSS put it earlier this year, must seek protection in the goodwill of the majority community, not in the laws of the land. The massive legitimization of an ideologically charged pogrom is a truly bruising embarrassment for all Indian liberals and a serious undermining of the pluralist national vision in Gujarat.[41]

Clearly, if the Gujarat model ever became a dominant model in India it would bring about the socio-political destruction of India's state nation. We hope that this will not occur, and we do not believe it is inevitable that it will.[42] Much of what we have discussed about India's institutions as well as the data we have presented here about the attitudes of citizens would support a more optimistic view.

Notes

1. For a classic book on these policies, see Eugen Weber, *Peasants into Frenchmen: The Modernization of Rural France, 1870–1914* (Stanford: Stanford University Press, 1976). Most nineteenth-century progressives and democrats, particularly those associated with the French Revolution, were profoundly opposed to federalism. For the normative advocacy of a unified, homogeneous nation state, see the entries on "Federalism". "Federation", "Nation", and "Department" in the extremely illustrative but not well known, Francois Furet and Mora Ozouf, eds, *A Critical Dictionary of the French Revolution* (Cambridge: Belknap Press, 1989), pp. 54–64, 65–73, 742–53.
2. See Juan J. Linz, "State Building and Nation Building", *European Review*, I, 1993, pp. 355–69; and Juan J. Linz and Alfred Stepan, *Problems of Democratic Transition and Consolidation: Southern Europe, South America, and Post-Communist Europe* (Baltimore and London: Johns Hopkins University Press,1996), chapter 2.
3. See "Stateness, Nationalism, and Democratization", in Linz and Stepan, ibid., p. 34, as well as Figure 2.1.

4. We accept Robert Dahl's definition of federalism as "a system in which some matters are exclusively *within* the competence of certain local units – cantons, states, provinces – and are constitutionally *beyond* the scope of the authority of the national government, and where certain other matters are constitutionally outside the scope of the authority of the smaller units." See his "Federalism and the Democratic Process", in *Democracy, Liberty and Equality* (Oslo: Norwegian University Press, 1986), pp. 114–26. Quote from p. 114.
5. A borderline case might be Sri Lanka, but while it may be a marginal democracy, it certainly is not peaceful. Also, the United Kingdom is a multinational society with Scottish, Irish, and Welsh assemblies but English is spoken by an overwhelming majority of the population in all three areas.
6. The concepts of "asymmetrical federalism" and "holding together federalism" are developed with greater detail and documentation in Stepan's chapter in this volume, and in his article cited in footnote 11.
7. For a thoughtful examination of the problems and promises associated with asymmetrical federalism, see Rainer Baubock, "United in Misunderstanding? Asymmetry in Multinational Federations", unpublished paper presented at the International Workshop on European Identities: Constructs and Conflicts, Austrian Academy of Sciences, 13–15 December 2001.
8. For example, Luxembourg is a unitary state but a "state nation", Ukraine, even though a unitary state follows many "state nation" policies because most political elites, both ethnic Ukrainian and ethnic Russian, were worried that strong ethnic Ukrainian "nation state" policies would generate conflicts with the Russophone population, especially in the eastern regions bordering Russia, where 90 per cent of the Ukrainian citizens speak Russian. Also, given the above, and irredentist sentiments in Russia, a policy of decentralisation, but not necessarily federalization, might be prudent. See Alfred Stepan, "Ukraine: Improbable Democratic 'Nation-State' but Possible Democratic 'State Nation'", *Post-Soviet Affairs*, vol. 21 (4), October–December 2005, pp. 279–308.
9. The analytical distinction between "nation state" and "state nation", as the terms imply, involves an affinity – since both include the term "nation", and certainly, for some theorists of nationalism, both terms would fit under their conception of a nation.
10. See, for example, Valerie Bunce, *Subversive Institutions: The Design and Destruction of Socialism and the State* (New York: Cambridge University Press, 1999).

11. For a more extensive discussion of these distinctions, see Alfred Stepan, "Toward a New Comparative Politics of Federalism, (Multi) Nationalism, and Democracy: Beyond Rikerian Federalism", in *Arguing Comparative Politics* (Oxford: Oxford University Press, 2001), pp. 315–62, esp. pp. 320–8.
12. For the original formulation of the concept of "constitutional patriotism", see Dolf Sternberger, *Verfassungspatriotismus*, Frankfurt am Main: Insel-Verlag, 1990. For a recent elaboration on the theme (in English) and adaptation of it to contexts outside of Germany, see Jurgen Habermas, "Citizenship and National Identity", in *Facts and Norms* (Cambridge, Mass: MIT Press, 1998), pp. 491–515.
13. On the very recent emergence of national consciousness in Austria, see T. Bluhm, *Building an Austrian Nation: The Political Integration of a Western State* (New Haven: Yale University Press, 1973), see esp. pp. 220–41.
14. A fine overview of the Swiss case can be found in Lidija Basta, "Minority and Legitimacy of a Federal State", in L. Basta and Thomas Fleiner, eds, *Federalism and Multiethnic States: The Case of Switzerland* (Fribourg, Switzerland: The Institute of Federalism, 1996), pp. 41–69. For another treatment that deals extensively with language policy in Switzerland, see Kenneth D. McRae, *Conflict and Compromise in Multilingual Societies*, vol. I (Ontario, Canada: Wilfred Laurier University Press, 1986).
15. See Linz, "State Building and Nation Building". *European Review*, vol. 1, 1993, pp. 355–69.
16. For the historiographical debates about the rise of peripheral nationalism in Spain, see Juan Linz, "Early State-Building and Late Peripheral Nationalisms against the State: The Case of Spain", in S.N. Eisenstadt and Stein Rokkan, eds, *Building States and Nations: Analysis by Region*, vol. II (Beverly Hills: Sage, 1973), pp. 32–116.
17. On the process of devolution to a federal state in Spain, see Juan Linz, "Spanish Democracy and the Estado de las Autonomias," in Robert A. Goldwin, Art Kaufman, and William A. Schambra, eds, *Forging Unity Out of Diversity* (Washington, DC: American Enterprise Institute for Public Policy Research, 1989), pp. 260–303. On electoral results in and public opinion about the Estado de las Autonomias during the first decade and a half of democracy, see Juan Linz, "De la crisis de un estado unintario al Estado de las Autonomias", in Fernando Fernandez Rodriguez, ed., *La Espana de las Autonomias* (Madrid: Instituto de Estudios de Administracion Local, 1985), pp. 527–672.

18. All the data we cite from Spain are based on the *Sondeo de opinion del Observatoria Politico Autonomico: 2003* (Barcelona: ICPS, 2004).
19. For a good synthesis of this historical process and an extended discussion of language policy there, see Kenneth D. McRae, *Conflict and Compromise in Multilingual Societies: Belgium* (Ontario, Canada: Wilfrid Laurier University Press, 1986, Chapter 1). For a study that focuses on linguistic conflict in the metropolitan region of Brussels, the only place where significant numbers of French speakers and Flemish speakers live side by side, see Jan de Volder "Le FN Brade Brussels", *Revue Francaise de Geopolitique*, no. 6, May 1998.
20. The data we use for Belgium are based on the 1995 *General Election Study*, conducted by the Interuniversitair Steunpunt Politieke-Opinieonderzoek, K.U. Leuven, and the Point d'appui Interuniversitaire sur l'Opinion publique et la Politique, U.C. Louvain. Results published in 1998.
21. The eleven federal countries that have been functioning democracies for at least the last fifteen years are India, the US, Switzerland, Germany, Austria, Belgium, Spain, Australia, Brazil, Argentina, and Canada. Belgium's long transformation from a unitary to a federal state was only completed in 1993 but it had increasingly functioned as a federal system since the 1970s.
22. All the above calculations are based on the population figures of the Census of India 1991. It should be noted that while the census provides the exact break-up of language and religion for each state, it does not provide religious break-up by language speakers. This has been estimated here by assuming that all the Urdu speakers in the Hindi heartland states are Muslims and that the rest of the language speakers are evenly distributed across religions. The total population of the country in 1991 was 838 million. Of these, 367 million were citizens of the Hindi states. The number of Hindi speakers in these states stood at 319 million. We estimate the number of non-Hindus among this group to be 27.5 million, thus leaving 291 million of Hindu, Hindi-speaking persons living in the Hindi heartland. This works out to 34.7 per cent of the population of India (*Source: Census of India 1991, Statement 3, Paper 1 of 1997 – Language: Registrar General of India*, New Delhi).
23. A case in point was the support by the communist parties for the suppression of Khalistani secessionism in the Punjab. The Indian communists did not extend any support in this instance to the demand of separation from the Indian state. The communist workers were among the

prime targets of the pro-Khalistan militants. A veteran leader of the CPI, Satyapal Dang, offers a defence of this stance in his *Genesis of Terrorism: Analytical Study of Punjab Terrorists* (New Delhi: Patriot Publishers, 1988). A statement by the Punjab state committee of the CPI(M) "expressed deep concern over the increasing activities of Sikh fundamentalists and extremists in the state and felt that they posed a threat to the hard-earned peace in the state and also to the unity and integrity of the country." *People's Democracy*, vol. XXIX (35), 28 August 2005.

24. Various human rights groups within and outside India have documented the denial of basic civil rights guaranteed by the Indian Constitution and law and the use of brutal repression by the security forces in the conflicts mentioned above. See the various annual reports and other India-related material of Amnesty International at http://web.annesty.org/library/eng-ind//index. Various human rights groups within the country have also extensively documented these violations. See the various publications of the reputed and independent Peoples' Union for Civil Liberties (PUCL) at www.pucl.org, especially its report, *Kashmir: A Report to the Nation,* published by PUCL and CFD, 1993. An academic compilation of these reports can be found in A.R. Desai, ed., *Violation of Democratic Rights in India* (Bombay: Popular Prakashan, 1986). For some recent reports, see Ram Narayan Kumar, Amrik Singh, Ashok Agarwal, and Jaskaran Kaur, *Reduced To Ashes: The Insurgency and Human Rights in Punjab* (New Delhi: South Asia Forum for Human Rights, 2003) (copy available at www.punjabjustice.org), and *Touch Kashmir: An Enquiry into the Healing*, a report by AFDR, HRF and OFDR, Hyderabad, 2003.

25. According to the Census of India 2001, the population of Nagaland was 1.9 million, just about 0.19 per cent of the Indian population, Manipur's population was 2.1 million and accounted for about 0.21 per cent. Jammu and Kashmir's population was 10.1 million. With this absolute number, Jammu and Kashmir had about 0.99 per cent of the total population of the country (of this 5.7 million or 0.56 per cent of the Indian population lived in the Kashmir Valley, the heart of political alienation). Of these states, only Punjab has a national population share of more than 1 per cent. (Source: Census of India 2001, Primary Census Abstract, Series 1 and 2 Registrar General of India, New Delhi.)

26. On the complex issue of pride (or lack thereof) in the German nation, see Elisabeth Noelle-Neumann, "Nationalgefuhl und Gluck", in Noelle-Neumann and Renate Kocher, *Die verletzte Nation* (Stuttgart: Deutsche Verlags-Anstalt, 1987), pp. 17–74.
27. Concerning Swtizerland, as the reader will see later (in Table 14), consistent with our idea of the state nation, of the eleven long-standing federal democracies Switzerland has the highest percentage of people with confidence in the government and the second highest percentage of people with confidence in the legal system. So while they may not have pride in being Swiss *as such*, they nevertheless have great pride in their Swiss institutions.
28. Mizoram's population is predominantly Christian: as per the latest census of 2001, 87 per cent of the population is Christian while less than 4 per cent are Hindus (Source: Census of India 2001, The First Report on Religion Data: Registrar General of India, New Delhi), In terms of language too, Mizoram is radically different from the rest of the country: in 1991 less than 2 per cent spoke Hindi, the national language, while 75 per cent of the population spoke Lushai/Mizo, a local language (Source: Census of India 1991, statement 3, paper 1 of 1997 Language: Registrar General of India, New Delhi; also see the website of Census of India: www.censusindia.net/religiondata and www.censusindia.net/data/15_miz.pdf). Mizoram was on the fringes of British India and did not have much of a nationalist movement against British rule. India's independence was followed by a refusal on the part of the Mizo leadership to accept India's sovereignty. The Mizo leaders waged a thirty-year-long bloody and, ultimately unsuccessful, armed struggle for independence from India. The long history of armed insurgency and state repression was brought to an end by the Mizoram Accord between the insurgents and the Government of India in 1987. This was followed by the institutionalisation of the routines of democratic politics with surprising success. The CSDS, Delhi, carried out a post-poll survey with a sample of 1116 following the state assembly elections in Mizoram in 2003. The survey findings indicate a surprisingly high level of integration into India's federal democracy: as many as 84 per cent expressed a preference for democracy. The majority of the respondents included India as constitutive of their identity: only 32 per cent of the respondents identified themselves as "only Mizo". Two-thirds of those who had an opinion supported the Mizo accord

of 1987. (Source: Mizoram Assembly Election Study 2003, CSDS Data Unit.) Stepan also carried out interviews with political leaders in Mizoram in January 2003 and arrived at similar conclusions.

29. Nagaland is home to at least sixteen major tribes that speak different languages but accept a broad modern political identity of being "Naga". Thus defined, the territory inhabited by the Nagas spills over to the state of Manipur and a bit of Assam and Arunachal Pradesh within the Indian Union and Myanmar across the international border. Disaffection with the Indian state dates back to the very foundation of independent India when Angami Phizo, the charismatic leader of the Nagas, refused to accept the authority of the Indian state. Thus followed decades of civil war and insurgency that severely limited the writ of the Indian state, formal state control being maintained only with the presence of the Indian army. Formally, the insurgency still continues and is led by the Nationalist Socialist Council of Nagalim (Isaac-Muivah) (NSCN[I-M]). But on the ground the situation has eased considerably since August 1997 when a ceasefire was announced between the Government of India and the NSCN(I-M). A series of informal dialogues outside the country paved the way for an official dialogue on Indian soil in January 2003. The peace talks have proceeded slowly since then but the ceasefire has continued. The NES, 2004, by the CSDS included a sample of 522 randomly chosen respondents from Nagaland and was perhaps the first-ever survey of political opinions and attitudes in the state. The survey brought out an unwillingness to accept Indian identity: about 57 per cent respondents identified themselves as "only Nagas" as against 9 per cent "only Indian", and 34 per cent "Indian and Naga". However, the alienation did not affect attitudes to the peace process: 85 per cent had heard about the negotiations and two-thirds of those who had an opinion were optimistic of a positive outcome. The survey also revealed a lack of strong support for the hardline agenda of "greater Nagaland" that has blocked the negotiations.

30. The limited survey evidence at our disposal does indicate a deep political alienation from India in the Kashmir Valley (which itself is a little over half of the population of the Indian state of Jammu and Kashmir) but it does not prove that there is widespread support for Pakistan in the Valley. In 2002, the CSDS (in collaboration with the Department of Political Science, University of Jammu) carried out a post-poll survey among a sample of 2195 adult persons, including 1118 respondents in the Kashmir Valley. Unlike other surveys of the CSDS, this survey was

not based on a strict probability sample. But the profile of the sampled respondents was a fair representation of the state's demographic profile except in terms of gender. In this first survey of its kind, the respondents were asked to choose from various options for Kashmir: as many as 79 per cent of the respondents from the Kashmir Valley opted for Kashmir on both sides of the border to be merged to form an independent country with the remaining respondents about equally divided between India and Pakistan. The situation in the Kashmir Valley has no doubt improved somewhat since this survey in 2002, given the reasonably free and fair elections in the state that led to the defeat of the National Conference government that was seen as an imposition of the central government. The NES 2004 records some of these changes. While nearly half of the sample of 954 respondents kept quiet on sensitive questions dealing with the fairness of the electoral process, an overwhelming majority of those who gave any response acknowledged a marked improvement: 76 per cent said that the 2004 parliamentary polls saw virtually no rigging, 71 per cent thought the level of electoral malpractice had gone down, and 90 per cent felt either no fear or said the fear had come down. These responses are for the entire state of Jammu and Kashmir, and not just the Kashmir Valley. Public opinion in the other regions of the state was sharply different. Only 7 per cent of the respondents in the Jammu region and 2 per cent of the respondents in Ladakh supported the demand for independence and none supported merger with Pakistan.

31. While there is a great deal of overlap between the linguistic divisions of India and the boundaries of the various states of the Indian union, there is no perfect match here. Most of the states have significant linguistic minorities. The language spoken by the largest number of people, Hindi, is the official language of eight states of the Indian Union. Most of the dominant languages are internally divided among various "dialects" that vary considerably.

32. This is a theme developed in Juan Linz, "Crisis, Breakdown, and Re-equilibration", in Linz and Stepan, eds, *The Breakdown of Democratic Regimes* (Baltimore: Johns Hopkins University Press, 1978).

33. For an elaboration on this theme, see Juan Linz, "Parties in Contemporary Democracies: Problems and Paradoxes", in Richard Gunther, Jose Ramon Montero, and Juan J. Linz, eds, *Political Parties: Old Concepts and New Challenges* (New York: Oxford University Press, 2002), pp. 291–317.

34. Among the other Latin American countries, Costa Rica sometimes, but not always, has a higher support for democracy than does India.
35. Pippa Norris, *Critical Citizens: Global Support for Democratic Governance* (Oxford: Oxford University Press, 1999).
36. The 2002 riots in Gujarat, and the 2002 electoral outcome in Gujarat raise many disturbing questions, which we discuss later. However, the central Election Commission emerged stronger in one respect. Against the ruling BJP's wish, the Election Commission managed to postpone the timing of the Gujarat ejections. The Election Commission also gained prestige due to the positive role it played in conducting reasonably fair elections in Kashmir in 2002.
37. See, for example, Sidney Verba and Norman H. Nic, *Participation in America: Political Democracy and Social Equality* (New York: Harper and Row, 1972), p. 97.
38. It should also be said that the reverse pattern in India is a long-standing one. See Samuel Eldersveld and Bashiruddin Ahmed, *Citizen and Politics: Mass Political Behavior in India* (Chicago: University of Chicago Press, 1978), Table 12.14, p. 195.
39. Yogendra Yadav, "Understanding the Second Democratic Upsurge: Trends of Bahujan Participation in Electoral Politics in the 1990s", in Francine R. Frankel, Zoya Hasan, Rajeev Bhargava, and Balveer Arora, eds, *Transforming India: Social and Political Dynamics of Democracy* (New Delhi: Oxford University Press, 2000), Tables 12.14 and 12.15.
40. See Juan J. Linz and Alfred Stepan, eds, *The Breakdown of Democratic Regimes* (Baltimore and London: Johns Hopkins University Press, 1978), p. ix.
41. Ashutosh Varshney, "Will the Stallion Baulk in Mid-Gallop?", *The Hindu Magazine*, 30 December 2002.
42. Let us briefly mention some reasons that make us more confident than many others that the "Gujarat model" is not bound to be successful in India's twenty-seven other states. Gujarat has many features that make it exceptional in India. One, the Gujarat electoral model was aided by the fact that the BJP was ruling in Gujarat without the actual, or at least potential, constraint of coalitional partners. In all other major states where the BJP was then in power, it was in a coalition with some other party or parties. Two, Ashutosh Varshney in his award winning book *Ethnic Conflict and Civic Life: Hindus and Muslims in India* (New Haven: Yale University Press, 2002, p. 9), presents data on deaths as a result of communal violence per 1,000,000 of urban populations in

seventeen major states in India from 1950 to 1995. Gujarat, by far, had the highest death rate. Three, of the seventeen states for which we have survey data on support for democracy, the state that had the highest number of explicitly anti-democratic responses in 1998 was Gujarat. Four, Gujarat had emerged as the safest electoral bastion for the BJP, and had witnessed the most intense Hindu-fundamentalist mobilisation of any state in the decade prior to the massacre. (See Yogendra Yadav, "The Patterns and Lessons [of Gujarat Election Verdict]", *Frontier*, 3 January 2003, pp. 10–16.) Five, the Godhra incident in which fifty-eight Hindus burned to death in a train returning from Ayodhya, one of the main symbols for Hindu fundamentalism, helped ignite the massacres. Without great complicity by incumbents, and unprecedented terrorism by civil society groups (whether Muslim or Hindu), a Godhra-type incident will be an extremely rare occurrence. More generally, we can say that the leaders of the BJP as a political party (who were in a governing coalition with twenty-three partners) for reasons of parliamentary, coalitional, electoral, and even very important national and international investment imperatives, might well want to distance themselves from full association or complicity with, the projects of such groups as the RSS, VHP, and the Bajrang Dal. Finally, a non-BJP government at the centre, as presently exists, would probably not allow this not only out of a commitment to value India's tradition of inclusiveness but also for reasons of party competition. This would contribute to governability, a strong Indian state, and widespread support for a state nation. Such a government at the centre, in all likelihood, would not tolerate an individual state leader's incitement of a Gujarat-type anti-inclusionary campaign and its attendant massacres. The BJP's defeat in the state assembly elections in Himachal Pradesh in February 2003 rapidly demonstrated some limits to the Gujarat model. The BJP's defeat in the Lok Sabha elections held in 2004 was widely seen as an indicator of the failure of the Gujarat model. Many of the key allies of the BJP like the Janta Dal (United) and the Trinamool Congress lost Muslim votes and blamed the BJP's role in Gujarat for their electoral reverses.

4

Democratic Paradox

Political Representation in Contemporary India

THINKING ABOUT POLITICAL representation in contemporary India requires simultaneous engagement with two levels of meaning embedded in this rich concept (Pitkin, 1967; Dovi, 2008). Political representation invites us to think, first of all, about the relationship between people or the citizens and their formal political representatives, between those who get represented and those who represent. But any sustained reflection on this relationship draws us into thinking about the setting, the mechanism, and the substance of representation – where, how, and what is being represented. An understanding of political representation in a narrow sense usually presupposes a larger understanding of the working of representative democracy. In the context of contemporary India, however, the relationship between these two levels is more intimate and constitutive: mechanisms of formal political representation have become a hinge that connects two largely disjointed arenas in the working of democracy in India. That is why the paradox of political representation in the narrow sense of the term has come to reflect a larger paradox of Indian democracy.

The paradox of political representation understood narrowly involves a tension between the profile, policies, and politics of those who represent and the desires and demands of those who get represented. On the one hand, the practice of representative democracy for over half a century has led to a widening of the pool from which political representatives are recruited, accompanied by a reduction in the mismatch between the social profile of the representatives and those who are represented. This deepening of descriptive representation coexists, on the other hand, with a thinning of "substantive representation". Progress on "who is the representative?" has been accompanied by a step back in "what does the representative do?" and eventually "what gets represented?"

This paradox is of course linked to the larger paradox of Indian democracy which takes many forms. It manifests itself in the form of the contrary pulls of the institutional design and workings of representative democracy. The institutional designs for authenticating claims to representation, accountability devices for popular control over elected representatives, and the mechanisms for linking the policy agenda of representative institutions with the needs and interests of the represented have not kept pace with the radical upheaval brought about by the democratic upsurge from below (SDSA Team, 2008). Sometimes the paradox appears in the form of a split: the domain of the formal institutions of parliamentary democracy does not quite reflect the dynamism of "popular politics" (Chatterjee, 2004). For historians of contemporary politics, the paradox takes the form of two contrary narratives, both of which appear simultaneously plausible: the story of the decline and demise of democracy and that of the deepening and strengthening of democracy (Khilnani, 1997; Mehta, 2003). From a different vantage point, this appears as a paradox of the promise and outcome of democracy: the radical promise of democracy continues to be subscribed to precisely by those who appear to have got little substantive outcomes from the working of this democracy (Bardhan, 2005). Or it can be seen as the paradox of democratic politics: political understanding and practices are thinning precisely when politics matters more and involves more people than before (Yadav and Palshikar, 2009b).

This essay does not aim to disentangle, far less resolve, this multilayered paradox. Rather, it seeks to spell out the background conditions that make this paradox analytically instructive and politically engaging. Accordingly, the first section takes a look at how the question of political representation has been approached in three cognitive fields to show how the limitations of each of these has stunted our collective ability to think about this question in a meaningful and integral manner. The second section offers an analytical account of the historical context of the inauguration of the institutions of modern representative democracy. This context enables us to appreciate why representative democracy has had deeper anchors in India than in many other post-colonial societies while providing a clue to why it has taken the shape that it has in India. The third section spells out the specifically Indian features of the working of modern representative democracy. The focus here is on how the institution of election has come to play a pivotal role in Indian politics. This enables us, in the fourth section, to bring out the consequences of the working of this kind of representative democracy for some of the key aspects of political representation in the narrow sense of the term, especially for regions, communities, identities, and issues like poverty. The deficits identified in this section lead to some concluding remarks on the theme of reforming the system of political representation.

Approach

Since a paradox lies in the eyes of the beholder, there is reason to suspect that a good deal of the contrariness that we noticed above might be a function of the received frames with which we study political representation in India. Much of what we take as "normal" in democracy and politics is of limited provenance (Kaviraj, 2003; Chatterjee, 2004; Chakrabarty, 2000). Therefore, we need to examine carefully if at least some layers of the paradox of political representation may arise from misplaced expectations. This requires us to pay some attention to three sites that have generated professional frames for understanding political representation: the interpretative dispute about assessing democracy in India, the dominant common sense on democracy, and democratisation and the academic scholarship on "election studies".

The interpretative dispute that lies at the heart of the democratic enterprise in today's India concerns the present and future course of Indian democracy (Khilnani, 1997; Kohli, 2001; Mehta, 2003). On the one hand there is the story of "the decline and fall" of Indian democracy. On this reading, democracy made a decent beginning in India, especially in the first two decades after Independence, but suffered a steady decline since then and a particularly steep erosion in the last two decades. Democracy faces difficult, if not bleak, prospects in view of governmental instability, proliferation of parties, regionalisation of politics and the rise in caste-based mobilisation, communalism, corruption, and criminalisation in the political arena. This reading often leads to a call for wide-ranging and urgent reforms, usually a series of reforms in the legal-constitutional design of democratic politics, to cleanse politics of its current ills (Kashyap, *et al.*, 2000).

Over the last few years, many voices have questioned this reading from different vantage points. Commentators have drawn attention to the elitist (upper-class, upper-caste) bias in this reading and argued that the story could look very different from a subaltern, especially dalit, vantage point (Jaffrelot, 2003). Much of the fresh empirical findings about political behaviour and attitudes of a cross-section of citizens have served to cast doubts on this dominant wisdom: they have shown that while citizens are quite critical of political actors and organisations, they do not share the sense of doom about democracy; that there has been something of a participatory upsurge notwithstanding claims of popular apathy (SDSA Team, 2008; Yadav, 2000). Some recent attempts to place Indian democracy in a comparative international perspective have had the effect of showing Indian democracy in a much better light than Indian political scientists have been accustomed to. Comparison with other democracies in the world has shown that unlike many other parts of the world, democracy has become here the "only game in town" and that support for democracy and the Indian nation-state is of a level higher than was normally supposed (Linz, *et al.*, 2006). These counter-readings have not produced a common alternative story of Indian democracy. They offer a variety of diagnoses of the current situation and varying prescriptions of what is to be done.

This larger interpretative dispute finds an echo in a split response to the state of political representation in the narrow sense of the term. One set of observers notes, quite accurately, the broadening of the base of political representatives, thanks to the inauguration of the constitutionally protected third tier of democracy. This expansion coincides with and reinforces a noticeable shift in the social profile of the elected representatives in the upper tiers as well (Jaffrelot and Kumar, 2009). This transformation can appear as nothing short of a social revolution through the ballot. Another set of observers of Indian democracy focus, quite appropriately, if narrowly, on the representation, or rather the lack of it, of popular issues and concerns in the political and policy agenda. If the exercise of legislative and executive power for redistribution of resources in keeping with the priorities of citizens is one measure of the working of the representational mechanism, Indian democracy's record would appear pretty dismal (Roy, 2009; Jalal, 1995). More often than not, a steep rise in the political representation of the "backward" castes has been characterised by a period of governmental mess and non-performance. No wonder this perspective draws attention to the severe deficits of representation. Add to this some ideological purism and an upper-caste vantage point, and the deficit appears nothing short of the failure or a crisis of representative democracy.

This interpretative dispute has deep theoretical underpinnings. An understanding of political representation in the Indian context not only makes strenuous demands on the empirical skills of packing millions of isolated bytes of information into a coherent story, it also presupposes a certain assurance about answering some foundational questions. These foundational questions have to do with the yardstick implicit in any attempt to measure the success or otherwise of the democratic enterprise. Thus discussions on representation often proceed as if we know what democracy is, that we agree upon what it means to advance or regress on the path of democracy (democratisation is the name for this presumably much traversed and well-mapped path these days), that we can measure the deficits of Indian democracy from the vantage point of an ideal that is within cognitive even if not practical reach, which then allows us to spell out a "roadmap" for democracy reform. The debates on this question take place as if it is a matter of differences about drawing the correct trend line, as if the coordinates are given and shared. A more distant view of debates on political representation invites us to entertain a suspicion that the dispute is as much about which axes to use in order to create a graph as about how to use the available information to plot India in the given space. In this view, the challenge of understanding political representation in contemporary India is as much a theoretical puzzle as an empirical task; it is deeply implicated in the larger dispute about the relevance of democratic theory received from Western academia.

The trouble with the dominant and received democratic theory is that it is rather narrow, if not downright parochial (Keane, 2009; Dunn, 2005). Based on the historical experience of democracy in a very small though privileged part of the globe, and increasingly distanced from the rich tradition of reflections on democracy even within the Western tradition, this theory threatens to marginalise different experiences and conceptions of democracy in different parts of the world. This imagination privileges form over substance and draws our attention selectively to a few elements in the democratic practice in India. Based on a formal "checklist model" of democracy that focuses on standard institutional requirements to qualify as democracy, this approach treats democracy as if it were a piece of hardware. You can pick it and install it anywhere you want. The dominance of this approach has marginalised another possible way of looking at democracy, one that treats democracy like software, a language, which must make sense to the users if they have to do things with it. It must be adapted to suit users' needs, their tastes, and their capacities. On this reading, popular common sense is not external to democracy; it is not one of the "factors" that aid or inhibit democracy: it constitutes the heart of the democratic enterprise (Taylor, 2007).

The academic discipline of "election studies" has served to reinforce the biases of democratic theory. Although the system of competitive elections is expanding to most of the world, election studies continue to interpret and evaluate electoral politics all over the globe in the light of the narrow historical experience of Western Europe and North America. This tendency often goes unnoticed, for the game of electoral politics appears similar all over the world (Klingemann, 2009). Since the end product of this game is recorded in a format that is universally recognised and lends itself to easy surface comparison, it is all too easy to believe that we are looking at the same game in all these cases. The familiar format or register distracts our attention from a more fundamental disjunction: the historical conditions in which the game is played are radically different. When placed in a new context, the same and familiar set of institutional rules lead to a radically different choice set, resulting in different meanings of the vote and very different outcomes.

This influence of "election studies" has meant that thinking about political representation tends to focus far too much on the "formal sector" of politics (national political parties, manifestos, electoral outcomes) to the neglect of the substance of politics, the meaning of the vote, shaping of the agenda and party political platforms, the back calculus of politics, and the role of money and crime in shaping and restricting political choices. This utterly messy aspect of politics is of course well known, but is not considered worthy of theoretical attention. It is noted as an embarrassment rather than a structural attribute. The critics see this as a negation of "free and fair" elections, rather than a constitutive element of elections in the Indian setting.

The existing body of knowledge on elections and voting behaviour (Narain, *et al.*, 1978; Hebsur, 1992) leads us to view the dynamics of political representation in India as a series of absences or "lacks", if not maladies. There is a lack of stable and enduring alignment of voters with political parties (low level of party identification, high aggregate and individual volatility, absence of safe seats). This is related to a lack of pure interest-based political identification and organisations. The choice of representatives is marked by ascriptive identities, ethnicities, politics of caste/community-based vote banks, group identification of interests and political preferences rather than individual voting. The lack of an informed citizenry and low levels of knowledge and awareness in the electorate make matters worse. This leads to lack of issue orientation and ideology as reflected in clientelistic as opposed to programmatic political orientations, pragmatic preferences instead of ideological considerations, an exaggerated role for charismatic personalities and the electoral game turning into an auction. Finally, this faulty mechanism results in the lack of policy outcomes as a result of electoral choices. Elections result in routine anti-incumbency that does not yield much. Those who get represented wield little control over those who represent them.

This dominant approach has suppressed an alternative reading of the apparently unique features of Indian elections. Instead of viewing these as deformities or lacks, the challenge is to capture the specificity of this encounter between the modern structure of formal political choice and the historically constituted public sphere with its own definition of politics and its patterns of organisation of political interest. This opens the way to reinterpret what is often seen as electoral "volatility", party "fragmentation", "casteism" in politics or the "absence of ideology", and the widespread "clientelism" in Indian elections. Such an interpretation would aim to provide a dynamic analytical narrative of the working of representative democracy in India, which recognises the historical and structural influences that shape and constrain institutional development and engagement, and relates them to a changing socio-economic environment that generates fluid patterns of political identity and association. The present essay takes this approach to understanding political representation in India.

Context

Modern representative democracy made a deceptively easy entry in India. Within two decades of the inauguration of democratic elections based on universal adult franchise, the phenomenon of elections had ceased to surprise students and observers of Indian politics. Like tea, cinema, or cricket, there is something about elections that make them appear like an age-old Indian passion. Like the ever-present piece of furniture in the household, elections only serve to remind everyone of the mundane and the quotidian routine of politics. It is therefore worth remembering that historically this apparently natural, taken-for-granted world of elections is a recent import and quite an extraordinary development in Indian society.

The modern practice of elections requires at least four sets of beliefs that had no currency in pre-modern times. It requires a specific kind of public arena, a set of actors with a given role definition, a purpose which orients the entire activity, and some agreed rules of the game.

The encounter with modern politics under conditions of colonialism laid the foundations of a new kind of public sphere in India, making it possible for the multitude of people living in this land to think of themselves as Indians (Kaviraj, 2003). The successful national movement ensured the passage from subjecthood to citizenship, thus creating the collective agency that participates in the election ritual. The creation of a republic in 1950 institutionalised the idea of popular sovereignty which in operational terms was translated in the form of universal adult franchise granted by the Indian Constitution. The constitution also met the final condition of specifying the procedures and protocols of representation, including the rules of deciding the winner in the electoral race and implicitly accepting the existence of organised political interests in the form of political parties. Thus, modern political representation came to India at the founding moment of the Indian nation-state along with the package of liberal democracy accepted at the time. Setting up a democratic state completed the process of reconstituting the public sphere in modern India that began with the colonial encounter. The democratic constitution formalised the sphere of modern politics, comprising institutions and practices of dealing with power that could not be traced back to operations of power in the pre-colonial past, as the prime mover in society. If the creation of a nation-state formalised the capacity of political power to act freely of external powers, the democratic state invested modern politics with a capacity to act autonomous of the logic of economy or that of the principal social divisions (Kothari, 1972). While there was some discussion about the nature of electoral rules to be adopted, there is no evidence to suggest that anyone in the Constituent Assembly seriously contemplated a non-competitive or non-representative form of democracy.

This is perhaps why representative democracy took roots in India but not everywhere else it was tried. A look at the experience of elections in other post-colonial societies of Asia and Africa helps to illustrate the alternative paths electoral democracy could have taken (Weiner and Ozbudun, 1987). In many of these countries, free and fair elections in a minimal sense still remain a distant aspiration. Even when elections are held in a more or less free and fair manner, party competition at the time of elections merely reflects the pre-existing ethnic divisions in society. One round of clean elections is not followed by another and elections fail to evoke popular interest and respect. In contrast, elections evoke deep public interest and passion and have come to be the hub of public activity, almost a public festival, in contemporary India. The system of elections has come to be a regular institution that commands a fair degree of public acceptance.

If elections in India did not take the familiar and tragic path in most former colonies, these also did not take the coveted path of Western democracies. The designers of Indian democracy had expected that the institution of a regular and fair system of elections would be accompanied by many features that they had seen in European democracies: the consolidation of political competition along the lines of a two-party system, electoral choices being made by individual voters along ideological lines, elections becoming an occasion for effective accountability of the rulers to the ruled and thus producing policy outcomes that work to the advantage of common citizens. More than half a century of representative democracy has not fulfilled this expectation (Yadav, 1999). We are beginning to be conscious that this expectation was not realistic in the first place. Elections in India did not and could not have produced the same outcomes as they did in the first world. This difference is not the result of any essential cultural difference or Indian exceptionalism; it is simply the outcome of the historically unique circumstances in which the game of universal adult franchise was instituted in India. The challenge therefore is to capture the specificity of this encounter between the modern structure of formal political choice and the historically constituted public sphere with its own definition of politics and its patterns of organisation of political interest.

Attributes

One of the first attributes of the Indian elections that strikes any observer is the role elections play in Indian politics, as reflected in their public visibility. Banners, posters, and hoardings fill the streets; massive processions and rallies are the norm; the media is full of election news and every street corner is buzzing with political gossip. Though on a steady decline of late, this kind of visibility symbolises the pivotal role elections have come to occupy in Indian politics. If a tension between the pre-existing social form and the borrowed legal-political structure provides the basic frame for understanding Indian democracy, the story of Indian politics is a story of the attempt by millions of ordinary people to write their own political agenda in an alien script. An encounter such as this requires, if it is to lead to meaningful outcomes, bridges or hinges which connect the two different worlds. The institution of elections came to perform this crucial role in India. It became the hinge that connected the existing social dynamics to the new political structures of liberal democracy allowing for reciprocal influence. Elections are often the site for a fusion of popular beliefs and political practices with high institutions of governance. Thus, the election is an occasion for the transfer of energy and resources from the "unorganised" to the "organsed" sector of democracy. This is the moment when the legal-constitutional order of liberal democracy makes contact with the messy social and political reality of India. The chasm that separates the two worlds and the absence or non-functioning of the other possible bridges has resulted in the unusual salience of the institution of elections. This unique role is what accounts for the continued dynamism of the electoral process in India, while a number of other imported institutions and processes are floundering.

Specifically, Indian elections are not merely about voters choosing their representatives, indicating their preferences on public policies, or selecting their governments. In the absence of well-functioning local bodies or accountable local officials, elections to Parliament and state assemblies also perform a routine municipal function of attending to local grievances and connecting the people to the administration. Notwithstanding a robust media that routinely uses public opinion polls, elections are still the principal occasion for the dissemination of political ideas and information and also the only reliable method to gauge public opinion on the big issues facing the country. Elections are also an occasion for the settling, unsettling, or resettling local equations of social dominance and the arena of struggles for social identity and dignity. Elections force political parties to take into account ideas, interests, and entities that do not lend themselves to easy aggregation through the instrumentalities of the "organised" sector. Thus elections often appear as the only bridge between the people and power, as the only reality check in the political system. This accounts for the festival-like character of Indian elections and the fierceness with which elections are contested here. At the same time this also means that elections are overloaded and the necessity of multiple processing leads to underemphasis on the representational functions of elections.

The second set of electoral attributes relate to the "electoral system" in the narrow sense of the term. Of course, the pivotal nature of elections is not written into the legal-constitutional design of Indian polity, nor is it directly a function of the electoral system chosen by the constitution makers. The Indian Constitution prescribed the first-past-the-post (FPTP) or the simple plurality method of election by all adults living in electoral constituencies, all of which now elect a single member (initially there were some triple- and a large number of double-member constituencies). This electoral system was chosen for its simplicity and familiarity. The danger of under-representation of social minorities was sought to be avoided by a system of "reserved seats", constituencies where all the candidates had to be from a designated community, for Scheduled Castes (SCs) and Scheduled Tribes (STs) in proportion to their share in population (McMillan 2005). The possibility of under-representation of religious minorities, which became a reality in the case of the Muslims, was shelved in the aftermath of Partition (Ansari, 2006). The choice of an electoral system may have added to the salience of elections indirectly: locality-based elections made for an easy transition to representative democracy and did facilitate the role elections have come to play in local politics.

In practice, the FPTP system did not produce the expected consequences, at least not at the national level. It did not produce anything like a two-party system; an extended period of one-party dominance has given way to a multiparty system with one of the highest effective number of political parties among the electoral democracies of the world. Accordingly, stable majority governments have given way to routine or coalition governments, much like in a system of proportional representation. In part, at least, this was a function of the scale of the Indian polity. With the intensification of electoral competition, the nation is no longer the effective unit of political choice; state-level politics is the real arena for political choices and partisanship (Yadav and Palshikar, 2009a). The national-level election is in many ways an aggregation of the verdict that is delivered at the state level. Thus some of the effects of the working of FPTP are visible at the state level: there is a tendency towards a bipolar competition and stable majorities in most of the states. In the Indian context, FPTP produced a different, unexpected, and under-analysed effect. The requirement of plurality in a single-member constituency coupled with the demographic mosaic forced political parties to forge social coalitions at the local level. Since no single caste or community tends to be in a majority in any of the state assembly or parliamentary constituencies, winning elections requires gaining support from more than one caste or community group. This unintended consequence has performed a significant integrative role in the Indian polity and constitutes the principal defence of the FPTP system. Indian elections are about a familiar game acquiring a character of its own and becoming virtually a new game.

Perhaps what contributed most to making this game different was a new condition that no one ever thought through. The design of representative democracy in India simply lifted a system of representation that was meant for much smaller political communities and applied it to a continental polity. This resulted in a manifold increase in the scale of representation and led to a qualitative difference in the nature of the relationship between the representative and the represented. An Indian member of the Lok Sabha typically represents a population over 21 lakh and a Member of the Legislative Assembly in one of the major states represents anything between 2 and 5 lakh. A comparison with the scale in Britain (less than a lakh for each member in the House of Commons), which served as the model, brings out the sharp contrast. The mega-scale of the system of representation had many consequences for the nature of political representation: the minimum requirements of resources and information needed for this kind of election result in a very high entry barrier for a new entrant to the system. This is related to the relatively fluid relationship between voters and parties that characterises Indian elections. Compared to some of the European polities, Indian elections witness a low level of voters' identification with political parties. Given the very high degree of aggregate and individual volatility that is routinely witnessed in Indian elections, concepts like alignment, realignment, or dealignment do not have much applicability in the Indian context. This is not to say that the changes are patternless, but that the lie of the land is very different in the Indian case (Yadav, 1996a).

The hinge-like character of elections is reflected in the set of attributes of electoral participation in India that defies global common sense in three respects. One, in an era characterised by global concern over declining electoral turnout, India is something of an outlier. After rising for the first two post-Independence decades, electoral turnout at the national level has remained fairly steady, but has registered a rise in state assembly elections. Two, as one goes down the tiers of democratic competition, turnout and political participation increases in India, rather than going down as it does in most established democracies. Panchayat elections tend to witness the highest turnout, followed by state assembly elections, and a much lower turnout for national elections. Three, India also defies the established common sense about a positive correlation between socio-economic status and electoral turnout. Dalits and adivasis (tribals) at the bottom or the margins of the Hindu social hierarchy have caught up with caste Hindus in their participation levels: a dalit has a greater likelihood of casting a vote than a brahmin. Since the Emergency, rural India tends to record a higher turnout than towns and cities. Within urban India, slums and working-class areas witness a higher turnout in elections than "middle-class" localities. The huge gap that existed earlier between male and female turnout has been nearly closed now. Religious and ethnic minorities do not generally record lower turnouts. Although this pattern of turnout does not hold for all forms of electoral participation and that in turn is not replicated in political participation, there is no doubt that India has witnessed something of a "democratic upsurge" from below and the social base of popular participation in turnout, electoral activities, and politics is much wider compared to what it was earlier (Yadav 2000; Palshikar and Kumar, 2004; Yadav and Palshikar, 2009b).

This distinctiveness in the level and patterns of electoral participation is in turn related to popular attitudes towards representative democracy in general and elections in particular. If the subalterns are using the vote as a weapon of the weak, it reflects a certain degree of approval of the system of representative democracy. Clearly, the weak do not view elections merely in instrumental terms; they associate something special, perhaps even sacred (Banerjee, 2007), with the occasion of elections and value the ritual of equal citizenship. Even though a significant proportion of electors do not vote, non-voters are not necessarily alienated from the system. Voters and non-voters all reject unequivocally the idea that elections should be dispensed with and record a surprisingly high degree of support for democracy (SDSA Team, 2008). Subaltern participation in politics has its flip side. When the weak use the vote as their weapon, they often do so in order to assert their group identity, to the detriment of considerations such as policy, representative, and government. Besides an act of participation is often simultaneously an act of co-option or a gesture of granting legitimacy to a system that often brings little to the people.

The linkage between inherited social cleavages and new political divisions provides a crucial mechanism to understand the hinge-like function of Indian elections. This linkage is often seen as a peculiar Indian pathology of "casteism in politics" or the operation ol "vote banks" in elections. Viewed in a more comparative light, the connection between caste and politics appears to be the Indian version of the more general phenomenon of the operation of social cleavages in voting behaviour almost all over the world. If caste appears to be omnipresent and omnipotent in Indian elections, it is partly due to two types of double-counts: several forms of social divisions (*jati, varna,* religious sect, occupational divisions, religious communities, migrant or linguistic groups, or even class) tend to get classified under the label of "caste" and multiple forms of possible linkages of the caste of voters and their political preference (caste of the candidate and the party leader, and the caste or caste group represented by the party) pass for "caste-based voting". In part this is also due to glossing over crucial analytical distinction between pattern and trend: while caste blocs often determine the initial level of support for a party, they do not explain changes across elections. Besides, the relationship between caste and politics does not necessarily mean that caste determines politics; very often it is the other way round (Kothari, 1970). In fact, if there is something distinctive about Indian elections it is not the existence and role of the institution of caste in elections but the capacity of electoral politics to forge social identities. The systemic imperative to forge local social coalitions for obtaining electoral plurality has led to the coalescing of several adjacent jatis into a single caste for purposes of politics, not to mention the more explicit political coalition of caste groups (Sheth, 1999).

The excessive and obsessive attention paid to the role of caste in Indian elections has often resulted in a neglect of other kinds of social cleavages. What is true of caste is also true of ethnicity: electoral politics shapes these communities as much as it is shaped by pre-existing ethnic groups. Gender difference has marked political opinions, attitudes, and behaviour for as long as there is evidence to trace it (Deshpande, 2004, 2009). Notwithstanding popular impressions, a substantial proportion of women do not vote the way the men in their family do. The gender gap in voting has not followed a simple trajectory but it is clear that this gap is big enough to make a difference, sometimes a decisive difference, to who forms the government. Class, understood not so much as a meta-historic agent of transformation but as an empirical phenomenon of either income-based strata or occupational division, is an important variable in voting behaviour and often overshadows caste or community in urban India (for example, for Delhi, see Kumar, 2004). In rural India too, class divisions provide a powerful clue to mapping the differences within caste and community groups. In the operation of these multiple and cross-cutting cleavages, India is not very different from the rest of the world. One of the distinguishing attributes in this respect is the near absence of a generational cleavage in political behaviour or even opinions in India. There are, no doubt, some age-cohort differences depending upon the political context when a person was socialised into politics, but there is virtually no life-cycle difference between different generations. Despite much hype in this regard, the Indian youth does not vote or think very differently from older people (Yadav and Palshikar, 2009b).

Finally, the hinge-like character of Indian elections means that elections are the site for an encounter between two very different kinds of belief systems, the high ideology of modern politics on the one hand and somewhat inchoate and home-grown belief systems on the other. Since the outcome is anything but neat, and there is little patience with the intricacies of the emerging hybrid language of politics, this gives rise to an impression that Indian elections are "devoid of ideology". Often the operation of patronage, interests, or social identity in Indian elections, as everywhere else, is seen as an evidence for the irrelevance of the ideological dimension in India. An alternative reading would suggest that Indian elections are as much about ideology as they are anywhere else, but this element cannot be captured by a single and familiar spectrum like the Left–Right dimension. Electoral politics is the site for a new hybrid language of politics, distinctly modern and specifically Indian, which does not fit easily into the reecived frames of political theory.

Establishment of a system of quite fair and largely free elections, at least in the more obvious sense of the term, is something India can legitimately take pride in. Compared to the rest of the world, including most electoral democracies in post-colonial settings, Indian elections are characterised by a very low degree of electoral disputes and frauds. There has been more than one instance where credible allegations regarding widespread fraud would lead one to doubt whether the party that won the election was indeed voted in by the people: West Bengal in 1972, Assam in 1983, Punjab in 1992, several elections in Nagaland and Jammu and Kashmir, including the most notorious election of 1987. This is an embarrassing but finite list and would still pass as an exception to the general rule of free and fair elections. The increasing independence of the Election Commission, the demise of one-party dominance, and the rise of media power have ensured that the trend is towards a sharp reduction in the more obvious instances of malpractices and fraud – all this is good news. If we proceed beyond this and ask what this system of elections has achieved for the ordinary citizen, the answers are harder to get and less encouraging.

Are Indian elections an effective instrument of meaningful political change? Indian elections have, in a sense, overcorrected for the first stage of one-party dominance where each successive election used to bring the same party back to power. The period since the demise of the congress system has witnessed a very high rate of regime alteration. At times the casualty rate of the incumbent state government was as high as three-fourths (Yadav and Palshikar, 2009a). This was linked to a very high level of aggregate volatility or a high degree of shift in the vote share for all the parties as well as a high level of individual volatility or the proportion of voters who changed parties across two elections (Heath, 2005). This was widely perceived to be an anti-incumbency reflex of the Indian voter. However, volatility need not be seen as synonymous with instability, or as an outcome of an anti-incumbency itch, or as a sign of a system which has not yet settled down, almost threateningly so. Volatility is best interpreted as voters' search for better governance or responsiveness, a sign of social churning, and a routine oscillation that takes place in the absence of social transformation. Viewed in this frame, the real difficulty with Indian elections is not that they lead to excessive change but that they offer little meaningful choice that can be the basis of political change. While the number of political parties has multiplied, this has not led to any expansion in the choices available to voters. Faced with this deadlock, the impulse for change degenerates into routine oscillation (Yadav and Palshikar, 2003).

Do elections offer an opportunity to reorganise political power or for shifting the locus of power? At least in one respect the participatory upsurge has resulted in very real changes in the locus of political power. Whereas the constitution of India provided for a weak federal system, and the post-Independence period was characterised by a clear centralisation of political power, a process of "electoral federalism" has seen the diffusion of some central power and a stronger role for state governments. As competitive politics has taken a decisive "regional" turn, the state has become the effective level of political choice in a Lok Sabha election. In the 1970s and 1980s voters voted in the state assembly elections as if they were choosing their prime minister; since the 1990s they vote in Lok Sabha elections as if they are choosing their chief minister. This has reduced the ability of national parties and governments at the centre to present or claim a general mandate, and has given greater power to politicians and governments at the state level.

This has been accompanied by a serious and substantial dilution of state representation in the Upper House of Parliament. As political parties freely shuffle nominations to the Rajya Sabha with little regard to domicile and little fear of loss of credibility, the constitutional design of the upper chamber as representing the interests of the states stands subverted. The Supreme Court's decision upholding the legal dilution of residential requirement in the Rajya Sabha was a fatal setback in this respect. This paradoxical development has produced a consequence that no one designed or anticipated: as the Lok Sabha, rather than the Rajya Sabha, becomes the principal arena for the representation of states, the onus of maintaining the federal balance has also been shifted to the Lok Sahha (Yadav, 2007; McMillan, 2001). This has served to legitimise an ill-conceived freeze in the Lok Sabha on the number of seats for each state which violates the basic principle of one-person–one-vote, besides working to the disadvantage of some of the already disadvantaged units of the Indian Union. A similar encounter between the political process and the institutional frame can be seen at the third tier of democracy. The passage of the 73rd and 74th Amendments to the constitution and the extension of constitutionally secured representative politics to the third tier set in motion a political process that appears to be gaining momentum. At the same time the state governments appear determined not to grant any real powers or resources to the new tier of political representation. Instead of redistributing resources and redirecting developmental policies at the local level, the principal function that the third tier performs now is to supply cadre and lower-level functionaries to political parties in desperate need of an organisation. Often it is much worse: the political energy released by this process leads to an intense, violent but vacuous quest for local political dominance.

How have the democratic upsurge, electoral volatility, and the shift in the locus of political power affected the pattern of social dominance?

Since participation in elections is seen to be an affirmation of citizenship, the very act of participation confers dignity on hitherto excluded segments of society. This opens up the potential for the mobilisation of group interests, and at the extreme the potential for the stoking of inter-group violence. But a substantive question here would be about whether elections offer an opportunity for changing and challenging the entrenched elites. If so, the potential for disturbing hierarchical structures can in itself be seen as an outcome of electoral politics. This brings us face-to-face with simultaneous advance and retreat in the political representation of the lower social order. There is no doubt that the post-Mandal era in our polity has led to some improvement in the presence of landowning or otherwise numerically large Other Backward Class (OBC) communities in the Hindi heartland states. Even though the quantum of change is much smaller than is popularly believed and the legislatures continue to massively over-represent the forward castes, there is a qualitative change in the political dynamics as the momentum has shifted away from the hitherto dominant communities (Jayal, 2006).

Yet this advance comes with built-in stagnation and retreat. The rise in the political representation of some backward communities has not led to a corresponding rise in the representation of many other communities that would be a part of the "lower social order". There is little awareness about or willingness to engage with the severe under-representation of the "lower" OBCs or the Most Backward Castes cutting across the north–south divide. Similarly, there is little attention to an equally severe under-representation of the "Maha Dalits", the dalit communities at the bottom of the SCs. The *Sachar Committee Report* has served to bring some attention to the gross under-representation of Muslims in Parliament and state assemblies, but the issue is yet to acquire the national salience necessary for any remedial action (Prime Minister's High Level Committee, 2006). There is little improvement in the political representation of marginalised social groups like women and the poor that do not possess a self-conscious political identity. The Women's Reservations Bill has drawn some attention to the fact that women's presence in legislatures has actually witnessed a marginal decline since Independence (Dhanda, 2008). There is no such data to track the presence of the "poor" in our legislatures. But if the episodic analysis of the disclosures of property filed by candidates at the time of their nominations is anything to go by, our legislatures are dominated by the super-rich (Association for Democratic Reforms).

Finally, do elections provide a forum for citizens' control over public policy? In a limited and direct sense they do: a whole host of populist schemes announced during every election testify to the need to respond to public demand. As the survival rate of governments has become respectable, this has led to serious competition among state governments to respond to people's needs such as electricity, water, and roads, things which the state has the capacity to deliver in a direct and visible manner. At the same time, electoral politics is still characterised by a lack of delivery, accountability, and responsiveness. Short-term interests are the only ones which can be realised, as survival becomes the only government imperative. There is a strong tendency towards populism rather than substantive politics so as to deliver long-term benefits in areas such as health and education.

This is related to the paradox of coexistence of democracy and poverty in contemporary India. The majority rules in democracies and we should be surprised if those who (can) rule do not use this power to improve their conditions of life. The paradox is even deeper in India than in many other societies. Some of the standard reasons why democracies do not care about poverty do not hold true in India (Bardhan, 2005; Varshney, 2004). One, the institutional design of Indian democracy (parliamentary system, asymmetrical federalism, flexible constitutional amendment) does not place significant obstacles to the democratic popular will. Two, the party system is highly competitive, with very high electoral volatility. Three, as noted above, the poor have not opted out of democratic politics, at least not from routine participation in electoral politics. Four, unlike some other poor democracies, India is not a failed state and its failure to address poverty cannot be put down to a more generalised incapability. All this makes it even more intriguing that representative democracy should not (be able to) do very much about poverty.

Before closing the discussion on the outcomes of the system of representative politics, it may be relevant to note one irony in the recent emphasis on the social profile of political representatives. The discussion on quality of representation is being reduced to the social identity of the representative precisely at a time when the political representative is increasingly marginal to the most vital decisions concerning legislation and governance. The passage of the amended anti-defection law has left only one answer to the classical question: Whom does the elected representative represent: they cannot but represent their political party. The rise of political families or the party supremo with a coterie within each political party complicates much of the routine discussion about the nature of political representation. True, political families come from a more diverse social background than before. But it would be facile to assume that these families represent the interest of the communities they come from. The rule of political families or the supremo from agrarian communities has proved to be more conducive for the capture of state power by organised industrial and business interests than was the case before. In any case, the issue of political representation itself is declining in salience due to a shift in the locus of decision-making from the legislature and executive to independent bodies and the judiciary. Simultaneously, the media has emerged as the key and not-so-neutral mediator in how any political issue is represented to the public and thus sets limits to the political agenda. It is not a coincidence that the judiciary and the media have remained nearly untouched even by the limited presence of the lower social order, as in the legislatures, and are thus immune to the pressures of the democratic upsurge.

Reforms

One way to summarise the argument offered so far is to spell out the implications of this reading of political representation for the issue of reforms in representative democracy, an issue that has occupied extraordinary public attention in India in the last two decades. If nothing else, this issue illustrates how a distorted reading of representative democracy can induce distortions in the practice of representative democracy. Over the last two decades, a good deal of well-intentioned, though diffused, enthusiasm for reforming democracy has turned into a conservative platform for refashioning the political structures to suit the interest of a small, hitherto entrenched, but now threatened class. The resultant agenda of political reforms amounts to nothing short of undoing the results of the democratic upsurge of the last two decades (Yadav, 1996b, 2001).

If the argument offered above has any merit, the agenda of political reform in India has to be different from the challenge in advanced industrial democracies, for our problem is not demobilisation and the slowing down of democracy. At the same time, unlike other new democracies of the third world, India does not face the challenge of democratic transition or consolidation. The real failure of the current phase of Indian democracy is not the failure to hold free and fair elections, nor the inability of the people to affect change in governments through the exercise of their free vote, but the growing distortion in the mechanism of political representation, the growing distance between electors and the elected, and the inability of the mechanism of competitive politics to serve as a means of exercising effective policy options. Clearly, the institutional frame of representative democracy has failed to translate popular participation and enthusiasm into a set of desirable consequences.

This is not merely a universal deficit in the promise of democracy. We are looking at a range of failures that are rooted more specifically in our experience. Some of them were written into the logic of democracy in a society like India. The fundamental contradiction – pointed out by Dr Ambedkar – that of instituting equal citizenship in a highly unequal society – lies at the root of many of the failures. Social inequality was further accentuated by unequal access to the means of forming and disseminating public opinion. Another contradiction was built into the act of importing political institutions, especially those that required autonomy in a cultural setting where attitudinal prerequisites were missing. There was the structural problem of constituting a polity to coincide with the boundaries of a civilisation when much of the meaningful political action and mobilisation could take place in micro-settings. Some other failures of the democratic experiments are not structural, but specific to the history of democracy over the last fifty years. The weak policy orientation of dalit–bahujan politics, a lack of emphasis on institution building, the decision not to change the character of the bureaucracy, and the retreat of the state in the face of the forces of globalisation were in no way neeessary to the design of Indian democracy. But these have contributed substantially to the democratic deficit facing us today. The litmus test for any agenda for reforming the system of political representation is its ability to deepen the ongoing process of democratisation for social groups and communities that have historically been denied access to political power.

This is not the place to begin offering such an agenda. It may be relevant though to note that such an agenda would require getting rid of some of the reigning superstitions or our times: the idea that there is a universally valid institutional design of liberal democracy; the suggestion that a set of best political practices can and should be replicated all over the world; the theory that the idea of democracy can be reduced to a standard "checklist". Once it is recognised that there is no universally applicable and valid package of political reforms or a model of democracy, it follows that a reasonable starting point for thinking about political reforms is here and now. We can thus take the next step of working towards an agenda that is anchored in time and space, is consequence-sensitive, takes the logic of politics as integral to thinking about institutional design, and is conscious of differing consequences for different social groups.

References

Ansari, Iqbal A., 2006. *Political Representation of Muslims of India: 1952–2004*. Delhi: Manak.

Banerjee, Mukulika, 2007. "Sacred Elections", *Economic and Political Weekly*, XL(17), pp. 1556–62.

Bardhan, Pranab, "Democracy and Poverty: The Peculiar Case of India", in *Scarcity, Conflicts and Cooperation: Essays in Political and Institutional Economics of Development*. Cambridge, Mass.: MIT Press.

Chakrabarty, Dipesh, 2000. *Provincializing Europe: Postcolonial Thought and Historical Difference.* Princeton, NJ: Princeton University Press.

Chatterjee, Partha, 2004. *The Politics of the Governed: Reflections on Popular Politics in Most of the World.* Delhi: Permanent Black.

Deshpande, Rajeshwari, 2009. "How did Women Vote in Lok Sabha Elections 2009?" *Economic and Political Weekly*, XLIV(39), pp. 83–7.

———. 2004. "How Gendered Was Women's Participation in Election 2004?", *Economic and Political Weekly*, LI(18), pp. 5431–6.

Dhanda, Meena (ed.), 2008. *Reservations for Women*, Delhi: Women Unlimited.

Dovi, Suzanne, 2008. "Political Representation", *The Stanford Encyclopedia of Philosophy* (Winter 2008 Edition), Edward N. Zalta (ed.), URL= <http://plalo.stanford. edu/arechives/win2008/entries/political-representation/>.

Dunn, John, 2005. *Democracy: A History*. New York: Atlantic Books.

Heath, O., 2005. "Party Systems, Political Cleavages and Electoral Volatility in India: State-wise Analysis 1998-1999", *Electoral Studies*, 24(2), pp. 177–99.

Hebsur, R.K. 1992. Studies on Indian Politics. Research Designs and Stragegies. A Trend report sponsored by and submitted to the Indian Council of Social Science Research. Unpublished.

Jaffrelot, Christophe. 2003. *India's Silent Revolution: The Rise of the Lower Castes in North India*. London: Hurst & Co.

———, and Sanjay Kumar (eds), 2009. *Rise of the Plebeians: The Changing Face of the Indian Legislative Assembly*. London: Routledge.

Jalal, Ayesha, 1995. *Democracy and Authoritarianism in South Asia: A Comparative and Historical Perspective*. Cambridge: Cambridge University Press.

Jayal, Niraja Gopal, 2006. *Representing India: Ethnic Diversity and the Governance of Public Institutions*. London: Palgrave Macmillan.

Kashyap, Subhash C., D.D. Khanna, and Gert W. Kueck (eds), 2000. *Reviewing the Constitution?* Delhi: Shipra Publications.

Kaviraj, Sudipta, 2003. "A State of Contradictions: The Post-colonial State in India", in Quentin Skinner and Bo Strath (eds), *States and Citizens: History, Theory, Prospects*. Cambridge: Cambridge University Press, pp. 145–67.

Keane, John. 2009. *The Life and Death of Democracy*. London: W.W. Norton & Company.

Khilnani, Sunil, 1997. *The Idea of India*. New York: Farrar Straus Giroux.

Klingemann, Hans-Dieter. 2009. *The Comparative Study of Electoral Systems*. Oxford: Oxford University Press.

Kohli, Atul (ed.). 2001. *The Success of India's Democracy*. Cambridge: Cambridge University Press.

Kothari, Rajni (ed.). 1970. *Caste in Indian Politics*. New Delhi: Orient Longman.

Kumar, Sanjay. 2004. 'A Tale of Three Cities', *Seminar*, 534.

Linz, Juan J., Alfred Stepan, and Yogendra Yadav. 2006. '"Nation State" or "State Nation"? Indian in Comparative Perspective', in Shankar Bajpai (ed.), *Democracy and Diversity: India and the American Experience*. New Delhi and Oxford: Oxford University Press, pp. 50–106.

McMillan, Alistair, 2005. *Standing at the Margins: Representation and Electoral Reservation in India*. New Delhi: Oxford University Press.

———. 2001. 'Population Change and Democratic Structure', *Seminar*, 506, October.

Mehta, Pratap Bhanu. 2003. *The Burden of Democracy: Interrogating India*. New Delhi: Penguin Books.

Narain, Iqbal, *et al.* 1978. *Election Studies in India: An Evaluation*. Mumbai: Allied Publishers.

Palshikar, Suhas and Sanjay Kumar. 2004. 'Participatory Norm: How Broad-based is it?', *Economic and Political Weekly*, XXXIX (51), pp. 5412–17.

Pitkin, Hanna Fenichel. 1967. *The Concept of Representation*. Berkeley: University of California.

Prime Minister's High Level Committee [Sachar Committee] 2006. *Social, Economic and Educational Status of MuslimCommunity of India*. New Delhi: Cabinet Secretariat, Government of India.

Roy, Arundhati. 2009. *Listening to Grasshoppers: Field Notes on Democracy*. London: Hamish Hamilton.

SDSA Team. 2008. *State of Democracy in South Asia: A Report*. New Delhi: Oxford University Press.

Sheth, D.L. 1999. 'Secularisation of Caste and Making of the New Middle Class', *Economic and Political Weekly*, XXXIV (34 and 35), pp. 2502–10.

Taylor, Charles. 2007. 'Cultures of Democracy and Citizen Efficacy', *Public Culture*, February.

Varshney, Ashutosh. 2004. 'Why Haven't Poor Democracies Eliminated Poverty?', in Ashutosh Varshney (ed.), *India and the Politics of Developing Countries: Essays in Memory of Myron Weiner*. New Delhi: Sage.

Weiner, Myron and Ergun Özbudun (eds.). 1987. *Competitive Elections in Developing Countries*, Durham, NC: Duke University Press.

Yadav, Yogendra. 2008. 'The Paradox of Political Representation', *Seminar*, vol. 586, October.

———. 2007. 'Epilogue: What does Fieldwork do in the Field of Elections?', in A.M. Shah (ed.), *The Grassroots of Democracy: Field Studies of Indian Elections*, New Delhi: Permanent Black, pp. 345–68.

——. 2001. 'A Radical Agenda for Political Reforms', *Seminar*, 506, October.

———. 2000. 'Understanding the Second Democratic Upsurge: Trends of Bahujan Participation in Electoral Politics in the 1990s', in Francine R. Frankel, Zoya Hasan, Rajeev Bhargava, and Balveer Arora (eds), *Transforming India: Social and Political Dynamics of Democracy*. New Delhi: Oxford University Press, pp. 120–45.

———. 1999. 'Electoral Politics in the Time of Change: India's Third Electoral System, 1989–99', *Economic and Political Weekly*, XXXIV (34 and 35), pp. 2393–9.

———. 1996a. 'Reconfigurations in Indian Politics: State Assembly Elections, 1993–95', *Economic and Political Weekly*, XXXI (2 and 3), pp. 95–104.

———. 1996b. 'Electoral Reforms: Beyond Middle Class Fantasies', *Seminar*, vol. 440, April.

Yadav, Yogendra and Suhas Palshikar. 2009a. 'Revisiting "Third Electoral System": Mapping Electoral Trends in India, 2004–2009', in Sandeep Shastri, K.C. Suri, and Yogendra Yadav (eds), *Electoral Political in Indian States*. New Delhi: Oxford University Press, pp. 1–45.

———. 2009b. 'Between *Fortuna* and *Virtu*: Explaining Congress' Ambiguous Victory in 2009', *Economic and Political Weekly*, XLIV (39), 26 September, pp. 33–46.

———. 'From Hegemony to Convergence: Party System and Electoral Politics in the Indian States, 1952–2002', *Journal of Indian Institute of Political Economy*, XV (1 and 2), January–June, pp. 5–44.

5

What is Distinctive about Indian Elections? A Hypothesis

I OFFER HERE A KEY to answering two simple, related, and rather obvious questions about the state of democracy in India.[1] What is wrong with representative democracy in contemporary India? And what can be done about it? Questions of this kind are considered too simple, too general, or perhaps too large for students of politics to answer. I suspect that in its search for *clever* questions and *novel* answers, academia often loses sight of *significant* questions and *good* answers. I suggest that good answers to these questions are not global answers. An attempt to answer these questions can help us understand the distinctiveness of electoral politics in India.

Let me first clarify the questions. The first one contains two sub-questions within it. Does the system of competitive elections succeed in representing the people in terms of what they demand, what they desire, or what they need? Without getting distracted by the distinction between these three terms and how they set up three different ways of measuring the gap between actual and ideal, if the straight answer is that competitive elections do not succeed in so representing the people, then the natural question is: why not?

There are many obvious candidates for an answer here – the quality of political leadership; the nature of the political parties and party competition; the institutional rules of electoral competition; and popular beliefs, attitudes, and values. How much weight do we assign to each of these possible explanations? An understanding of what and why should give us some clues about how we can go about correcting the democratic deficit. Where should the thrust of the attempts at political reform be directed? Does the situation call for constitutional and legal redesigning? Should we look at institutional modifications? Or does the answer lie in the domain of political action?

I cannot hope to answer all these questions here, even if I were to pretend to know the answers. But I do wish to suggest a general way of thinking about and answering them in the Indian context. In this sense, my argument is specific to India.

Established academic wisdom plays little role in shaping political common sense on this issue in contemporary India. Scholars may of course put it down to the illiteracy of politicians and public intellectuals. But it could also, equally plausibly, be read as a sign of the disconnect between political science and political sense. India has rich, almost obsessive, public debates on what is wrong with representative democracy and what can be done about it. Political common sense on this question is forged by debates in legislatures and committees, jurisprudence and legal discourse, "civil society" recipes for political reform, and media debates around specific instances of the lack of accountability and responsiveness in politics. Yet this debate has virtually no point of contact with the professional knowledge of politics.

Three Objections Met

Let me begin by responding to three possible objections to the line of inquiry that I have undertaken here. It could be argued that the questions I ask are not worth pursuing because: (a) India is not quite a democracy; (b) there is nothing really wrong with the outcomes of democracy in India; (c) one should not expect democracy to address issues like mass poverty.

In defining democracy, I follow the "minimalist" tradition and define it as a form of government in which those who rule are elected by the people through competitive elections and run the risk of losing power in regular elections. In this definition, the election of rulers by the people is subject to some qualifications:

(a) The election should be competitive in that there should be more than one serious contender

(b) The opposition should have a fair chance of winning if it has popular support
(c) The electoral mandate cannot be revoked by the loser and the winner should get to exercise the highest political power
(d) The elections should be held at regular intervals irrespective of the wishes of the incumbent

Keeping these minimal rules in view, it seems fair to categorise India since Independence as a democracy. To be sure, there has been more than one instance of one or the other of these rules having been violated. The illegitimate – though strictly speaking not unconstitutional – extension of the term of the Lok Sabha during the state of national "emergency" imposed by Indira Gandhi (June 1975 to March 1977) was one such instance at the national level. At the state level, there have been several equally gross violations of these minimum requirements of democratic rule, all suggesting that the overall verdict of that particular election could not be described as a fair reflection of popular choice. Into this category I would put all elections in the state of Jammu and Kashmir before 2002, excluding the election of 1977; all elections in Nagaland before 2003 and in Mizoram before 1987; and the state assembly elections in West Bengal in 1972, Assam in 1983, and Punjab in 1992. This is an embarrassingly large but fortunately finite list of exceptions that serve to prove the rule that India since Independence must be characterised as a democracy in the minimalist sense of the term.

The second objection – namely, that there is nothing really wrong with the outcomes of democracy in India – can be countered by pointing to one gross failure in India since Independence – the continued existence of a vast population well below a floor of minimum goods and services required for dignified living.

This leads directly to the third possible objection, namely, that one should not expect democracy to address issues like mass poverty. To counter this view, perhaps we may begin by asking: Why are we surprised by the coexistence of democracy and mass poverty? The reply, to put it simply, is that the majority rules in democracies, and it seems logical to be surprised if those who rule do not use their power to improve the general conditions of life. This is not to say that the desire or demand of every kind of majority is routinely fulfilled in all democracies. In fact, clearly, the strong desire of an overwhelming majority of the electorate in all democracies to get clean, accountable, and efficient government is routinely frustrated. The point here is that the non-fulfilment of this specific expectation calls for an explanation. There is nothing new in this expectation: democracy was always seen as the rule of the poor by the rich. Before the recent spread of the democratic form of government all over the globe, democracy was the dread of the propertied classes and the hope of those who believed in a radical redistribution of power and resources.

An explanation seems called for in this specific context because the paradox of the coexistence of democracy and mass poverty is deeper in India than in many other societies. Some of the common reasons for democracies not caring for their poor do not obtain in India. First, the institutional design of Indian democracy (parliamentary system, asymmetrical federalism, flexible constitution amendment) is not "demos-constraining" – in that it does not put significant obstacles to the democratic popular will. There are not too many veto points that could be seen to account for the failure of floor-securing social policies to be legislated and implemented. Second, the party system is intensely competitive, with very high electoral volatility. The first-past-the-post system accentuates the effect of voters' volatility into dramatic change in seats and government formation. Though the level of volatility has come down in this decade as compared to the previous one, any ruling party in any Indian state has a just about 50 per cent chance of coming back to power. Parties cannot afford to be complacent and overlook issues that might concern a significant proportion of the population. Third, state capacity in India is higher than in most comparable poor countries. The state can impose its will and is not crippled by the absence of resources to complete some of its key projects. All this makes it even more intriguing that ruling parties and coalitions should not be able to muster adequate political will to carry out anti-poverty policies.

Finally, what makes it truly intriguing is that the poor have not opted out of democratic politics in India, at least not from routine participation in electoral politics. The evidence put forward by National

Election Studies in India shows that the participation level and the faith in the efficacy and legitimacy of the system is still fairly impressive among the poor. While electoral participation rates are declining in older democracies, turnout at the state assembly level has risen in India. Turnout in Indian elections goes up as one goes down the multiple tiers of democracy – the highest turnout is recorded in local-level elections. Unlike Europe and North America, participation rates do not decline in India as one travels down the social hierarchy. Citizens at the lowest rung of the hierarchies of caste, class, and education turn out to vote in numbers as great, if not greater, as those at the top. Villagers vote more than city dwellers and women's participation level is catching up with men's.

To sum up, the coexistence of a functioning democracy and mass poverty constitutes a paradox that we need to think about in relation to India. A meticulous way to respond to this paradox would be to take up each link in the chain of argument summarised above and specify at each level the mechanisms that do not allow this expectation to be realised. Many of these mechanisms would turn out to be nearly universal and fairly well understood. Grossly unequal distribution of private wealth and the constraints it imposes on the nature of democratic politics are good examples of such universal factors. I take these into account while proposing the way forward, but let me focus here on some of the mechanisms that are distinctively Indian.

The Specificity of Indian Elections

As regards the impact of the electoral system, across countries the key factors in making sense of elections are: the structure of political choices offered by the party system; the social basis of political preference; agenda setting and public opinion formation; and the invisible role of issues and ideologies, interests and identities. Because of these structural similarities we simply assume that elections perform the same role everywhere. The end result is that the experience of electoral politics in societies like India is interpreted in light of the narrow historical experience of Western Europe and North America. Hence the need to understand the distinctiveness of the Indian experience of elections.

One of the first things that strikes any observer of Indian elections is their centrality in India's political life. Banners, posters, and crowds fill the streets; massive processions and rallies are the norm; the media is full of election news and every street corner buzzes with political gossip. Though steadily declining of late, this kind of visibility symbolises the pivotal role elections have come to play in Indian politics. If tension between pre-existing social form and borrowed legal–political structure provides the basic frame for understanding Indian democracy, the history of Indian politics is a story of the attempt by millions of ordinary people to write their own political agenda in an alien script. An encounter such as this, if it is to lead to meaningful outcomes, requires bridges or hinges that connect the two different worlds. The institution of elections has come to perform this crucial role in India. It has become the hinge that connects the existing social dynamics to the new political structures of liberal democracy, allowing for reciprocal influence.

An election is often the site for a fusion of popular beliefs and political practices with the high institutions of governance. It is an occasion for the transfer of energy and resources from the "unorganised" to the "organised" sector of democracy. It is the moment when the legal–constitutional order of liberal democracy comes into contact with the messy social and political reality of India. The "formal" sector is highly visible, it leads a legal–constitutional existence, it involves "civil society" groups and NGOs or a certain segment of political parties, it speaks a familiar modern language, mobilises secular identities, and is easy to incorporate into a global register of democracy – even if it draws modest energy and participation.

Every political actor is aware of another – an "informal" – sector, often seen as a source of embarrassment. Political organisations and movements that inhibit this sector speak a homespun hybrid language and fall back upon identity-based mobilisation. Though political practices in this sector lead an invisible, often para-legal, existence below the radar, this remains the most happening political site in terms of popular mobilisation and energy. The chasm that separates the two worlds, and the absence or non-functioning of the other possible bridges, have resulted in the unusual salience of elections.

This unique role is what accounts for the continued dynamism of the electoral process in India, even as a number of other imported institutions and processes are floundering.

Elections in India perform many more functions. For a post-colonial country like India, successful elections are still a symbol of a national political community, something of a festival of collective identity. For the poor and the marginalised, who are excluded from the normal functioning of the state, elections are an affirmation of their citizenship and seen as a sacred ritual of political equality. Notwithstanding a robust media that routinely uses public opinion polls, elections are still the principal site for the dissemination of political ideas and information, and the only reliable method to gauge public opinion on the big issues facing the country. Elections force political parties to consider ideas, interests, and entities that do not lend themselves to easy aggregation through the instrumentalities of the "organised" sector. Thus, elections often appear as the only bridge between the people and power – the only reality check in the political system.

Elections are also an occasion for settling, unsettling, or resettling local equations of social dominance and the arenas of struggle for social identity and dignity. They are a site for contestations over dominance within a locality, leading to assertion by dominant social groups and protests by subaltern groups. Attempts by clever political entrepreneurs to manufacture a social majority often involve building a local coalition of castes and communities. This frequently leads to the invention of community boundaries, and sometimes to the gerrymandering of settled boundaries. In a micro as well as macro setting, elections are an occasion for the distribution and redistribution of resources. This is the time for patronage distribution as well as for ordinary citizens to collect their "dues" from the political class. All this accounts for the festival-like character of Indian elections and the fierceness with which they are contested. At the same time, this compression of multiple decisions into a single act also results in an underemphasis on the representational function of elections.

Two other structural features of Indian elections have accentuated this difficulty. One of these has to do with the problem of scale in politics. The design of representative democracy in India entailed lifting a system intended for much smaller communities and applying it to a polity of continental size. This resulted in a manifold increase in the scale of representation and led to a qualitative difference in the nature of the relationship between the representative and the represented. A member of the Lok Sabha typically represents a population exceeding two million and a member of the state legislature in one of large states represents anything between 200,000 and 500,000 people. A comparison with the scale in Britain (less than 100,000 for each member in the House of Commons), which served as the model, makes the contrast clearer. The mega-scale of the Indian system of representation has had many consequences for the nature of political representation. The minimum requirement of resources and information needed for this kind of election result is a very high entry barrier for new entrants into the system. The impossibility of face-to-face interaction between representative and represented has necessitated an army of rent-seeking intermediaries and is beginning to lead to the mediatisation of constituency-level politics.

Finally, a system with multiple levels of government, and its corollary of multiple non-corresponding electoral cycles in a parliamentary system, has introduced a peculiar disjunction between different levels of government and elections. Over the years, state-level politics has become the principal arena of political contestation, whereas the design of Indian federalism allocates much of the power and resources to the central government. Most of the principal or at least immediate problems faced by citizens, however, require solution at the level of the local government. In the absence of well-functioning local bodies with matching resources or accountable local officials, elections to parliament and state assemblies also perform the routine municipal function of becoming the site for voicing local grievances and connecting people to the administration. Parliamentary elections often reflect the verdict for or against a state government. This conflation in levels has meant that the central government is simultaneously under-account able and over-accountable. It is over-accountable in the sense that every round of state assembly elections is politically sensitive for the national government. At the same time, the central government can be under-accountable in the sense that its fate is largely determined by things that some of the state governments do.

Political Lessons for Our Times

An overwhelming majority of India's population still lives below the acceptable minimum level of access to goods, services, and dignity. It uses every available opportunity offered by universal adult franchise and open political competition to secure better conditions of life for itself. Very often it does not succeed, for the political menu on offer is very narrow and hard to alter, especially at a time when mainstream political parties are insular and party organisation is very fragile.

What, then, needs to be done? If the argument offered above has any force, it points in two directions. The first and most pressing need is a package of political reform that reduces some of the institutional constraints that prevent the requirements of the majority from being translated into the political will necessary for social policies. Let me provide here a checklist of the changes required. The basic idea is not to bring India in conformity with global practices, for deviation from the Western norm has been the strength of the Indian system. Nor do we need to change India's electoral system or uncrowd the electoral arena of contestants – as many enthusiastic reformers have recently suggested. What we need is, first of all, a decentralisation of political power by creating smaller states; greater assured resources to state governments; autonomous district-level governments; and enhanced funds, functions, and functionaries for local bodies. Second, we need measures to strengthen other mechanisms of accountability and responsiveness by instituting independent regulatory institutions, and by reforming the bureaucracy and the police to bring them closer to the people. Third, we need measures to reduce the asymmetry of information – such as a genuine public service broadcaster, the regulation of cross-media ownership, checks against private treaties, and stronger disclosure norms for public functionaries. Fourth, we need measures to reduce the inequality of resources in politics – such as the public funding of elections by vote-linked cash reimbursement on a non-discriminatory basis and tax support for political contributions. These reforms are urgent, for their absence hurts not just the prospects of social democracy but also the existence of democracy itself.

A fairly common way to think about representational deficits in India is that representative democracy in India has not yet evolved to the level of "advanced" democracies. There are too many parties, too much caste-based identity politics, and too little ideology, all of which allows political entrepreneurs to take advantage of ill-informed citizens. This view invites us to be patient with the maturing of Indian democracy and encourages legal interventions to nudge it in the right direction.

Such a reading gives a different perspective on what is wrong with representative democracy in India. The problem is not that the people are uneducated and lack ideological orientation; the problem is that popular preferences do not get translated into politically relevant signals by the media. The problem is not that caste mobilisation subdues other cleavages, but that the multiplicity of cleavages fractures the majority. The problem is not that the proliferation of parties leads to fragmentation, but that an increase in parties is compatible with a shrinking of political choices and the capture of parties by special interest groups. Finally, the problem is not with the first-past-the-post (FPTP) system, but with the massive scale and multiple levels of representation.

This reading recognises the need for some corrective measures: lowering the scales, reducing the asymmetry of information, monitoring the media, and levelling the playing field in terms of resources. At the same time, it also reminds us that democracy cannot be made responsive and accountable by tinkering with institutional design alone, that the quality of democracy is in the last instance a function of the intensity and nature of politics.

Note

1. This essay is a revised version of a talk delivered at the Wissenschaftskolleg, Berlin, in 2010, as the concluding presentation of a year-long fellowship.

6

The Decline of Political Judgement

Comparing Regimes and Parties

THE END OF THE year 2010 may appear to be a particularly inappropriate moment to assess the state of Indian politics.* The context of near-zero sessions in both houses of Parliament in the midst of a fulsome national spectacle of political corruption is not designed to cultivate a discerning appreciation of the practice and practitioners of politics. The activity of politics and the institutional sites where this activity is carried out appear to be in an exceptionally sorry state.

There is something surprising and therefore systemic about the current state of politics. The United Progressive Alliance (UPA) II government is at once legislatively more secure and politically more incoherent than most coalition governments of the recent past. A clean prime minister appears to be more debilitated in dealing with the muck that surrounds him than his predecessors. A regime that shows flashes of social conscience – real if short-lived – simply cannot muster the political will to give effect to it, even when the calculus of electoral gains happens to weigh on the same side as conscience. A ruling party that has started attracting back marginal social communities – by default rather than design – remains largely indifferent to their interests,

*This essay is the beginning of an enquiry. It draws upon parts that I had developed with Suhas Palshikar and others and presented to the group on India's Intellectual History at Wissenschaftskolleg, Berlin. My thinking on political judgement has benefited greatly from the reading of and discussions with John Dunn, and from an unpublished paper on this by Sanjay Ruparelia.

unsure of what to do with this windfall. Far from being an effective agency for managing the collective interests of the capitalists, the state appears paralysed by intra-corporate wars, vulnerable to predatory capital, and unable to see the "big picture" in the larger interest of the capital.

Something is clearly amiss here. This is not the story of politics that political science tells us about – political agents fail to realise their career objectives, parties do not move towards the median voters, regimes do not care for their political constituency, classes cannot see or pursue their "objective" interests. Nor is it simply a story of individual stupidity, collective muddle-headedness, organisational confusion, or suicidal political moves that constitute the everyday stuff of political gossip in any place or time. Perhaps we are witnessing a sharp decline of a crucial element in politics, something we have forgotten to name. What is amiss in the scenario described above could be paraphrased as political judgement.

This essay later suggests that the present moment, far from being particularly inappropriate, allows us to see more starkly a process of decline of political judgement that has taken place over a long period in post-Independence India and has acquired a qualitatively different dimension after the turn of the century. An examination of some of the recent political developments brings out some attributes of this process. Lest these instances be seen as peculiar to the UPA government, this essay looks across the political spectrum to find that the malaise is more widespread than would appear to be the case. Finally, it uses a long-term historical lens to understand the decline of political judgement.

Policy Political Judgements

The Kashmir policy is admittedly a difficult test to subject any regime to. If the two UPA regimes should be put to this test, it is only because they inherited a better situation than any other regime in the previous two decades. By the time UPA I came to power, Vajpayee had brought down the political heat, Lyngdoh had delivered fairly credible elections, Mufti and Mehbooba Sayeed had released a safety valve, and the Pakistani elite was busy digging its own grave. The constellation of political opportunities could not have been more favourable to the resolution of the six-decade-old dispute. Six years down the line, instead of a forward movement, we have definitely moved away from any resolution of the problem.

Some day historians will tell us a fuller story of this spectacular disaster in Kashmir. But we can anticipate what might puzzle them most: it is hard to see any evil design of the rulers behind this disaster. No doubt there was considerable ill will, suspicion, and animosity from the foot soldiers and local political agents. But it is difficult to discern just what the Congress could have gained from playing the games it did in Kashmir.

Unless there is some staggering piece of evidence hidden in the archives for historians, we can guess that their story would read as a story of the poverty of political judgement. The rulers in Delhi underestimated the high stakes in the Kashmir crisis, did not appreciate the need for a political bridge between mainstream politics and separatists, failed to take into account the accumulated resentment of the people of Jammu, and, in effect, handed over the state to political actors and middlemen who played for their petty stakes.

The performance of the UPA stands in sharp contrast to that of the National Democratic Alliance (NDA) government led by Vajpayee, which inherited a highly troubled legacy, faced a tougher cross-border situation, and yet left behind a lot of residual goodwill, if not peace. Perhaps the future historian would see the UPA's mishandling of Kashmir as a textbook illustration of why benevolence must not be seen as the highest virtue in politics.

Telangana is not as tough as Kashmir, or should not have been so. Here the UPA's handling had all the elements of a poverty of politics: bad faith, poor timing, indecision, shoddy choices, and loss of nerve. After promising a second SRC (States Reorganisation Commission) in its 2004 manifesto, the party slept over the matter as Chief Minister Y.S. Rajasekhara Reddy (YSR) found ways to keep Chandrashekhar Rao, leader of the Telangana Rashtriya Samiti, silent. It showed that the national leadership was not bothered about keeping its word to the people of Telangana. The political drama over the selection of YSR's successor, following his "accidental" demise, exposed a national leadership that had at best a remote connect, not just with workers but even leaders of its own party. And finally, the flip-flop over the declaration of Telangana showed a government that had lost sense of direction and nerve.

While the Union government may hope that the Srikrishna Committee will help it find a way out of its own indecision, the state of Andhra Pradesh has already undergone an emotional and political partition. The story of Telangana resembles the fable of a man who opted to eat a hundred onions over getting a hundred shoe strikes as punishment, failed to eat beyond ninety-nine onions, and then was subjected to a shoe beating as well. Barring a political miracle, the Congress appears to be courting a similar fate in Telangana as well as the rest of Andhra.

The government's decision to go in for a caste census brings out yet another facet of a loss of political judgement. One would expect the Congress to be anxious to court the Other Backward Class (OBC) voters, given that the party has finally started regaining some OBC support that it lost after Mandal. An OBC enumeration in the 2011 census should have been an easy decision: administratively sensible, legally defensible, and politically advantageous. But instead of working proactively for an OBC enumeration, the government adopted every trick to block, delay, and deflect any decision on this matter. By the time a parliamentary consensus – which took the government by surprise – forced the government to change course, the concession looked like a surrender to political blackmail. The final outcome is thus the worst of all possible worlds: those opposed to a caste census feel betrayed, the OBC lobby feels cheated by the delinking of the caste count from the main census, and those with a policy interest in the caste census feel infuriated with the final decision that, given the two-stage process now adopted, serves no purpose.

The three instances here depict different types of errors in political judgement. The misjudgement in Kashmir was the result of a lack of fine-grained contextual understanding of what was going on in and outside the valley, and a deficit of strategic acumen. The flip-flop in Telangana flowed from a poor practical sense or prudence, besides a lack of steadiness in judgement. The misjudgement about the caste census came from a lack of "synthetic" judgement, an inability to combine a good principle of unmarked citizenship with the specificities of the case and the balance of other policy considerations. But there is one attribute that all the three misjudgements share: these were not caused by a common error of lack of dispassionate assessment; if anything, they originated from a lack of passion.

Party Political Judgement

It is possible to agree with the story so far and yet not see it as reflecting a systemic trend. After all, the misjudgement of the UPA II government can easily be attributed to the peculiarities of this dispensation. It may be unfair to expect an exercise of political judgement from two leaders who have not risen from the ranks in the political process, who cannot be described as political animals. Besides the unusual split of the political executive into the prime minister, who plays chief executive in governance, and the party leader, who has the final word in things political, is designed to produce discordance. Their misjudgement may, thus, not be anything more than a historic accident specific to the current government. Let us, therefore, shift from the level of government to that of the entire spectrum of party politics. Let us examine a crucial moment – how various political parties responded to the electoral verdict in the Lok Sabha election of 2009 – to understand the nature of political judgement that is clearly more systemic in nature.

The "victory" in the Lok Sabha elections of 2009 opened up a historic possibility for the Congress party. The opportunity was not so much to re-emerge as the once-dominant party and to rebuild the famous rainbow coalition of the Congress system. In systemic terms, the Congress had been given an opportunity to internalise and accommodate the political diversity that enriched Indian democracy in the 1990s. Equally, here was an opportunity to reconstitute itself as a political vehicle of the bottom of the pyramid.

Viewed differently, the real opportunity for the Congress party was to inherit various legacies of which it was not a natural heir. The legacy of "reaching out to the last man" could be connected to the politics of "garibi hatao" in the early 1970s, when the party made an effort, however short-lived and instrumental, to renegotiate its relationship with the poor. Having missed the Mandal bus, the party had the opportunity of inheriting the second wind of Mandal by appealing to the social constituency of the lower backwards and mahadalits, among others. With political imagination, the Congress could have turned the windfall of 2009 into an enduring political asset.

It is no surprise that the Congress party has done little in the last year and a half to realise this possibility. Like the first UPA regime, this one too is shy of making "political capital" out of its large welfare programmes like the Mahatma Gandhi National Rural Employment Gurantee Act (MGNREGA) and creating a long-term support base. Unlike in the first regime, there is no left to arm-twist the Congress into doing things which are, in the last instance, in the Congress' own interest. In the absence of any coercion from outside or pressure from within the party, it is left to a largely non-political National Advisory Council to connect the government to those who voted it to power. The ruling party appears to have convinced itself that its renewed talk about the *aam aadmi* had already made it a party of the *aam aadmi*, that it has already made a generational transition, that it has a vision for the future. It has misconstrued the weakness of its opponents to be its own strength. The Congress party, in so far as it is meaningful to talk about the party as a thinking creature, appears to have mistaken its *fortuna* for its *virtu* and is well set to squander a historic opportunity, which it has done little to earn.

The Bharatiya Janata Party (BJP) has displayed little will and capacity to benefit from the Congress' complacency. Working under a mistaken assumption – that the party had lost an election that it could have won – much of its post-mortem of the 2009 defeat focused on short-term and at best secondary factors. Since the implosion in the party happened to coincide with a transition in leadership, it was easy to conclude that the crisis was one of leadership. It could thus avoid facing the more fundamental issues of its political placement and organisation. The 2009 election showed that the BJP's "new social bloc", the strategy of overdrawing from a smaller social pool comprising the upper end of the caste-class continuum, had hit a dead end. It failed to realise that this strategy was always vulnerable to small shifts of some key and historically fickle or unattached social groups – upper caste, middle class, and lower OBCs. Moreover, it was dependent on the political fragmentation of the bottom of the social pyramid. The BJP could not use its six-year rule to convert this loose and temporary coalition into an enduring political bloc.

The BJP's inability to hold allies and court new social groups was partly a function of its exclusivist political platform. The real challenge for the BJP thus was to expand the pool of its potential voters by re-adjusting its platform to appeal to the sensibilities of the centrist voter. Instead, a significant section in the party wanted to go the opposite way towards hard Hindutva. This erroneous response to its stagnation goes back to a fundamentally flawed reading of the BJP's rise to power.

The party had gained in the early 1990s through a coincidence of opportunity and adversarial mobilisation – the post-Mandal social churning, the organisational decline of the Congress, and an anti-Congress sentiment among the electorate – but read it as a purposive coming together of the supporters of Hindu nationalism. Hence, the temptation to fall back upon the hard Hindutva line. Even as this may pay some local and regional dividends, at the national plane in today's political context it is only a recipe for its further political marginalisation. The latest victory of the Nitish Kumar-led Janta Dal (United)–BJP government in Bihar is likely to push back this tendency, at least for some time, but it is not clear if it would push a rethink of a reading that reinforces the Hindutva line.

The left faced a challenge that was much deeper than a coincidence of the low point of the electoral cycle in Kerala and West Bengal. Its reverses in 2009 were largely unrelated to the farcical but limited attempt at putting together a "third front" at the national level. The real problem was that the left did not have the language to make sense of and respond to the real political challenge posed by its electoral reverses.

Some of these challenges were not difficult to spot: the left was not gaining new voters and cadres in the younger generation or in regions where it did not already have an effective presence; it had suffered steep erosion in its robust base among the rural poor, especially in West Bengal; its critique of the economic policies of the mainstream parties sounded full of duplicity; and its claims of being different from other parties and their leaders appeared increasingly suspect.

Like the BJP, the left too faced the challenge of a shrinking social and political base. In the long term it faced the challenge of reconciling its revolutionary ideological postures to the political reality of being a left-of-centre democratic party. If so, adherence to pure ideology could be more a part of the problem than a solution. Last heard, the Communist Party of India (Marxist), i.e. the CPI(M), has planned a special meeting to educate its leaders into the party's ideology.

The Bahujan Samaj Party (BSP) problem was not that it faced a "crisis" or a "saturation point". Notwithstanding an inability to convert its victory in the assembly elections in Uttar Pradesh in terms of Lok Sabha seats, the party continued its onward march in 2009 in terms of popular support across the country. Its problem was that it simultaneously created premature expectations of its rise to power in Delhi. Besides, the attempt at expanding its base beyond Uttar Pradesh and supplementing its dalit social base has not yielded the kind of dividends the party needed for consolidation.

Of all the non-Congress parties, the BSP had the best opportunity for creating a counter coalition of the bottom of the social pyramid. Yet, it seems that the party may be moving in the opposite direction. It appears to have read its reverses in Uttar Pradesh as a failure of the mythical dalit–brahmin alliance and become wary of the task of expansion. Worse, it has a leader ready to barter long-term national gains for immediate benefits in Uttar Pradesh and compromise the political for the personal, and does not appear keen to take the decisions necessary for pushing the party towards realising this opportunity.

Finally, while the obituaries of regional parties and the discussion of the demise of Mandalite politics were premature, the verdict of 2009 contained several serious lessons which these parties could ignore at their own peril. Clearly, the first wave of Mandal politics was nearly exhausted. While the parties that emerged out of the first flush of empowerment of the backward castes in North India were not about to disappear into thin air, they faced the challenge of retaining and consolidating their political inheritance. They needed to deliver outcomes in terms of better quality of government in order to retain their political constituency; a simple one-dimensional appeal to one's caste was no longer adequate.

Similarly, the prevailing strategy of stapling additional social constituencies on to the existing core support needed to give way to an appeal to a cross-section of citizens. The Bihar verdict of 2010 has reinforced both these messages of 2009. But it is too early to say how far the Nitish model will be adopted by other regional parties. Bihar also shows the opposite example of parties like the Rashtriya Janata Dal (RJD) and the Lok Janshakti Party (LJSP) that clearly failed to read the writing on the wall and persisted with a one-dimensional politics of caste and community.

The poverty of judgement at the level of party competition may not be as obvious or blatant as in the case of governance, but it is more ominous precisely because it cuts across parties and regimes. To be sure, each party misconstrues the electoral verdict in somewhat different ways. If the Congress overlooked the historic opportunity of building a winning coalition of the bottom of the pyramid, the BJP was inattentive to the disintegration of the social bloc that brought it electoral success. The left and the BJP have a tendency to go back to its ideological core that may have brought them to where they are, while the BSP and the regional parties have a tendency to stick to a social core that constrains their expansion. Across the political spectrum, we find parties either out of touch with their own social constituencies, or unable to reach out to their potential voters. There is a widespread inability to revise older tactics in the light of new realities. It is to be noted that most of these misjudgements arise out of a lack of intimacy with ground-level political realities.

Conclusion

In concusion, let me take a leap from the two levels we have examined so far and offer some general observations about the state of political judgement today, even if this article does not offer all the necessary evidence.

We tend to think of political judgement as an attribute of persons or, at most, of organisations. An analysis of the decline in political judgement in contemporary India invites us to think of political judgement as a collective attribute, as a quality shaped by political and intellectual context and shared by actors within a political community. That is why the decline in political judgement is not confined to the quality of reflection in one or the other register of political thinking, nor to one or the other tradition of thought. Cutting across familiar political divides, political actors, organisations, and institutions of governance are losing touch with ground realities, failing to "sense" the public mood, are incapable of making political moves that secure their own long-term interest, and are increasingly unable to establish cause–effect relationships that guide their political action. This spills beyond the political arena and affects political judgement, or rather its absence among social movements, the media, and academia. The problem is clearly more structural, for it relates to how the relationship between ideas and politics is shaped.

Thus, the decline should not be seen as either accidental or temporary. Since judgement draws its resources from traditions of thinking, a significant change in the collective political judgement is obviously connected to the fate of the tradition called modern Indian political thought. A sudden discontinuity in this tradition in post-colonial India resulted in a drying up of the resources of political judgement. This rupture got further accentuated by a decline of bilinguality and the growing linguistic division of intellectual labour, which placed the world of theory and experience into two separate compartments. It is too early to argue this with some confidence, but this decline may also be part of a much bigger story of the decline of that specifically twentieth-century Indian activity that we call politics.

7

How Good is the Rise of States? Ten Theses on State Politics

THE BEGINNING OF THE election season is a good occasion to note the rise of state politics to the centre stage of Indian politics.* We all have silently accepted that the Lok Sabha election is nothing but an aggregation of state-level elections. Our mind goes over at least two dozen parties, many of them statewide, as we do a back-of-the-envelope calculation of the coming elections. We have travelled a long way from the 1970s and 1980s when this was not the case, when national electoral waves swept across states, and electoral projections were about how the national mood was swinging for or against a nationwide party.

The rise of state politics as an autonomous domain invites and requires theoretical attention by students of comparative politics. This essay offers a preliminary frame for such a comparative analysis by identifying some key issues that need to be enquired into and offering working hypotheses for each of these lines of enquiry. Before turning to these it may be useful to understand what we mean by the autonomy of state politics and why it needs more attention than it has so far received.

Autonomy of State Politics

Clearly, when we talk about the autonomy of state politics, we are talking about autonomy from national politics. In the last two decades,

*This essay is co-authored with Suhas Palshikar.

state politics has broken free of the logic of national politics and has acquired a rhythm and logic of its own. This manifests itself in many ways related to one another.

First, states have emerged as *the* effective arena of political choice. If the people voted in state assembly elections held in the 1970s and 1980s as if they were choosing the prime minister, they now vote in the parliamentary elections as if they are choosing their chief minister. In their eyes an individual constituency is too small and the country too big; it is at the level of the state that the voters make their choice.

Second, the nature of political choice now varies from state to state. We have moved a long way from the old Congress versus opposition scenario that was replicated all over the country. Nor have we entered a multiparty system in all the states. The Lok Sabha may present the picture of an intensely fragmented multi-party system, but at the state level we can find all kinds of contests: bipolar, triangular, four-cornered, or even more fragmented.

Third, "regional parties", or statewide parties, have become more salient than ever before. One cannot even begin to play the favourite national sport of "*kaun banega* PM" without factoring in the prospects and the proclivities of the All India Anna Dravida Munnetra Kazhagam (AIADMK), Telugu Desam Party (TDP), Samajwadi Party (SP), Bahujan Samaj Party (BSP) and the Trinamool Congress (TMC), even if one overlooks the regional parties that are now somewhat stable allies of the United Progressive Alliance (UPA) or the National Democratic Alliance (NDA). The state units of national parties too are more independent, at least in terms of the issues, strategies, and styles, if not leadership, than used to be the case. In some non-trivial ways the Communist Party of India (CPM) units in West Bengal, Kerala, and Tripura are three different parties.

Fourth, following from the first three, if the unit and the nature of political choice varies from state to state, so does the outcome. The changing fortunes of political parties are not replicated across state boundaries in ways that held good in the past. For instance, currently the four big states of South India are being ruled by four very different political formations: Congress in Andhra Pradesh, the Bharatiya

Janata Party in Karnataka, the Dravida Munnetra Kazhagam-led alliance in Tamil Nadu, and the Left Democratic Front (LDF) in Kerala. The Hindi heartland that used to swing together is now a political mosaic. In terms of pattern, anti-incumbency is the norm in many states, but not everywhere.

Fifth, governmental outcomes have become more variegated at the state level. Citizens' access to various goods and services varies across the country, within each state, district, and town, and even village. But the most significant variation now is the one among different states, which is a function of how everyday politics, including social movements and political struggles, relates to the governmental apparatus.

Sixth, state-level politics is freer of the control of national politics and is often in a position to dictate terms to national politics. This happens in the most visible manner when statewide parties determine the agenda of national politics or enjoy an upper hand in their bargain with national parties.

Finally, a long-term process of differentiation of political community has ensured that citizens' identity has crystallised around states. The reorganisation of states along linguistic lines had set off this process. But a political community had not emerged by that time along the boundaries of states. The recent era in the evolution of democratic politics has witnessed the emergence of states as markers of political identity. Each state has developed a distinctive political culture, its own vocabulary of politics. Some of the long-term political trends and patterns have also differentiated along state lines.

The Study of State Politics

Interest in and study of state-level political processes is not new. Even in the 1960s and 1970s, when the focus was on the "all-India" patterns, attention was indeed given to state-specific processes. However, most studies of state politics tended to emphasise the peculiarities of each state and thus develop a state-specific story.[1] Somehow, state politics was seen in terms of developing political trajectories that were independent of all-India politics. Elsewhere, we have dealt with these developments.[2]

The 1980s and the early 1990s witnessed a lull in the study of the states and state politics though the developments of the 1990s forcefully brought back the states into the consciousness of the student of Indian politics. But this development did not really receive the kind of attention it deserved: states were now recognised as the main theatre for the unfolding of the drama; state parties became the focus of attention; and state-level electoral verdicts came to be analysed for explaining national electoral outcomes. But all this still happened within the confines of state-specific stories rather than by weaving the threads together.

Myron Weiner, one of the pioneers of the study of state politics in India, had long back recognised the need to go much beyond this approach.[3] He made a powerful plea for using state-level studies to develop a comparative perspective on state politics in India. In retrospect it is clear that Weiner was ahead of his times. The comparative frame that Weiner proposed was only an initial sketch. The contributors to his volume found it difficult to follow his suggestion. Nonetheless, his early work does underscore the need to adopt a comparative framework. More recently, following the lead of Kohli,[4] many more comparative studies of state politics have emerged.[5] Most of these involve two or more states in a comparative design. This welcome development might benefit from some reflections on the overarching framework.

Such a reflection must begin with some consideration of what the objective of comparison is. Discussions of India's tryst with democracy repeatedly show that this has not produced uniform results across time and space: there have been moments of concern, hiccups, bleak disappointments, and jubilation; there have also been terrains where these moments were strongly or weakly experienced. In other words, the quality of democracy has varied over time and across states. This is not the place to go into the vast literature on the subject. Suffice it to indicate here that by quality of democracy we mean not just the smooth functioning of the basic legal-constitutional apparatus of democracy but also the fulfilment of essential regulative tasks and providing access to symbolic and material resources to citizens in a way that opens up the possibility of a further deepening of the democratic norm.

Thus, it is not difficult to see that different states of the Indian union have a variegated record on these aspects of democracy. We propose that a comparison across states might help us better understand this variation as also in developing an explanatory framework. It might also salvage the study of state politics from primarily focusing on state-specific engagement. Thus understood, the subdiscipline of comparative politics could be transformed in the Indian context into a comparative study of the quality of democracy across Indian states.

In what follows we suggest some themes that could become the focus of such a comparative study of democracy across states in India. Each of these themes invites us to ask a question that permits a meaningful comparison. For each of these we also propose an initial working hypothesis, boldly and baldly presented here as theses. The basic idea is to provoke discussion and stimulate further studies that might challenge the initial formulations offered here.

Thesis 1: Impact of legacy: The very first question concerns the burden of history or the impact of political legacy. To what extent can the differentials in the quality of democracy be explained with reference to the conditions that existed at the time of Independence? Which aspects of political legacy continue to have a greater imprint on the state of affairs today?

With the benefit of hindsight we can make a distinction between two aspects of political legacy. Most states began their democratic political journey around 1950 and some even later. As we move away from the founding moment, we see a gradual erosion of the impact of the erstwhile institutional and administrative histories in ways that are not apparent at the national level. At the time of Independence, one of the major differences was between the areas under princely rule and areas under direct British rule. The former had less intense popular struggles generally and somewhat higher levels of influence of the feudal social and political order. This distinction clearly mattered in the early post-Independence period, as witnessed in the success of many ex-princely rulers and the Swatantra party in those areas. These differences accounted for the structure of political competition in these areas, often between the Congress and Rightist forces in many parts of the country.

Today it would be hard to detect the boundaries of princely and British India in the map of democratic politics. The nature of party competition has changed radically. The Congress has been marginalised in many states that it dominated in the 1950s. Although most of the big parties of today trace their legacy to one or the other party that existed in 1952, the structure of party competition is entirely different. The inherited map of politics has thus more or less faded away. Perhaps to a lesser extent we can say the same about the quality of democratic governance. The "laggards" of today are not necessarily the states with poor quality of governance sixty years back. Today we are used to distinguishing between states in the south and west on the one hand and those in the north and the east on the other. This line dividing the "advanced" and "backward" states did not exist in 1947.

It would, however, be hasty to conclude that the past does not matter. The political impact of movements and ideas appears to be more enduring. Areas that came under the influence of communist or socialist movements in the 1930s or 1940s still bear the legacy of that influence, either as a dominant political force (Kerala, West Bengal, Tripura, Bihar, Uttar Pradesh) or as protest movements and forces that shape politics (Andhra Pradesh, Orissa, Karnataka, Maharashtra).

Politics in areas that were marked by social justice movements (Tamil Nadu, Kerala) is different today from the politics of other areas; areas influenced by the Ambedkarite movement (Maharashtra, Uttar Pradesh) continue to throw up different patterns from other areas. States that witnessed separatist or secessionist movements (Nagaland, Mizoram, Punjab) or those which experienced major political movements (Bihar, Gujarat, Assam) still bear the legacy of those movements. Even when the structure of political competition appears familiar, the terms of competition are very different across different states and reflect the ideological contestations of the past.

We can thus present the first thesis: *The political legacy of movements and ideologies at the state level has proved more enduring than that of institutions and organisations.*

Thesis 2: Political integration: The second set of questions has to do with the nature of integration of the state with the Indian union, integration within the state, and its distinctiveness from other states. To what extent has the state become a political community conscious of its identity and existence? How well has this community integrated with the larger national political community? Does such a community mark its boundaries from its neighbours on the basis of the political boundaries of the state? Does the community face serious challenge from smaller, subregional communities?

Writing forty years ago, Myron Weiner commented upon the fact that most states, especially those in the Hindi heartland, had not emerged as a political community. Today we have passed that stage. Regional histories, a common cultural-linguistic universe, and political experience have combined to ensure that the boundaries of the modern public sphere are often coterminous with the boundaries of the state. This is the level at which political choices are made and intelligible contestations emerge; it is the terrain where people meaningfully relate to the "political". Compared to the condition fifty years back, every state has become more conscious of its regional identity and its existence as a self-contained political community.

No doubt there are differences in the level of identity consciousness. This consciousness is weaker in Hindi heartland states like Madhya Pradesh and Uttar Pradesh that lack a distinctive language or political culture. The struggles for a linguistic state sharpened this process in states like Andhra Pradesh, Maharashtra, and Punjab, while regional identity found expression through other movements in Tamil Nadu (Dravida movement), Assam (anti-foreigners movement), Mizoram (insurgency), and West Bengal (communist movement). The states have also witnessed different trajectories in this respect. Maharashtra and Gujarat are both becoming more regional than before (though the expressions and the political outcomes are different). At the same time, regional self-consciousness is no longer a central factor in driving the politics of Tamil Nadu, Andhra Pradesh, and Punjab.

Finally, regional consciousness combines with other identities in different ways: caste, class, and religion both compete with region as also strengthen the region as the basis of political competition. Therefore, in some states – Tamil Nadu or Punjab – caste and/or religion play a crucial role in shaping the regional, whereas in Gujarat the regional has facilitated the rise of religious consciousness. As a rule we can say that the strengthening or otherwise of political community is less a function of pre-existing cultural unity in the state and more an outcome of its political articulation in recent times.

The rise of statewide political communities has not, however, weakened the ties of the states with the Indian union. If anything, the more fully integrated a state is within itself, the greater is the ease with which it exists with the larger union. It is important to note that almost all the states that have witnessed a long-standing separatist strand are marked by deep internal divisions of different kinds, be these linguistic (Nagaland), religious (Punjab), ethnic (Manipur), or linguistic and religious (Jammu and Kashmir) that feed into separatist politics. Nevertheless, since the political leadership at the centre has accepted a legitimate role for regional identities, the states are more integrated with the Indian union than was the case fifty years ago.

At the same time, the rise of state-level political communities has not suppressed the rise of subregional consciousness. Since region is a product of political experience, and because many states include smaller regions that are incongruent with the dominant regional experience, almost every big state now has identifiable and backward subregions: North Bengal, Western Orissa, Poorvanchal, Bundelkhand, besides the famous instances of Telangana and Vidarbha. Whenever economic grievance and the availability of a political instrument have combined, the sub-region constitutes a more salient basis of local politics as in Telangana and Vidarbha. Sometimes it even allows for a rather painless creation of new states, such as the three new states in the Hindi heartland.

Thus statewide or subregional consciousness is neither the natural nor permanent basis of politics; such a consciousness is partly a result of the project of cultural homogenisation and political consolidation in each state or region. Nor can we think of regional or subregional identifications as protonationalisms that are bound to subvert national unity and suppress smaller identities.

Second thesis: *The emergence of states as real and imagined political communities has intensified political regionalism without weakening the ties with the larger national unit or suppressing the emergence of subregional communities.*

***Thesis 3: Power-sharing mechanisms*:** The third set of questions has to do with institutional mechanisms and practices for devolution of power at two different levels. How has the relationship of the states with the union changed in terms of distribution of powers? And to what extent have the states shared their powers with their administrative and political sub-units?

In general a common political institutional frame has ensured that institutional difference is not a key factor in understanding the differences in the quality of democracy across different states. Some "special provisions" for a few states did facilitate greater autonomy for the government and greater space for respecting their specificity, but *only* when these provisions were given free political play (Sikkim after the merger and Mizoram after the accord, but not in Jammu and Kashmir). At the same time, special provisions have perpetuated local oligarchies, not exactly strengthened democracy in those areas, and often weakened the links between the people and political power.

For the rest of the country, the relationship between the states and the centre has been defined by the balance of two opposite forces: politics has ensured greater federalisation of the Indian union, while the working of economic processes and security apparatus has tended to flatten the differences across various states. Both these forces have also led to differentiation among states: the logic of politics has of late tended to favour states like Tamil Nadu that get to play a pivotal role at the centre while the logic of economy has worked to the advantage of the more developed states and those with greater capacity to attract investment.

As for sharing of power within a state, the real tension lies between legal-constitutional advances and lack of political will. Though there have been a few institutional innovations for subregional autonomy, the regional development boards in Maharashtra, the Darjeeling Hill Council in West Bengal, and the Bodoland Development Council are instances that have made only a cosmetic difference in the absence of political will to share power.

Another area of post-constitution innovation is the evolution of panchayati raj institutions (PRIs), but so far their impact on the quality of democracy is debatable. Till the 1990s, this was the responsibility of the states and the states did come up with different strategies of addressing the challenge of democratic decentralisation. There were first-generation PRIs in states like Maharashtra, Gujarat, Rajasthan, and Tamil Nadu where, though the initiatives were formally speaking bold, they turned out to be politically and administratively harmless since the existing political establishment managed to convert the PRIs into their extensions. Kerala, Karnataka, and West Bengal constitute the second generation of PRIs where the initiative strengthened local political mobilisation and also generated support for state-level players to ward off their political adversaries at the centre.

After the 73rd Amendment, though the initiative slipped out of the hands of the states in terms of institutional innovation, the difference in implementation remained and proved to be crucial. This third generation of panchayati raj is characterised by a temporary coincidence of political design emanating at the top and the demands of party functionaries at the bottom. This initiative did create political space for grassroots activists of political parties, particularly women, dalits, and OBCs. But panchayati raj is yet to account for serious differentials in the quality of democracy as it remains hostage to the machinations of governments that may be indifferent (Bihar, Jharkhand, Uttar Pradesh) or to sabotage from above (as in Andhra Pradesh during TDP rule), or political hijacking (West Bengal).

Thesis three: *The greater political clout of the states and their unwillingness to share power with their sub-units has blunted the democratising impulse of institutional reforms and accentuated inequalities across states instead of reducing differences in access to power.*

Thesis 4: Political culture: The fourth question relates to the domain of political culture, including political ideologies and public opinion. How distinct is the culture of democracy in each state? How does this distinctiveness affect the nature of political choice and the quality of democracy?

At the time of Independence, different states began with a very different political ethos or mass political attitude depending upon the nature of pre-modern culture, the depth of the nationalist movement, and the impact of other social and political movements. But soon a culture of democracy crystallised everywhere. This development did not mean that democracy wiped out all regional differences; instead, states evolved their varying cultures of democracy depending on the presence of different parties and the nature of ideological contestations in the public sphere. Thus the culture of democracy reflects neither a continuity of the pre-modern ethos nor an imitation of the borrowed ideas of democracy; the new cultures of democracy are distinctly modern yet specific to the state concerned. At the state level, for instance, the pressure to maintain high ideological form is somewhat relaxed. Hence, the seemingly non-ideological and pragmatic character of the culture of democracy at the state level and its emphasis on "getting the work done".

Yet, woven into these cultures of democracy are various elements. In some situations one of these becomes the key or defining element. In sharp contrast to the dominant ethos of pre-modern values and cultures, the ideas of dignity, equality, and emancipation constitute a very important element of democratic cultures across states. These have emerged from the anti-colonial movement and struggles against the caste system and acquired a strong Indian content. It is possible to posit that public discourse in states like Kerala, Tamil Nadu, or Maharashtra has been dominated by these concerns for the major part of the last half-century. This, however, does not preclude the rise and spread of a strong populist element in the public culture – as in the case of Tamil Nadu and to some extent Maharashtra. States like Andhra Pradesh too have shown a turn towards this culture based on the key role of a semi-charismatic leadership.

The third element visible in the cultural expressions of many states is based on a strong sense of community-based majoritarianism. Many states of the North East as also Jammu and Kashmir are examples of this trend; parts of Uttar Pradesh too exemplify this trait and, more recently, Gujarat has also turned towards this majoritarian norm. Fourth, as discussed above, region and regionalism also constitute the bases of political culture and formative elements of public opinion. In fact, the impact of equality, populism, and majoritarianism is filtered by the regional element.

Thus, in Andhra Pradesh and Tamil Nadu populist culture is strongly associated with the regional element while in Gujarat more recently, or in Punjab historically, the rise of a majoritarian norm is filtered through the regional element. In Jammu and Kashmir too, the regional and religious combine to give the state its sharp sense of "difference". The key point here is that these cultural expressions and features of public opinion shape political activity and the democratic enterprise in the states more than traditional or pre-given values and norms about the public sphere and power.

Thesis four: *The spread of a distinctive culture of democracy has given a regional flavour to political practice without ensuring a democratic culture, as emancipatory ideas confront majoritarianism and the populist tendency faces pragmatism.*

Thesis 5: Political participation: The fifth question relates to the degree, intensity, and quality of political participation at the state level. How does political participation in the electoral and the non-electoral arena at the state level compare with national-level politics? What accounts for the substantial state-wise differences on this count? To what extent does higher political participation lead to better democratic access?

The democratic enterprise has successfully attracted popular participation at the state level. The emergence of the state as the principal locus of political choice has meant that electoral participation at the state level is higher than at the national level. For the same reason, much of the political protest and movements are played out in the arena of state politics rather than that of national politics.

Over the years, participation has gone up both in terms of electoral turnout and in election-related political activity.[6] The extent of participation varies from state to state. On the whole, smaller states seem to have higher participation. Other states with high participation rates are those dominated by communist parties where the party machine is employed to mobilise the people. States like Gujarat, Rajasthan, and Andhra Pradesh, as also larger states like Bihar and Uttar Pradesh, record lower levels of participation in elections and election-related activity, but it may not be appropriate to say that they are low in terms of overall political participation and engagement.

There does not appear to be a direct relationship between electoral and non-electoral forms of political participation. On the whole, high rates of participation are indicative of an expansion of democracy. This expansion is often *not* accompanied by any improvement in the outcomes democratic enterprises produce, nor is there any evidence of a deepening of democracy. And yet, low system response does not discourage people from participating in politics and this helps the system in generating legitimacy for itself.

Thesis five: *Higher and more intense political participation at the state level has widened the base of democracy and sustained its legitimacy without enriching the quality of democratic outcomes.*

Thesis 6: The social basis of political power: The sixth set of questions is about the sociology of power. Who controls political power at the state level and how? How narrow or wide, stable or unstable is the social profile of those who control political power? What are its consequences for the character of the democratic regime?

One of the common expectations about democratic politics in India has been that it will erode the power and legitimacy of the traditional structure of domination in the form of caste. This was expected to happen in a democratic transition of power from the forward "upper" castes to the "lower" and backward castes. Overall, this process has been under way for quite some time, more visible at the state level than in national politics, but in quite dissimilar ways. In some states the transition has flown to the relatively more backward castes, while in others it slowed down after reaching the middle castes, and in yet others the transition more or less failed to take off and the upper castes retained their power.

The main story here is, of course, the rise of the middle peasant castes – either one caste or a combination of middle castes through a formidable cluster – as the main claimants of power in the democratic set-up. Gujarat, Maharashtra, Andhra Pradesh, Karnataka, Haryana, and Punjab represent this development. In states like Kerala, Tamil Nadu, Bihar, and Uttar Pradesh, this transition has gone beyond the middle castes; while in West Bengal, Orissa, Madhya Pradesh, Chhattisgarh, Rajasthan, Himachal Pradesh, and Uttarakhand, the dominance of traditional upper castes has persisted.

Often, in states where the traditional patterns of domination persist one witnesses relatively low levels of improvement in the quality of democracy coupled with low levels of politicisation (with the exception of West Bengal). On the other hand, states where the transition has gone beyond the middle castes reveal a mixed evidence of improved quality of democratic governance. In the South where this transition has stabilised, we find improvement in the quality of governance, while states that are undergoing this transition only recently are less well governed and unsure of the outcome of this democratic transition.

Whenever a middle caste or caste cluster has emerged as a dominant political configuration, it is often associated with the rise of a political machine that ensures the electoral victory of this caste cluster as also the emergence of patronage networks through which the advantages of democratic transition are invariably routed. This development gives a semblance of stability to these regimes. Democratic politics acquires legitimacy because of the transition away from the upper castes; and yet this same development has the potential of turning itself into a system of bondage. It arrests further spread of the democratic norm and puts a halt to democratisation. The dominant middle castes become both the harbingers of democracy and bottlenecks in the progress of democracy.

Thesis six: *Political regimes at the state level acquire their anchorage as well as bondage from the rise of dominant castes to power, which represents as well as halts the transfer of power to lower social orders.*

Thesis 7: The economic limits to politics: The seventh question is one of political economy. How autonomous or otherwise is the democratic regime in dealing with organised economic interests? Who controls political power and for whose benefit?

The autonomy of state politics is clearly not to be confused with autonomy of state power *vis-à-vis* dominant economic interests. If anything, the rise in the autonomy of state politics in recent times has been accompanied by a decline in their autonomy in the economic sphere. First, while states have gained political clout and bargaining capacity, this does not translate into greater economic freedom from the controls of the central government. Federal fiscal relations remain heavily loaded against the state and the centre continues to dictate many key economic policies irrespective of the political preferences of the state government (e.g. the current LDF government in Kerala).

Second, as the state governments get more power to negotiate directly with multilateral and private actors, it appears that each of them is weaker in terms of collective bargaining and more vulnerable to capital blackmail (competing offers to Tata for the Nano cars is an example). Third, a lower degree of transparency and weaker mechanisms of accountability in the states also mean that state-level political decisions are more likely to be governed by the vested interests of the dominant classes, if not reflect a naked use of political power for plundering economic and natural resources.

Fourth, the shift in many states from an alignment of political power with the interests of big farmers to those of industrialists and capitalists has meant a shift from indirect to direct intervention in political decision-making, for big farmers lacked the wherewithal to monitor and control a vast range of economic decisions. And finally, the historic coincidence of the rise in the autonomy of state politics in the era of the New Economic Policy has meant that the states have to simultaneously deal with a limited range of policy options, a media climate hostile to pro-people public action, and multi-pronged interventions of the various arms of global economic players.

The results of all these developments are for everyone to see. Some states have had political leadership that almost openly represents the dominant economic interests (Haryana, Gujarat, Orissa, Jharkhand); others do it less brazenly. Even big state governments have little option but to accept the logic of dominant classes for fear of losing out on investments and development (Uttar Pradesh, Bihar); in some other states, the political elites have quietly abandoned agrarian interests (Maharashtra, Andhra Pradesh). In state after state, governments are openly adopting policies that restrict the choices available to the people, and bypass ordinary democratic procedures in arriving at crucial decisions about relocating large sections of society or depriving them of their livelihood, often restricting their right to resist or even protest.

The political terrain is no more the arena where crucial economy-related decisions are made; instead, it has been reduced to an arena of formally adopting and implementing economic policies that appear to be pre-given and without any alternative or option. If one was looking for evidence for the famous quip that governments are nothing but the executive arm of the capitalist class, many states in contemporary India would fit the bill.

Thesis seven: *As state politics gains greater autonomy* vis-à-vis *national politics and the central government, its capacity to resist corporate and other organised interests appears severely eroded, often producing regimes that act as agents of the dominant classes.*

Thesis 8: Party political competition: The eighth question concerns the nature and consequence of party political competition. How different is the emerging party system from the national system of party political competition? Does it offer a greater and more meaningful choice to citizens?

Just as the "congress system" was a point of attraction for many observers, many today appear convinced that the rise of coalitions in itself augurs well for democracy. Therefore, much of the writing on Indian politics during the late 1980s and 1990s was full of expectation about the new party system. In general, however, while the format of party competition has somewhat opened up over the years, the nature of choices available is quite narrow and often narrowed down further. This is the paradox thrown up by the 1990s: state after state experienced the rise of competitive politics that witnessed the entry of new occupants in the political space, but this competition rarely led to new policies, programmes or institutional devices. We describe this system as a system of competitive convergence.[7]

Within this broader framework of convergence, we can identify four major types of party political competition in contemporary times: (i) bipolar convergence (Rajasthan, Madhya Pradesh, Gujarat, Chhattisgarh, Delhi, Himachal Pradesh, Uttarakhand), (ii) multiparty–bipolarity (Tamil Nadu, Punjab, Kerala, Maharashtra, Orissa, Bihar, Tripura), (iii) stable multi-polar convergence (Andhra Pradesh, Karnataka, Uttar Pradesh, Assam, Jharkhand, Jammu and Kashmir, Manipur), and (iv) fluid multipolarity (Arunachal Pradesh, Mizoram, Haryana, West Bengal).

Notwithstanding the general cynicism prevailing about political parties, the arena of party political competition has greater autonomy in determining the quality and outcome of democracy. What matters in this domain though is not so much the format of party competition which has attracted much analytical attention, but the range of substantive choices available. We hypothesise that the shrinking of choices negates the gains made by expansion in numeric choices that emerged in the last two decades.

Thesis eight: *A system of competitive convergence has meant that the opening up of the format of party competition has not led to greater and more meaningful political choices for the citizen.*

Thesis 9: People's movements and struggles: The ninth question takes us beyond party politics. How active and powerful are the various people's movements and struggles in the state? In which ways do they affect the political agenda and the quality of democracy?

The limitations of the party system of competitive convergence can be overcome by the non-party sector, especially social and political movements. At the state level, peoples' movements and popular struggles can be more effective, especially if the state is small in size. But this possibility is differentially realised through very different channels and with strikingly different outcomes. States with more dense social and political movements tend to experience a more vibrant democracy, both because these movements act as a check, feedback, and resource for the political parties, and also because civil society organisations draw their vibrancy from these movements (Kerala, Tamil Nadu). There are, of course, states that have witnessed social and political movements and yet await their turn to a qualitatively better democratic environment (Uttar Pradesh and Bihar) and states that once boasted of a vibrant legacy of movements and civil society but have lately lost the momentum (Maharashtra).

When the principal channel of popular protest is a violent movement, it often succeeds in shaking up the established consensus (though not always, as in Punjab) and the political elite, but at a very high cost to the people, democratic norms, and the character of state power, at both the local and national level. This is borne out by examples of Jammu and Kashmir, Punjab, Nagaland, Manipur, Jharkhand, Chhattisgarh, and so on. In places which have not witnessed any serious social and political movements (such as Rajasthan, Haryana, much of Uttar Pradesh, and Himachal Pradesh), politics remains insulated from societal concerns and is unable to receive societal feedback and inputs.

Thesis nine: *Struggles and movements seek to rupture the convergence of the political establishment but their non-political character limits their capacity to affect the political agenda.*

***Thesis 10: The politics of violence*:** Finally we need to ask a question about the emerging phenomenon of the politics of violence in many forms. What is the impact of various forms and degrees of political violence in the state? How does it affect the space for democratic politics?

The last quarter of a century has seen the rise of all forms of violence in public life: violence as an instrument of electoral mobilisation, violence as an instrument of achieving high political objectives, secessionist violence, and so on. Much of this violence, directed at state machinery and functionaries, only results in a further brutalisation of the state machinery. The standard response of the state has been to meet violence with tough military measures. This, however, does not ensure the use of state force when more or less organised mob violence is staged to target and hound minority communities.

Except in cases of communal violence, the state has routinely adopted a militarist approach to terrorism and violence. This has given birth to issues of state repression in Manipur, Nagaland, and parts of Assam. The response to militant violence in Punjab, and terrorist violence more recently, has also been one of flexing the repressive state apparatus. In addition to using state repressive machinery, Chhattisgarh has also witnessed the formation of a civil militia to combat collective violence.

Apart from these instances of violence, there are many other areas of concern – everyday coercion in Haryana, Uttar Pradesh, or Bihar, party violence in West Bengal, and frequent recourse to vigilantism in Maharashtra. All these have a common effect: they erode democratic space; implicitly justify the use of coercion by the state; provide justification for "strong" laws and draconian powers to the police *without* any guarantee that governance will improve if political actors engaged in violence and coercion are put down or that civil society will be the stronger by employing strong state protection.

The growing concern about security and terror has led to increased emphasis, cutting across states, on the security apparatus to the detriment of civil and political rights and a democratic culture. This has affected politics in the states more severely, for human rights institutions and independent media tend to be weaker at the state level. Peripheral states in the North East and Jammu and Kashmir find greater corrosion of their autonomy due to greater focus on internal security.

Thesis ten: *A rise in the politics of coercion and state response to it leads to a spiral of shrinking space for democratic politics.*

Wider Implications

What are the likely effects of these developments in terms of the expansion and deepening of democracy in India? Does the rise of the state as a serious and autonomous platform of politics strengthen or weaken the hope for advance in the direction of democratic governance? In other words, is this rise good news for democracy?

By now, it has been almost two decades since this development started taking shape and we believe that it will now stabilise. Some consequences of the rise of states as an autonomous platform of politics are clearly good with the potential of steering democracy towards further expansion. Not only is the possibility of greater autonomy for the states in itself a welcome feature, it has also led to a differential party system that reflects the social context more clearly than was the case earlier. A new set of elites has been able to enter politics through the rise of regional parties, and gates have been opened up for higher participation in politics by more diverse sections than before.

However, it may be too early to celebrate this development without keeping in mind the constraints within which it takes shape. In the first place, this development does not help us overcome the indifferent record of India's democracy in making institutions function properly and effectively. Nor can it help overcome the fundamental constraint of being bound to a social context that is mired in complex grids of domination and exploitation. The emergence of the states as the central platform of politics might actually weaken the capacity of democratic politics to withstand the pressures of organised economic interests; and may open the doors wider for the consolidation of oligarchic control by dominant social groups, reducing the real political choices available to the citizen.

But then, it is precisely this mixed balance sheet of possibilities and anxieties that makes the study of state politics an exciting and important enterprise.

Notes

1. Iqbal Narain, *State Politics in India*, Meerut: Meenakshi Prakashan, 1976; John R. Wood, *State Politics in India: Crisis or Continuity?* Boulder: Westview Press, 1984.
2. Yogendra Yadav and Suhas Palshikar, "From Hegemony to Convergence: Party System and Electoral Politics in the Indian States – 1952–2002", *Journal of the Indian School of Political Economy*, January–June 2003, pp. 5–44.
3. Myron Weiner, *State Politics in India,* Princeton: Princeton University Press, 1968.
4. Atul Kohli, *The State and Poverty in India*, Cambridge: Cambridge University Press, 1987.
5. Rob Jenkins, *Regional Reflections: Comparing Politics across India's States*, New Delhi: Oxford University Press, 2004; John Harriss, "Comparing Political Regimes across Indian States: A Preliminary Essay", *Economic and Political Weekly*, 27 November 1999, pp. 3367–77.
6. Yogendra Yadav, "Understanding the Second Democratic Upsurge: Trends of Bahujan Participation in Electoral Politics in the 1990s", in Francine R. Frankel, Zoya Hasan, Rajeev Bhargava, and Balveer Arora (eds), *Transforming India*, New Delhi: Oxford University Press, 2000, pp. 120–45; Suhas Palshikar and Sanjay Kumar, "Participatory Norm: How Broad Based is It?" *Economic and Political Weekly*, 18 December 2004, pp. 5412–17.
7. Yogendra Yadav and Suhas Palshikar, "From Hegemony to Convergence", *vide supra*.

8

On the Necessity of Politics

MODERN POLITICS IS inherent in the very constitution of modern society. Any society which is large-scale and complex requires a specific force/activity which coordinates/ties up its various segments/aspects/sectors: politics is born out of this necessity. In that sense politics is the central driving force or integrative mechanism of a modern society. The same logic applies to societies like India which did not opt for modernity. Even though a "modern", large-scale, and complex collective life was thrust upon India through colonialism, there is no way it can now escape the logic of politics.

This apparently theoretical point has a simple though far-reaching practical implication: either you determine and control the character of politics or politics determines the character of your life and action. It is possible to make significant short-term changes in one or two aspects of society without entering politics, but those who wish to transform the character of public life *in totality* or those who wish to transform one aspect in a fundamental sense cannot but enter politics. In that sense, keeping out of politics is not really an option available to us.

The experience of peoples' movements in the recent past confirms this point. To be effective and authentic, these movements have to be "micro" in the sense that they have to focus exclusively on one or two issues and work intensively in a small area to realise it. This compulsion applies even to the best and most authentic of movements. They have made an invaluable contribution to Indian public life by bringing fresh issues and energy into it. But it is equally true that their success has

*Co-authored with Kishen Pattanayak.

always been issue specific and could therefore be politically contained. Whenever these movements have tried to enter the political/electoral area *without changing their character*, the masses have rejected them, but not because of the attempt by hitherto "pure" people to enter the "corrupt" arena of politics. The reason is that people think that these single-issue movements/organisations are not capable of handling the complex task of managing political power. And they are right, unless these movements can do something to prove to the contrary. Moreover, once that single issue is resolved or dies a natural death, the movement also faces a near-certain death.

In other words, the very logic of the constitution of our society makes it impossible for non-political movements to affect its character. Even if different movements come together, they cannot make a large impact unless they transform their character, that is, unless they turn political. A "political" intervention will have to be "comprehensive" in a dual sense: it will have to take up all the issues concerning the people and develop a framework which puts all these issues into perspective; and it will be "macro" in the sense of aiming at expanding to the state or national level.

There is another kind of necessity of politics for those who wish to serve the deprived sections of society. In contemporary India the dominant sections of society have access to information, decisions and power through elite bureaucratic connections and money. But the only possible channel available to the "masses" is politics. Unless they can be represented in politics, their voice will never be heard. The apparently contradictory trend in Indian politics – on the one hand there is a steadily growing politicisation of the masses, on the other hand a growing cynicism among elites regarding politics – should be viewed in this context. If we want the growing politicisation of the masses to be matched by their increased empowerment, the only option is political intervention through a political organisation.

A political party is best suited to fulfil this role. Its mobilisation and mode of action is qualitatively different from that of a movement. It cannot remain satisfied with winning the partial allegiance of the masses on the few issues it espouses. It has to win their trust, their total allegiance, and be accepted as their representative on all the issues in public life. Moreover, its appeals must be widespread: it must extend to practically all sections of society so as to be able to win the support of a plurality. These two compulsions transform the character of a political party irrespective of its ideological leanings. A party has to evolve a comprehensive agenda for all the issues and problems facing society. It has to assign them in order of priority and resolve their mutual contradictions – a task which a movement can easily evade. And it has to undertake macro actions in order to come to power: it has to listen to the demands and aspirations of different regions and sections. If it fails in any of these respects, it faces rejection in a democratic contest which can serve as a corrective mechanism. In other words, those who wish to bring about a fundamental transformation of the existing society through democratic means must, of necessity, move towards a political party. They may call it by a different name, or design it in ways different from the corrupt political parties which exist today, but if they are serious about their purpose, there is no way they can escape performing some of the basic functions which political parties perform in today's democracy.

Needless to add, forming a political party is by itself no solution, though it is a necessary step towards a solution. As we all know very well, political parties perform the above-mentioned functions in a grossly distorted manner, because for most of them attaining power has become an end in itself. Their internal organisation is anything but democratic. Their contact with the masses is remote.

This pushes them into "short-cuts" – into policies which can win popular support for themselves, in a short time, but at the expense of the people's long-term interests. Instead of reflecting popular aspirations, these parties suppress popular initiative. All this indicates that there is a fairly strong intrinsic tendency among political parties towards corruption. Yet it is not inevitable. The present corruption is not because of the logic of a political party but because of the organisational structure of all the existing political parties – the kind of political culture which has come to dominate India's polity and the degeneration of political ideologies. If we have a clear perspective and concrete plan regarding these three challenges, there is no reason why political parties must degenerate into their present state. We have to believe in this possibility and work towards its realisation if we believe in the future of democracy in India.

9

On Theories of the Indian State

A Review Essay

A SURVEY OF THE THEORIES of the Indian state promises to be a tidy if lengthy exercise in plotting the available answers to a given set of questions. Or so it would seem until one takes a closer look at the key concepts, namely, state and theory, and realises that these do not tell us with any precision what is to be surveyed. They merely point towards an essentially contested terrain of ideas. There are simply no given questions to which answers might be located. The theoretical dispute about the Indian state turns out to be one where the participants do not recognise any common questions; indeed, many of them might even deny that theirs is a theory of the Indian state. As in what the philosophers of science call an "inter-paradigmatic debate", the evidences, standards of verification, value preferences, and vocabularies differ widely. It is as much a dispute about the very idea of a state and what it means to theorise about it as it is about the nature of Indian political reality.

The problem is compounded by the relative lack of conscious and systematic theorisation on this subject. Scholarship on Indian politics has been dominated by empirical-descriptive studies which do not raise theoretical issues. Moreover, the concept of state was not in currency outside Marxist circles until recently. It seems natural, therefore, to confine oneself to the few, mostly Marxist, theorists who have consciously put forward a "theory of the Indian state".

A better alternative is to cast the net wider by opting for more open and richer notions of both state and theory. In its contemporary narrow usage, "state" has come to mean an institutional apparatus which is the locus of sovereignty. In operational terms, "state" has become an impressive way of talking about government and its allied agencies. Yet, in assigning enormous significance to the idea of the state, we have at the back of our minds the classical, wider notion of the state as political community, as coterminous with the very domain of politics, as the criterion to define what is political. The tension between these two notions can be reduced by defining the *state as a continuous public power, distinct from and above both rulers and the ruled.* The question of understanding the Indian state is accordingly that of appraising the character of this continuous public power in contemporary India.

The concept of theory can be similarly rescued from popular usage which restricts it to casual explanation. To theorise is to make sense of something. It involves looking at a phenomenon from within as well as without, placing its present in a narrative of past and anticipated future, judging its significance, and choosing the worthy course of action.

From this relaxed standpoint we can now see that most of the major arguments about Indian politics clearly concern the ground covered by the concept of the state and that they are very much theoretical. But their potential theories have mostly remained in the twilight of implications; these have to be brought to the discursive level and placed alongside other theories of the Indian state.

Three Perspectives

Like the rest of the social sciences, it is customary to divide reflections on the Indian state into two schools: the liberal and the Marxist. This ready and useful classification covers at least three sets of differences: the different aspects of the state to be focused upon, the different techniques and training of analysts, and different political values. But its tendency to subsume the first two differences under the third dimension of ideology puts limits to its analytical value in this case.

Perhaps it would be more fruitful to redraw the lines of division a bit so that these are more attentive to the differentiation and allow complex responses. This may be done by giving primacy to the first dimension and by unpacking the unhelpful category of "liberal". On this reading the theories would fall into three groups which may be called, for want of better terms, political-institutional, political economy, and cultural perspectives on the Indian state.

In the first group would fall theories which focus on political institutions and processes as the key to understanding the character of public power in India. These are usually put forward by political scientists who hold liberal-modernist values. The second set of theories would be those that regard political economy as holding the clue to the nature of the state. Coming from students of social sciences with an emphasis on economics, these theories are mostly of Marxist persuasion. And finally, there is an amorphous group of theorists trained in sociology or anthropology who focus on the interaction of polities with the belief system of society. Some of them stand for "traditional" values, others for "modern".

The Political-Institutional Perspective

This perspective was the first to suggest itself, in keeping with the dominant mood of both the newly independent country and contemporary political science. Both the reality and the theory seemed to indicate that India was reliving the experience of the modern West with a time lag. Thus the new constitution and Western liberal-democratic institutions seemed the most crucial entities for understanding the vast domain of politics. At a normative plane, too, the evolution of a desirable political order in India seemed to depend on the success of these institutions.

This clearly set a European agenda for theorising about the Indian state, based as it was on the gross assumption that the contingent historical experience of the modern European state supplied both the tools to analyse and the standard by which to judge the experience of the newly independent states. With the passage of time the terminology changed – from plain "westernisation" to the more euphemistic "modernisation" and "political development"; but the underlying spirit did not.

W.H. Morris-Jones' *The Government and Politics of India* was one of the early attempts to advance an overarching argument about

Indian politics. For Morris-Jones, its "fascinating features" result from a contrast between the political institutions of a nation-state and the structures of an ancient society – a contrast symbolised by the various idioms of Indian politics. The triumph belongs, inevitably, to the former. Thanks to the legacies of a stable administration, the one-dominant-party system, and representative institutions, the record of the operation of public power in India has been "impressive" in accomplishing "vast social and economic changes" as well as establishing the legitimacy of the state. The judgement, shared by many Western observers then as now, had unmistakable elements of being both innocent and patronising.

Not all observers, however, were as impressed with the Indian state as Morris-Jones. In his classic *Asian Drama*, Gunnar Myrdal characterised India, like other South Asian countries, as a "soft state" for its failure in relation to mass poverty. The term was meant to highlight the severe limits to the scope of public power in India: the inability of the state to enforce policies and to place obligations on the people.

Robert Hardgrave's *India: Government and Politics in a Developing Nation* identified the major problem in the domain of public power in India as "the revolution of rising frustration": demands and aspirations have increased in the process of modernisation but the capacity and the will of the government to respond effectively has not kept pace. But if it was difficult to translate Myrdal's plea for a more disciplined nation into concrete terms, Hardgrave's concrete suggestion of higher institutionalisation did not pay adequate attention to the specificities of the Indian situation where early institutionalisation had in fact taken place.

The most ambitious and to date the most impressive attempt to understand the nature of public power in India is, of course, Rajni Kothari's *Politics in India*. To be sure, Kothari did not challenge the foundation of the European agenda, the belief that the modern European state was the telos of development. But through a series of innovative middle-order conceptualisations, he did posit an alternative to the Western way for reaching there. This was the "Indian model", at once a device to interpret what was happening in Indian politics and an independent norm. His was the most innovative theorisation within the limits of the European agenda.

According to Kothari, the Indian model consisted of establishing a "dominant political centre" – this comes close to "state" as defined here in a society characterised by plural identities and segmental distances. The state had the following attributes: autonomy in dealing with demands and pressures, a high degree of legitimacy and authority, an elaborate institutional edifice, and the capacity to perform. Combining planning from above with open and representative politics, the state was to perform a central role in bringing about an "incremental revolution" through a simultaneous pursuit of several goals: political democracy, social mobilisation, economic development, and a consolidation of the polity by integrating the peripheries with the national mainstream. He thought the model had performed "creditably" in the face of political crisis. So the model is the right one: the task is to pursue it imaginatively and pay more attention to some problem areas.

In retrospect, some of the problems in Kothari's theory seem obvious. The performance of the system was not so creditable in many crucial areas, the limits of the state's autonomy were more rigid than he was prepared to acknowledge, the institutional edifice was more fragile. On the whole, Kothari seems to have read many of his wishes into his picture of reality – a common human error. But it is still not readily recognised that in the last instance most of these analytical weaknesses and blindness resulted from his commitment to the European agenda.

The Emergency marked the definite decline of political-institutional theories of the Indian state. Since then, there has been no systematic articulation of this perspective. Instead, there are occasional voices of discontent, less coherent and certainly less confident than before. Here, again, Kothari is the best representative. In his recent writings, he views the Indian state as having lost its autonomy to the narrow interests of the neo-rich and its allies who control and manipulate it. This has resulted in the crumbling of the institutional edifice, criminalisation of politics, and violence and repression by the state both in its internal functioning and its dealing with the people. The ray of hope now is the mass movements developing outside the framework of political parties. At the level of ideals, the task is to search for alternatives to the capitalist and communist models.

This theorisation, closer to reality but less attentive to specificities, is best seen as a fragmentary amendment to the earlier one. It seems difficult as yet to separate two things: change in the perspective and change in the nature of the Indian state itself. Above all, while a challenge has been posed to the European agenda at a normative plane, its corollaries in terms of new analytical tools are almost absent. Any future political institutional theory has to attend to these problems first.

The Political-Economic Perspective

Most of the conscious theories of the Indian state are from the perspective of political economy. Once the inadequacy of the political-institutional perspective was exposed, the Marxist theory of the state and the discipline of political economy provided a ready alternative. This legacy of the received theory was both an asset and a liability. It sensitised analyses to the systematic linkage between the operation of public power and the dominant interests of society, but it also tended to draw their attention away from the non-economic aspects of society.

Moreover, this understanding was rooted in a theory of history which generalised as necessary and progressive the path taken by Europe since the rise of capitalism. Developments in the rest of the world could be measured by the extent to which they conformed to or deviated from this norm. Understanding India was simply a matter of plotting it appropriately on the graph of history. In other words, the European agenda surfaced here too.

This relative insensitivity to India's specificity, coupled with the economic determinism of the orthodox Marxists, made their analysis of the Indian state a mechanistic exercise. The state is the agency of the ruling classes, and classes are homogeneous and conscious entities. They ally, conspire, and act to control and dictate the state. To enquire into the character of the Indian state is to ask: whose state is this? One has to identify the classes, their combination and order, and place these along the progressive–regressive divide. Given these shared assumptions, the rest of the debate was no more than an exercise in their permutations and combinations.

The theories put forward by the Indian communist parties illustrate this. For the Communist Party of India (CPI), the national-bourgeoisie is the ruling class: the state can hence resist pressure from the big bourgeoisie and landlords to play a progressive role. The Communist Party of India prefers a different combination: the big bourgeoisie and landlords are the ruling classes, with the former dominating this alliance and collaborating with foreign finance capital. The state tends to be reactionary. But for the "Naxalites" it is a "semi-feudal, semi-colonial" state, out-and-out reactionary. The big comprador-bureaucrat bourgeoisie and landlords are only nominally the ruling class: in reality they depend on US imperialism and Soviet social imperialism.

Academic Marxists improved the terminology and introduced a few new nuances, but the rules of the game remained unaltered. A.R. Desai seeks to demonstrate that despite appearances to the contrary the state in India is a capitalist state. For Ajit Roy it is essentially the organ of the dictatorship of the Indian monopoly bourgeoisie and the rural bourgeoisie. C.P. Bhambhri allows for conflict within the ruling classes and the consequent weakening of the state, but the latter is seen simply as a vehicle of capitalism.

Of late, some Indian Marxists have sought to rise above this level of theorising. Thanks to a belated discovery of Gramsci there is a greater willingness now to recognise the "relative autonomy" of politics – ironically, the recognition came when the Indian state was rapidly losing its autonomy – and multiple ways, including "passive revolution", to build capitalism. Hamza Alavi was among the first to argue that a post-colonial state like India has relative autonomy in mediating the competing interests of the dominant classes. Two recent arguments have taken this awareness further.

In *Political Economy of Development in India*, Pranab Bardhan views the Indian state as an autonomous actor in that it acts neither at the behest nor on behalf of the ruling classes, as capable of shaping class re-alignments, and which plays a catalytic role in industrial-technological transformation, and is an important part of the economic base itself. But the conflict within the heterogeneous ruling classes, which ensures democracy, is such that this autonomy is reflected more in the regulatory than developmental functions of the state.

A significant attempt to refine the Marxist tools for an analysis of Indian politics can be seen in the recent writings of Sudipta Kaviraj. Starting with the premise that a Marxist study of politics should not merely collect the political corollaries of the arguments of Marxist economists, he recognises the need to write a narrative of the Indian state in terms of actual political actors, in addition to a structural analysis of Indian politics. On his reading, the Indian state today faces a structural crisis which results from the very success of the social form on which it is based.

These recent advances in the Marxist theory of the Indian state are mainly in the nature of theoretical clarification. It is to be seen how the ground prepared by these is used for substantive theorisation, and whether that turns out to be significantly different from the orthodox accounts in the specificity of the Indian state. Besides, the Marxist theories have to overcome the narrow notion of the state they operate with and their reluctance to engage in normative theorisation.

Not all political economy arguments are from the point of view of Marxists. Francine Frankel's narrative, *India's Political Economy, 1947–1977*, views India's public power as a "paradox of accommodative politics and radical social change", though not many would agree with her about the latter. Recently Susanne and Lloyd Rudolph have presented an elaborate and in some ways innovative argument in their book *In Pursuit of Lakshmi: The Political Economy of the Indian State*.

To the Rudolphs, India is a paradox of a "weak strong state" for, in the past four decades, the Indian state has "alternated between autonomous and reflexive relations with the society". Drawing strength from various historical legacies, the state acts as the "self-determining third actor", independent of both capital and labour, and has served at different times the capitalist, socialist, and liberal-constitutional objectives, or sometimes its own partisan interests. Highly mobilised albeit fragmented social forces are its sources of weakness. The paradox is reflected in the realm of economic policy in the alternation between two models: "command polity", when the state makes authoritative allocation, and "demand polity", when the state surrenders to popular sovereignty and fulfils societal interests and values.

The Cultural Perspective

As political economy theorists begin to recognise the autonomy of the state, a reminder of its limits come from another direction – the social anthropologists who relate the domain of public power to the belief system of the society. Although this perspective has not been articulated as frequently or consciously in the Indian context as the first two, it needs to be taken seriously for two reasons. First, it corrects the structural bias of the first two perspectives by reminding us that ideas about the state, both commonsensical belief and academic theories, are not external to state: they are constitutive of the entity called state. Second, with their cultivated sensitivity and respect for societal differences, students of culture are well equipped to counter the ethnocentric bias of the European agenda.

Methodological suggestions for applying this perspective to the Indian state can be found in Clifford Geertz and Louis Dumont. But not many scholars have followed them up. Some contributions to the "modernity-tradition debate" in political science in the 1960s, especially those of the Rudolphs and Kothari – already showed an amorphous awareness of the issue by rejecting the stereotype that modernity and tradition are monolithic entities, diametrically opposed to each other. Recently, the historian Ravinder Kumar and the sociologist T.K. Oommen have shown a similar awareness and applied it directly to the question of the state by arguing that the idea of the nation-state is inappropriate for India.

Common to all these arguments is a suspicion that the view of India's culture implicit in the usual theories of Indian politics is grossly mistaken, and that these theories go wrong mainly because of this error. Two recent statements which bring this suspicion to a discursive level deserve closer attention. T.N. Madan's paper, "Secularism in its Place" makes a bold statement about one of the central ideas which constitute the Indian state: ". . . in the prevailing circumstances secularism in South Asia as a systematically shared credo of life is impossible, as a basis of state action impracticable, and as a blueprint for the foreseeable future impotent" (748).

The reasoning behind this judgement is of greater and general interest: secular ideology and institutional structures are based on a belief of the modernist minority which is not shared as a world view by the overwhelming majority. To be sure, Madan consciously desists from generalising this argument, but it certainly lends itself to a broader application so as to cover the whole gamut of modern institutions and ideas underlying the Indian state. Are all of these condemned to meet the same fate as secularism? What is the alternative? Many students of culture like Ashis Nandy believe that the only alternative is to begin afresh a dialogue with the Indian tradition in search of new principles for ordering the Indian polity.

A similar analysis can yield a different conclusion, as can be seen in the work of Satish Saberwal, a sociologist-cum-historian, entitled *India: The Roots of Crisis*. His comparison of the long-term processes in India and the West leads him to conclude that the roots of the contemporary crisis in India lie in a lack of fit between the principles underlying our institutions of Western origin and those which have informed traditional Indian institutions.

Colonialism made India a "mega-society" by giving it a techno-social frame of a very large scale, but the segmented Indian society did not produce a unified set of beliefs in accordance with such institutions. The continuation of multiple codes over a long period has tended to destroy the modern mega-societal institutions. The only solution lies in evolving the skills to reduce the multiplicity of codes, in providing a belief system to match modern institutions. Unlike Madan, Saberwal is prepared to extend his argument to all the major political institutions and to the state.

Both these statements, seemingly marginal to the Indian state, promise a lively debate about the nature, limits, and prospects of public power in contemporary India. Some Indian Marxists working under the rubric "Subaltern Studies" are already prepared to take questions of culture and ideas very seriously. Perhaps one can hope for a dialogue between the "traditionalists" and the "radicals", a dialogue about what it means to be radical in the Indian context. The recent inclination among social scientists to take up questions of culture, power, and interests together is a welcome step in this direction.

Towards an Indian Agenda

Theories of the Indian state have been cast for far too long in the European agenda at the analytical as well as normative plane. The specificity of the Indian state has only been seen as a deviation from the European norm; the differences have been conceptualised as distortions and hence only partially understood. The result is obvious to us all: the Indian state continues to puzzle and spring surprises at its theorists.

What is called for is a serious reconsideration of the received theoretical apparatus and perhaps a bold shift in analytical strategy. Above all, what is needed is a shift from the European agenda to an Indian agenda for understanding the Indian state. Such an assertion is liable to be misunderstood. It must be clarified that the agenda need not be Indian in its theoretical inspiration and personnel. Also, it need not overlook the European legacy insofar as it is constitutive of many structures and institutions of contemporary India. But it must be Indian in the sense that the task of theorisation must be situated in the context of the specificity of India.

It is easier to see what is being asked for if it is spelt out in the form of some concrete demands. First, any investigation into the realm of public power in India must see that realm as Indians themselves see it; it must establish a dialogue with the categories, beliefs, and world view of the actors. Of course, it need not and should not be confined to that. Second, the specificity of the Indian must not be conceptualised merely in terms of exceptions to a norm; the theorists must learn to see Indian politics as "normal". Third, while comparison with other states is a must, it needs to be made explicitly, historically, and not with Europe alone. Finally, at the normative plane there is a need for explicit debate on whether India's search for a good political order *must* end with what modern Europe has been able to, or hopes to, achieve.

References

Alavi, Hamza, "The State in Postcolonial Societies: Pakistan and Bangladesh", *New Left Review*, no. 74, July–August 1972.

Bardhan, Pranab, *The Political Economy of Development in India*, Delhi: Oxford University Press, 1984.

Bhambhri, C.P., *Politics in India, 1947–1987*, New Delhi: Vikas, 1988.

Dumont Louis, "Nationalism and Communalism", appended to *Homo Hierarchicus*, Delhi: Oxford University, 1988.

Frankel, Francine R., *India's Political Economy, 1947–1977: The Gradual Revolution*, Princeton: Princeton University Press, 1978.

Geertz, Clifford, ed., *Old Societies and New States: The Quest for Modernity in Asia and Africa*, New York: Free Press, 1963.

Hardgrave, Robert L., *India: Government and Politics in a Developing Nation*, New York: Harcourt, 1970.

Hasan, Zoya, S.N. Jha, and Rasheeduddin Khan, eds, *The State, Political Processes and Identity: Reflections on Modern India*, New Delhi: Sage, 1989.

Kaviraj, Sudipta, "On the Crisis of Political Institutions in India", *Contributions to Indian Sociology*, no. 2, 1984.

———, "A Critique of the Passive Revolution", *Economic and Political Weekly*, November 1988.

Kothari, Rajni, *Politics in India*, Orient Longman, 1970.

———, *State Against Democracy*, Delhi: Ajanta, 1987.

Kumar, Ravinder, "India: A 'Nation-State' or a 'Civilization-State'". Occasional Papers on Perspectives in Indian Development, no. VIII, Nehru Memorial Museum and Library, 1989.

Madan, T.N., "Secularism in Its Place", *Journal of Asian Studies*, November 1987.

Mathew, Kurien K., ed., *India – State and Society: A Marxist Approach*, Bombay: Orient Longman, 1975.

Morris-Jones, W.H., *The Government and Politics of India*, 3rd edn, Bombay: B.I. Publication, 1971.

Myrdal, Gunnar, *Asian Drama: An Inquiry into the Poverty of Nations*, London: Allen Lane & Penguin, 1968.

Oommen, T.K., "Political Alienation and the Internal Threats to Indian Nation-State: Towards a Non-alarmist Perspective", *Indian Journal of Social Science*, 2(2), 1989.

Rudolph, Susanne, and Lloyd Rudolph, *In Pursuit of Lakshmi: The Political Economy of the Indian State*, Hyderabad: Orient Longman, 1987.

Saberwal, Satish, *India: The Roots of Crisis*, Delhi: Oxford University Press, 1986.

Vincent, Andrew, *Theories of the State*, Oxford: Basil Blackwell, 1987.

10

On Rajni Kothari

The Enigma that is *Politics in India*

POLITICS IN INDIA is a classic waiting to be read. If a classic is "a book to which you cannot remain indifferent, and which helps you define yourself in relation or even in opposition to it", *Politics in India* attained this status instantly upon its much awaited arrival in 1970. Its publication was described as "something of an event". Much and justly celebrated, the book has retained this iconic status as perhaps the only classic so far on India's democratic experience (Kothari, 1970; unless specified, all page citations are to this book).

Yet there is something odd about this status. For one thing, very few actually read this book in its entirety. Dated jargon and dense prose make sure that very few survive the first chapter. No wonder the book has been known more through hearsay than actual reading. Or, to be precise, the book is skimmed through in search of the one or two capsule-like formulations – the "Congress System" and "politicisation of caste" are the top contenders here – that were already famous through Kothari's writings in the run-up to *Politics in India*. The book was widely admired (for early and positive reviews, see Morris-Jones, 1971–2; Narain, 1970; Palmer, 1971; Weiner, 1974). Norman D. Palmer was being matter of fact when he described the book as "by far the most sophisticated general study of Indian politics that has yet been written". A Marxist critic chided Rajni Kothari for "producing an ideological justification for the decaying Indian polity" (Chopra, 1972, p. 76; see also Khaliq, 1978). But it is not clear whether the book was really understood by its admirers or critics. It may have sedimented in our collective unconscious even before it was properly digested. All this makes *Politics in India* odd, but what makes it unique – in the club of oddballs that classics are – is the peculiar indifference of the creator to his creation. Although there is no trace of authorial reticence in the book itself, Kothari appeared to have turned his back to his magnum opus soon after its birth. This commercially successful product never had a second edition; apparently the author was reluctant to allow reprints. It had to be substantially rewritten for a recent Hindi trans-creation. The book gets passing mention in his *Memoirs* (Kothari, 2002, pp. 113, 121–2) and other autobiographical reflections. Although he did not repudiate the book, much of his subsequent writings effectively distanced him from many of the substantive positions in *Politics in India*. There is no clear moment of epistemic rupture, yet his post-Emergency writings move beyond the frame set out in the book. It would be hard to recognise the same man as the author of *State against Democracy* and *Growing Amnesia*.

Some reasons for the author's apparent unease are not hard to guess. There must have been awkwardness about the inability of the book, just as of most other academic writings of that time, to anticipate the dramatic events that were to unfold almost immediately after its publication: Indira Gandhi's spectacular victory in the 1971 elections, the resurgence of one-party dominance, protest movements in Gujarat and Bihar, the Emergency, and the extraordinary elections of 1977. In retrospect, it seems that Kothari read 1969 as if it was 1989, the beginning of the era of multipolar competition, regional parties and coalition governments. More than the inability to predict the short-term political future, the author may have felt awkward about the value slope of the book. Though couched in a language of value-neutral social science, the book was held together by an unstated Nehruvian ideology. As in the case of many of his contemporaries, his naïve faith in the Indian state upholding this ideology was shattered by the developments beginning with the Emergency. This disenchantment made Kothari move away from some normative beliefs. His new willingness to question the benevolence of the liberal state, attentiveness to the ways in which this state can turn against its people, sensitivity to the poor and the marginalised, and openness to alternatives must have made him look at his magnum opus from a greater distance than was warranted by the passage of time.

There are some other reasons why this book's status as a classic appears enigmatic. First of all, although the book has a theoretical orientation and was welcomed as "an essay in empirical democratic theory", it appears to have limited its theoretical ambitions. It opens with a theoretical framework, but on first reading its theory appears a modified version of the then dominant and now largely forgotten systems theory of politics. The author appears keen to eschew theoretical ambitions and willing to settle for a "case study" which is not in the business of dealing with "broader issues of theory" (p. 295). Second, though the book was then seen to be empirical, if not positivist, it may not have met rigorous standards of empirical work in its own time. The book has many tables that present some fresh evidence from the newly instituted survey research at the Centre for the Study of Developing Societies, yet the author has fairly limited sources for techniques, and, indeed, interest in quantitative data analysis. Therefore, empirics mainly serve to illustrate his experiential and intuitive understanding of politics rather than form its principal basis. Third, the method followed in the book remains under-specified. While the book was perceived to be a part of the behavioural revolution in the discipline, and does prioritise substance over form, it follows an eclectic method that draws upon various resources and comes up with its own way of analysing these. As we will see below, the methodological status of the "Indian model" – the centrepiece of the book – remained unclear. Thus, behavioural persuasion was more a gesture than a method. Fourth, and following from the first three, the book has not had the kind of legacy for students of Indian politics that one would expect from a classic. While it is mandatory for every major study of Indian politics to refer to Kothari, there is hardly a tradition or school of interpreting Indian politics that can be traced back to *Politics in India*.

We are thus dealing with an intellectual puzzle. We know that *Politics in India* is a classic, but we are unable to specify why. More than four decades later, it is unclear as to how one can place the book in the journey of Indian democracy, in the evolution of the discipline of political science, and, indeed, in the intellectual biography of its author. In the absence of a living intellectual tradition that might follow in its footsteps, the book has not had the benefit of exegeses. Therefore, as long as we confine our search within the frame and the language provided within the book, we are unlikely to understand Kothari's magnum opus. We need to look at the book from outside and read it against its grain to understand its meaning and the reasons for its lasting significance. Perhaps the best tribute to this classic is to prise it open, look for apparent cracks that may offer a clue to the unstated assumptions that operate in it, and point the way to resolving this enigma. That might tell us what makes this book a classic and how to recover and reconstruct its intellectual resources for our times.

An Unresolved Tension

There is a tension that runs through *Politics in India* and in a sense through Kothari's intellectual biography. Reading the book more than four decades later, its analytical frame and normative preferences seem to pull in opposite directions. The Nehruvian ideological preferences appear rather complacent, while his analysis of India's political modernity promises a radical departure from the established ways of thinking. In some of his subsequent writings it comes up as a tension between his alternative vision and his preferred political modalities, except that here the vision is radical but the political understanding is somewhat flat-footed.

The "Indian model" that constitutes the core of the book also lies at the heart of this tension. The perspective that informs the entire book and holds it together is that India's route to modernity is distinct from the European route. While modernity is the "central tendency of our times" (p. 1), both in Europe and outside it, the principal vehicle of modernity in India is politics. The form, substance, and trajectory of this Indian political modernity is quite distinct from those of Europe or elsewhere. Since modernity does not erase the pre-existing social and political order but builds on it, the historical absence of a "political centre" in India played a vital role in shaping modern politics in the

Indian context. It meant that political modernity in India was about creating a "political centre" that included a powerful state and equally powerful political forces that would ensure a wide and deep reach of this state in order to bring out simultaneous change in multiple dimensions. Thus, famously:

> The Indian model of development is characterized by politicization of a fragmented social structure through a penetration of political forms, values, and ideologies. Operating against the background of an essentially apolitical condition of society, such a process involves the building of a political center, the diversification of this center through a network of benefits and obligations, and the mobilization of diverse sections of society in this network. (p. 11, also summarised at p. 193; for a detailed exposition, see pp. 420ff.)

This "Indian model" helps in understanding much of what this book espouses and warns against. At a general plane the book argues against "doctrinaire complacency" (p. 144) in thinking about modernity that is often reflected in "a simple-minded, unicausal, unilinear, and largely dichotomous view of the developmental process" (p. 12). In the Indian context, it leads Kothari to argue forcefully against the idea of a predetermined sequence of political development that rules out simultaneous change and leads to a paranoid concern with stability (p. 163). His general insistence on the autonomy of politics has a specifically Indian angle to it, for the tendency to view political institutions as superstructure and political elites simply as recipient of inputs from society is what prevents observers from acknowledging the creative role of politics in the Indian context. Specifically, the Indian model enables Kothari to view Indian politics in terms of a series of absences. He seeks to replace this "empty" understanding by articulating and defending the specifically Indian forms of political modernity. Kothari's genius lay in demonstrating that what appeared to outsiders as the distortions and maladies of Indian politics were more often than not just historically different forms that modern politics took in the Indian context.

The "Indian model" was indeed a new and illuminating way of organising insights and evidence about recognising the specificity of the working of democratic politics in India. The brilliance of the move, however, prevented readers from asking two basic questions about this model. First of all, what kind of a model was this? Initially it appears as no more than an analytical construct, an ideal type that summed up the specific form that Indian modernity happened to have taken. But soon it becomes clear that the Indian model is something of a norm that the author approves of, indeed recommends to the Indian elite. The success or failure of India's historic transformation, a "race with time itself" (p. 452), depends on living up to this model. He believed that the success or failure of this model would have larger repercussions beyond India (p. 451).

This prompts the second question. Given how crucial the model is, both as an analytical construct and as a normative standard, how do we know that we got this right? Or, to put it more starkly, whose model is this? Again, a cursory reading of Kothari's formulation might suggest that he thought of the Indian model as something India's modernising elite, Nehru included, believed in and consciously pursued. But a careful reading dispels this notion. He firmly rules out the claim that the Indian model was a conscious design:

> Modern India's history – like the history of most nations – is full of vague intentions, dim perceptions of reality, and a lack of clear anticipations even while thinking in terms of a "strategy" of progress. What is relevant for us is not the intent but the content of the strategy. (p. 151)

This makes the Indian model at once more robust and fragile: robust because it is not tied to a history of ideas, but fragile because it now needs an independent justification. The questions now are: How do we verify the analytical construct? And how do we justify the normative standards?

Asking these questions brings us face to face with the tension between the normative and the analytical frame built into the Indian model. The core analytical frame of the Indian model in *Politics in India* follows a hermeneutic method and offers an insider's account. It is an attempt to explicate the logic of the system from within, recognise its features as such and not as deviations or distortions of another expected path. Such a reading could not but have a normative slope.

It invited the reader to affirm the path India had taken so far. To be sure, there was room for criticism of the practice of this model, for the inability of the elites to understand the spirit of the model, but not of the model itself. The insider's account did not prevent a recording of some of the worst effects of the performance of the system, but it did prevent a recognition that these were systemic effects and not aberrations. The Indian model opened fresh and radical possibilities of the specificity of political practices in a young democracy, yet it pushed him into being what Kothari himself was to describe later as a "spokesman" of the system. This version of the Indian model was ill-suited to absorb external shocks that arrived in the form of the Emergency or to insulate itself against the harsh but everyday realities of poverty, deprivation, and degradation for the vast majority of India's citizens.

A cataloguing of the systemic deficits came from an external or outsider's standpoint. Such a critique tended to draw its normative standards from a universalist theory, Marxist or liberal. The universalist theory in both its analytical and normative versions tended to draw its model from the historical experience of European and North American societies. It provided a critique alright but did not leave enough imaginative room to permit recognition of the historical specificity of the Indian experience. *Politics in India* firmly rejected such an external critique, but largely by turning its eyes away from some of these harsh realities or by a somewhat naïve acceptance of the wisdom of pro-establishment economists that this hardship was transient.

Kothari did not overcome this tension between the "insider" and the "outsider" perspective on India; his writings oscillated between the two. *Politics in India* stayed with the hermeneutic at the cost of appearing conformist in values. With the passage of time, Kothari was to shift the burden of his argument to an external critique of the Indian state, often at the cost of losing his analytical grip over the inner working of the system. For all its limitations, *Politics in India* carried the promise of an immanent critique, one that drew its standards from within the practices that it sought to evaluate, even if it fell short of realising this promise.

It is only fair to recognise that reconciling both these perspectives is incredibly difficult, and was far more difficult four decades ago than it is now. Kothari's intellectual context was defined by high modernism: the aspiration for law-like universal generalisations in the field of the social sciences, teleological accounts of stages of modernisation, and the narrow procedural models of democracy. *Politics in India* could not have drawn upon post-positivist philosophies of the social sciences to connect the analytical to the normative. Kothari was not writing in the wake of post-colonial theory, or following in the footsteps of formulations of alternative modernity, which made it possible to capture the specificity of the modern experience in the ex-colonies. Nor did he have the benefit of current theorisations on the role of the social imaginary or "culture of democracy" that would allow democratic norms to be localised. Yet *Politics in India* forged ahead in this direction, without waiting for a neat theoretical articulation to emerge, and opened the possibility of an immanent critique. It did so before Indian democracy had experienced its post-Emergency consolidation and entrenchment in the post-Congress phase. It made a bold intellectual move much before there were any signs of the shift in the global balance of power away from the US and Europe. A classic work of ideas needs a context for it to emerge and be recognised. *Politics in India* was a classic that arrived well before there was a context for its production and reception. This, perhaps, is what accounts for its enigma, its unresolved tensions, its peculiar reading, and its oddity as a classic.

An Unrealised Promise

How do we then relate to *Politics in India*, more than four decades after it was published? If the argument so far has any merit, this enigmatic classic has more to offer than was realised by its initial readers and the author himself, much more than has been mined so far. But what it has to offer is not self-evident. We need to excavate carefully, remove not just the layers of earth but also the shell that covers the pearl, before we can recover the ideas and insights that this book has to offer. This requires a focused approach that needs to draw its tools from a history of ideas. Students of intellectual history have often drawn attention to how modern Indian thinkers creatively adapted Western concepts and theories that they deployed. What might appear to an outsider as a derivative transfer of political theory could involve a subtle transformation of the received theory. Very often it could be "new wine in old bottles" and "strange objects masquerading under familiar names", to quote Sudipta Kaviraj's inimitable expression.

This may be a useful frame to understand Kothari's relationship to the American science of politics that travelled to India under the label of "behaviouralism", "systems theory", and "structural-functionalism". On the face of it, *Politics in India* is shaped by this new vocabulary of politics. This is also how it was perceived by its first set of readers, admirers as well as critics. Myron Weiner began his otherwise favourable if a tad patronising review of this book in the *American Political Science Review* by presenting Kothari as "our man in India". His critics too condemned him for being an agent of an alien and conservative American science of politics (see, for example, Chopra, 1972). But a careful rereading of the book shows that Kothari was far more selective and creative, if not strategic, in his relationship to the received wisdom of the new political science than has been granted so far.

Notwithstanding popular impression to the contrary, Kothari had at best a modest investment in the structural functionalist account of society and systems theory politics. He used its vocabulary quite liberally – and that is what caused the popular confusion – but he wore its theory lightly. To be sure, his was not a consciously strategic use of a dominant language in order to subvert it. His use ranged from genuine theoretical conviction to purely pragmatic deployment. On balance, it is fair to say that he deferred to the dominant language of his time to package his new way of looking at Indian politics, but at no stage did he allow this language to alter his substantial observations. He did not allow the dominant theory to frame his enquiry. The chapter scheme and the organisation of each chapter followed a very loose theoretical frame. He carefully eschewed meta-theoretical debates. Instead of engaging with theoretical debates that could distract him from his observations, he often took shelter under barefoot empiricism by way of a randomly organised laundry list of his observations (see, for example, his listing of the characteristics of the party system, pp. 160–7). In retrospect, this apparent weakness of the book turns out to be a hidden weapon: this was his way of subverting the neat but derivative analytical structure that he was unable to fully challenge at that time.

The excavation proposed here would thus involve stripping this book of the dominant vocabulary of its time so as to recover lasting conceptual, theoretical, and methodological resources for the study of Indian politics. Briefly, such a project could take us in four directions. First of all, Kothari's uncanny ability to read broader trends and patterns implicit in everyday developments of politics provides a rich resource and a model for empirically grounded political judgements and middle-range generalisations. In more ways than is realised, the book has stood the test of time. Above all, the book stuck to a bold assertion that India's democratic experiment was here to stay and that it will not follow either the fate of other post-colonial polities or the Western script. He stuck his neck out to argue that the crisis of mid-1960s, especially after the 1967 elections, posed no threat to the democratic order. The book anticipated, too early, the differentiation in the patterns of state politics, the rise of regional parties, regionalisation of national parties and regionalisation of party politics, and the rise of coalition governments at the centre (pp. 189–92). His reading that Panchayati Raj leads to "integrating [Indian polity] into a common frame of institutional allegiances" and the creation of a national continuum of power (pp. 132–5) is another example, not just of insights that have stood the test of time, but of linking the micro to the macro. This remains on the agenda of the student of Indian politics.

This takes us to the second aspect. Kothari's preference for empirically understanding political behaviour as the starting point of understanding Indian politics needs a fresh look. This move was presented and perceived as a privileging of survey research-based quantitative analysis in political science. Kothari initiated and used survey research in political values, attitudes, opinions, and behaviour. But, as we noticed above, much of the empirical sense in the book does not draw upon this resource; instead he derives his insights from his own extensive travels, conversations with political actors, and his intimate observation of political reality. Thus, his empirical moves beyond the positivist prescription; it is as much hermeneutic and phenomenological as "scientific" in a narrow sense. Thus reinterpreted, this book is an invitation for a new generation of empirical work that encompasses ethnography, history of ideas, case studies, and survey research, among other things.

Third, the book offers a rich and readily accessible resource for contemporary efforts at uncovering the logic of political modernity. The approach to modernisation that he spells out in the third chapter offers an alternative account of modernity. He simply assumed that the trajectory of modernity was going to be different in India and could not be derived from elsewhere: "Analogies from other countries . . . have little relevance in understanding [India's] problems. Nor are conceptual categories or empirical insights drawn from the European experience of the nineteenth century of great relevance" (p. 322). His critique of the "colonial mind" (p. 7), the idea of a "pre-ordained path" (p. 14), and the insistence on necessary sequence and stages implicit in the dominant modernisation theory of his time anticipated and paved the way for contemporary perspectives on alternative modernities in a post-colonial setting. He provides a painstaking inventory of how political modernity was carved out, piece by piece, from blocks of tradition, how in each case the pre-existing facilitated and resisted this change, and how, despite significant difficulties, the task was accomplished. More than his more famous formulations of the Congress system, etc., it is his nuanced cataloguing of how an encounter with India's pre-modern context provided political modernity its unusual "depth, flexibility and maneuverability" (p. 83) that constitutes the richest intellectual legacy of *Politics in India*, a legacy that can inspire a new generation of scholarship.

Fourth, although the book does not discuss the concept and theory of democracy at length, it can help us think of a new democratic theory that draws upon the varied experiences of the real life of democracy in most parts of the world. Kothari's insistence on an "empirical" view of politics implies that democratic theory may take political practices as its point of departure. He consciously resisted two tendencies prevalent among students of Indian democracy prior to him. He avoided the pitfalls of treating India as an underdeveloped democracy on its way to the proper path taken by Western democracies, and, at the same time he resisted the essentialist reading of India that drew upon India's uniqueness. It was not an easy position to take in his time; it is still not an easy position to spell out. It required, and still does, intellectual, cultural, and political self-confidence for which the objective grounds were much weaker then. *Politics in India* was among the first books to overcome the "Euro-normal" assumptions of democratic theory. In one stroke the book shifted the locus of normality away from the global North to the rest of the world. The grand achievement of this book was simply this: it made it possible to think of India as yet another "normal" democracy. This achievement did not become the collective unconscious of his time and is still an unfinished intellectual agenda for our times.

The methodological, theoretical, and substantive resources that this extraordinary book can offer to students of Indian politics in particular and democratic theory in general are still a promise. The indifference of the author and the peculiar trajectory of the discipline of political science in India has meant that this resource was neither discovered nor utilised. The promise of a critical hermeneutics, of an immanent critique that dissolves the dilemma of insider/outsider, is yet to be realised. To the extent to which democratic "*politics in India*" is a work in progress, *Politics in India* is also a work in progress. It is a classic waiting to be (re)written.

References

Calvino, I. (1986). "Why Read the Classic?" *New York Review of Books* (9 October).

Chopra, N. (1972). "Book Review of Politics in India by Rajni Kothari". *Social Scientist*, 3 (1), 76–81.

Dube, A. (ed.) (2003). *Rajniti ki Kitab: Rajni Kothari ka Kritatva* (A. Dube, trans.), New Delhi: Rajkamal.

Kaviraj, S. (2009). "Marxism in Translation: Critical Reflections on Indian Radical Thought". In R. Bourke (ed.), *Political Judgement: Essays for John Dunn*. Cambridge: Cambridge University Press.

Khaliq, Z. (1978). "Review of Democratic Polity and Social Change in India by Rajni Kothari". *Social Scientist*, 7 (3), 80–5.

Kothari, R. (2005). *Bharat Mein Rajniti: Kal Aur Aaj* (A. Dube, ed., and A. Dube, trans.). Delhi: Vani.

Kothari, R. (ed.) (1969). *Caste in Indian Politics*. New Delhi.

—— (1993). *Growing Amnesia: An Essay on Poverty and the Human Consciousness*. New Delhi: Viking.

——(2002). *Memoirs: Uneasy is the Life of the Mind*. New Delhi: Rupa.

—— (1970). *Politics in India* (rpnt 1985 edn). Hyderabad: Orient Longman.

—— (1988). *State Against Democracy: In Search of Human Governance*. New Delhi: Ajanta.

—— (1964). "The Congress 'System' in India". *Asian Survey* , IV (12).

Morris-Jones, W.H. (1971–2). "Review of Politics in India by Rajni Kothari". *Pacific Affairs*, 44 (4), 624–6.

Narain, I. (1970). "Ideology of Consensus". *Economic and Political Weekly*, V (39), 1601–6.

Palmer, N.D. (1971). "Review of Politics in India by Rajni Kothari". *Journal of Asian Studies*, 30 (3), 698–700.

Taylor, C. (2007). "Cultures of Democracy and Citizen Efficacy". *Public Culture*, 19 (1), 117–50.

Weiner, M. (1974). "Review of Politics in India by Rajni Kothari". *American Political Science Review*, 68 (3), 1363–4.

11

On Election Forecasting

Polls, Predictions, Psephology

Anthropologists tell us that cultural goods always come in packages. There is no logical reason why phenomenon A must go with phenomena B and C, but it so happens that it does. What connects A, B, and C is that they happened to be together. And were then expected to.

Something of this insight is relevant, or so I believe, in making sense of the phenomenon of psephology in India. Like any other cultural product, "psephology" is also a package. In its contemporary Indian usage the word has come to refer to a combination of at least three things: one, systematic election-related opinion polls based on carefully drawn samples from a vast population; two, the high-profile and highly exciting game (or rather business) of predicting the electoral outcome and thus preponing its knowledge by a week or so; and three, a highly statistical interpretation of election data.

Psephology as Prediction

Now, strictly speaking there is nothing that necessarily connects the first and the third to the prediction business. Sample surveys to ascertain popular opinion are a standard item in a social scientist's toolbox, used more by sociologists than political scientists. Getting to know who people will vote for is but one minor application of this technique. Similarly, a narrowly statistical interpretation of the entire phenomenon of elections is also a widespread form of enquiry. At least one generation of Indian political scientists, and their counterparts in South Asia departments of American universities, spent all their energies doing just that. And none of them ever attempted an election prediction.

But, as I said, what matters is conventional association. It so happens that educated TV-watching Indians have been exposed to opinion polls and election data analysis through election prediction, especially the more successful ones in 1984 and 1989. Generalisations drawn from statistical interpretation of past election results provide the "theory" component while nationwide opinion polls supply the "field report" for high-profile media predictions, the "real stuff". This whole package is called psephology.

I do not mean to pick a quarrel with this popular usage, or to show the typical scholar-like impatience with the popular misuse or "pollution" of the "neat" concepts which they presumably own. Scholars might as well start taking it seriously, treating it as a starting point rather than the dead end of their investigation. In other words, we can begin by accepting what everyone means by psephology and then see what made it necessary, what it has done and can do for us, what is wrong with it, and what can be done about it.

Nor do I wish to suggest that this entire package of psephology is shallow show business, an intellectual counterpart of the *filmi* dance, as it were. For it is not that a pure form has been corrupted in application, but rather that the application has drawn our attention to some new possibilities of theorisation. Psephologists might be superficial or business-minded: psephology is not – that is, not necessarily. It has some extremely valuable and otherwise inaccessible tools for comprehending what is still the best-known mechanism to give effect to the most favoured form of government known to our age – democracy.

My basic point is very simple. The new techniques of opinion polls and psephological reasoning have till now remained overshadowed by the prediction game. Therefore, in its present prediction-oriented form, the psephology package seems to have little value once elections are over and we have the results. Here lies its basic problem. In fact, the real and more important role of the new techniques begins after the results are known, for it is only with their help that we can understand what the electoral verdict means. The task of serious students of elections, then, is to analytically separate the valuable data and insights from the prediction game and incorporate these into a political interpretation of elections.

The official election result in terms of seats won and lost by different parties or candidates tells us very little about all that went into its making, too little to be able to draw political conclusions from it. We need to know, for instance, whether the verdict in terms of seats really reflected the popular will, or who voted for whom (not individually, but in terms of social groups and parties) and why. It is here that opinion polls and psephology can help us.

Both pollsters and psephologists share the concern to go behind the electoral verdict and thus unpack it, as it were. Psephology enables us to take the first step in the interpretation of results by uncovering the crooked logic of our first-past-the-post electoral system. It tells us about the extent to which an electoral victory reflects real popular support. Opinion polls help us take the second step. Their informal data based on small, representative samples give us otherwise inaccessible knowledge of the pattern of voting, its relationship with the age, caste, community, and sex of the voters, and their reasons for voting the way they did.

This is not to dismiss predictions altogether. I must confess to enjoying them and participating in the game once in a while. But this is no reason to confuse pastime with serious business. There is one reason, however, why even serious students of elections must keep tabs on prediction. It is a good test of the tools one is employing and can be used as that. A grossly mistaken prediction is a sure indication of either an unrepresentative sample in opinion polls or mistaken psephological reasoning.

Psephology as Post-mortem

The Lok Sabha election in Uttar Pradesh in May and June this year is a good example of the need for and role of psephology. The result looked like a saffron thunderstorm: the Bharatiya Janata Party (BJP) won 50 out of 82 seats which went to the polls, the Janata Dal (JD) and allies got 23, while the Congress got only 5. Analysts were quick to observe that Hindutva/communalism dominated Uttar Pradesh's voters, that it was a popular verdict for the Mandir, and so on. The result was contrasted to Madhya Pradesh where the voter had "rejected" the BJP.

Now consider this simple analysis of the BJP victory. Its share of popular vote was only 33 per cent (as against the over 60 per cent seats it won); two-thirds of Uttar Pradesh's voters had voted against the BJP. (Its vote share in Madhya Pradesh was 42 per cent.) The JD and its Liberal Party allies got about 24 per cent votes in Uttar Pradesh while the Congress got 18 per cent (JD + LP + Congress = 42 per cent). So much for the "saffron wave". The BJP's victory was due more to disunity among its opponents than its own popularity. On an average the leading opponent of the BJP in Uttar Pradesh got less than half of the non-BJP votes in a constituency.

A much better example of the use of psephological skills was the problem of interpreting the difference in electoral outcome between those parts of the country which went to the polls on 20 May and those which did so in June after Rajiv Gandhi's assassination. There were several questions here. Did Rajiv Gandhi's assassination result in a sympathy wave for the Congress? What was its strength? What would the outcomes have been had the assassination not taken place? Any comparison of seats won or lost or total votes gained in pre- and post-assassination constituencies would have been too crude an assessment. For the nature of these constituencies was different. In Rajasthan and Madhya Pradesh, for instance, the post-assassination constituencies were traditional Congress supporters and could not be compared with the rest.

A psephological analysis in terms of "swing" (change in a party's votes in a constitucncy over two elections) revealed the actual picture. The Congress had gained in all the six states where elections were split, but its gains varied from 4.3 per cent in Madhya Pradesh to 12.3 per cent in Rajasthan. This gain was mainly at the expense of the National Front and its allies, except in Rajasthan and Bihar. The analysis also threw up a possible explanation for this difference between the two phases in Bihar, Madhya Pradesh, and Rajasthan, namely, a significant rise in voter turnout.

In overall terms, a psephological analysis brings out the most significant but hidden fact of this election. The Congress' improved electoral performance (from 197 to 225) was not based on increased popular support. In fact, its all-India share of votes fell by more than 2 per cent (from 39.5 to 37.3 per cent). It did better because its opponents were hopelessly divided. The Index of Opposition Unity (IOU) for this election read 66, as compared to 77 in 1989 and 74 in 1984.

What made this analysis possible was a new psephology established in India about a decade ago, thanks to the pioneering efforts of two professional economists – Ashok Lahiri and Pranoy Roy – in collaboration with the famous British psephologist David Butler. The basic idea was to take a macro view of elections instead of focusing on micro details of each constituency in order to explain and predict the overall outcome. It suggested that basically there were two things which affected electoral outcome: the way people voted and the way political parties aligned themselves. In the Indian context both these could be measured with reference to the Congress. Any movement of votes could be measured as a move in favour of or against the Congress. Hence the concept of swing was tied to the Congess: it expressed a positive or negative change in the percentage of votes secured by the Congress over two elections.

The concept of the IOU was more complex and a genuine innovation. The challenge here was to devise a quantitative measure of alignment of political forces. Everyone knew that the Congress tended to perform worse in the face of a united opposition than if these parties fought against one another, but the question was how to measure it. The number of total candidates did not help. You could have a straight contest in real terms where there were more than a dozen candidates. Even if one took into account only the candidates put up by various parties, matters did not improve very much. Think, for instance, of parties like the Samajwadi Janata Party, the Bahujan Samaj Party or the Doordarshi Party which put up a large number of candidates whose presence hardly mattered.

The IOU sought to circumvent this problem by evolving a post-facto measurement, something you could measure once you knew the results. The basic idea was to see how many of the opposition votes went to the leading opposition candidates in one constituency irrespective of the total number of candidates or of who won or lost. In 1977, for instance, about 90 per cent of those votes which did not go to the Congress went to the leading opposition candidates all over India. In the next election, in 1980, this came down to 65 per cent due to a highly disunited opposition.

This bit of conceptual innovation was very helpful in making sense of the general elections from 1977 to 1989. The concepts of swing and IOU provided a clear explanation of the changing political fortunes of the Congress, especially in the most volatile electoral zone – the Hindi heartland. And it became the basis of some fairly successful predictions, especially those in 1989.

Psephology as Pollstering

The other component of the psephology package, opinion polls, also acquired a new prominence during this election. So much so that we nearly had a flood of opinion polls. Their sponsor-publishers (above a dozen) and research agencies (over half a dozen) varied, as did their scope, sample size, and aim. There were as many as four nationwide opinion polls (*India Today* – Marg, *Sunday* – Marg, *Frontline* – Mras, *Week* – Mode) on the eve of the May elections, two weekly/fortnightly series of polls (*Week* – Mode Barometer, *Times* – Marg Poll-meter), one massive nationwide exit poll (*India Today* – Marg), and umpteen other polls of a local/regional character. Future historians of Indian elections might remember this as the first war of opinion polls in India.

The wealth of information thrown up by opinion polls in this and the previous elections easily outmatches all previous mini-sized surveys conducted by academic students of Indian politics. Hence it is nothing less than ironic that political scientists have not yet condescended to incorporate this evidence in their understanding of Indian elections and politics. Of particular significance is the evidence of the

India Today– Marg exit polls in 1989 and this election for its huge sample size (above 77,000 and 90,000 respectively), extensive coverage (51 and 72 constituencies respectively), and an unusually high level of accuracy. All this evidence falls into two areas: relationship of voting to voters' social background, etc., on the one hand and voters' opinion on various national issues on the other.

The results challenge many widely held beliefs and theories about elections. One of these is the myth of "vote banks". The 1989 exit poll came out with decisive evidence against it: Congress votes among all age, sex, caste, community categories were within 5 per cent of its national average. Even the 1991 election shows a very minor variation from this pattern. The backward castes' vote for the Congress falls slightly below the "5 per cent band" and Muslim and SC/ST vote slightly above it. But one hardly finds any vote bank anywhere.

Other evidence is also very valuable. The BJP is more popular among urban, upper-caste, young and male voters, and the Janata Dal among rural and Muslim voters (its failure to even bring over a substantial share of Other Backward Classes voters is a very significant indicator here). As for the difference in voting in the two phases, women and Muslim voters swung most sharply towards the Congress after Rajiv Gandhi's assassination; urban and upper-caste voters were the least influenced.

The evidence on people's opinions on various questions and their reasons for voting is less unambiguous and requires careful interpretation. Yet some of the conclusions are striking. In people's eyes the issues usually regarded as the lead issues of this election (secularism, stability, and reservations) have very little value. For them, the main issues are price rise and unemployment. Another surprise awaits us as we go through responses to the Ayodhya dispute in various opinion polls. There is much larger support for the BJP stance (over 40 per cent) than its share of votes. Yet when people are given the specific option of demolishing/removing the Masjid, less than 30 per cent approve it. And less than half of these hardcore supporters turn out to be BJP voters!

This election may or may not prove to be a watershed in Indian politics. But it can hardly be doubted that it will prove so in the use of opinion polls in Indian politics and elections. We have certainly come a long way since the mid-1950s when the Indian Institute of Public Opinion began its pioneering work led by E.P.W. da Costa, father of pollstering in India. Methodological innovations in pollstering are not as striking as in psephology, but the entry of market research organisations in this field in the last decade has certainly led to a substantial improvement of skills, especially on the crucial question of ascertaining people's voting intention.

Whither Psephology?

Now that these techniques are here to stay, how can we improve upon them? What is wrong with their contemporary form and application? How can we make these more relevant to our needs and conditions? India is perhaps the first country in the "third world" where these techniques have been applied on such a large scale and with this degree of success. The main problem, however, is that these new techniques have become a world unto themselves, intellectual enclaves immune to outside influences. Especially sad here is the absence of any meaningful interaction with academic social science in general and political science in particular.

To take psephology first, the basic challenge is to respond to the changing political reality in recent times, especially during this election. Psephological innovations of the 1980s were based on the assumption of Congress versus opposition as the main contest of the Indian electoral arena. This is no longer the case in the electorally most volatile zones of North India. In that sense the real psephological challenge of theorising multiparty contests in a first-past-the-post system begins now. Specifically, Indian psephologists must address themselves to the following tasks:

- How do we measure the fragmentation of political forces in a truly multiparty situation where no single party can be used as a measuring rod? This calls for a new, comprehensive measure to improve upon the IOU.
- How do we take into account some of the specific features of the Indian party system such as the discontinuous existence of different parties and short-term electoral alliances?

- How do we measure, explain, or predict the electoral performance of non-Congress parties? This is one front on which even the most "successful" psephologists have not done too well.

The challenge faced by pollsters is somewhat different. The basic problem here is the rather narrow focus pollsters have set for themselves. The central focus of pollsters and their methodological innovations has been the single question of how best to ascertain people's voting preferences much before they actually cast their vote. How to catch the right set of voters in the poll's sample? How to get the true answer? How to prevent or detect lying? Which is quite understandable, given that this is the only testable item in an opinion poll and that the commercial success of the poll and the concerned agency depends entirely on this. But its result is an unfortunate neglect of other parts of an opinion poll, those related to people's perceptions and opinions. This is what makes these polls of great interest to social scientists and it is precisely here that these polls are least reliable. The main tasks for the pollsters could be listed thus:

- Methodological research on how best to measure people's perceptions through opinion polls in the context of a semi-literate, culturally heterogeneous society like India.
- Research on the impact of opinion polls on society itself, especially of prediction based on opinion polls on the electoral outcome.
- Some institutional initiative on two fronts: one, better internal organisation of the trade on the lines of a guild so as to evolve a badly needed code of opinion poll conduct; and two, the collating of the vast amount of opinion poll data from different sources and different points of time – as done, for instance, by the social science research establishment in Britain – for purposes of academic use and scrutiny.

12

On Sample Surveys

Reflections on the State of Survey Research on Politics in Most of the World

Survey Research Then and Now

When I was a student, doing my master's in political science, the worst thing you could say about any political scientist was that he or she "did survey research". The label "survey research" stood for what was considered to be most inappropriate in third world imitations of the American science of politics: it was methodologically naive, politically conservative, and culturally inauthentic. Perhaps my academic socialisation bore a strong impress of the institution where I studied then: the Jawaharlal Nehru University (JNU) in general and the School of Social Sciences in particular were strongly left wing in their orientation. In those days a radical orientation in political science was associated with a taste for certain kinds of subjects (revolutions rather than constitutions, land reform rather than affirmative action, protest movements rather than voting behaviour), preference for some approaches (political economy over analysis of political institutions, history of ideas over conceptual analysis), and strong methodological partisanship (theoretical and not empirical, diachronic and not synchronic, qualitative and not quantitative). In retrospect it is less obvious why these preferences were associated with radicalism. But it should not be hard to see why "survey research" did not then fit into what a young political scientist wanted to do then.

Some of it may have been specific to JNU or to political science in India. But it may not be unfair to say that milder or stronger versions of this orientation towards survey research characterised the cutting edge of third world political science, such as it was. Survey research was not merely a technique of data gathering, as keeping a beard was not merely a hairstyle, it was a cultural package with a political orientation. It meant focusing on mainstream politics of parties, elections, and voting. It went with a liberal political orientation; to be "liberal" was as conservative as one could get in a self-consciously left-wing discipline. It also meant relying on sample surveys of political opinion and behaviour and drawing simple-minded, often harmless if inane, conclusions from the quantitative data thus gathered.

I must confess that I shared with my contemporaries much of this disdain for survey research.[1] After completing my master's, I took to political theory and did research on the history of the idea of socialism in modern India. It was not surprising therefore that my professional friends and well-wishers were quite puzzled and upset when I started doing survey research, and that too on voting behaviour. Many of them tried to dissuade me from this strange move of "giving up" on political theory and "taking to" something as crass as survey research. Some of them have never understood why I did so; some have never forgiven me for doing so.

As I received the news of my selection for the Malcolm Adiseshiah Award, my thoughts went back to that initial response of my professional colleagues. Not because this honour vindicates my choice, as would be clear from what I say. I continue to harbour a deep unease with the practice of what is often called survey research. In any case I have never managed to gather enough energy to participate in methodological crusades in the social sciences and could not care less if one or the other carried the day. The reason I turned to my initial encounter was that my initial reaction and that of my professional colleagues was very typical of those times. This award recognises some of my work and much of the work done by other colleagues in the Lokniti network, for which I get underserved credit – in gathering and analysing empirical data on Indian politics. It occurred to me that perhaps this recognition marks a silent shift in the discipline from largely derivative "theoretical" debates to addressing our own agenda with the help of systematic gathering and sifting of information, maybe with some of our own conceptual tools. In that sense my work happens to be a part of a much larger body of work – as much a product of the work by political theorists as of empirical studies on Indian politics that has ushered the discipline of political science in India to come into its own. I take this award not so much as recognition of work already done but as an encouragement to work in this direction so as to earn this honour and as a signal about the direction in which the study of politics in our country should proceed.

From what I said about my disposition towards survey research in my student days, you might expect my lecture to be a story of conversion, a story of how I discovered the virtues of survey research and found that the charges against it were unfounded or irrelevant. I'm afraid I am not going to do that today. It is true that a closer encounter with the practice of survey research has made me appreciate some of its subtle aspects more than I did initially. I do believe that some of the criticism against survey research reflected (and continues to do so to this date) the fear and the prejudices we all have against things we know little about. Ignorance about the basics of survey research is not confined to public and media; I have found that my fellow political scientists are no less innocent and often give in to the temptation of making a virtue of it. But that is not the burden of my argument this evening. As I said earlier, fighting disciplinary crusades on behalf of the survey research cult doesn't engage me.

Looking back at it a quarter of a century after I first encountered survey research and as someone who has come to be seen as a practitioner of survey research, I am not sure if the charges against it were mistaken. Nor can I say with any confidence that these charges do not apply to the practice of survey research today, including to some of my own work. I would suggest instead that the encounter between the package of cognitive practices that we call "survey research" and the socio-political reality of what used to be called the third world continues to be a very difficult encounter, full of pitfalls and possibilities. I would therefore seek your indulgence to use this opportunity that you have been so kind to provide me to think aloud about the dangers and the promise of this epistemic encounter.

A quick word of clarification about what I mean by survey research here. I do not use the word in its generic sense that covers census as well as sample survey.[2] I use it in the sense in which it is used commonly by political scientists, as a technique of data gathering in which a sample of respondents is asked questions about their political preferences and beliefs to draw conclusions about the political opinions, attitudes, and behaviour of a wider population of citizens. In this sense survey research is associated with but not limited to election studies and research on voting behaviour on the one hand and public opinion research on the other. It includes academic as well as commercial use of this data gathering technique.

In my remarks today I draw upon two contexts that I am somewhat familiar with. The first, the more obvious and familiar context, is that of political science in India. In sharp contrast to many other social sciences, the discipline of political science in India has had a fraught relationship with things empirical.[3] The unease originated in conditions that are not difficult to understand with hindsight. The empirically oriented study of politics came to our country as a part of the package of the American Science of Politics which was understandably viewed with deep suspicion by students of politics in our country. This suspicion initially released creative energies that involved philosophical and political interrogation of the newfangled science of politics.[4]

As a first reaction, this was understandable. Arguably, this response saved the discipline of political science in our country from becoming an intellectual colony of American Political Science. But protests have a tendency to degenerate into rituals and serve as shields for vested interests. This I think is what happened to the early critique of positivist political science in India. Since this critique was not backed by a vigorous and creative search for alternative modes of thinking about politics, the discipline of political science soon degenerated into a loose if fashionable way of talking about politics, poorly grounded in theory and devoid of anchors in reality.[5] As radical posturing replaced serious thinking, every empirical enquiry was dubbed empiricist, anything to do with numbers was shunned.[6] In this intellectual climate there was simply no space for developing skills for data analysis, though the universities continued with the ritual of teaching some abstract statistics as a part of the research methodology courses. As political scientists in India try to come to terms with survey data, they face a larger question that has relevance beyond the disciplinary context: Must the latecomers to survey research confine their intellectual ambitions to "catching up" with the advanced survey research tradition and data analysis techniques offered by the dominant discipline of political science? Or can they use the latecomers' advantage to reflect on the state of the discipline and chart out a course of their own?

This question acquires a wider significance if we turn to the other context that I draw upon for my reflections today. This is the context of expansion of survey research on politics outside academia and beyond the boundaries of India. One of the by-products of the global march of democracy in our times is the expansion of public opinion research all over the globe. Much of this research takes place outside academia and is driven by the institutional imperatives of the opinion polling industry in close collaboration with the mass media. Often the focus of this industry is very narrow. In India, survey research on politics has become synonymous with the "exit poll" that has come to be the generic name for all pre- and post-election polls that aim at predicting electoral outcomes.[7] This is occasionally supplemented by analysis of electoral outcomes and by opinion polls that are not election related.[8] In most of the newly democratising countries, a similar pattern is being replicated, except that there is even less academic input into opinion polling than in our country. Opinion polling organisations, often the local branches of global corporate companies, are rapidly spreading in all these countries, introducing polling into the newly developing democratic culture. This has had its academic counterpart: some countries with social science capacities have evolved public opinion research. But much of serious public opinion research in these countries has been carried out by cross-country international surveys by academics in the global North with local collaborators. A little later I will say something about the nature and effect of this type of expansion of survey-based public opinion research. But at this stage, let me just use this to pose a question: What happens when survey research is taken to "most of the world"?[9] Must the growing research on public opinion in most parts of the world replicate the dilemmas and infirmities of the art in the older democracies? Worse, must the practice of polling citizens' opinions, attitudes, and behaviour in the global South follow the intellectual and political agenda set in the global North?

To anticipate, I shall argue that public opinion research can take one of the two paths as it expands beyond the global North to "most of the world". The first – the more likely and decidedly less promising – path is that public opinion research in the rest of the world will replicate a discipline that is yet to come to terms with its foundational assumptions. This expansion might expose and accentuate the inherited flaws of survey research, especially its Eurocentrism and political conservatism. Instead of serving democracy, public opinion research can become a tool of powerful local and global interests. I do not, however, think that this is the only path possible. The encounter between the inherited toolkit and the new political reality opens up a second path as well. This would involve not just reflecting on how the techniques should be "applied" to a new setting but to rethink and reshape the methodological self-image of public opinion research. This encounter offers an opportunity to rescue survey research from its unreconstructed positivist self-image and to learn from the "linguistic turn" of the social sciences. It invites us to consciously bracket many of the Western assumptions and meanings that have crept into the standard toolkit of public opinion research. This encounter also provides us with a powerful tool to restore the "public" that is increasingly elusive in the "public opinion" manufactured by the mass media.

A Case against Survey Research

Let me go back to the three charges that I mentioned right at the beginning and try to review where we stand on each of these today. I would not even attempt to offer an overview of the vast literature that exists on debates and controversies concerning survey research on political opinions, attitudes, and behaviour.[10] I am interested here in summarising the basic questions and the answers that these elicited or failed to elicit. Just to remind you, the three charges levelled against survey research in the early days of survey research were that it was methodologically naive, politically conservative, and culturally inauthentic or neo-colonial.[11]

Right from the beginning, survey research was imagined within the four walls of the larger project of developing a "positive" science of society on the lines of the natural sciences. That its findings could be presented in terms of hard numbers and therefore that it lent itself to a lot of the precision and sophistication that comes with quantification tended to confirm the self-image of the survey researcher as a scientist in the mould of a natural scientist. Ironically, largely unknown to the practitioners of survey research in political science, this grand project was interrogated and its methodological foundations rendered suspect just when survey research was beginning to take off. This is not the place to offer a bird's-eye view of the positivist debate in the philosophy of social sciences; the debate is very well recounted in more than one place.[12] Suffice to say here that the critique of the positivist claim did not come only from intellectual traditions like hermeneutics and phenomenology that have offered strong reasons why social phenomena could not be treated like natural objects. Some of the most powerful critique came from historians of natural sciences and philosophers of language who questioned the impression that the kind of science that students of society sought to imitate was ever practised in the natural sciences or could in principle be achieved in any branch of knowledge.[13]

Survey researchers in general and survey researchers in the discipline of political science in particular offered very little by way of a response to this critique. The critique and the "linguistic turn" in social science did dent the prestige of survey research and served to subordinate these within American academia to the theoretical enterprise within which surveys could measure whatever they sought to measure, but it is not clear if this critique changed in any way the practice of survey research on political opinions, attitudes, and behaviour. The study of political opinions, attitudes, and behaviour was split between two groups that coexisted in a relationship of back-to-back neighbourliness. Most radical students of politics went in for ethnographic case studies, completely disregarding whatever information was gathered by survey researchers. For survey researchers it was business as usual, as if the Emperor Science still had his clothes on. There was no doubt methodological sophistication, but this was largely confined to data analysis. Search for a grand theory of value shift in the contemporary world did bring some conceptual sophistication as well, but this was confined to Anglo-Saxon political culture. Arguably, the currency of large-N studies and search for cross-national data actually led to a decline in the quality of survey data in post-colonial countries. Survey instruments conceptualised and designed in North America and Europe were lifted and hastily transferred to other parts of the world, generating many a dubious insight. Be that as it may, the fact is that survey researchers and those who shunned surveys have largely been two different subdisciplines, almost two different sects, that hardly spoke to one another. One could say that the methodological dispute regarding a science of society has left political science on the whole a wiser and a more modest, if fractious, discipline, but it would be difficult to make a similar case about the subdiscipline of survey research. It may be unkind, but not very unfair, to say that we stand on this question exactly where we did twenty-five years ago.

The second charge, of political conservatism, may not stick as easily today as does the first one. But that is not necessarily a function of learning or improvement in survey research practices. One could argue that this critique was always somewhat misplaced. It was a critique of the political conclusions of the scholars who happened to do survey research; the method itself was free of political bias. It is true that in the heat of the methodological debate it was argued that the method itself was tied to status quo, but it is hard to see the merit in that reasoning today. Survey research on political opinions and attitudes is bound to be a surface investigation, but it is not clear why a conversation in a survey setting is more likely to be status quoist than textual interpretation or ethnographic description. All one can say is that (like in all other branches of knowledge) established routines of knowledge tend to favour the existing configuration of power and that one needs to be very creative to be able to break this.

There is another, weaker, version of this charge that deserves closer scrutiny. It could be argued that the association of survey research with status quoist politics may not be a necessary function of its method, yet this association is not just a coincidence. It reflects a theoretical inadequacy or laziness that has always characterised survey research. The community of survey researchers has not been vigilant while interrogating the values implicit in its measures. The absence of caution has led to a wholesale and unconscious importing of unexamined political values that reflect the dominant values of the society that exports survey research. This is what accounts for the evident political conservatism of much survey research on politics. The question we need to answer is whether the practice of survey research has improved in this respect in the last quarter-century. I am not very sure of my judgement on this score, for such a judgement presupposes a familiarity with substantive conclusions of survey research-based studies of politics in different parts of the world that I do not possess. I look forward to corrections and refutations of my reading. But on balance it seems to me that the verdict cannot be very positive on this score as well. Survey research continues to be imprisoned within the frame of liberal democracy that may not appear conservative in Europe and North America, but that has a built-in drag in the context of post-colonial societies. I think it is possible to counter this drag while using the survey method, but I am not sure the community of survey researchers has done very much about it. From a largely passive application of "modernisation" and "development", we have moved to equally uncritical application of "democracy" and "civil society". A checklist model of democracy dominates the discourse on democracy; survey research applies it to different parts of the world to measure how they measure up to it. Cross-sectional surveys use more or less the same framework as was used by elite measures like the Freedom House index; the Washington Consensus on democracy dominates both of these. I see very little attempt to use survey research to expand the meaning of democracy. Let me reiterate that I do not see this as a limitation inherent in survey research but as a weakness of the way it has been practised.

Let me now turn to the third charge, that of cultural inauthenticity. To be sure, this is not how the charge was originally framed, and this is not how many critics of survey research will like to articulate it: the charge presupposes a notion of authenticity that is not shared by all. Some critics might wish to call it the neo-colonial nature of the survey research enterprise; others might point to the intellectual heteronomy in the practice of survey research. Whatever the label, the substance of the criticism is not very different: survey research is accused of a mindless imitation of ideas and of using concepts of one society in a different and inappropriate context. This criticism in similar to the previous one in that it is political in its substance, but that is different from calling it politically conservative. The charge of political conservatism could apply in any context, but that of cultural inauthenticity is specific to the practice of survey research in a post-colonial setting. It involves three related arguments: that survey research has external origins, that its currency draws its strength not from its intrinsic intellectual charm but from the field of power, and that its application creates an incongruence or a mismatch between the method applied and the reality that it seeks to capture. Please note that the criticism about cultural inauthenticity is not confined to a simple-minded complaint about its external origins alone; at the heart of this charge is an intellectual criticism. I am not sure if survey researchers have responded to this criticism seriously. It might be useful to contrast the response of survey researchers with the response of anthropologists to the charge of being instruments of colonial knowledge;[14] survey research on political opinions has never undergone that kind of self-criticism and transformation.

This is not just an academic point. The link between survey research and colonial power is not just a matter of archaeology of knowledge, as it were. It is a contemporary and pressing political concern. It is not a coincidence that there has been a proliferation of comparative survey research precisely at a point when the world is more unipolar than was the case before and when the US is on a mission to export liberty and democracy by using, shall we say, rather unconventional means. In a world where knowledge is power, the sudden proliferation of US-sponsored research on mass political opinions cannot be an unmixed blessing. At least the students of politics cannot pretend that this is a pure diffusion of scientific knowledge. Not to put too fine a point on it, I fear that survey research on political opinions and attitudes can serve as an instrument, more effective and therefore more dangerous, of neo-colonial surveillance of global populations. In this respect, I'm afraid we do not stand where we stood a quarter of a century ago; we may be in a much more precarious position today.

That much of survey research in the global South is done now by "local" researchers does not take away from what I am saying. We know that colonial power (or for that matter any white racist regime) was defended by largely "native" armies.

Transfer as Transplantation

The extension of democracy to most parts of the world following the third wave of democratisation was also accompanied by the expansion of polling and other forms of survey research in most parts of the world. This globalisation of survey research took many forms, but in each case it meant a transfer of the established survey practices from the global North to the rest of the world. This may be called "transfer as transplantation". The expansion of survey research has meant an extension of field sites but it has not been matched by a corresponding expansion of theoretical and methodological imagination. Before turning to the deficiencies of this mode of transfer as transplantation, let us first understand the dynamics of globalisation of survey research.[15]

The demand for more and better survey research outside the global North has been fuelled by a shift in the agenda of media, academia, and global financial institutions. The fall of the Berlin Wall was accompanied by the opening up of a new world that was both accessible and newsy. Similarly, the story of rise and fall of democracies in other parts of the world also served to shift media attention in the global North to politics in most parts of the world. This was particularly so for the "emerging economies" that now held the key to economic transformations all over the world. All this meant greater media attention to political developments in democracies outside North America and Western Europe. This was accompanied by a shift from area study to comparative design in the academic research on politics, especially within the discipline of political science in the US. This has meant greater comparative attention to democracies outside the US. The methodological premium on putting theoretical models to empirical test fuelled the need for greater data from these parts of the world. Partly as a result of these two, there occurred a shift in the thinking of global lenders and donors. They discovered that politics mattered, perhaps in fundamental ways, to economic and human development. It began with the World Bank's emphasis on what it called "governance". But the agenda, and the number of institutions that subscribed to it, expanded rapidly. An intellectual desire to understand quality of governance soon gave rise to a quest to index and rank countries by their quality of governance. Thus came together curiosity, intellectual tools, and the funds to support public opinion research in most parts of the world. While the initiative may have come from within in some cases as in India that can boast of a large economy, mature media, and social science academia, for most countries the push came from outside.

The supply side of globalisation of survey research took three forms. First, there was a rise of cross-national surveys in a comparative design. Some of these surveys were one-off cross-national comparisons of political behaviour, attitudes, and opinions. But this gave rise to some very large and regular cross-national surveys that have increased their scope. The trend began with the World Values Survey (WVS)in 1981.[16] By the time the WVS carried out its fourth wave in 2004, it had covered as many as eighty countries. Over the years it has also tried to shed its dependence on North American concerns and vocabulary, though it continues to retain a large residue of that. One could add the Pew Global Survey and the Transparency International Survey to this list.

The second source of cross-national survey data is the rise of regional barometers all over the world that offer at regular intervals a reading of political opinions, attitudes, and values of a cross-section of citizens in several countries. Taking its inspiration from the Eurobarometer that began in 1960 and that covers countries of the European Union, a series of regional barometers started in the 1990s. Beginning with 1991, the New Europe Barometer has come to cover sixteen post-communist countries. The Latinobarometer has run continuously since 1995 and covers seventeen countries of Latin America.[17] The Afrobarometer began in 1999 and covers nineteen democracies in Africa.[18] Finally, the East Asian Barometer began in twelve countries of East and South East Asia in 2001,[19] and has joined hands with the

State of Democracy in South Asia study that covered five countries of South Asia in 2005.[20] The regional barometers of the global South, beginning with the Latinobarometer, have tried to foreground different concerns and are sensitive to the vocabulary of politics in each region. Although the regional barometers began independent of one another, they have come to ask a core set of comparable questions on political participation, institutional trust, support for democracy and its alternatives, and sources of political information.[21]

The third source has been the rise of commercial opinion polling in most of the new democracies. While some of these countries witnessed local companies taking the initiative in this regard, the general trend has been the entry of some big global corporations like Gallup, MORI, and A.C. Neilsen in most of these countries. Commercial opinion polling works closely with market research and draws some support from local media.

There is no doubt that the globalisation of survey research has widened the base for generalisations about public opinion on some key issues of our time. We have comparable data from more countries than ever before on what the citizens think about, say, democracy. We have data on many new issues of global concern, such as global warming, corruption, and terrorism. At the same time it is only fair to say that the expansion of survey research has as yet not brought corresponding theoretical dividend to social sciences. Much of the quest in cross-national research is about confirmation of the existing wisdom drawn from a small part of the globe. There is some attempt at statistical sophistication in analysing data from different countries, but it is hard to avoid the conclusion that much of this sophistication is at the expense of contextual understanding of each of these countries. Anchored in the "democratisation" paradigm, much like the modernisation paradigm that characterised the first wave of studies of "developing societies", the new wave of survey research shares the same naive teleological approach that expected the rest of the world to traverse the golden path taken by Europe and America. In sum, more than presenting us with an opportunity, the globalisation of survey research brings us face to face with a real danger of a new "parochial universalism".

Transfer as Transformation

By now some of you must be wondering where this onslaught on survey research is headed and whether it does not in fact cut the branch on which I am perched. If survey research faces such fundamental questions and if these are only deepened as a result of the recent globalisation, isn't it time to give up on it? If the advanced and well-funded academia in the first world could not respond to these questions, how would practitioners of survey research in the global South cope with the challenge?

But as many of you can guess, I do not share this line of reasoning. Let me say with all the emphasis at my command that doing survey research on the political opinions, attitudes, and behaviour of citizens is not an optional activity in modern democracies. If we are at all serious about the democratic project, we cannot but record and register public opinion. And if we are even marginally aware of the contemporary setting when exposure to mass media and homogenising political practices shape rapid shifts in mass political opinions, we cannot but need an instrument like survey research that can sketch the broad contours of changing public opinion. Those of us who have chosen to or are condemned to live under conditions of modernity that are usually not of our making have simply no choice except to use modern cognitive tools that enable us to make sense of the world that we inhabit. In that sense modern social science and survey research on public opinion is essential for those who wish to make sense of modern politics, democratic or otherwise.

There is a stronger, democratic, argument for taking survey research seriously. We face a paradox in the global discourse on democracy: while democracy is expanding all over the world, our notion of what it means to be a democracy is shrinking. A one-dimensional checklist model of democracy seems to dominate our imagination today along with institutional quick fixes about how to build democracy. Survey research can play a very significant role here by recovering and foregrounding "public opinion" in an age where democracy is all about institutional forms and correct rituals. As a tool for recovery, reconstruction, and amplification of subaltern/marginal voices, survey research can become an ally of the project of radical democracy. This is not to say that every form of survey research is an ally of radical democracy. Such an enterprise would require considerable change in the dominant mode of comparative survey research. Surveys will have to be not just carried out but also imagined in different parts of the globe. Designing surveys specific to the political culture might mean giving up on some universal questions and checking some of our global theoretical ambitions. Above all, it would mean focusing surveys to excavate the "social imaginary" that envelops democratic practice in different parts of the worlds and gives a different character to this word in different political settings.[22] By pluralising the concept of democracy to reflect the diversity of opinions across the globe, we might forge one of the strongest counters to neo-colonial domination of the world.

In the post-industrial societies of the global North, public opinion polling as an institution may have become a way of shutting out critical voices by drowning them into the mainstream voice of the majority. But in the global South, the real challenge is to establish that the opinion of the public and the voice of the majority are heard. In this context, a simple-minded aversion to "positivist" social science and complete abandoning of empirical enquiry into political behaviour, attitudes, and opinion has done a lot of harm to the understanding of politics in many countries of the global South. I know I am making a fairly strong and largely unsubstantiated case here, but I hope that by now I would not be accused of being partisan to survey research.

I do not believe that survey research in the global South is condemned to producing a poor copy of the comparative survey research practised in the global North and thus reproducing its fundamental flaws in its worst form. I think what appears to be a grave problem, of carrying the tools of survey research to a radically different situation, is in many ways a big opportunity for tackling afresh some of the foundational questions that have always dodged survey research on public opinion. This would require us to diverge from the prescription of a pure methodologist in the global North: giving up omnibus surveys, better sampling, living up to standards set by "proper" surveys, and greater emphasis on sophisticated data analysis. Instead the approach we need to pursue may be described as "transfer as transformation". This involves innovation in a different direction so as to explore the distinct character of public opinion research in the South. This calls for nothing short of rethinking the method, substance, and protocols of survey research in a radically different setting and reflecting on the political practice embedded in survey research. In what follows I offer a synoptic overview of this approach. I do so in the hope that these remarks will generate a debate that can lead to a more careful consideration and reflection on the future direction of survey research.

First of all, the truth claims of survey research could do with some clarity and modesty. If the current state of philosophy of social science dictates a mood of methodological modesty, survey research too needs to partake of this modesty. While methodological debates have shaken the foundations of survey research, they have questioned other hallowed ground as well. Philosophy is seen as no more than a form of writing.[23] If hermeneutic engagement with texts or ethnographic involvement with subjects was not assured of recovery of meaning, survey research had all the less reasons to pretend to provide it. It is time we saw and presented survey research as a craft, as an art form, rather than get entangled with claims of scientificity. This can help survey research get rid of a lot of excess baggage that the previous generation of survey researchers carried on their shoulders. In particular this would free survey research from carrying the burden of the positivist project of a science of society. This would also alert researchers to the profoundly political nature of survey research on politics. Survey research on political opinions, attitudes, and behaviour is no different from any other form of enquiry on this subject in that it is inextricably enmeshed with concepts that are "essentially contested". Embedding such concepts in a questionnaire and presenting the evidence in statistical tables does not absolve the researcher from the responsibility of demonstrating that the concepts are appropriate to what they seek to measure. This would necessitate establishing a conversation between survey-based enquiries with political theory.

This reorientation would affect the design of surveys as well as the analysis of survey findings. Survey research in most parts of the world need not adopt the latest, the most fancy state-of-the-art techniques; "appropriate technology" is a good slogan in this context. In the last few years, the routine and flat-footed understanding of causality deployed by mainstream researchers has attracted serious criticism within American Political Science.[24] This awareness of the complex nature of causality is vital for the study of most parts of the world. Since the formal models of politics "are usually distilled from the historical experience of European and North American societies, they can be specially debilitating in the study of other societies. There is a need therefore to build in an understanding of the context of different countries, especially in cross-national surveys. In this effort some state-of-the-art techniques can be quite useful. I have in mind the use of vignettes as a way to control for the variations in baseline expectations in different societies and the use of field experiments.[25] But we need to resist the have-data-will-regress mood of the discipline and the fad for the latest techniques of data analysis. No matter how sophisticated the technique of data analysis, it offers no more than an interpretative suggestion that needs to be fitted with other links in the logical chain to arrive at a causal inference. Regression by itself is not causal determination, though carefully testing models with sophisticated techniques is necessary for arriving at any serious conclusion about mass political behaviour. The outcome may be even weaker in the case of survey data on opinions and attitudes, for what one can conclude from such an enquiry is severely constrained by the conceptual design and interpretative frame.

The second change would have to do with how survey research relates to other forms of enquiry. Once we give up the monopolistic claims of survey as a method to understand the structure of mass beliefs, survey research can serve as a reality check for much of social science research on democracy and democratisation. It can do so by sketching the big, if rough, picture of the changes in mass political behaviour or mass opinions and attitudes. Even if survey-based investigation does not offer a satisfactory explanation of the phenomenon, it can set the agenda for what needs to be explained. The nature and pattern of political participation in contemporary India provide an apt illustration. Earlier, both popular and academic commentaries had assumed that India had followed the global pattern of a growing disinterest and apathy among the citizens, especially in the lower orders. It took survey-based investigation to show that this was simply not true: the levels of political participation in India were good by global standards, did not experience a secular decline, and that citizens from the lower order of society actually participated as well if not more than the upper castes and classes.[26] This finding does not by itself explain this outlier, but it does specify what needs to be explained. It now opens itself to ethnographic enquiries of what goes into political participation,[27] comparative investigations of the patterns and theoretical disputes about the meaning and significance of political participation. Similarly for a country like India where we have some credible survey-based data for several points in its post-colonial history,[28] there needs to be a better conversation between political historians and survey researchers. The need for dialogue is more pronounced if we take the instrument of survey research to newer democracies in most parts of the world. Research designed on formal models of politics is unlikely to be of much help here, simply because these models have not been distilled from the political realities of these societies. If one has to pose meaningful and researchable questions in the survey, one has to draw from anthropology, political history, and in some cases post-colonial studies. The less insular survey research on politics becomes, the more will be its dialogue with other related disciplines, and the higher we can expect from its yield in terms of a better understanding of politics.[29]

The third domain of "transformation" is really about the restoration of a fundamental tenet of survey research, namely, its privileging of probabilistic sampling. Random sampling is usually seen and discussed in technical terms, as the ideal method for selecting a sample that mirrors the attributes of the larger universe. It is time we viewed this technical practice through a political lens. In the new democracies of the global South, random sampling is a radical device to ensure that subaltern and suppressed opinions are made public. This is a way to find out if collusion between political elites and opinion makers may have kept public opinion out of public policy. The introduction of the policy package of "liberalisation" in many countries including our own is a case in point. In most cases these new policies have been pushed with the help of a political consensus. In our own country the New Economic Policy was a political surprise; it was a matter of political contention but has over the years come to be seen as a subject of political consensus for all parties that govern at the centre or at the state level. However, a series of studies of public opinion on this question has demonstrated that the public does not share this political consensus, that public opinion is still for state intervention in the economy, for the public sector as a provider of basic services and uneasy with, though not hostile to, globalisation.[30] The Afrobarometer found a similar dissonance between public policy of structural adjustment programmes and public opinion in many countries of Africa. I am not here to make a case for or against neo-liberal economic policies. My only point here is about ensuring that public opinion really reflects the opinion of the public.

In this context sticking to random sampling acquires a new salience. If opinion polling in India is any indication, the expansion of polling in most parts of the world has meant a step back in methodological terms. Crude quota samples, where even the quota does not represent the population profile, are the norm. Much worse are urban or metro polls that do not even try to cover the national population that they seek to represent. Even academic surveys do not use the principle of randomness; purposive sampling is the norm as and when researchers use survey methods to study public opinion.[31] Well-regarded global surveys accept utterly unrepresentative samples when it comes to countries outside the global North. Insisting on random sampling in this condition would require some innovations. We need to work on sampling techniques in conditions where background information is very low and the listing of the population is not always available. Another area of attention will be devising a protocol of reporting the sample profile that takes into account the various dimensions of exclusion and marginalisation. In India, for instance, it should be mandatory for every poll to make public its sample profile in terms of the urban–rural divide, gender, and major caste-community groups.

The fourth transformation is about ensuring that survey research is imagined and conceptualised in the language of the subjects whose opinions it seeks to capture. It is ironic that nearly two decades after the "linguistic turn" in social sciences was recognised, survey research is yet to take that linguistic turn.[32] Surveys on political opinions, attitudes and behaviour are still imagined and conceptualised in the languages of the global North. Concepts distilled from the political practice of Europe and North American democracies are often applied all over the world without serious debate on their appropriateness or otherwise to most parts of the world.[33] And this applies not just to cross-country surveys. The entry of global firms in the polling industry all over the world has meant a mechanical replication of survey items designed in the older democracies to all other countries. In this respect as well the expansion of survey research has meant methodological regress: some of the elementary rules of survey research are given the go-by when exporting them to most parts of the world. Methodological discussions on cross-national surveys rarely mention language as a key issue. In a multilinguistic context like ours, the challenge is multifold: the survey instrument needs to be developed in several languages and dialects.[34]

The challenge is not merely that of accuracy of translation that can be checked by back-translation; the real challenge is of conceptual translation and the appropriateness of the concept itself. I would like to reiterate emphatically that we are not discussing nuts and bolt issues here: if the enterprise of survey research derives some of its relevance from the project of pluralising the idea of democracy, then recovering the "social imaginary" embedded in political practices is one of its key tasks, one that it cannot even begin to take up unless the surveys are imagined and designed in the languages of the subjects. Survey research must recognise the language of political practice as a conceptual resource.

The fifth and related domain is that of survey fieldwork protocols. Here is another area where the survey research tradition has experienced a decline in recent times. Since face-to-face interviewing has become prohibitively expensive in North America and Western Europe, the focus of methodological sophistication has shifted to telephonic and now internet-based interviews. As a result very little attention is paid to refining the original and the best practice of the face-to-face interview, which is still possible in most parts of the world. Anthropology has produced a good deal of reflection on how an "outsider" should gain entry into a new culture, but there is no equivalent reflection in survey research on how to establish a rapport with a respondent who is from a very different class, caste-community, or gender and speaks a different register of the same language, as is often the case while doing surveys in India. There is a real need to develop fieldwork manuals and training modules to attend to these questions.

Let me pick up two questions for special attention here. Survey researchers often approach respondents who are either not literate or are not exposed to media and draw a blank when they ask them questions about controversies of national politics or questions involving remote institutions. The standard protocol requires them to put these responses under a dustbin category of "Can't say/Don't know". This category actually masks three different kinds of responses: when the respondent is unable to comprehend the question, when the respondent understands the question but has no clear opinion about it, and when the respondent has an opinion but does not wish to disclose it. Since the proportion of those who fall in this category can be anything from a quarter to half of the respondents for some of the complex questions, we need much more reflection on fieldwork protocols for identification of these different responses. A related issue is that of survey research in conflict zones. The current protocols of fieldwork are about the ordinary or normal situation that simply does not obtain very often in our setting. Think for example of survey researchers in the Maoist-controlled areas in Nepal before the restoration of democracy, or for that matter in Salwa Judum-affected areas of Chhattisgarh today.[35]

Finally, let me turn to the externalities of survey research: Who carries out surveys? At whose behest? To what end? These questions are more pertinent to survey research than any other form of social science enquiry, for survey research is a resource-intensive team game. More than any other kind of research, surveys require institutional support. The needed evolution of surveys in the older democracies has meant a close collaboration of public opinion research with private interests. Opinion polling is done by private companies and is dictated by their bottom line. Mass media and political parties are the biggest funders of public opinion. A good deal of public opinion research never makes it to the public domain, for it is for-clients-eye-only. No wonder the agenda of "public opinion" is dictated by organised private interests. The situation gets even more complicated when we look at public opinion research in the global South. The agenda is not just dictated by private interests, but by those situated outside the country. Very often the nationally owned media simply cannot afford to sponsor or does not see value for money in such surveys. The surveys are supported by media outside the country, global corporate houses, instruments of global finance, or multilateral donor agencies. While the investigators are local, the intellectual leadership and toolkit comes from outside. No wonder survey research of this kind is viewed within these countries with deep suspicion if not active hostility.

It is time therefore that we start thinking of the questions of funding and the institutional setting of survey research as political questions that require policy responses. First of all it would require infusing some public funds into the collection of public opinion on some key questions on a regular basis. Our country has a rich tradition of data collection on economy and demography thanks to institutions like the Census of India and the National Sample Survey Organisation. I am not suggesting that a governmental agency should be set up to investigate public opinion on politically sensitive questions. We are fortunate to have autonomous agencies like the Indian Council of Social Science Research that can be used to funnel public funds into regular monitoring of public opinion. Other countries that do not have a similar set-up will have to think of different mechanisms. Nor am I arguing for banning private or foreign funding: such bans are either superfluous or counterproductive. What we need is greater public-spirited philanthropy and at any rate more transparency in the reporting of funding sources for every kind of survey. Besides funding we also need to think of other resources like institutional space, intellectual capacity, and skills. Very often a rapid expansion of polling in the absence of trained personnel leads to a decline in the quality of survey research. I believe that this is what has happened in our country in the last decade or so. Pioneers of academic survey research and commercial opinion polling in our country had achieved for their time fairly high international standards of quality of research. The expansion of commercial opinion polling in the last decade has led to a visible decline in the quality of research, accuracy of findings, and extent of transparency. There is clearly a need to invest more in the R&D of survey research and the training of personnel. Improving the standards of survey research would also require learning across national boundaries. In this respect survey researchers in the global South can learn quite a lot from one another.

Conclusion

I began by talking about the days when I was a student. It may be appropriate therefore to conclude by reflecting on what it could mean to be a student of politics today and what role, if any, survey research could play in that. We live in different times today and the world of political science in our country has, at least partly, moved with the times. There is a grudging acknowledgement that the students of political science should study politics, and not just socio-economic structures. There is a desire to understand popular opinions and attitudes, and not merely as false consciousness. There is also a willingness to entertain a suspicion that understanding India may require modification in some of the received categories and theories of social science. All this has happened at a time when Indian politics has witnessed a democratic upsurge, new social groups are making claims to political power, and new social alliances and political coalitions are being forged. These are exciting, times to be a student of politics in India.

It is not my case that survey research has to be at the fulcrum of the engagement for a student of politics in India today. As would be clear by now, I would consider it nothing short of an intellectual catastrophe were the entire discipline of political science to swing now to survey research of the kind that we have received. My plea, rather, is that theoretically oriented yet empirically grounded engagement with politics should be at the fulcrum of the future of the discipline of political science in India. This engagement can and should take multiple forms: conceptual analysis, intellectual history, political history, comparative analysis, ethnography, and survey research, among others. I believe that survey research of the kind suggested above would constitute one necessary ingredient of the toolkit for a student of politics in India. I hope at least some of those who are students of politics today will make it their business to not just transfer but transform the tradition of survey research and make it relevant for most parts of the world.

Acknowledgements

This was delivered as the Malcolm Adiseshiah Memorial Lecture on 21 November 2008 at Chennai. Some of the ideas here were presented as a plenary speech at the session, "Probing Public Opinion, Interpretations, Deliberations" of the 38th World Congress of the International Institute of Sociology at Central European University, Budapest, 27 June 2008. An earlier version was presented as a talk, "Setting Standards for International Survey Research", Afrobarometer Round 3, Planning Workshop, Accra, 7–11 February 2005, and as a valedictory address to the Summer School in Research Methodology in Political Science organised by the Indian Institute of Advanced Study (IIAS) Shimla, with Lokniti, Centre for the Study of Developing Societies, Delhi, at IIAS, Shimla, 2–14 July 2007. Comments and feedback from participants at Budapest, Accra, and Shimla are gratefully acknowledged.

Notes

1. I think I was only reflecting this common sense in one of the first essays that I published on a critique of positivist ambition of creating a science of politics. "Political Science: Positivist Method and Philosophic Critiques", *Indian Journal of Political Science* (October–December 1986), 502–17.
2. A recent textbook defines survey in this generic sense as follows: "A 'survey' is a systematic method for gathering information from (a sample of) entities for the purposes of constructing quantitative descriptors of the attributes of the larger population of which the entities are members . . ." Robert M. Groves, *et al.*, *Survey Methodology*, New Jersey: John Wiley, 2004, p. 2.
3. The contrast is, for example, with the discipline of history in India that has been robustly empirical without giving up on theoretical ambitions. Irrespective of their ideological hues, Indian historians are very attentive to their "sources", in sharp contrast to the attitude of most political scientists to the nature of "evidence". Marxist economists in India have never shunned quantitative information, unlike their counterparts who study politics. The most influential tradition of social anthropology has also been deeply empirical in nature, with "fieldwork" being seen as a rite

of passage. The discipline of political science did not develop any such protocol of external reference to archive, ethnographic fieldwork, or surveys.

4. For two examples of this initial energy, see Sudipta Kaviraj, *et al.*, *State of Political Theory: Some Marxist Essays*, Calcutta: Research India Publications, 1978; and Randhir Singh, *Reason, Revolution and Political Theory: Notes on Michael Oakeshott*, New Delhi: PPH,1967.
5. These remarks are aimed at the mainstream of the discipline of political science. Needless to say, there were some exceptions and creative interventions from within the Marxist and the non-Merxist camps that defied the limitations of the mainstream.
6. Ironically, one of the biggest casualties of this radical orientation in the discipline has been a systematic study of class in Indian politics. While Marxist economists and political practitioners spent a good deal of their intellectual labour going over empirical data, including a lot of survey data, on land relations to understand the structure of class in the agrarian economy of India, Marxist political scientists have never cared to sift through the existing evidence on how class operates in the domain of politics. If anything the irony has deepened in the last decade or so: as evidence of the operation of class as a variable in electoral politics begins to mount in these years, political analysis of radical persuasion has moved further away from any attention to this kind of evidence. It is not surprising that one of the few attempts at using empirical information for the study of the class character of Indian politics came from an economist. See Pranab Bardhan, *Political Economy of Development*, Delhi: Oxford University Press,1984.
7. I have had the misfortune of commenting repeatedly on this art of the so-called "psephology" in our country without much success. See my "Polls, Predictions, Psephology", *Seminar*; 385 [Beyond the Vote: A Symposium on 1991 Election and After], September 1991. For a more technical analysis of election forecasting models, see Rajeeva L. Karandikar, Yogendra Yadav, and Clive Payne, "Predicting the 1998 Indian Parliamentary Elections", *Electoral Studies*, 21 (2002), 69–89.
8. Although the number of such polls is now huge, there is little academic reflection on the findings of these polls or on their methodology; there is not even a simple compilation of the reports of such surveys. India Today's Mood of the Nation Poll done in association with ORG-MARG is one of the most reputed and long-standing series of public opinion polls in the country. In recent years, CNN-IBN and the Centre for the

Study of Developing Societies (CSDS) have come together to institute a six-monthly State of the Nation Survey that combines the functions of political barometer and general-purpose public opinion research.

9. I borrow this phrase from Partha Chatterjee who uses it to draw our attention to the fact that what used to be described as the "third world" or the global South is not just a small appendage; this comprises most of the world. See Partha Chatterjee, *The Politics of the Governed: Reflections on Popular Politics in Most of the World*, Delhi: Permanent Black, 2004.
10. For a quick overview, see Slavko Splichal, *Public Opinion: Developments and Controversies in the Twentieth Century*, Lanham: Rowman & Littlefield, 1999. For a summary of theoretically informed critiques of survey research on public opinion, see James R. Beniger, "The Impact of Polling on Public Opinion: Reconciling Foucault, Habermas and Bourdeieu", *International Journal of Public Opinion Research*, 4 (3) (1992). For a political critique of the polling industry, see Peter V. Miller, "The Industry of Public Opinion", in T.L. Glauser and C.T. Salmon (eds), *Public Opinion and the Communication of Consent*, New York: Guilford, 1995.
11. The literature on the philosophy of social sciences and method in political science, which the current section draws upon, is so vast that I have avoided making specific references. Some of the classical critiques aimed generally at the follies of the new empirical science of politics were Charles Taylor, "Neutrality in Political Science", in Peter Laslett and W.G. Runciman (eds), *Philosophy, Politics and Society*, Oxford: Blackwell, 1967; Alasdair MacIntyre, "Is a Science of Comparative Politics Possible?", in Alan Ryan (ed.), *The Philosophy of Social Explanation*, Oxford: Oxford University Press, 1973. For extracts from the larger philosophical debate in the philosophy of social sciences, see Gerard Delanty and Piet Strydom (eds), *Philosophies of Social Science: The Classic and Contemporary Readings*, Maidenhead: Open University Press, 2003.
12. Anthony Giddens, "Positivism and Its Critics", in *Studies in Social and Political Theory*, London: Hutchinson, 1977. Richard Bernstein, *Beyond Objectivism and Relativism: Science, Hermeneutics, and Praxis*, University of Pennsylvania Press, 1983. For extracts from the larger philosophical debate, see Gerard Delanty and Piet Strydom (eds), *Philosophies of Social Science: The Classic and Contemporary Readings*, Maidenhead: Open University Press, 2003.
13. The critique surfaced with Thomas Kuhn's classic *The Structure of Scientific Revolutions*, Chicago: University of Chicago Press, 1962.

For an examination of the implication of the debate following Kuhn's work, see S. Fuller, *The Philosophy of Science and Its Discontents*, 2nd edn, New York: Guilford, 1993.

14. See, for example, the powerful critique of Western descriptions of the non-West in anthropology in *Writing Culture: The Poetics and Politics of Ethnography*, James Clifford and George E. Marcus (eds), *School of American Research*, Santa Fe: University of California Press, 1986. Edward Said's classic *Orientalism* had already had this influence on the humanities in general and on literary criticism in particular.
15. This section draws upon the limited literature on globalisation of survey research on politics. See Tom Smith and Jibum Kim, "The Globalization of Survey Research", paper presented at the annual meeting of the American Sociological Association, TBA, New York, New York City, 10 August 2007. Online <PDF>. http://www.allacademic.com/meta/p175569 index.html. International Organization for Standardization/Technical Committee 225, Market, Opinion and Social Research Draft International Standard, Madrid: AENOR, 2005. J. Harkness, "In Pursuit of Quality: Issues for Cross-National Survey Research", *International Journal of Social Research Methodology*, 2 (1999); Anthony Heath, Stephen Fisher, and Shawna Smith, "The Globalization of Public Opinion Research", *Annual Review of Political Science*, 7 (2005).
16. For an introduction to the World Values Survey and access to its data and findings, see http://www.worldvaluessurvey.org.
17. http://www.latinobarometrro.org. The Latinobarometer also serves as the headquarter for a coalition of all these regional barometers called Global Barometer Surveys. See http:///www.globalbarometer.net/
18. http://www.afrobarometer.org/
19. http://www.asianbarometer.org/
20. http://www.democracy-asia.org/ for an introduction to the survey and to the State of Democracy in South Asia study.
21. For some of the findings from the barometers on support for democracy, see articles in the symposium on Democracy Barometers, *Journal of Democracy* (January 2008).
22. This concept is drawn from Charles Taylor, *Modern Social Imaginaries*, Durham: Duke University Press, 2004.
23. Richard Rorty, *Philosophy and the Mirror of Nature*, New Jersey: Princeton University Press, 1979.
24. Charles M. Cameroon and Rebecca Morton, "Formal Theory Meets

Data", in Ira Katznelson and Helen V. Milner (eds), *Political Science: State of the Discipline*, Washington: APSA, 2002. For a critique of mechanistic models of explanation that dominate statistical analysis of survey data in political science, see Christopher H. Achen, "Lets Put Garbage-Can Regressions and Garbage-Can Probits Where They Belong", *Conflict Management and Peace Science*, 22 (4) (January 2005).

25. For suggesting the use of vignettes within surveys, see Gary King *et al.*, "Enhancing the Validity and Cross-Cultural Comparability of Measurement in Survey Research", *American Political Science Review*, 97 (2003). For field experiments, see Donal P. Green and Alan S. Gerber, "Reclaiming the Experimental Tradition in Political Science", in Ira Katznelson and Helen V. Milner (eds), op. cit.

26. Yogendra Yadav, "Understanding the Second Democratic Upsurge: Trends of Bahujan Participation in Electoral Politics in the 1990s", in Francine R. Frankel, Zoya Hasan, Rajeeva Bhargava, and Balveer Arora (eds), *Transforming India: Social and Political Dynamics of Democracy*, Delhi: Oxford University Press, 2000; for subsequent modification, see Suhas Palshikar and Sanjay Kumar, "Participatory Norm: How Broad-based is It?", *Economic and Political Weekly*, 39 (51) (18 December 2004).

27. Mukulika Banerjee, "Sacred Elections", *Economic and Political Weekly*, 42 (17) (2007).

28. Much of this data is available at the CSDS Data Unit, perhaps the richest data archive on politics anywhere in the global South. See *www.lokniti.org*. For an introduction to its flagship survey series, see Lokniti Team, "National Election Study 2004: An Introduction", *Economic and Political Weekly*, 39 (51) (18 December).

29. For a plea for such a dialogue between ethnographic and survey research on elections, see Yogendra Yadav, "Epilogue: What Does Fieldwork Do in the Field of Elections?", in M.N. Srinivas and A.M. Shah, *The Grassroots of Democracy: Field Studies of Indian Elections*, Delhi: Permanent Black, 2007.

30. K.C. Suri, "Democracy, Economic Reforms and Election Results in India", *Economic and Political Weekly*, 39 (51) (18 December).

31. The CSDS surveys have been an exception in this regard. Ever since the 1960s when the survey tradition started there, the CSDS teams have followed multistage random sampling procedures and have used the official electoral rolls to draw samples. For discussion of the

evolution of sampling practices, see Lokniti Team, "National Election Study 2004: An Introduction", op. cit.

32. The expression is used widely to refer to the move in social and human sciences away from objectivist orientation to one that takes language and subjectivities more seriously. Richard Rorty, *The Linguistic Turn: Essays in Philosophical Method*, Chicago: University of Chicago Press, 1992. There is very little reflection on the question of language in survey research. For a few examples of some technical work, see O. Behling and K.S. Law, *Translating Questionnaires and Other Research Instruments: Problems and Solutions*, Sage, 2000. J. Harkness, B-E Pennell, and A. Schoua-Glusberg, "Survey Questionnaire Translation and Assessment", in S. Presser, *et al.* (eds), *Questionnaire Development Evaluation and Testing Methods*, Wiley Series in Survey Methodology, New Jersey: John Wiley and Sons, Inc., 2004.

33. The wide currency of concepts like social capital and civil society, and the battery of questions on trust and membership of organisations in most global surveys appear to me to be an example of this trend. The application of the concept of "self-expression values" drawn from post-industrial societies is another instance of the lack of fit between the concept and the world that it seeks to capture. For the latter, see Ronal Inglehart and Christian Welzel, *Modernization, Cultural Change and Democracy: The Human Development Sequence*, New York: Cambridge University Press, 2005.

34. The question of "dialects" or languages without a script or state recognition is a vital question waiting to be attended to in our context. The National Election Study, with its research instrument in eighteen languages, has attempted to address this question with the help of transliteration in the case of Kok-Borok, a language spoken by the adivasis of Tripura. The real challenge is to attend to more than a dozen "dialects" of Hindi that can be mutually incomprehensible.

35. For some reflections on survey at the height of the Maoist insurgency in Nepal, see SDSA Team, *State of Democracy in South Asia*, Delhi: Oxford University Press, 2008. CSDS teams have carried out surveys in the Kashmir valley, Manipur, and Nagaland in recent years but the lessons remain to be written about.

13

On Ethnography

What Work Does "Fieldwork" Do in the Field of Elections?

INTERESTING ANSWERS, but what exactly was the question? That was my first reaction on reading the rich collection of anthropological studies of Indian elections put together in this book. There is something refreshing about shifting our gaze in terms of time and space, in going back from the present to a different era in the past, and in moving from aggregate countrywide electoral statistics to the nuances of how the game was played out in a village or an urban neighbourhood. As I tried to formulate what I had learnt from encountering a radically different way of looking at elections in a very different time, I kept coming back to some basic questions: Are these essays about what electoral politics does to society? Or are they about how local social dynamics shape elections? Do these seek to sketch the context of voters' choices? Or do these offer an explanation of the electoral outcome? It soon became clear that the various authors in this volume were not only studying varied locations, they were also asking different kinds of questions. It was not going to be easy to tease a common question or a set of questions that informed the answers offered here. What exactly then was I to respond to?

The second reaction was of course more personal: what was my qualification for writing an epilogue to this book? The studies in this book are about the 1967 and 1971 elections, a period and events on which I have done no primary research. More importantly, much of my research about India's elections since 1989 has used quantitative data and survey research techniques, something I should be ashamed of if the introduction to this volume is right. Perhaps the decision of the editor and the publisher to invite a younger colleague from a different tradition to comment on the book was generous to a fault.

Or so it seemed on my first reading of these essays. It took another reading (and I am afraid many more months) to realise that my double handicap in reading this collection might not in the end be a source of weakness. I had unwittingly placed myself in the classical situation of an anthropologist who seeks to leverage his status as an "outsider" to gain insights into unfamiliar territory. "A Political Scientist Among the Anthropologists" may not be as exciting as "An Anthropologist Among the Historians",[1] but it is not a bad position to be in if one wants to ask questions about the nature and limits of a fieldwork-based study of elections. Ever since the study of elections became a serious social scientific pursuit, there has been a professional consensus among its students that it is essential to study elections by the fieldwork method. The various disciplines have, of course, varying understandings of what fieldwork means. Which field should one choose? Once in the field, what kind of work does one do? And how does one make sense of what one gets through fieldwork? These questions have divided the various disciplines and schools of thought. So, the invitation to contribute this epilogue looked like a perfect opportunity to reflect on an old methodological dispute. It was also a good occasion to map continuities and changes in Indian elections and thus revisit some of the substantive debates on the subject.

This is pretty much what I do in this epilogue, and I do it by coming to terms with both my handicaps one by one. First, I engage with the substantive question by mapping the distance between the elections that these essays describe and elections today. I discover that the continuities are much stronger than we imagined, and that a range of attributes that we suspect to be of recent origin are actually much older. These studies thus enable us to go beyond the familiar common sense on Indian elections.

Recognition of the immense value of the material presented in these essays prompts a question: Do these insights originate from the methodology deployed by the authors? This brings me face to face with the radical methodological difference that lies at the heart of the disciplinary agenda that informs many of these essays. It appears to me that the methodological claims implicit in the editorial introduction may have overstated the case. I argue that much of the missionary zeal of believers situated in the different methodological religion of the 1960s was rather misplaced. What we need is a dialogue among various methodological pursuits for studying elections. Drawing these thoughts together, I conclude by offering some remarks on a future agenda for election studies that may perhaps emerge from the dialogue proposed here.

Elections: Past and Present

The case studies in this book focus on a period that was a turning point in the history of Indian elections. Students of Indian politics remember the period up to 1967 as the epitome of "the Congress system", the phrase coined by Rajni Kothari to describe the unique party system that evolved in post-Independence India.[2] The point about calling the politics of that period "the Congress system" was not that the Congress was strong then and weak thereafter. In fact, in electoral terms the Congress scored some of its most impresive victories – take the electoral waves of 1971, 1980, and 1984, for example – in the period after 1967. The real point about calling it "the Congress system" was that in that period the Congress occupied the role of the ruling as well as the opposition party. The factions within the Congress served to articulate political dissent. Initially seen as yet another example of Indian exceptionalism, this type of intra-party competition is best interpreted as characteristic of the phase of transition from a national movement to a full-blown multi-party competition within a polity characterised by elite-driven politics and a low level of political consciousness and participation by ordinary citizens. Elections in the pre-1967 era carried the stamp of this phase of Indian politics; this was to undergo a significant change by the 1971 elections. The "Garibi Hatao" campaign led by Indira Gandhi's "new" Congress, the plebiscitary nature of the elections, the leader's direct appeal to voters – bypassing political middlemen – and the arrival of countrywide electoral waves inaugurated a new era in Indian elections.

The studies in this book happen to have captured this critical moment of transition in Indian politics. Although they do not seek to be representative in a simple sense, the story of the Congress candidate challenged for the first time by an opposition candidate or by a Congress rebel, told in many essays of this book, is typical of its time. These essays enable us to recognise the larger story behind the changing fortunes of political parties during this period. The change between 1967 and 1971 was also a transition from the elite-dominated first phase to the second phase of mass politics, corresponding to the change from the first to the second electoral system.[3] By combining evidence from other sources and with the help of hindsight, the essays collected here help us understand the key elements in this transition.

First, there is a gradual disappearance of the middleman from elections. The study of Chomu and Thanjavur in this volume brings out how political middlemen, who could be trusted in earlier times to get bulk votes for parties and candidates, were losing their role in this new era when political leaders were establishing direct contact with the electorate. In the remote hill area of Bageshwar, the practice of paying money to middlemen continued into the 1967 election, but it was not clear whether the middlemen were able to deliver votes. Indira Gandhi's plebiscitary politics was to put a decisive end to this practice. More than one essay in the second half of this book registers the presence of *hawa* – the general national mood shared by an imagined community of voters – which translates into a similar pattern of voting behaviour unmediated by local brokers, that made all the difference, overriding all the local factors.

This is related to a second crucial change. The period covered by these studies records a shift of electoral contestation from micro issues specific to locality to macro, national issues. "Development" was already becoming the trope of election campaigns. Jayaraman reports from Thanjavur that "people had come to look upon a member of the assembly as a kind of 'broker' in their dealings with the external world, particularly with the state government." Various studies of the 1971 elections record how national issues such as bank nationalisation and the elimination of the privy purses, and slogans like "Garibi Hatao", travelled to various localities and changed local political alignments.

Third, these studies reflect the changing nature of political mobilisation and campaigning. One of the considerations for Ram Kishore Vyas getting the Congress ticket in Chomu in Rajasthan was that he was "a man of means who would be in a position to meet the high financial demands of an election campaign." This is echoed in many studies in this volume. Clearly, elections were no longer just about popularity and issues. The election machine was beginning to become very important. Both the articles from Tamil Nadu capture the emergence of the Dravida Munnetra Kazhagam (DMK's) powerful election machine, which was to ensure many victories. Dua's analysis of the Jullundur South constituency reminds us of a forgotten factor in the famous victory of 1971, namely, the role of the Communist Party of India (CPI) in giving Indira Gandhi's Congress an organisational network in many parts of the country.

The research reported in this book shows that many of the ills of electoral democracy that we think of as being of recent origin can be traced back to the 1960s. We find many instances here of the role of money and lineage, and of the corresponding decline of party organisation. Dua's study of how the Congress' vote bank among the Dalits was dented in Jullundur South shows that all the routine ills associated with electoral politics had come into operation by then: wheeling and dealing in micro-level alliance-building, the role of money, the appeal to religion for voting, and the use of dummy candidates to damage rivals. We have also the report of the use of liquor by the Swatantra Party candidate in Chomu in Rajasthan in 1971.

Of course, the scale of things has changed radically. Anjum reports that each Congress candidate was paid by the party a sum of Rs 1000 to Rs 2000, a tiny amount going by prices prevailing at that time. The instance of "inducement in kind" noticed by Jayaraman in Thanjavur in 1967 – "a small tray filled with a small tin of vermilion powder, flowers, and a coconut" – makes for amusing reading today. The role of money in the more prosperous areas of Maharashtra was already reaching serious proportions. Baviskar discovered that both the leading candidates had spent around Rs 50,000 in their election campaigns at a time when the legal ceiling of expenditure was only Rs 8000.

The fourth dimension of change, namely, the changing profile of leaders, is best captured by the story of Pushpa Behenji, the Congress candidate from the Prithviraj Road Metropolitan Council constituency in New Delhi. Her personality is a fascinating mix of the generation that was passing out and the one that was coming into electoral politics. Hers is a typical story – of what the entry into electoral politics did to Congress workers of the national movement, a change extensively noted and commented upon by the literature in Indian languages but rarely captured on the radar of social sciences. Pushpa Gupta brought impeccable credentials to public life: an Arya Samaji by orientation, she was active in the nationalist movement, engaged in constructive work, wore khadi, and did not marry. However, participation in electoral politics drew her back into her upper-caste and upper-class origins as she ended up making use of her family and caste connections as well as the resources of a public institution for her victory in the elections.

Fifth, we discern an incipient trend suggesting the rise of political consciousness and activism among the subaltern classes. The study by Sanwal and Sanwal identifies a very interesting pattern of political participation that foreshadows patterns established in the 1990s: "Elections provide the members of numerically small and economically dependent castes with an opportunity to feel the glory of being associated, however indirectly, with the societal power apparatus." This was to lead to a democratic upsurge among the lower orders of society in the 1990s.

More than one essay in this book comments on the changing political status of the Harijans of that period. The study of the Bageshwar constituency in Uttar Pradesh (now in Uttaranchal) demonstrates the coexistence of three generations of politics among the ex-Untouchables. The Congress candidate Das was a typical "Harijan" politician: hailing from a traditional drummer community, he had "not allowed his education or economic independence to turn his head" and could be relied upon to respect the traditional status norms. Tamta, the Jan Sangh candidate, can be described as a "Scheduled Caste" or SC: a *patwari* by occupation and well entrenched in the local administration and its ways, he was a man of some education and greater resources who was interested in pushing his political career. The third candidate, Arya of the Samyukta Socialist Party (SSP), was what we today call a "Dalit": politically conscious and militant, he had "not only been alienated from his traditional caste occupation but had actually repudiated his caste" and thus could not be relied upon to uphold the *maryada*. These three nomenclatures capture the differences over three generations of political leaders from the ex-Untouchable communities. "Harijan", a name coined by Mahatma Gandhi, became associated with patronising, if not downright condescending, upper-caste attitudes. "Scheduled Caste" or "SC" was more neutral and gestured towards legal constitutional status, although over the years this word too acquired negative connotations. The current expression "Dalit", though negative in origin, is a marker of political aspiration and identity. Over the last few decades, political "Harijans" have given way to "SCs" and then to "Dalits".

The last, but perhaps most important, conclusion emerging from this book pertains, as a social anthropological study of politics should, to the nature of social cleavages that operated in electoral politics. The prevailing popular and academic common sense on this question holds India to be a very special case where political behaviour is still imprisoned in primordial loyalties of caste and community.[4] A common saying in political circles is that in India voters "do not cast their vote but vote their caste". This common sense is captured in the expression "vote bank": the idea that each party or candidate has a pool of voters who can be relied upon to serve as a bank irrespective of issues, evaluation of performance, or intra-party politics.

In this context, it is extremely important that not a single essay in the present book discovers anything like a vote bank in operation. Several studies support this reading, although the insight remains under-theorised. The study of the Chomu constituency in Rajasthan concludes that "Caste did not seem to play an important role in the elections"; however, going by the evidence in the essay, perhaps it is fair to say that while there were no vote banks, caste did matter during voting. Jayaraman's essay on Thanjavur in 1967 argues that the simple association of caste blocs with political parties did not hold: "the groupings in terms of Brahman, Non-Brahman and Adi-Dravida did not function as the basis for political support at the village level." The essay is a convincing description of the fluidity of political alignments. Panini's revisit to Rampura, the village made famous by M.N. Srinivas, shows that political leaders of the younger generation were busy establishing "ties of friendship cutting across the links of caste", indicating the loosening of patron–client ties. Panini finds "no evidence of voting along lines of caste". Gupta argues to the contrary and suggests that "voting was influenced by caste and economic consideration", but the evidence she puts together does not indicate caste-based voting except for the Republican Party of India (RPI). Mittal's study of the Sarojini Nagar constituency in New Delhi provides glimpses, despite the author's inattention to this fascinating process, of how political identities were being forged in an urban context through regional associations, such as the Bengali Association and the Uttar Pradesh Association. Even in the most extreme case of the Manipur Outer constituency, where the Meitei tribal tensions and the Naga–Kuki conflict tended to polarise the elections along ethnic lines, the evidence presented in the paper by Rohit Singh does not warrant the label "vote banks".

The evidence put together by all these caste studies can be subsumed under what Imtiaz Ahmad calls "situational solidarities": "there were a number of loyalties which served as a basis of organization of political support in the rural areas. These loyalties were those of religion, caste, kinship, and faction. All these loyalties were operating simultaneously, but they were situationally determined, and operated at different levels." Ramaswamy makes a similar point based on his study of a working-class area in the Singanallur constituency in Tamil Nadu. He identifies several "aggregates" of the electorate: factions, castes, local groups, groups of unionists, groups of millworkers, supporters of a political party, and kin groups. "The individual voter was at the same time a member of more than one aggregate and was exposed to competing pressures. Which of these proved more compelling was not a matter of individual choice. At least in Singanallur it was possible to work out a rough hierarchy of loyalties which influenced voting behaviour." Recent social scientific recognition that political identities are multiple, and that what gets foregrounded at which moment depends on the context, is only a different way of stating this insight.

Interestingly, this conclusion is supported by another kind of evidence that anthropologists do not normally look at. The National Election

Study of 1971 carried out by the Centre for the Study of Developing Societies (CSDS), Delhi, based on a post-poll survey of a national representative sample of electors, asked the respondents: "Is there a person in this village who has influence over how others vote?" Only 27.4 per cent respondents replied in the affirmative, and less than 1 per cent mentioned caste or religion as the basis of influence. Ordinary voters did not believe that vote banks existed: only 35 per cent respondents said that most members of their own caste or religion voted for one party. Analysis of voting behaviour by caste and religious community in this survey showed that for most caste and religious communities the level of support for any one party was within 10 percentage points of the average vote share of that party.[5]

This is no doubt indirect evidence, for aggregation at the national level can mask many local effects. The evidence gathered by researchers in this volume is more direct and to the point. The question, of course, is: What kind of inference does one draw from these studies regarding the changing nature of social cleavages in electoral politics? Can we say, as with the other points made above, that they capture a decline of vote banks? That would be a difficult claim to sustain for, unlike the phenomenon of middlemen, one cannot say that the operation of caste cleavages in electoral politics is a thing of the past. One could argue an opposite reading and suggest that the trajectory is the other way round in the case of caste and community, that what these studies capture is an initial point in the career of caste politics which has since acquired monstrous dimensions.

Perhaps the most fruitful way of interpreting the evidence presented in this book is to resist both these simple readings. The operation of caste cleavages was and continues to be one of the determinants of electoral politics. Yet this operation never took the form that is suggested by the metaphor of vote banks. In that sense, vote banks were always something of a myth. What we should be debating is the change in different forms and levels of caste-based voting. Has the location of caste-based voting shifted from the micro to the macro level? Most of the studies in this book identify the candidate's caste or village-level caste dynamics as the determinant of caste voting. In recent years, the caste of the party's top leader, or the dynamics of caste at the state level, decides which caste votes for whom. While the present book opens up this field of enquiry, we do not have here comparative anthropological studies to prove or disprove any of these hypotheses. Political science literature is also not very helpful on this question.[6] A dialogue between the two disciplines can open the way for fresh thinking on this subject.

Methodology of Election Research

Before returning to the theme of the dialogue outlined in the previous section, let me attend to the question of the methodology of election research – something that has prevented a dialogue between the various disciplines. The editor's introduction views the common thread running through the various studies in methodological terms. It identifies the distinguishing feature of the book as the fact that these are election studies carried out by sociologists and social anthropologists using the method of intensive fieldwork or participant observation in small communities, with a minimum of quantification. The introduction goes on to place this approach within a tradition of research developed at the Department of Sociology at the University of Delhi under the disciplinary leadership of M.N. Srinivas. The editor finds in this tradition of research nothing short of a new approach to the study of political phenomena: "Our department had developed by then a distinct approach to the study of various aspects of society, including the political aspect. This approach lay in the study of small communities by the method of intensive fieldwork often associated with social anthropology. Srinivas often said that this approach provided the worm's-eye view of society that contrasted with the bird's-eye view offered by most other social scientists."

The introduction raises more questions than it answers: What was distinctive about the approach of Indian anthropologists to the study of electoral politics? How was this approach different from an application of anthropological techniques to policies, or from what students of politics study as "political sociology"? It is fair to assume that this approach drew upon the existing methodological literature, both worldwide and in India, on the fieldwork method adopted by social anthropologists. The only difficulty is that this method was originally not designed to capture a phenomenon such as modern politics. The possibility of this extension is precisely what makes the claims in the introduction both interesting and somewhat wanting in the spelling out of distinctiveness. Yet the last part of the quotation above already hints that this approach was a conscious departure from and critique of other approaches to the study of this subject. The introduction contains many passing remarks providing glimpses into the methodological polemics that informed anthropological attempts to understand politics: the superficial character of the "hit-and-run method" of survey research versus the in-depth nature of ethnographic work; the artificial assumptions about voters' rationality deployed by political scientists versus a realistic model of how context-bound human decisions are; and surface statistics versus qualitative interpretation. Ethnographic fieldwork, it appears, is the only way of getting it right. Perhaps it is only natural that no other tradition of "fieldwork" finds mention in this book's introduction.

This self-consciousness about disciplinary boundaries and the touching faith in discipline-specific methodologies to deliver the truth is very much the stuff of the 1960s. In that era of the rise of social sciences, the practitioners of the various disciplines or sub-disciplines, and adherents of various schools of social science often exhibited deep methodological conviction without always spelling out what their method really was, or explicating the presuppositions of their methodological creed, or offering good reasons why someone should believe in them.[7] This was true of the ethnographic method of anthropologists, but it was no less true of survey researchers in the discipline of political science, of Marxist historians, of econometricians, and so on. Arguably, social anthropologists were better off than their counterparts in other disciplines for they did produce some texts on their method in the Indian context.[8] Practitioners of survey research failed to produce even basic textbooks on the specificities of the method in the Indian context.[9] No wonder methodological disputes took curious forms: differences over sites and techniques of information collection were presented in a grand way, as though they constituted methodological debates. Very often these disputes were merely a shadow of battles being fought elsewhere. One could argue that the dispute between the ethnographic versus the survey method was largely a reflection of a dispute internal to the empirical tradition of Western social science; it mirrored to a great extent the dispute between mainstream British anthropology and political science on the one hand and the dominant tradition in American sociology or political science on the other.

In many ways, the methodological dispute in Indian social science was a debate that never was. It was carried out by the exercise of the authority of disciplinary establishments rather than through an open and written exchange across disciplines that could have allowed free and equal participation by a larger group. This was responsible for a virtual non-communication among the various disciplines – something that can be seen in this book as well. While the editor is justified in complaining of lack of attention to anthropological research on elections by political scientists, most of the authors in this volume reciprocate the lacuna by taking little note of the political science literature on the area they are writing about.

This absence of a meaningful dialogue leads to mistaken or simplistic representations. For instance, the "political science" that anthropologists wished to resist simply did not have a significant presence in the Indian context. Far from being the dominant and overbearing style of studying political phenomena, election study and voting behaviour analysis was actually the least sought after subdiscipline in political science (see Hebsur, 1992). A trenchant critique of quantification was out of place here, for Indian political science never achieved any degree of quantitative sophistication, let alone any obsession with quantification.[10] Far from being a prisoner of models of voters' rationality devoid of social context, political science in India could in fact be accused of dissolving voters in their social contexts of caste and community. In fact, the idea that research done by political scientists followed the survey method, in contrast to the ethnographic method adopted by anthropologists, is simply not borne out by a look at the history of the discipline. An overwhelming majority of the early research on Indian elections deployed the case study method. If anything, Indian political scientists could be accused of ignoring survey research and overreliance on the case study method.

But let us put these forms of misunderstanding aside and examine the methodological claims made on behalf of anthropology in terms of the three components of the approach identified by the editor: choice of small community as the unit of analysis; participant observation as the technique of data collection; and the non-quantitative technique of data analysis. The methodological claim made here can have a weak or strong version. The weak version would merely suggest that the non-quantitative study of a small community by using the participant observation technique is a useful, or even a necessary, supplement to the study of elections. The strong version would suggest that it is not merely useful and necessary but also in some way better than other ways of studying elections. The editor's introduction vacillates between these two claims. But let me focus on the stronger claim, for it informs much of the common sense of the discipline.

Take the question of unit of analysis first. There is no doubt that studies of how elections are played out in the context of local community can be a very useful supplement to studies of electoral politics at the constituency and state levels. These studies are no doubt essential to a fuller understanding of elections. The difficulty arises when any one level is considered not only necessary but also sufficient, or when strong methodological claims are made on behalf of any study of local community. The editorial introduction does not quite make this claim, but it is worth discussing here since a version of this claim is implicit both in the introduction and in many anthropological studies.

The difficulty with a case study of a small community is that we do not know what to do with it unless we know why that particular case was selected. This problem is particularly severe in studying a macro phenomenon like elections. In an event that takes place simultaneously all over the country, it is possible to come up with all kinds of cases at different levels of what would be considered local – village, *mohalla*, constituency, district, and so on. We do not know whether the conclusions from such a study can have wider application unless we know how typical the case is of larger trends and patterns. That does not render case studies irrelevant or useless. But it does require that a case study must offer careful justification of the choice of the case, or at least give sufficient post facto information allowing anyone to see how that case was placed in the entire universe of analysis – just as any survey research must offer a rigorous defence of its sample selection. In this respect, many of the studies in this volume do not make a case for the case study method. Most authors have studied elections in a community merely because they happen to have studied that community earlier, for some other purpose. We are not told enough about what makes these cases illuminating for a study of electoral politics. This is not to say that these studies are not illuminating – I have argued exactly the opposite in the previous section – but simply to insist that this question cannot be addressed without placing the case under examination within a broader matrix.

Related to the question of unit of analysis is the issue of the nature of causality. A focus on local community that does not take note of its linkages with the world outside it is unlikely to offer a robust causal understanding of a process such as elections. There is no doubt that the macro phenomenon called elections is lived in its micro setting, and that we cannot understand elections without making sense of the act of voting in its micro context. In the typical situation where national political parties do not control local-level politics, there is a kind of autonomy of local politics that transforms the character of electoral competition, something that any macro analysis cannot begin to comprehend. Hence the need for and relevance of ethnographic research on elections. Yet the explanatory enterprise remains incomplete without taking into account what Rao, writing in this book, calls "interaction between the wider political processes and local-level politics".

Many studies in this volume end up misreading their own material in the absence of an understanding of how their case was related to wider political processes. The study of Chomu in Rajasthan in the 1967 elections actually demonstrates that macro level resentment against the Congress party proved decisive in ensuring the defeat of the Congress candidate in that constituency. The local factors and social equations that the author emphasises actually favoured the losing candidate. Similarly, Dua's narration of the election campaign in Jullundur South misses the point of the story: of how the Congress' Harijan vote bank was dented by a protest of young, educated persons (emerging Dalits?) in that community at a moment of overall dissatisfaction with the Congress party. Ironically, the one case where the candidate's personality and local campaign did make a difference – the Prithviraj Road constituency in New Delhi, where the Congress candidate won despite an anti-Congress wave – is seen by Anjum as a case where the candidate won "because of her party".

It could be argued that it is not the anthropologist's task to offer a causal explanation of electoral outcomes. But that defence does not work in real life, for most anthropological studies do get into the business of offering explanations and thereby invite scrutiny regarding their causal claims. Ramaswamy's meticulous account of the complexities of trade union and party politics in Singanallur does not help us understand electoral outcome, for the outcome in this constituency was a function of the state-level macro alliance rather than of the local rivalries and hostilities so carefully sketched in his paper. Mishra's study of the defeat of Charan Singh in Muzaffarnagar concludes that the "national issues raised by the candidates and parties in this constituency had a rather limited impact on the people of Jatpura", but the evidence presented by the author points to the role of the macro context in the absence of which local issues could not have become decisive. Similarly, Vishwanath emphasises the role of local factors in the victory of the Old Congress in Gujarat, but his narrative provides enough evidence of how the national context was transforming the nature of Gujarat politics. Chakravarti presents the shift from 1967 to 1971 in the Chomu constituency as a shift from local issues to national issues. A model of interaction between the macro and the micro would allow us to read the same material differently: in both these elections we have national issues filtered through the local context.[11] The only difference is that in the previous election both these sets of issues were working at cross-purposes, while in 1971 they were aligned.

The second aspect of the methodological claim concerns the technique of data collection, specifically the choice of a structured questionnaire administered by an outsider versus participant observation by an outsider-insider. Perhaps no one would deny the superiority of the ethnographic technique in gathering *some* kinds of information: those pertaining to beliefs and meanings and the complex web of social relations. The real question is whether participant observation is necessary for understanding the act of voting. Now, it is not necessary for every study of elections to get into a study of voting behaviour, but a large majority of them do – including most case studies in this book. And if that is one of the research foci, the value of a sample survey is undeniable. Often, the disadvantages of gleaning surface information through a structured survey questionnaire are outweighed by the large number of observations that survey research offers. Arguably, even mediocre hit-and-run surveys are not bad at offering an insight into patterns of voting behaviour, something that cannot be said of all participant observations. Many participant observers in this book fumble when it comes to describing or anticipating patterns of voting behaviour. If ethnographers substitute survey research on voting behaviour by simply recycling prevailing notions about who voted for whom (as in Dua's essay on the 1967 election), their analysis does not contribute to the ethnographic method.

Part of the difficulty here may be the ethnographer's unfamiliarity with the nature of survey methodology. Gupta's "pre-election opinion poll" and Mittal's use of a sample survey of the voters in her constituency are examples of the risks inherent in deploying unfamiliar methodological tools. It also shows that structured questioning done by a participant observer brings no special insights that a casual investigator will not pick up. Both these experiments may provide a clue as to why surveys may not have been popular among anthropologists.

If the yield of participant observation has to be compared to that of survey research, perhaps a more fair comparison would be to look at the findings of the National Election Study carried out by the CSDS immediately following the mid-term poll in 1971. This survey of a national representative sample of 3800 electors, both men and women, carried out in nineteen states and union territories, provides a mine of still underutilised information on the mind of the Indian voter at that point. This survey found that even after the famous victory of Indira Gandhi at the height of her popularity, 43 per cent of adult citizens did not know who the prime minister was. This first "wave election" in post-Independence India had as many as 72 per cent of the electors completely uninterested in the elections.[12] Here was survey research providing something of a worm's-eye view of the ordinary routine of elections. Unfortunately, we have no signs of any interaction between these two forms of enquiry in the existing literature, nor in the present book.

In this respect, the problem is not the method but how it is deployed. Many essays in this book tend to read off election issues by surface analysis of the content of election speeches, hardly a method the anthropologist would recommend in the study of any other ritual. This is almost like trying to understand the social meaning of an Indian wedding by restricting one's attention to the priest's utterances. In that sense we do not always get here the promised worm's-eye view of how issues get shaped in the arena of electoral competition.

There are some exceptions. Imtiaz Ahmad's distinction between the formal and the informal campaign begins to take this into account, but his description of the informal campaign limits it to appeals to the caste, community, and religious background of voters. Attention must be drawn here to a methodological innovation little noticed in the study of Bageshwar by Sanwal and Sanwal. They use village gossip, information slips issued by polling agents, and a format post-poll survey to reinforce information about voting behaviour. Here is an example of utilisation of the participant observer's skills to foreground the distinct methodological advantage of ethnographic fieldwork over survey fieldwork in a way that could provide lessons for political research.

Finally, let us turn to the question of quantification as a method of analysis. Disciplinary disputes of the 1960s presented the use of numerals as an epistemic choice; accordingly, the world was divided into the quantitative camp and the qualitative camp. Many authors in this book share this consciousness, though some of them do make astute use of election statistics. Perhaps one can use simple common sense against the advocacy of non-quantitative techniques in this book. Common sense would suggest that resisting quantification can scarcely be a virtue when studying a phenomenon to which numbers are intrinsic and quite fundamental (e.g. market prices, lotteries, calendars, etc.). As long as votes are counted, those who study the act of voting have no option except to take counting seriously.

Many of the essays in this book prove this point. Ramaswamy's careful analysis of village-wise voting figures in the Singanallur constituency, Baviskar's analysis of the results of all the booths in the Shirdi constituency, Rao's use of intelligent local guesswork, and Imtiaz Ahmad's approach of putting voting data side by side with the data on the caste composition of the electorate are examples of quantitative analysis that do not take away from the depth of ethnographic analysis. Gupta's essay on Sasni is also something of an exception for its effort to gather caste-wise voting data at the booth level, though there is a hiatus between her data and her argument. Her data actually shows the absence of caste-based voting blocs, contrary to her interpretation. These attempts can be contrasted with the almost casual attention paid by some of the authors to the statistics of electoral outcome in that constituency which introduce disconnection between the explanation and what is sought to be explained.

Thus, on all three counts – unit of analysis, technique of data collection, and data analysis – the strong version of the methodological claim, namely, of the exclusivity and superiority of anthropology, is far from convincing. This is not to say that similar claims by another discipline – say, survey research in political science – are any more secure. Barring a few honourable exceptions, the first generation of election studies based on survey research in the Indian discipline of political science were something of an embarrassment, yielding neither theoretical insights nor even robust empirical measures. Some of these problems have continued to persist: survey research in political science – including, I must hasten to add, my own work – continues to be deficient in relating to the larger theoretical developments in social sciences. Rich discussions in the philosophy of social sciences over the last three decades have suggested the need to move beyond discipline-based methodologies in favour of problem-oriented methods. Such a perspective would recommend that studies of elections combine research on local communities with the study of the macro context, participant observation with formal surveys, and quantitative with qualitative analysis. The methodological toolkit of the social anthropologist thus needs to be reinforced with those of the survey research, political history, and political economy of the context of elections.

Proposal for a Dialogue

The substantive and methodological reviews of the rich material in this book both point to the need for a dialogue between the different disciplines, especially between political science and anthropology. Let me conclude this epilogue by making a concrete proposal on such a dialogue.

In my opinion the constituencies covered in this book provide a wonderful site for such a dialogue, should a group of anthropologists and political scientists choose to revisit them after three and a half decades. I have already said that these constituencies provide a good glimpse of political change from 1967 to 1971. I should add that seen in a longer time frame, too, the constituencies reflected in this volume stand the test of time. The changes in these constituencies reflect larger change in the political landscape over the last three decades.

A quick look at where some of the constituencies discussed in this volume stand in 2006 may be a convenient starting point to register how much the world has changed since 1967. Some of these constituencies have simply disappeared. Both the constituencies of the Metropolitan Council in Delhi have disappeared, along with the Metroplitan Council itself, and been submerged in the new and large assembly constituencies in the National Capital Territory. The assembly constituency of Bannur in Karnataka also disappeared in the redrawing of the electoral map in the mid-1970s – the areas in that constituency now fall under Puttur, a new constituency. But most other constituencies have survived and illustrate very well the changes in party political competition.

Some of these constituencies are very useful sites to investigate the rise of political Hindutva in the last two decades or so. The Swatantra Party has disappeared from the political horizon, giving way to the Bharatiya Janata Party (BJP) in the Chomu assembly constituency in Rajasthan and in Bannur in Karnataka, though as it happens the Jan Sangh was not a force in either of the two places during 1967–71. In Chomu, the demise of the Swatantra Party was followed by the short-lived presence of the Janata Dal, which gave way in that entire region or Rajasthan to the BJP in the 1990s; the BJP won this seat from the Congress in 2004. The Puttur constituency in Karnataka, where a Congress candidate could be opposed only by a rebel Congress candidate in 1967, is now a BJP stronghold, returning that party's MLA since 1994. This area has thus become one of the early entry ports for the BJP in south India. It is a sign of the expansion of the BJP in recent times that it now registers its presence even in the Outer Manipur parliamentary constituency, something unthinkable in 1971.

Both the constituencies of Uttar Pradesh discussed in this volume have seen the decline of the Congress and the rise of new political actors in state politics. New actors have made their presence felt in some of these constituencies. Given the history of Jan Sangh organisation in Sasni town, it is hardly surprising that the Sasni constituency has turned into a BJP stronghold, a seat the party has held for the last three assembly elections. At the same time, the Bahujan Samaj Party has been able to build upon the marginal presence of the RPI there and is the major rival of the BJP. Similarly, given the presence of socialist parties in the 1960s and a significant share of Muslims, it is not surprising that the Rudauli seat in Uttar Pradesh is currently held by the Samajwadi Party. The Thanjavur assembly constituency in Tamil Nadu, where the Congress managed to defy a DMK wave in the state in 1967, is now just another place that witnesses a straight contest between the DMK and the All India Anna Dravida Munnetra Kazhagam (AIADMK), and where the Congress gets a space only when it is in alliance with one of these two.

Only a few of these constituencies present a picture of continuity, though not without subtle changes. Shirdi in Maharashtra, a Congress bastion then, continues to be a Congress bastion – the Congress candidate got nearly 80 per cent votes in the 2004 elections. It was breached once, in the 1999 assembly elections, when the split between the Congress and the Nationalist Congress Parry of Sharad Pawar enabled the Shiv Sena to win this seat. The hill constituency of Bageshwar may have changed its state (it is now a part of Uttraranchal) but the nature of political contest has not changed: it continues to be a Congress versus BJP contest, more so with the elimination of the then SSP. The same is the case with the Jullundur South constituency in Punjab. Here, the religious composition of the electorate has ensured that the earlier support for the Jan Sangh has now shifted to the BJP, in alliance with the Akali Dal. The Singanallur constituency in Tamil Nadu continues to reflect the influence of the trade union movement on electoral politic. The CPI (M), and not the original CPI, maintains a strong presence here and holds the seat in the current assembly.

These constituencies do not cover all the dimensions of political change since 1971 worth analysing. For example, there is nothing in this book from West Bengal and Kerala that could allow us to understand the presence of the Left in those parts of the world. One would also wish for a greater number of case studies from the geographical and social periphery: studies form the Adivasi regions of middle India and the north-east, for example. These gaps can be filled by linking up with some ongoing studies and some case studies undertaken by political scientists.[13]

Notwithstanding these limitations, an attempt to revisit the constituencies covered in the present collection can offer a rich unpacking of political changes across time. I believe such a collaborative research by a group of social scientists cutting across disciplines can push the frontiers of our understanding of democratic politics. Such an attempt needs to begin by recognising that the current state of knowledge on the subject is very inconclusive. At least in India both survey researchers and ethnographers are far from securing the insights associated either with survey research or ethnography. Therefore, a beginning has to be made by learning from the respective disciplinary orthodoxies. The tradition of voting behaviour research in the discipline of political science can offer many insights for developing a model of the Indian voter. Advances in the discipline of anthropology can help us attend to shifting political identities, the construction of meanings, and, of course, the impact of social stratification on politics.

While it is important to begin by mining what the existing disciplines have to offer, a dialogue must go beyond that. Social scientists from varying disciplines must come together to combine their insights in order to explore a common set of questions. These questions will include but not be limited to the classic voting behaviour question: Why do voters vote the way they do? There is a need to ask questions that go beyond routine political behaviour and ethnographic enquiries. These must include some larger questions about the political context of electoral choice, the nature of electoral choice itself and the process of agenda setting. These questions cannot be answered either by survey research or by ethnographic fieldwork alone.[14]

Such a dialogue will be premised on methodological pluralism. It will not and cannot eschew quantitative analysis – including analysis of available official statistics, such as the results of panchayat elections, membership of political parties and pressure groups, and above all booth-wise voting figures that are available once again thanks to the introduction of electronic voting machines.[15] This will include a component of survey-based analysis that maps the basic profile of voting behaviour and its relationship with demographic attributes, as well as political opinions and attitudes. Survey data analysis needs to be linked to analysis of participation patterns, legitimacy of democracy, social basis of leadership, and issue cleavage. Ethnographic studies will be an essential component of such an attempt to understand elections. But, for this to become meaningful, we need to know what function ethnographic fieldwork performs in the field of elections. If the argument offered above is useful, ethnographic fieldwork is uniquely placed to fill three slices in this big picture: a study of political beliefs of ordinary citizens; a study of the making and unmaking of social blocs operating in politics; and a thick description of the local context of electoral choice. An integrated approach to the study of elections can not only provide insights into the functioning of Indian democracy, it can also rescue the discipline of election studies from the intellectual exhaustion that it faces currently.[16]

Acknowledgements

Written as the epilogue to M.N. Srinivas and A.M. Shah (eds), *The Grassroots of Democracy: Field Studies of Indian Elections* (2007), the dialogue that this paper advocates first began as a dialogue with D.L. Sheth, one of the few Indian social scientists at ease within the multiple methodologies of social science. I am grateful to him for his insights into the context of methodological disputes of the 1960s. I am also grateful to A.M. Shah for his exemplary patience and perseverance in putting up with this criticism from outside, not to mention the inordinate delay in delivering him this epilogue. I would like to thank Anindya Saha for his critical reading which cautioned me against overdrawing the contrast between the two disciplines, and for drawing my attention to many references. Thanks are due to Kanchan Malhotra for helping me with data on some of the constituencies studied in this volume.

Notes

1. The reference is to Bernard Cohn's self-description of his professional location, in his essay "An Anthropologist Among the Historians" (1987).

2. Kothari's idea was implicit in "Form and Substance in Indian Politics" (1961) but was fully developed in "The Congress 'System in India' (1964)". It is surprising that there is little attempt in *The Grassroots of Democracy* to engage with this formulation, for it subsequently defined so much of the common sense on Indian politics. Kothari revised his formulation in "The Congress System Revisited: A Decennial Review", 1974.
3. The first and second electoral systems refer to the configurations of party-electoral competitions. For elaboration, see Yadav and Palshikar, 2003.
4. One of the early attempts to think carefully about the relationship between caste and voting was Bashiruddin Ahmed, 1970. But this pioneering attempt to empirically verify some of the models of caste voting was not noticed even by political scientists, let alone scholars outside the discipline.
5. See National Election Study 1971, unweighted data set, CSDS Data Unit. Unfortunately, we do not have a single full-length analysis of this pioneering study. For a detailed analysis of some of the findings of this study, see Sheth, 1975.
6. One of the simple reasons for this inability is the absence of time series data. The National Election Study series at CSDS is the only systematic evidence that allows comparison across time. But the early studies do not have a sample that allows analysis of data at the state level. Besides, there are huge gaps in the series between 1971 and 1996.
7. As a rule, participants in these methodological debates showed little awareness of the debates in the philosophy of social sciences that were shaking the foundations of some of the naive empiricism that informed these disputes. This is precisely the time when positivist notions of the truth were being challenged by hermeneutics, phenomenology, critical school, and post-empiricist philosophy of science. For an overview of these debates, see Delanty and Strydom, 2003.
8. Indian anthropologists went a step ahead of others in reflecting on the methodology of their craft. See Srinivas, Shah, and Ramaswamy, 1979: Béteille and Madan, 1975, Panini, 1991, Nita Kumar, 1992, and Thapan, 2002. There are a few equivalents of these reflections in the study of politics. Narain, *et al.* (1978) did not go beyond a formal review of the various studies. Hebsur (2000) is methodologically more self-conscious but yet to see the light of day.
9. For one of the few exceptions to this, see Hursh-Cesar and Roy, 1976. However, there is very little in this book on surveys of political opinions

and attitudes and on the specific challenges faced in this regard in the Indian context.

10. See Kothari, 1967. This includes the famous study of the Modasa constituency by Ghanshyam Shah and Rajni Kothari. The same is true of early works on Indian politics by Paul Brass and Myron Weiner.
11. I am not suggesting that a weakness in understanding the micro–macro interaction is intrinsic to the fieldwork method or is bound to the discipline of anthropology. Bailey's study of politics in Orissa (1970) consciously moved from the village to the district and then to the state. Cohn's work (1987) is a good instance of integrating not just the micro with the macro but also the here and now with a long-term historical view.
12. See also in this context the unweighted data set of the National Election Study 1971, CSDS Data Unit.
13. I am thinking here of Mukulika Banerjee's ongoing research on West Bengal, and that of Lucia Michelutti's and Craig Jefferey's on Uttar Pradesh. For some recent case studies by political scientists, see *Economic and Political Weekly*, 13–20 January 1996.
14. For a good recent example of research on elections that combines ethnographic fieldwork with careful quantitative analysis and rational choice theory, see Chandra, 2004.
15. The first generation of studies of Indian elections made a lot of use of booth-wise voting data to circumvent the problem of data inadequacy. After 1971 the Election Commission of India made it a policy not to release booth-level data. The practice of mixing ballots from all booths before counting the votes made this information inaccessible. The introduction of electronic voting machines since 1999 has made the booth-wise data public information, though it is still not easy to access it. This opens a gold mine of information for scholars interested in studying elections in their local context.
16. See Franklin and Wlezien, 2002.

References

Ahmed, Bashiruddin. 1970. "Caste and Electoral Politics". *Asian Survey* (10:11), November.

Bailey, F.G. 1970. *Political and Social Change: Orissa in 1959*. Berkeley: University of California Press.

Béteille, André, and T.N. Madan (eds). 1975. *Encounter and Experience: Personal Accounts of Fieldword*. Delhi: Vikas.

Chandra, Kanchan. 2004. *Why Ethnic Parties Succeed: Patronage and Ethnic Head Counts in India*. Cambridge: Cambridge University Press.

Cohn, Bernard S. 1987. *An Anthropologist Among the Historians and Other Essays*. Delhi: Oxford University Press.

Delanty, Gerard, and Piet Strydom (eds). 2003. *Philosophy of Social Sciences: The Classic and Contemporary Readings*. Maidenhead: Open University Press.

Franklin, Mark M., and Christopher Wlezien (eds). 2002. *Future of Election Studies*. Elsevier: Pergamon.

Hebsur, R.K. 2000. "Studies on Indian Politics: Research Designs and Strategies". Unpublished manuscript submitted to the Indian Council of Social Science Research (ICSSR), New Delhi.

Hursh-Cesar, Gerald, and Pradipto Roy (eds). 1976. *Third World Surveys: Survey Research in Developing Nations*. Delhi: Macmillan.

Kothari, Rajni. 1961. "Form and Substance in Indian Politics". *Economic Weekly* (XII: 3), June.

———. 1964. "The Congress 'System' in India", *Asian Survey* (4: 12), December.

———. 1974. "The Congress System Revisited: A Decennial Review". *Asian Survey* (24:12), December.

———. et al. 1967. *Party System and Election Sudies*. Bombay: Allied. On behalf of Centre for the Study of Developing Societies, Delhi.

Kumar, Nita. 1992. *Friends, Brothers, Informants: Fieldwork Memoirs of Banaras*. Berkeley: University of California Press.

Narain, Iqbal, *et al.*, 1978. *Election Studies in India*. Delhi: Allied. On behalf of ICSSR, New Delhi.

Panini, M.N. (ed.). 1991. *From the Female Eye: Accounts of Female Fieldworkers Studying Their Own Communities*. Delhi: Hindustan.

Sheth, D.L. (ed.). 1975. *Citizens and Parties: Aspects of Competitive Politics in India*. Delhi: Allied.

Srinivas, M.N., A.M. Shah, and E.A. Ramaswamy (eds). 1979. *The Fieldworker and the Field: Problems and Challenges in Sociological Investigation*. Delhi: Oxford University Press. Second edition, 2002.

Thapan Meenakshi (ed.). 2002. *Anthropological Journey: Reflections on Fieldwork*. Delhi: Orient Longman.

Yadav, Yogendra. 1999. "Electoral Politics in a Time of Change: India's Third Electoral System, 1989–99". *Economic and Political Weekly* (34: 35), 21–28 August.

——— and Suhas Palshikar. 2003. "From Hegemony to Convergence: Party System and Electoral Politics in the Indian States, 1952–2002". *Journal of Indian School of Political Economy* (15: 1&2), January–June.

14

A Radical Agenda for Political Reforms

What is Not to be Done?

IS THERE A RADICAL agenda for political reforms in contemporary India? Does politics of social transformation have a readily available checklist of what needs to be done in the sphere of political institutions and practices? Or, at the very least, does it have a robust sense of the direction in which to move? I wish to suggest that such an agenda is not available, even in the minimal sense of the term.

The present essay begins by defending this suggestion and exploring why we find ourselves in such a sorry state. The latter half of the essay is an attempt to fill this gap. It offers some thoughts on how to go about constructing such an agenda, or perhaps on how not to think about political reforms. The essay concludes by separating what I call the "old" and the "new" arenas of political reforms and offering a rough checklist of what needs to be done in each of these. The principal ambition that underlines this enterprise is to rehabilitate political common sense as an appropriate mode of thinking about political reform.

The Absence of a Ready-made Agenda

We begin to get a sense of the absence of a radical agenda on political reforms by contrasting it with the radical agenda on the economy. The latter is in no great shape today. The last decade has certainly shaken radicals out of the complacent belief that this agenda will be realised for them by a benign movement of history. The agenda seems to be fast disappearing from the horizon of realisable dreams. Its empirical assumptions and institutional expression are increasingly under serious dispute. It turns out that some of the critical details of this agenda were never clearly worked out.

Yet there is a sense in which we still possess a radical economic agenda: there are some guiding values, a sense of the direction to move towards, and a shared understanding of what to welcome and what to resist. A similar focus on the social and environmental question would also bring out the existence of such an agenda, notwithstanding all the attendant complications.

One could argue similarly that there is a radical political agenda which radical political mobilisation must aim at. But no such agenda is available to us on the question of reforming the institutional design and practices of politics so as to improve the chances of politics yielding whatever we expect of it. It is unclear as to what the radicals should stand for in this realm.

It is not uncommon for practitioners to speak as if everyone knows what needs to be done. But efforts at spelling it out rarely go beyond the facile consensus of a drawing room conversation: that there is something radically wrong with the national enterprise, that politics is at the heart of our ills, and that it must be reformed to resurrect the wonder that could be India. There could be agreement on some isolated items – appointing a *lokpal* or state funding of elections. But the various items do not fit into an integral whole that displays some internal coherence, nor is there a hierarchy of significance at work in such thinking. In this sense there is no radical agenda for political reforms in contemporary India.

There is nothing new about this absence. The current mismatch between the significance attached to political reforms and the cognitive attention paid to it has characterised this subject right from the beginning. Thinking about political reforms has been seriously debilitated from two directions in post-Independence India. The mainstream or establishment thinking has been caught in the prison-house of realism. A fascination with the new constitution and the entire gamut of constitutional practices prevented mainstream thinking from going beyond considerations of minor tinkering with the legal-constitutional framework. There was a latent anxiety, no doubt, about the inability of

Indian democracy to attain the "correct" form of Western democratic institutions – the non-emergence of a two-party system, the non-correspondence between the Indian Parliament and Westminster, and so on.

It must have been depressing for them, for the establishment did believe in what Roberto Unger has described as "institutional fetishism", the idea that political values have a unique, single, and necessary institutional expression. In a post-colonial setting institutional fetishism mixed with an awe of the West produced a set of cognitive and practical impediments to thinking about political institutions. But this anxiety did not result in a comprehensive set of proposals to reform the polity.

The critics of the establishment too, on the other hand, never thought carefully about political reforms. For left-wing critics, the word "reform" always carried a tinge of suspicion, the fear of being caught in a reformist trap. In their worldview it made little sense to think about reforming the existing political design, for they aimed at nothing less than a complete overhaul, nothing short of revolution. The trouble was that the political design of the post-revolutionary state was never attended to beyond some vague and poetic gestures in Marx's writings. There was little attention paid to how political institutions of the future would relate to the existing gamut of social and political institutions in a society like India. Thinking about these subjects, like so much else, was relegated to the "last instance" that never arrived.

At the other end of the spectrum of critics of the liberal democratic set-up, the Gandhians too shared the communists' temptation to write on a clean slate. Shrimannarayan's alternative constitution for independent India was not quite a proposal for political reform. It was an alternative design for a new polity. Perhaps Jayaprakash Narayan's "A plea for the reconstruction for the Indian polity" was the only comprehensive set of proposals for radical political reform. In retrospect his critique looks ahead of his time. It is striking how many of the ills of our political system were seen by him in a climate much less conducive to discussing such issues.

Unlike other reformists of his time, JP did not lack for bold imagination. What he perhaps did lack was realism, not in the sense of being non-practical and unfeasible but in the deeper sense of not connecting to sociological reality, of being insufficiently grounded in a sense of power and causality of everyday life. The village community on which JP rested his entire communitarian model may never have existed. Like the communists, JP was unwilling to spell out his model in relation to the existing gamut of modern political institutions and practices.

In that sense the Lohia socialists were something of an exception. Lohia's vision of a *chaukhamba raj* or a four-pillar state was a much less radical departure from the existing institutions than was the case with his other radical contemporaries. His plea for the centre, and state, district, and village-level governments as the four pillars of a decentralised state structure anticipates much of the discussion on political decentralisation in the 1990s. But, like so many of his ideas, his proposals remained in the realm of broad gestures that were never worked out.

The challenge of thinking about political reform fell between the two stools of conservative constitutionalism and its visionary critiques. Political reforms came to be an area where our convictions were insufficiently grounded and even less sufficiently worked out. Something of a cross between these two tendencies also accounts for the common sense on political reforms that developed between the 1970s and 1990s. This common sense was first articulated in the arena of electoral reforms by the Tarkunde Committee and then in documents like "An Agenda for India" (*Seminar*, 245 and 251, January and July 1980), the Dinesh Goswami report on electoral reforms and the writings of L.P. Singh and S.L. Shakdher.

All these efforts created something of a consensus on at least some familiar items of political reforms: thinking about a proportional or mixed electoral system as a substitute for the first-past-the-post (FPTP) system, an anti-defection law, the institution of a lokpal, and state funding of elections. More than these specific items, common sense also defined some basic attributes of the dominant thinking about political reforms. Like the establishment and the revolutionaries, reformers also focused on institutions of high national politics: the national legislature and the executive. The objectives of reform were still quite generalised: to clear the system of corrupt practices and to ensure free and fair elections. The favoured instrument of political reforms was legal-constitutional change. At the same time it was recognised that these changes needed to be backed by political action.

The Rise of a Conservative Perspective

The last decade has changed all that. The question of political reform has never enjoyed as much public attention as it did in the last decade. Greater public attention and priority to political reforms did not, however, produce a radical agenda for political reforms. On the contrary, there has been a clear shift to a conservative agenda on political reforms. To be sure this shift is not a direct outcome of the rise of the Bharatiya Janata Party (BJP) during the same period; the new conservative agenda is not communal. Yet the rise of the political right makes it possible to articulate positions that were impermissible earlier.

The change in India cannot also be directly linked to the changing global paradigms of democracy. The global vocabulary of good governance has not yet come to dominate our thinking on politics the way it has in Africa and other parts of the third world and the way its economic counterpart dominates our thinking on the economy. Yet the intellectual climate of globalisation has played a deep role in eroding our collective sense of alternative possibilities in the realm of politics too. Coupled with the domestic anxieties of a highly articulate "middle class" (a euphemism for the urban, upper-caste, consuming class in India) in a post-Mandal phase of democratic politics, best captured in the rhetoric of Seshan or the prescriptions of the Law Commission, this new discourse on political reform has quietly taken over the popular imagination. The formation and the preliminary output of the National Commission to Review the Working of the Constitution falls squarely within this imagination.

Let us look at some attributes of this conservative perspective that dominates thinking on political reforms. First, it shares with its predecessors the preoccupation with institutions of high politics: national legislature, executive, and possibly judiciary. There may be an occasional reference to panchayati raj, but the principal focus of the intellectual and practical energy is on changing the design of the central government. Second, there is a universal search for a good political or electoral system with a view to importing the best political practices to India. Although there is a ritual reference to contemporary malpractices in Indian democracy, the proposals are not anchored in any analysis of here and now. No wonder the result is a kind of Internet shopping in a global constitutional superstore (American two-party system, German constructive vote of confidence, French mix of the presidential and parliamentary systems, and so on).

Third, there is a simplistic belief in the magic of design. All that is required to solve a problem is to change the law. Once you have the right design, the desired set of consequences will follow as a matter of course. What it does not consider is the phenomenon of unintended consequences, and that these are not random or accidental. The idea that all constitutional and legal designs have political consequences that can largely be anticipated is alien to this mode of thinking.

This is related to a fourth attribute. The conservative perspective has a very narrow understanding of design itself. An institutional design is understood as a legal-constitutional design alone. Politics is external to this design of democracy, if not seen as an outright nuisance. Much of the contemporary discussion on political reforms proceeds as if democracy can flourish without politics. No wonder many of these designs reflect a deep fear of politics and are an attempt to wish it away. Finally, the dominant perspective is not anchored sociologically; it does not sufficiently differentiate between the various sections of society that stand to benefit or lose from specific acts of political or electoral reforms. No wonder an undifferentiated discussion about "citizens" does not turn out to be a view from nowhere. Much of the ethical anxiety underlying the dominant perspective on electoral reforms reflects the concerns of the so-called middle class.

The consequences of this approach are by now familiar. The political doctor identifies the symptoms of the disease that afflicts our body politic: the role of money and muscle power, political opportunism, decline in the moral fibre of the leadership, and so on. The tone reflects a deep hatred, not just of politicians and political parties but of politics itself. A new item now enters the list: political instability, understood in terms of the stability of governments. The diagnosis for all these ills is simple: an absence of effective legal controls on politicians and political parties. As for instability, proliferation of political parties is seen as the root cause of the malaise.

The prescription naturally follows from this diagnosis: a strict regime of legal controls on the entry of criminals and the role of money in electoral politics, plus a series of measures to ensure that the political arena is de-crowded and governmental stability ensured (increase in security deposit, additional conditionalities for contesting elections, banning independents, denying seats to small parties, fixed term for the legislatures, and so on).

Thus the mainstream perspective now threatens to turn into a conservative platform for refashioning the political structures to suit the interests of a small, hitherto entrenched but now threatened class. This agenda amounts to nothing short of undoing the results of the democratic upsurge of the last decade. It is all about sanitising democracy for decent citizens "like us", saving democracy from the people. In this version political reform is a corollary of and an effective vehicle for the "economic reforms" package of liberalisation, privatisation, and globalisation, a prerequisite for rolling back the state.

Faced with this onslaught, the radicals have retreated into a defensive battle for preserving the basics of a liberal democratic framework. Those who spent a lifetime highlighting the deficiencies of the Indian constitution are now busy defending its progressive features and investing it with a newly discovered sanctity. At this rate it is not inconceivable that the radicals may be reduced to defending the bare minimums of universal adult franchise. The cognitive ambition of restructuring the polity in line with some dreams about a future society and economy has been surrendered, not dissimilarly to what has happened in the economic arena. However, in the political arena radicals cannot even demand what Unger calls a "ten per cent discount". Their fragile intellectual heritage on this subject leads them into unthinking collaboration with their adversaries.

It is not uncommon to see well-meaning democrats share the middle-class angst about politics and parrot an anti-political vocabulary. Their institutional agenda is not too dissimilar from the conservative agenda in its focus on a regime of legal controls. With the sole exception of a consistent (and, typically, institutionally ill-designed) advocacy of women's reservations, radical democrats have contributed little to the agenda of political reforms in recent times, never mind a comprehensive proposal on institutional redesigning.

There is hardly a serious challenge to the emerging conservative agenda on political reforms. In the resultant imaginative deficit, radical gestures of political reform take a strange turn. There is a misplaced moral outburst when salaries and perks for MPs are raised to a level lower than those of senior bureaucrats (see Yadav 2001). There is an innocent belief that providing for a "negative vote" on the ballot or arming voters with a "right to recall" will solve the ills of our democracy. A sense of deep pessimism that informs radicals today is self-evident. What is not clear to them is that their lack of imagination is partly responsible for the narrow horizon of political possibilities open to them.

A brief comment on the contribution of the academic discipline of political science to thinking about political reforms is in order at this point. If it has contributed little to a radical agenda for political reform, it is not because the discipline lacked a radical orientation, at least in the obvious sense of political affiliation. The top intellectual and institutional spaces in this discipline were dominated by academics with progressive, if not left, affiliations in the last couple of decades. The problem was that they simply did not find the challenge of institutional redesign worthy of their attention.

The dominance of political theory resulted in trivialising any academic work that dealt with real-life institutions and policies. This came from a mix of Marxist superstition that the revolution will look after everything and the brahminic arrogance in dealing with the nitty-gritty of institutional functioning. Those who did not share the radical orientation and its resultant indifference to the question of political reforms shared in some form or the other the fetishism of Western institutions. The state of the discipline of public administration is living testimony to this intellectual catastrophe.

All in all, professional practitioners of political science either reproduced the prejudices of the politics they espoused or, worse, the social class they came from. Far from providing an intellectual design for political practitioners, the discipline failed to provide even the empirical information on which such designing and innovation may take place. The closest the discipline came to contributing to national debates on political reforms was recently when some political scientists allegedly wrote one of the most embarrassing consultation papers of the National Commission to Review the Working of the Constitution. None of the recent initiatives on political reforms – the Mazdoor Kisan Shakti Sangathan's (MKSS) campaign on the right to information, Lok Satta's various initiatives on electoral rolls and finance reforms, and Nagarpalika Network's efforts at rejuvenating local democracy – could draw upon any idea, information, or insight from the discipline.

An Approach to a Radical Agenda

Let me not dwell any more on how not to think about political reforms. It is time to explicate the hints embedded in the above critique and offer constructive suggestions on approaching this subject. If the critique offered above has any merit, what we need is nothing less than a paradigm shift from a state-of-the-art view of political technology to the "appropriate technology" view of things, from thinking of democracy as hardware to recognition that it is a software that depends on protocols of reception.

We begin to clear the conceptual ground for thinking about political reforms by getting rid of some of the reigning superstitions of our times: the idea that there is a universally valid institutional design of liberal democracy; the suggestion that a set of best political practices can and should be replicated all over the world; the theory that the idea of democracy can be reduced to a standard "checklist".

Once it is recognised that there is no universally applicable and valid package of political reforms or a model of democracy, it follows that a reasonable starting point for thinking about political reforms is here and now in India, AD 2001. We can thus take the next step of working towards an agenda that is anchored in time and space, is consequence sensitive, takes the logic of politics as integral to thinking about institutional design, and is conscious of the differential consequences for different social groups. Working out such an agenda means asking some fundamental questions: Why do we need political reforms? Why at this stage? What should we prioritise? And, who is this "we", the bearer of this responsibility?

This paradigm shift has another fundamental implication that must be noted. If here and now is the only starting point available to us, there is not and will never be a clean political slate to write our dreams on. The existing gamut of political institutions and practices is the building bloc available to institutional innovators. What exists can be transformed – and the whole point of institutional innovation is to transform these in the right direction – but it has to be replaced or repaired brick by brick. It follows that the entire range of modern political institutions formally inaugurated by the Indian constitution and the patterns of competitive politics cannot simply be wished away. Once introduced, the compulsions of organising political life on the scale of a nation state cannot be rolled back at will.

It is a terrible thought for those who are conscious of the human costs of political modernity. But it may be tempered by the recent recognition that modernity has had multiple trajectories in history and can be made to have many more in the future. This abstract idea has a concrete corollary for those who take JP's critique of parliamentary democracy in India seriously. The point of his critique and the vision underlying it can still be rescued if we see the challenge of political reforms as not that of going back to any traditional model but as one of forging a different kind of modernity suited to our requirements and values.

The agenda of political reform in India has to be different from the challenge in the advanced industrial democracies, for our problem is not demobilisation and slowing down of democracy (contra Unger's diagnosis of Western democracies). At the same time, unlike other new democracies of the third world, India does not face the challenge of democratic transition or consolidation (see Linz and Stepan 1996). The problems in Indian democracy are not the result of a failure of the modern idea of democracy to take root in an alien setting. Rather we are faced with problems arising out of an apparent success of the democratic experiment.

People accepted the democratic invitation and over the years popular political participation has only gone up. The last decade has seen something of a democratic upsurge. Popular participation is not devoid of a sense of legitimacy and efficacy of the democratic system. The elections are free and fair in the minimal sense that the rulers are not assured of a return to power; they are at least more free and fair than in most third world democracies. Yet the existence of this democracy does not deliver what democracies are supposed to: people's control over how collective decisions affecting their lives are arrived at.

The real failure of the current phase of Indian democracy is not the failure to hold free and fair elections, nor the inability of the people to affect change in governments through the exercise of their free vote, but the growing distortion in the mechanism of political representation, the growing distance between the electors and the elected, the inability of the mechanism of competitive politics to serve as a means of exercising effective policy options. Clearly, the institutional frame of democracy has failed to translate popular participation and enthusiasm into a set of desirable consequences.

This is not merely a universal deficit in the promise of democracy. We are looking at a range of failures that are rooted more specifically in our experience. Some of them were written into the logic of democracy in a society like India. The fundamental contradiction pointed out by Ambedkar, that of instituting equal citizenship in a highly unequal society, lies at the root of many of the failures. Social inequality was further accentuated by unequal access to the means of forming and disseminating public opinion. Another contradiction was built into the act of importing political institutions, especially those that required autonomy, in a cultural setting where attitudinal prerequisites were missing. There was the structural problem of constituting a polity to coincide with the boundaries of a civilisation when much of the meaningful political action and mobilisation could take place in micro settings.

Some other failures of the democratic experiments are not structural, but specific to the history of democracy over the last fifty years. The weak policy orientation of dalit-bahujan politics, a lack of emphasis on institution building, the decision not to change the character of the bureaucracy and the retreat of the state in the face of the forces of globalisation were in no way necessary to the design of

Indian democracy. But these have contributed substantially to the democratic deficit facing us today.

The principal task of political reform is to address the democratic deficit and some of its root causes. Specifically, the challenge is to strengthen devices that facilitate popular mobilisation and its effective expression in the formation of political agendas, the formulation of governmental policies and their effective execution. In the context of the retreat of the state there is a need to bring back the primacy of politics and restore its capacity to act as the principal vehicle of social change. The litmus test for any proposal of "radical" political reforms is its ability to deepen the ongoing process of democratisation for social groups and communities that have historically been denied access to political power.

If this understanding of the deficits of Indian democracy and the need for political reforms is not entirely off the mark, some conclusions about the arena and the instruments of political reform follow. First, it needs to be recognised that political reform constitutes a critical part of the agenda of social transformation in today's India. Radicals of all hues have by now accepted that democratic struggle is the only path to social transformation. But they have not fully understood its implication: it requires bold institutional imagination with eyes and wings to be able to use the existing democratic apparatus for radical ends.

The second set of conclusions relates to the arena of reforms. They should not be confined to or focused on electoral reforms, as has often been the case. The scope needs to be expanded to include the entire range of political reforms in the comprehensive sense of the term. Similarly, the focus should shift away from the high arena of national politics towards the intermediary and lower levels where democratic governance meets, or rather fails to meet, the people. The "lower" levels in the political and administrative hierarchy must not occupy a low position in the agenda for political reform.

Finally, the question of instruments. There is a case for thinking beyond law as the privileged agent of political reform. While a substantial part of institutional innovation must be carried out through or at least reflected in legal changes, there is a need to shift the emphasis of analytical energy to thinking about other instruments (public opinion, media, social movements) that must accompany or supplement legal-constitutional changes so as to yield the desired institutional practices. This is crucial, for there are the unrealised possibilities of existing institutions. As the example of the Election Commission of India itself shows, institutional practices can improve substantially even within the given legal-institutional framework.

And now, finally, to the agenda itself, to a quick overview of the items that should find a place in the radical agenda for political reforms in contemporary India. Let us first revisit the "old arena", the high ground of national politics that has in the past attracted most political reformers and see if some familiar items appear in a different light today. We can then try to outline the "new arena" of political reforms. I simply present the bare conclusions rather than offer detailed reasoning for each of these.

The Old Arena of Political Reforms

Redesigning the electoral system has figured prominently in the agenda for political reforms even before the Tarkunde Committee. The first generation of reformers were quite persuaded by the merits of proportional representation as against the existing FPTP system. I think there is a need to rethink whether panchayati raj (PR) needs to figure on the radical agenda and if the issue of the electoral system deserves the salience in the agenda of political reforms that it has enjoyed in the past. The changing pattern of politics, the rise of region-based parties, and the decline of national parties have automatically corrected the vote–seat imbalance at the national level and rendered harmless some of the classic arguments in favour of the PR system.

Besides, there is insufficient recognition in radical circles of the virtues of the existing system, especially its impact on the politics of social cleavages. By forcing political actors to form social coalitions at the constituency level, the existing system promotes social cohesion, while a PR system can easily turn into a system of separate electorates. It seems much of the enthusiasm for a PR system emanates from a lack of careful analysis of the political consequences of this system (see Sridharan 2001, for an exception) and an insufficient awareness of its disastrous consequences in countries like Sri Lanka. It only illustrates how an agenda of political reforms can get distorted by attractive global imports.

If there is any need to tinker with the electoral system, it is with a view to address two specific problems: under-representation of women and Muslims. In both cases the under-representation is gross and structural, and therefore unlikely to be overcome in the normal course. Both these are fit cases for redesigning institutions. But it needs to be ensured that the proposed change would achieve the objective and that its side effects will not outweigh the benefits. The Women's Reservation Bill (WRB) that proposes to reserve one-third of the seats in the legislatures does not meet these elementary criteria. It is not clear if the reservation of geographical constituencies is the best route in this case, especially given all the attendant effects of the rotation system. The WRB illustrates the lack of attention to the challenge of institutional design in radical circles (see, for example, otherwise very insightful and valuable articles by Nivedita Menon [2000] and Mary John [2007]. It seems to me that, on balance, the alternative of mandatory quota of tickets for women by every recognised party better meets the objective of the WRB: for details, see Madhu Kishwar, *et al.* 2000).

The first difficulty with addressing the problem of under-representation of Muslims is the inability and unwillingness of radicals to discuss it openly. Once we overcome that, we come across a real dilemma. It is possible to design a system, either through careful delimitation that produces Muslim-plurality constituencies or through a "top-up" arrangement of a semi-proportionate system to ensure that Muslim representation in the legislature goes up substantially. But in both these cases the result will have been achieved at the cost of reducing the clout of the Muslim electorate in the remaining constituencies. And some of these measures may not have healthy effects for the entire polity. Working a way out of this dilemma is one of the most pressing challenges of institutional innovation in India.

Like with the electoral system, changing the basic design of the executive legislature relationship has attracted reformers right from the beginning. A desire to flirt with some form or the other of US-style presidentialism is not new. But what was earlier an innocent if sad desire to copy everything American has taken a specific political hue in recent years. Now it is a not-so-innocent design to tilt the political scales in favour of a national political party like the BJP. The arguments for the presidential system show little understanding of what this system was originally designed to produce. It also reveals a complete ignorance of the disastrous record of the presidential system all over the world, especially in Latin America (see Linz and Valenzuela 1994).

The same is true about a fixed tenure for the legislature that goes against the basic spirit and functional requirements of the parliamentary system. The system of a constructive vote of confidence would solve a minor problem, only to create a much bigger constitutional deadlock (see James Manor). As of now there seems to be little reason to doubt or revise the wisdom of our constitution makers on the choice of a parliamentary form of government. In fact, a resolute opposition to any proposal for change should be on the agenda for political reforms.

A small suggestion worth considering about executive powers is that the appointment and accountability of high constitutional offices should be ensured through a constitutional appointment committee comprising the leader of the opposition, the speaker, the chief justice of the Supreme Court, besides the prime minister. Giving more powers to the lokpal and the *lokayuktas* is a suggestion in the same direction.

Another set of proposals have traditionally focused on the composition of the legislatures, either on the question of allocation of seats in the legislatures or preventing party switch after elections. On the former, the 91st Constitutional Amendment Bill has already been passed by Parliament without sufficient national debate and awareness of its implications. Alistair McMillan is quite justified in arguing that the decision to freeze interstate allocation in the name of population control violates the basic one-person one-vote principle of our constitution. His suggestion that federal political balancing should be attempted by restructuring the Rajya Sabha to give greater representation to smaller states needs to be taken seriously.

The anti-defection law represents one of the few cases of successful institutional innovation in post-Independence India. While it would be sad to give up its gains, it would be fatal to try and "tighten" it up by banning defections altogether. The disastrous implications of such a provision for inner-party democracy must be weighed against any presumed gains. The anti-defection act needs fine-tuning by making the Election Commission rather than the speaker the adjudicator of any dispute. The political horse trading and money games played before the Rajya Sabha elections could be discouraged by allowing political parties to inspect the record of how their legislators voted.

Another favourite subject of old-style political reforms was to legislate on the nature of the party system, mainly to determine the number of players and to bring it close to the "ideal" of a two-party system. It was often driven by the idea that a party system can be picked from the supermarket of political designs. Historically, party systems evolve partly in response to the nature of the electoral system and partly in response to the nature of society and political traditions. We can only tinker with it by encouraging or discouraging a certain growth, but any attempt to genetically modify the entire system is likely to be disastrous, as in Nigeria. It is not clear why the evolution of the party system in the last decade or so needs to be viewed as pathological. What looks like the fragmentation of the party system has in fact brought parties closer to the ground and facilitated the practice of accountability (see Yadav 1999). Since none of the region-based parties have a separatist agenda, it is not clear why this development poses a threat to the nation.

The focus of attention on the party system should shift from the number of parties to what they do. There is a case for two kinds of reforms here:

- There is a need for minimalist legislation to regulate the internal functioning of political parties. The legislation could require political parties to follow their own constitution, to allow for external adjudication in the last instance, maintain an open register of membership, and provide for regular and democratic election to the highest decision-making body. At the same time the temptation to legislate on every aspect of the functioning of political parties must be resisted (see Mehta 2004).
- Contrary to dominant opinion, there is in fact a special need to protect small political formations, along the lines of saving small-scale industry from big monopoly houses in the economic realm. The experience of the last few decades shows that the compulsions of large-scale and huge resources built into our

existing system tend to kill smaller political formations, forcing them to become part of one of the big parties. Not only should any attempt to further discourage smaller parties (as suggested by the Law Commission) be resisted, institutional innovations should be made to enable the smaller formations overcome unfair competition of scale and resources. This could be done by not allowing recognised parties to participate in the panchayat elections or by making available monetary and other resources on a non-discriminatory basis.

Some old and long-standing suggestions for controlling electoral malpractices need to be noted and endorsed here, while remembering that in the last instance it is the popular verdict that controls such malpractices:

- Electoral rolls should be put under the charge of local post offices, as suggested by Lok Satta's campaign on electoral roll reforms.
- The proportion of tendered votes should be linked to the requirement for repolling in the booth.
- Candidates should be made to declare the cases pending against him or her involving charges of criminal conduct or corruption at the time of filing nominations.
- Similarly, candidates should declare property and income for the last three years at the time of filing nominations. False declaration on both these should be a ground for disqualification.
- The returns of expenses filed by the candidates and the tax returns filed by political parties should be made public.
- The ceiling on election expenditure should be regularly increased and fixed only at a point where one candidate's expense affects all the others.
- Political advertising on television should be banned before it can take off and develop vested interests.
- The new delimitation exercise should be made more professional and transparent along the lines of the recommendations of an experts workshop held this year.

The New Arena of Political Reform

Valuable as these reforms in the old arena are, I have suggested that a radical agenda for political reforms must not foreground these. The attention should now shift to the new arena of reforms that has opened up, thanks to the issues highlighted by social and non-party political movements in the last decade or so. Some of these go beyond the traditional boundaries of political reform and spill over into "administrative", "judicial", and "media" reforms. But then the point of the new arena is to question the rationale of the earlier boundaries. The new arena reforms can be divided into four parts: (i) measures to safeguard the primacy of democratic governance; (ii) measures for decentring the polity and reducing the compulsions of scale; (iii) measures to ensure a less unequal access to resources in politics; and (iv) measures to encourage democratisation of political information and opinions.

Not all of these suggestions are new. The Agenda for India, for instance, did anticipate some of these suggestions, especially the second set, way back in 1980. But as a package this articulates a new thinking implicit in some of the recent attempts at political reforms.

Let us consider these four areas one by one. The first set of measures try to respond to the anxiety about the erosion of democratically elected authorities in the last decade either to the bureaucratic and the technocratic establishment or to international economic institutions. These erosions threaten to undo many of the gains of the democratic upsurge in the last decade. Some possible suggestions:

- It should be mandatory for the government to get any international economic agreement ratified by Parliament. This would cover not only the treaties under the World Trade Organization but also the memorandums of understanding signed with bodies like the International Monetary Fund.
- Similar treaties that affect the subjects in the state list must be ratified by a majority of state legislatures.
- Every non-elective regulatory authority should be subjected to public accountability.
- The recent practice of Groups of Ministers to short-circuit decision-making in the ministries should be discouraged.

The need for political decentralisation is clearly not a new subject. It has been commented upon and spelt out at length and in the last decade our polity has moved in that direction thanks to the 73rd and 74th Amendments and the change in our party system. What is required is to press for the consolidation of these gains and to see these as measures of political reform:

- Greater financial powers for the state governments as suggested by the Sarkaria Commission.
- Strengthening the new PR framework by making it mandatory to devolve greater powers and financial resources to panchayats and nagarpalikas and ensuring the role of gram sabhas.
- Constitution of another State Reorganisation Commission to go into the various demands for small states.
- Include within the purview of such a commission the question of greater political autonomy to backward regions within large states by expanding the scope of the institution of Autonomous Councils beyond Scheduled Tribe areas.

The issue of unequal access to resources in politics has conventionally been taken up in the old arena as a measure for reducing the role of "money power" in politics with its typical emphasis on a regime of controls to ensure a ceiling on political expenses. The emphasis should now shift from the issue of ceiling to that of securing a floor, from a regime of controls to a package of enabling measures to ensure adequate and equal supply of resources. Contrary to popular impression based on highly publicised cases of national- and state-level political elites, there is a serious dearth of legitimate resources in politics, made worse by grossly unequal distribution of what is available. The problem is not that spending more money ensures victory in elections, but that lack of money denies an entry into the political arena. This area acquires new salience in the context of the democratic upsurge from below and the rolling back of the welfare state. Some measures to rectify this inequality are:

- State funding by way of reimbursement of election expenses for each candidate or party at the rate of, say, Rs 10 for each vote secured.

- Funds to be given on a non-discriminatory basis to all the candidates/parties, and not only to recognised political parties as suggested by the Indrajit Gupta Committee.
- Funding to be available in cash rather than kind (again, contra the Gupta Committee) so that it could be used for political activities between elections.
- Tax exemption up to a certain limit to individuals and companies for contributions to political parties.
- Civil society initiatives to set up public funds for political workers.

Finally, the arena of democratising information promises to be one of the most critical for political reforms in the years to come, an arena where traditional state legislation is a weak instrument of reforms. Some proposals are:

- Struggle for "right to information" not only in the sense of demand for central and state legislation, but in the wider sense of movement for direct and democratic accountability of state functionaries to the people by organisations like the MKSS.
- Measures like the Kerala initiative for direct participation of the people in policy formulation and developmental planning.
- Restoring the spirit of the independent public broadcaster behind the Prasar Bharati legislation and removing all recent distortions.
- Measures to democratise the ownership of private media and curb monopolistic practices, and to ensure easy access to cheap media to small groups and movements.
- Restrictions and regulations on the operation of foreign media, whether in print or otherwise.
- Measures to change the social profile of media practitioners and to ensure the entry of communities that were denied access to higher learning.
- Evolving a self-regulatory code for opinion polls, prescribing greater methodological transparency and rigour, so that the views of a small section cannot be imposed in the name of public opinion.

- Greater public investment in democratic knowledge enterprises, so that information about trends and patterns in democratic politics is regularly gathered and made available publicly.

The agenda outlined above is only a rough sketch that hints at the areas rather than present a plan of action. By its very nature, it suffers from an inattention to details that are critical to the success of an enterprise like this. And, above all, it does not even begin to address the issues of agency and strategy: Who would carry out this agenda? Under what conditions does it have a chance of being accepted? It does not offer any thoughts about a minimalist coalition that is necessary to carry out a radical agenda of political reforms. In this context it leaves unattended the vexed relationship of attempts to bring about political reforms with substantive radical or alternative politics. The question is: Must a radical agenda for political reform wait for the triumph of radical politics? On the other hand, can radical politics succeed without any political reforms that precede it?

References

An Agenda for India, 1980. *Seminar* (245), January.

John, Mary E., 2000. "Alternate Modernities? Reservations and Women's Movement in 20th Century India", *Economic and Political Weekly* 35 (43 & 44), 28 October, p. WS-22.

Kishwar, Madhu, Jayaprakash Narayan, D.L. Sheth, and Yogendra Yadav, 2000. "Call for Support: An Alternative Bill for Women's Reservation". Forum for Democratic Reforms, Rammanohar Lohia Samata Vidyala Nyas.

Linz, Juan J., and Arturo Valenzuela (eds), 1994. *The Failure of Presidential Democracy: Comparative Perspectives*, vol. I. Baltimore: Johns Hopkins University Press.

Linz, Juan J., and Alfred Stepan, 1996. *Problem of Democratic Transition and Consolidation*. Baltimore: Johns Hopkins University Press.

McMillan, Alistair, 2000. "Delimitation, Democracy and End of Constitutional Freeze", *Economic and Political Weekly* 35(15), 8 April.

———, 2001. "Constituting 91st Amendment Bill: A Constitutional Fraud?", *Economic and Political Weekly* 36(14&15), 14 April.

Mehta, Pratap Bhanu, 2001. "Reform Political Parties First", *Seminar* (497), January.

Menon, Nivedita, 2000. "Elusive 'Women': Feminism and Women's Reservation Bill", *Economic and Political Weekly* 35(43 & 44), 28 October, p. WS-35.

"Multiple Modernities", 2000. *Daedalus*, 129(1), Winter.

National Commission to Review the Working of the Constitution, 2001. "Review of the Working of Political Parties Especially in Relation to Elections and Reform Options: A Consultation Paper". New Delhi.

———, 2001. "Review of Election Law, Process and Reform Options: A Consultation Paper". New Delhi.

Report of the Committee on Electoral Reforms, 1975. Tarkunde Committee, Delhi: Citizens for Democracy.

Saberwal, Satish, 1986. *India: The Roots of Crisis*. New Delhi: Oxford University Press.

Shakdher, S.L., 1980. *Electoral Reforms for India*. Delhi: The Voters' Council and Citizens for Democracy.

———, 1984. "Electoral Reforms", *Journal of Constitutional and Parliamentary Studies* 18(1–2), January–June.

Singh, L.P., 1986. *Electoral Reform: Problems and Suggested Solutions*. New Delhi: Uppal.

Sridharan, E. (forthcoming). "Does India Need to Switch to Proportional Representation", in Paul Flathur (ed.), *Indian Politics: How to Refresh Democracy*. London: Macmillan.

Yadav, Yogendra, 1996. "Electoral Reforms: Beyond Middle Class Fantasies", *Seminar* (440), April.

———, 1999. "Politics", in Marshall Bouton and Philip Oldenburg (eds), *India Briefing: A Transformative Fifty Years*. New York: M.E. Sharpe.

———, 2000. "Understanding the Second Democratic Upsurge: Trends of Bahujan Participation in Electoral Politics in the 1990s", in Francine R. Frankel, Zoya Hasan, Rajeev Bhargava, and Balveer Arora (eds), *Transforming India: Social and Political Dynamics of Democracy*. New Delhi: Oxford University Press.

———, 2000. "Whose Democracy? Which Reforms? A Plea for a Democratic Agenda for Electoral Reforms", in Subhash C. Kashyap, *et al.* (eds), *Reviewing the Constitution?* Delhi: Shipra.

———, 2001. "Let's Find an Alternative", *Indian Express*, 19 June.

———, 2001. "Saansadon ke Vetan Bhatte" (Hindi), *Hindustan*, 13 September.

15

An Agenda for Political Action in Our Times

What is to be Done?

1. THE IDEA OF INDIA faces an unprecedented challenge. Preventing irreversible damage to the Republic of India, as we have known it, is the most pressing political task of our times, our *yugadharma*. So far the response to this challenge has been marked by intellectual lethargy and political paralysis. A better response would require that we appreciate the dangers, acknowledge the depth of the challenge, and then prepare a road-map that combines short- and mid-term strategies with a long-term vision. This is what the present essay offers.

It argues that the challenge is at once more serious and deep-rooted than we care to admit. We are up against nothing short of a hegemonic regime that enjoys power with legitimacy. Having said that, it suggests that at least some of the sense of doom and gloom that surrounds the defenders of the idea of India is self-created, that we have more resources to take on the present challenge than we imagine, and that this challenge requires us to respond creatively. Paradoxically, this crisis could well be an opportunity.

The Challenge

2. First, a candid look at the nature and extent of the challenge. There can be an argument about whether we have reached the lowest point

of democratic freedoms in the history of post-Independence India. But not about the fact that we are passing through the most trying time, so far, for the ideals that the Republic of India stood for.

2.1. While the current challenge is unprecedented, it is not the first time that one or the other constitutive element of the idea of India has faced a serious challenge. India's democratic record was tainted by the Emergency and regularly smudged by many milder but chronic failures. Our commitment to diversity has been punctured by episodes of majoritarian excesses like the Sikh massacre of 1984 and Gujarat carnage of 2002 and by failures in regions like Kashmir and Nagaland. There is not much to write home about the idea of development for the last person, an ideal that has been practised mostly in the breach.

2.2. Yet the present juncture represents an unprecedented challenge to the idea of India in multiple ways. One, all the core ideas – democracy, diversity, and development – are under simultaneous and vigorous challenge. Two, this challenge does not arise from a mere failure or violation of the vision; rather it is informed by a vision that stands in opposition to the idea of India. Three, for the first time the onslaught enjoys considerable popular backing; there is a real danger of the republic being undone by the public.

2.3. The challenge has caused more damage than we are willing to admit. This onslaught has already downscaled constitutional commitment to diversity, halted the deepening of democracy, and further distorted the developmental trajectory. The present juncture has not just exposed the long-standing weakness of the institutional edifice of our democracy, it has taken deinstitutionalisation to a new low. The gains from a deepening of democracy in the 1990s have largely been reversed.

Many higher education institutions have been politically captured with little resistance from the top. Anti-corruption agencies have either been packed with yes-men or put in deep freeze. The higher judiciary has been part infiltrated and part tamed, though not without some flashes of dissent. The Election Commission too appears weaker than ever in the post-Seshan era. The regime has found ways to circumvent the Rajya Sabha. The national security apparatus as well as intelligence and investigation agencies have been aligned, more than ever before, with the demands of the ruling party. Extralegal actions by security agencies face less scrutiny than ever before, even as vigilante groups on the street and social media trolls enjoy visible political patronage.

There is a brazen shift to a "growth-only" paradigm of economic development. Most of the welfare measures introduced in the post-liberalisation era face a quiet but effective rollback. The environmental safeguards built over the last three decades are being dismantled, one after another. There is a naked disavowal of commitment to diversity; Muslims have de facto been reduced to second-rung citizenship, though without a change in their de jure status.

2.4. All these changes have been accompanied by a significant shift in the spectrum of public opinion in favour of a majoritarian consensus, achieved through a mix of image positioning, aggressive ground action, and media control. A Modi cult has been carefully built up with the help of communication, media amplification, spin doctoring, and social media management. A series of critical events were engineered for the assertion of aggressive nationalist rhetoric so as to brand and silence all voices of dissent. Above all, the mainstream media has been compromised through a mix of clever spin doctoring, meticulous capture of key media positions, misuse of state patronage alongside the brazen use of money power, blackmailing, and arm-twisting.

2.5. The real challenge is, however, much deeper. If this onslaught continues for a significant duration, we may well be looking at a fundamental disfiguration of the Indian enterprise. The end product may not be "fascism" in a textbook sense, but likely something different if not worse. It is hard to outline the features of this evolving deformity, but some of the elements can be anticipated. The political system could be "competitive authoritarianism" where representative democracy and party competition would be limited to episodes of elections, with the playing field severely skewed in favour of one party. In between elections, it would resemble an authoritarian system with a presidential form of governance, severe curtailment of civil liberties, and a higher threshold of tolerance for deviations from constitutionally mandated procedures.

Concentration of power will likely take many forms: state power into the Union government, governmental power into the ruling party, and the power of the party into the hands of one person. Development will likely mean a no-nonsense rule of the capital, with the occasional populist discount but minimum "hindrance" from ecological considerations. On the diversity front, it will likely be a non-theocratic majoritarian rule with minor tweaking of some of the secular laws but effective delineation of the hierarchy of religious communities. The existing system of affirmative action may be diluted in a series of small steps. For its survival and popular endorsement, this regime will probably depend on occasional electoral endorsement, informal regimentation of the media, crushing of dissent, ongoing crusades against "internal enemies", and a possible military adventure. To sum up, we may be looking at the mutilation of the idea of India.

2.6. For all these dangers, this challenge also presents us with an opportunity. The struggle against this onslaught must not be a battle for restoration, of going back to an India that existed prior to 2014, for that will not succeed. It must simultaneously be a battle for transformation. A successful response to this challenge would open up space to renegotiate settled equations in multiple spheres. It can force a reconfiguration of the party system, making way for the emergence of alternative political forces and a realignment of voters with parties. It can also provide an opportunity to fortify democratic institutions, push through radical electoral reforms, loosen up economic limits to politics, redefine the paradigm of development, reform our clearly flawed practice of "secularism", and reimagine the existing frame of social justice. This crisis may facilitate, indeed necessitate, a radical rupture with the business as usual of democratic politics.

The Roots of the Challenge

3. The current challenge has deeper anchors than is normally conceded. Narendra Modi is no doubt the face of this challenge, yet he is not the challenge. He happens to occupy a unique point of intersection of multiple lines and embodies the opposition to the idea of India. As such, he represents a constellation of forces, not all of which draw energy from the Rashtriya Swayamsevak Sangh (RSS) Jan Sangh–Bharatiya Janata Party (BJP) lineage.

While there was nothing inevitable about his ascent to power in 2014, Modi is not an accident or aberration. We are not just dealing with someone who happens to have won an election and captured state power. His popularity has faced its first crisis in the fourth year of his government. The BJP's victory and Modi's rise to power has been accompanied by a realignment in the social basis of politics and a shift in the spectrum of public opinion. Thus, the challenge to the idea of India comes from a force that is at once widespread, well entrenched, and popular. The Modi regime should be characterised as a hegemonic power since it combines state power with street power, electoral dominance with ideological legitimacy.

3.1. The Modi regime wields far greater legal and extralegal coercive power than enjoyed by any ruling party in post-Independence India. It uses every possible constitutional-legal power *sans* the constraints imposed by democratic conventions: dismissal of unfriendly state governments, use of the Central Bureau of Investigation and other investigative agencies, and, of course, use of the armed forces. This is supplemented by the use of the state apparatus for extralegal coercive measures: harassment and persecution of political and ideological adversaries, protection of vigilante groups, and the misuse of anti-terror laws. The most pernicious aspect of the BJP's use of coercive state apparatus is the silent, everyday form of surveillance, intimidation, and infiltration.

3.2. This coercion draws its legitimacy from the BJP's growing electoral dominance. The BJP may not match the Congress in its heyday of one-party dominance, but it does resemble the Congress during its one-party salience period in the 1980s. Despite reversals in Delhi and Bihar, the story of the BJP since its spectacular performance in the Lok Sabha election of 2014 is one of expansion and growth. It has spread to virtually every nook and cranny of India, including the hill states of the North East, and is a force to reckon with even in the coastal belt from Kerala to Bengal, though it is as yet in no position to win elections. The organisational machine, the election machine, and the propaganda machine put together make the BJP the most formidable political force to emerge in recent times.

3.3. It would be a mistake, however, to think that Modi's power rests only on political dominance and a coercive state apparatus. The Modi regime enjoys a hegemonic position because it has also successfully secured moral, cultural, and ideological legitimacy. The BJP's and Modi's continuing popularity in opinion polls draws upon something deeper than an approval of its governmental performance. The packaging and positioning of the prime minister's image as "hard-working", "tough", "selfless", and "driven by larger national goals" has more takers than many would care to admit.

The BJP has successfully shifted the entire spectrum of public opinion towards its ideology. It has more or less captured key symbols of nationalism, Hinduism, and our cultural heritage. The demons invented by the BJP troll brigade – "anti-national", "westernised", "secular", "enemies within" – have come to acquire a life of their own. To be sure, Modi's legitimacy is categorically different from the deeper ethical appeal of a Gandhi or a Nehru, or even the legitimacy of the Congress in the post-Independence era. In a sense, a typical BJP supporter is saying, "We may not be ethical as per the highest standards; but what the hell, why do we need to be saints?" A latent societal meanness has found a legitimate political outlet.

3.4. It needs to be underlined that the BJP's hegemony is far from total – no hegemony ever is. Its coercive power is frustrated by the endemic inefficiencies and the notoriously modest capacity of the Indian state. Its electoral dominance peters out at the geographical and social peripheries. The BJP is not a serious contender in Kerala, Tamil Nadu, Andhra Pradesh, Telangana, West Bengal, and smaller states like Tripura, Mizoram, Meghalaya, Nagaland, and, of course, the Kashmir Valley.

This hegemony is predicated on the exclusion of the Muslims and mostly Christians as well. The inclusion of dalits is still tentative, the peasantry's association is still tenuous as is its hold over the youth. For all its seeming ideological dominance, it is yet to find acceptance among the intellectual elite, both in English and Indian languages. None of this takes away from the fact of the BJP's hegemony. But it does point to spaces available for counter-hegemonic action.

3.5. Modi's rise to hegemony has deeper historic causes which we cannot detail here. While certainly not the only possible outcome, long-term failure of political action and imagination combined with structural deficits in our capitalist modernity clearly contributed to it. First, our democratic institutions have always been weak, subject to routine indifference and occasional capture. At the best of times we have shown little respect for the rule of law and institutional autonomy. This was partially made up by a deepening of our democratic practices, especially in the wake of "the second democratic upsurge". But the gains of the deepening of democracy were not consolidated. The earlier system was unsettled without being replaced by a new one, thus opening the space for a sudden capture.

Second, the failure of economic growth to deliver well-being to the vast majority of our population created a political constituency that could be easily mobilised by populist promises. Rising inequality and growing media density in a society gradually coming out of absolute poverty in the post-liberalisation era has created a class whose aspirations are completely out of sync with reality. This underclass is easy prey for miracle masters as well as hatemongers.

This was reinforced, third, by the cultural logic of modernity in a post-colonial society. The imitative character of India's modernity created a shallow public sphere marked by envy and anxiety. The modern Indian citizen, pushed into urban experience, craved for a sense of belonging and self-respect. The failure of the so-far-dominant liberal-secular ideology to fulfil this need gave rise to a huge vacuum.

Fourth, the weakening of the existing instruments of political action contributed to the vacuum which Modi occupied. Over the last few decades, political movements have declined and are forced to exist in an agitational mode, useful for sectoral gains but not worthy of general trust. This period has also witnessed a hollowing out of political parties as they essentially turn into election machines, indispensable yet illegitimate.

Finally, the sudden death of modern Indian political thought in post-Independence India resulted in a drying up of intellectual resources in politics and the disjunction of political ideology from popular imagination. The task of making sense of reality was left to university-based academics and high-end media with little feel for or touch with ground realities. The challenge of shaping public opinion was thus completely neglected, leaving the field open to a lowbrow media, ever amenable to propaganda, hate speech, and myth-making.

What is Not to be Done

4. Cogent thinking about what is to be done must begin with clarity on what is not to be done. So far, this clarity has eluded Modi critics. It is a sign of our times that those who seek to uproot the republic are proactive, innovative, and energetic, but the defence of the republic is reactive or knee-jerk, if not lethargic or paralysed. Opposition to the Modi regime is marked by an inability to fathom the extent of the challenge it poses, unwillingness to recognise its deep roots, and failure to think beyond quick fixes. No wonder, anger at history has replaced serious criticism, fearmongering is the only response to hatemongering, fright has prevented any far-sighted action.

So far, the Modi regime has evoked a series of predictable responses from its opponents: a passive wait for the bubble to burst; simple-minded anti-Modiism, attempts to take on the regime on its own turf, and trying to build a grand anti-BJP coalition. None of these strategies is likely to succeed.

4.1. The actions, or rather inactions, of the Congress party symbolise the first approach, that is, wait for an unravelling of the Modi regime by its own blunders, for the Modi bubble to burst thanks to the sheer magnitude of its original lie. Now, it is true that Narendra Modi made irresponsible and impossible promises – *achche din*, Rs 15 lakh in each account – giving rise to unreal expectations. Even as the public is sharp enough to perceive the gap between promise and delivery, it is also quick to scale down its expectations to "realistic" levels and overlook some rhetorical excesses of a power seeker.

By now the Modi regime has accumulated a big heap of blunders, arguably bigger than its counterparts in the recent past. Even as its mismanagement of the economy is staggering – with incontrovertible evidence of all-round economic failure such as falling growth rates despite a favourable climate, job shrinkage, aggravation of agrarian crisis, decline in manufacturing and fall in exports made worse by the demonetisation disaster and goods and services tax (GST) mismanagement – the government's failures in other domains are only waiting to be exposed, be they of its highly publicised missions or of its foreign policy initiatives to yield results when needed or indeed the counterproductive nature of its internal security measures.

Yet, a blunder is a blunder only when seen to be such and there are layers of mediation between reality and popular perception. The Modi government's "brilliant" management of perceptions to turn the demonetisation disaster into at least short-term political dividends is a textbook illustration of this eternal truth of politics. Besides, usually, governance blunders have political consequences only when there is an assurance that an alternative will be better. There are occasions when the people could not care less for an alternative, when they just want to "throw the rascals out" as they believe that no one can be worse than the incumbent. But it would be fanciful to think that the Modi regime's popularity has already hit that point.

4.2. When the opposition graduates from not doing anything to doing something, more often than not it takes the form of simple-minded "anti-Modiism". A typical opposition tactic in competitive politics, it involves countering the ruling party in anything and everything that it does in the hope that some of the criticism will stick. The luxury of playing opposition obviates the need for coherence and consistency in these oppositional manoeuvres. So, the opposition can criticise the prime minister for spending time abroad; if he did not, he would be accused of relinquishing his international responsibility.

Deeper maladies that have afflicted the country across all regimes – railway accidents, malnutrition, farmer suicides – are now attributed to the Modi regime as if they are happening for the first time. The Congress party that drafted and pushed for a GST, not too different from what this government has implemented, can happily blame the BJP for its consequences. Unfortunately, such short-sighted criticism soon loses legitimacy as the public begins to see it for what it is – opposition for the sake of opposition. These tactics may work once the regime has lost public confidence, but cannot be deployed to undermine the legitimacy of an otherwise popular government. In fact, they could end up eroding the legitimacy of the opposition.

4.3. A more proactive and consistent form of anti-Modi politics has tried to take on the BJP on its own turf. Over the last three years, ideological and political opposition to the Modi regime has focused on its jingoist nationalist rhetoric, its anti-minority stance, and its promotion of obscurantism. Hence, the campaigns against cow vigilante-led lynching, award *wapasi* to protest against the murder of rationalists, opposition to the move for a uniform civil code, questioning of the "surgical strikes", a critique of brutality by security forces in the Kashmir Valley and elsewhere, mobilisation against the murder of Gauri Lankesh and rejection of anti-Romeo squads, and so on. There is no doubt that each of these acts of opposition is in itself worth undertaking and necessary. Yet, taken together, an obsessive focus on these issues plays into the hands of the *sangh parivar*. The Modi regime might even welcome criticism on these counts as it could bring desired publicity for the regime. An indictment of the Modi regime for its anti-minority orientation sends a positive signal to the majority community that the regime stands with them.

The opposition to a uniform civil code usually ends up as evidence of the politics of "minority appeasement". Any questioning of the regime for its jingoist nationalism ends up reconfirming its nationalist credentials. It is not that the regime cannot or should not be confronted on its cultural agenda. The present essay goes on to suggest several long-term measures to this end. Yet, we must admit that as of now the opposition does not possess the cultural weapons to match the BJP in this battle. A premature battle on this ground can be counterproductive.

4.4. Finally, much of the oppositional politics falls back on forging a grand coalition of anti-BJP parties. As we inch towards 2019, this anti-BJPism (to replace anti-Congressism) seems to be the default strategy, or perhaps a response of helplessness that the opposition is drifting towards. The logic is self-evident. On the face of it, there is an arithmetic advantage to a pre-election coalition in a first-past-the-post system. Aggregation of non-BJP votes can help the opposition edge past the BJP, even if it retains its peak vote share of the 2014 parliamentary elections. This can be decisive in states like Uttar Pradesh and Karnataka where the non-BJP parties enjoy a distinct and complementary vote base, provided it is transferable. Besides actual aggregation, opposition unity can also help create a perception of inability and the possibility of an alternative to the BJP at the national level.

But these possible advantages of opposition unity may not translate as well in a real-life scenario. For one, the benefits from an aggregation of votes are overstated. First, opposition unity is irrelevant in a large number of states. These states either witness a direct BJP–Congress contest, with virtually no other party for the Congress to align with, or do not have the BJP as one of the top two parties. Second, the mechanical advantages of aggregation of votes may be overstated in many cases where votes of non-BJP parties are either non-complementary (Congress and the Janata Dal [Secular] in Karnataka) or non-transferable (Communist Party of Indian [Marxist] and Congress in West Bengal and Kerala, also the Samajwadi Party and the Bahujan Samaj Party in Uttar Pradesh). Third, the benefits of opposition unity may be uncertain when possible allies – parties like the Telangana Rashtra Samithi, Telugu Desam Party, Dravida Munnetra Kazhagam, Jammu and Kashmir National Conference, Biju Janata Dal, and Bahujan Samaj Party – could as easily shift their loyalty to the BJP in a post-poll scenario.

Moreover, the calculus of arithmetic advantage of opposition unity fails to add up some serious minuses. One, the unity of major parties (e.g. Rashtriya Janata Dal and Janta Dal United in Bihar, regional party and Congress in Odisha, Telangana, and Andhra Pradesh) tends to create a void, as many voters of either party feel "orphaned". This space vacated by the opposition could result in a consolidation of votes in favour of the BJP. Two, the perception of everyone "ganging up" against Modi can create sympathy for him. He could well improvise upon the famous retort used to deadly effect by Indira Gandhi *vis-à-vis* the Grand Alliance against her in 1971: "*Woh kehte hain Indira hatao, main kehti hoon garibi hatao*." The bottom line on a grand anti-BJP alliance is simply this: a carefully crafted unity of major oppositional forces may yield some dividends for opposing the Modi regime in 2019, but a ragtag coalition of all non-BJP parties cannot be an alternative to Modi; an electoral alliance cannot substitute for a coherent vision, a credible leadership, and a clear road map.

What is to be Done?

5. What, then, is to be done? In one word: think. Those of us who are serious about taking on this challenge to the foundations of the republic urgently need to move from kneejerk reactions to a plan of action

that incorporates smart tactics which draw upon a coherent anti-hegemonic strategy that reflects an alternative vision. While much of the action aimed at countering the Modi regime will understandably focus on the Lok Sabha election of 2019, it is critical to reserve some mind space for the deeper challenge beyond Modi, beyond electoral politics and beyond 2019.

If the understanding of the challenge proposed here has any merit, it is here to stay with us in one form or another, irrespective of the outcome of the 2019 polls. Therefore, we need a more coherent and calibrated response. The plan of action must link various fields and sites of action. The tactics need to weave the familiar moves with new and surprising manoeuvres. The strategy must harmonise the immediate with the mid-term and long term. The vision that guides it must recast the foundational vision of the republic for our times.

Short-term Tactics

6. Let us begin with a short-term perspective on what can be done to preserve some available spaces and open up possibilities of resistance within the current regime.

6.1. There is some space available for a battle of institutional autonomy. As mentioned earlier, the judiciary, media, and universities constitute three sites where complete control still eludes this regime. While the Modi regime has succeeded in curbing judicial independence more than any other regime since Indira Gandhi in the 1970s, the presence of judges with conscience and spine and the residual strength of procedures and precedents in an otherwise liberal constitutional system sustain the possibility of resistance.

While the owners of private media are more compromised than ever before, an average journalist feels suffocated and the majority of opinion makers are still not aligned with the regime. These are silent allies in the battle for truth. Notwithstanding the regime's massive investment in dominating social media, the very nature of this media resists control and provides avenues for alternative articulations. While most university administrators have caved in all too easily, the faculty remains circumspect, if quiet for now. The real resistance has come from the students, both in the form of organised groups and as a community.

All these three are critical sites, especially for their impact on many other sectors and sections of the population. Thus well-thought-out action here could have a multiplier effect. This may not take the form of organised protests; techniques of silent solidarity are more likely to be effective here. Equally, action for institutional autonomy cannot afford to be silent on the rather shoddy record of the earlier regimes, including the Congress and the left, on this score.

6.2. Picking another low-hanging fruit would entail mobilisation of spontaneous outrage against the political and cultural excesses of the Modi regime, especially among youth and marginal social groups. These include protests against lynching and other restrictions in the name of cow protection; building on the youth unease with attempts to impose "love jihad" or vigilante activities of anti-Romeo squads; dalit upsurge against atrocities or caste-based discrimination; and local unrest against the killing of rationalists and dissenters like Gauri Lankesh. As mentioned above, all this has to be done with caution, or else it could backfire. Even as these local and sectional protests cannot be the fulcrum of counter-hegemonic action, as they may not enjoy widespread support, a careful stitching together of such protests could bring to fore our home-grown liberalism and prove critical to defending the republic.

6.3. A relentless and credible exposé of corruption at all levels could also be a critical element in countering the hegemony of the Modi regime. The *lokpal* movement created a legitimacy crisis for the previous regime and paved the way for the BJP's rise to power. However, more than three years into its term, this government has little to show by way of an anti-corruption record. On the contrary, it has diluted anti-corruption laws and institutions: amendment to the Prevention of Corruption Act, non-implementation of the whistle blower act, appointment of compromised officers to the Central Vigilance Commission, and non-appointment of a Lokpal are cases in point.

At the ground level, there has been little difference in the experience of everyday corruption, or in the persecution of corrupt officers. Gradually, various corruption scandals of this government are beginning to breach the media's wall of silence. To be sure, we should not expect a repeat of the Lokpal movement type of anti-corruption agitation, yet a consistent and credible campaign can take off the residual moral sheen of the Modi regime.

The Mid-term Strategy

7. The thrust of counter-hegemonic action, however, needs to be on proactive mobilisation of two key constituencies: farmers affected by agrarian distress, and the unemployed youth. There are good reasons why, unlike communalism and nationalism, these two issues have put the regime on the back foot. One, agrarian distress and unemployment are not short-term difficulties arising out of a faulty policy or poor execution; both flow out of the nature of economic policies pursued in the post-Independence period. In both cases the condition has got much worse under the current regime.

Two, both these issues are very hard to address in the short run; it is virtually impossible for the Modi regime to improve the outcomes on either of these fronts in the next year and a half. Three, unlike many other issues, agrarian distress and unemployment have a clearly identified social group – farmers and youth respectively – that can be mobilised for action. Both these groups are large enough to make a difference. Their mobilisation is among the best antidotes to possible polarisation along communal lines. Finally, the regime's commitment is suspect on both these counts. The BJP was always seen to be a party of urban traders, even though it has now acquired a fair share of the farmers' vote. The youth has always been attracted more to the left than to the right. All this makes it easier and more rewarding to build counter-hegemonic mobilisation on these two issues.

7.1. If there is one class whose "objective" interests almost entirely match the political project of counter-hegemony, it is the farmers. Structural contradictions of the economy make it impossible to incorporate and retain farmers into the fold of the new hegemony. It so happens that at this juncture the farmers' movement is poised at a historic turn. This coming together of the "objective" and the "subjective" situation means that in the short to medium run, the ongoing farmers' movement across the country offers the greatest possibility for mass mobilisation against the Modi regime.

The agrarian crisis – a combination of economic, ecological, and existential crisis – has been around for a long time. But an overlap of climate-, market-, and policy-induced disasters in the last three years has pushed the agrarian crisis to a flashpoint. The response of the central and state governments is no match to what the farmers need; the governments have continued with business-as-usual governance, platitudes for policy, and indifference where political will is needed. That is why the spontaneous eruption of farmers' protests across the country since June this year and the formation of an umbrella coalition to fuse these could prove to be a turning point in the history of farmers' movements. After a very long time the stage has been set for an all-India farmers' movement.

The realisation of this possibility depends upon the successful fusion of two streams of agrarian struggle that we have inherited from the twentieth century: "farmers' movements" for intersectoral parity between agriculture and non-agricultural domains on the one hand, and "peasant struggles" for intra-sector justice for small farmers, sharecroppers, and farm labour. The growing and starkly visible rural–urban disparities, increasing pauperisation of all sections of the peasantry, including the erstwhile well-off sections, and the increasing overlap between farm labour and sharecropper farmer has created objective conditions for this political unity of the "big" and "small" farmers with sharecroppers and farm labour. The point now is to turn this possibility into a reality.

This requires a historic project of uniting farmers' movements as well as different classes and both genders, various ideological shades, and conflicting charters of demands. Specifically, it would mean bringing "green" as well as "red" flags together, getting the farmer green to speak to the ecological green, bringing dalit and adivasi struggles within the fold of farmers' movements and foregrounding women farmers cutting across all divisions.

All this is not just in the realm of a theoretical possibility: this fusion has already begun. The All India Kisan Sangharsh Coordination Committee (AIKSCC) has already brought both shades of green with red, along with dalit, adivasi, and women farmer organisations under one umbrella. Farmers' movements all over the country, even those outside the fold of the AIKSCC, have adopted the twin agendas of remunerative prices and freedom from debt.

Forging this unity will also be an ideological challenge: the traditional farmers' movement needs to acknowledge that marginal farmers and women farmers are the typical Indian farmers; left-wing peasant movements need to set aside the tendency to view class distinctions within the peasantry as the principal contradiction. There is a real danger of the farmers' movement degenerating into typical trade union-style "economism". Thus, the political challenge before it is to become an all-encompassing movement for the regeneration of rural India. Such a movement can be the vanguard of counter-hegemonic politics to defend the republic.

7.2. Unemployed youth are at once more powerful and more difficult agents of counter-hegemony at this point in history. The youth movement is more powerful by virtue of the sheer energy, speed, and visibility that it can bring to counter-hegemonic politics. Yet, it is also currently much weaker and more fragmented than the farmers' movement. Consequently, it is difficult to find issues and sites that can bring together the various sections of India's youth.

The "objective" conditions appear ripe as in the case of farmers: an extended period of jobless growth, possible shrinkage of job opportunities, contractualisation of organised sector employment, widening gulf between work conditions of organised and unorganised sector workers, an educational system that fails to provide skills or knowledge, and growing disparities in educational opportunities.

The "subjective" conditions are also, on balance, favourable. The crisis is seen and felt by the affected group: take any opinion poll and unemployment tops the chart of problems that the youth would like the government to address. There is enough evidence of a latent youth unrest that occasionally comes out in campus protests across the country. Clearly, a significant section of the youth is uncomfortable with the cultural politics of this regime.

The real challenge at this moment is to marshal this latent energy into counter-hegemonic politics. Campus politics is in deep freeze: since elected student unions are an exception in the institutes of higher education, politics has long been an episodic aberration. While there are thousands of student organisations across the country, there has been a marked decline in vigorous and ideologically oriented all-India students' organisations.

There are very few independent organisations of the youth other than students that could launch a nationwide movement for employment. A new generation of youth leadership is emerging from among women, dalits, Muslims, and other marginalised communities. But there is no large platform for this leadership. The creation of a nationwide youth movement on the two issues of equal access to quality education and dignified employment to all is thus a historic possibility and a historic challenge.

The Long-term Vision

8. In the last instance, the success of counter-hegemonic politics depends not so much on the short- and medium-term action plans and strategies mentioned above, but on its capacity to offer an alternative vision. We need a long-term strategy of counter-hegemonic ideology. The heart of the challenge lies in the creation of a new vision of India that can capture the popular imagination. This requires careful deliberation, as the defenders of the republic need fresh moral, cultural, and intellectual resources. Today it would be imprudent to foreground counter-hegemonic politics on issues of nationalism, secularism, and culture since any contestation on conventional terms would end up strengthening the Modi regime. But an inability to take on these issues for long would be fatal to counter-hegemonic politics.

Fortunately, we need not begin in thin air. Many of the resources needed for the counter-hegemonic project are available. Modern Indian political thought is an extraordinary repository of moral, intellectual, and cultural resources that can help us collectively negotiate our present. This tradition can help us access the wisdom of our cultural traditions and also the heritage of modern European thought. But we can draw upon this tradition only if we give up the insistence on any of the twentieth-century ideological labels or icons as the starting point. We must recognise that many of the ideological battles of the twentieth century – violence versus non-violence, state versus market, class versus caste – are pointless today. Instead of carrying on the dead wood, we need to learn from all the major streams of modern Indian political thought.

Specifically, we need to bring together two strands in twentieth-century Indian political thought: the modern egalitarian strand represented by the socialists, communists, Ambedkarites and feminists on the one hand, and the indigenous strand represented by Gandhians, sarvodayaites, and environmentalists on the other.

What we need is a new ideological integration of both these strands under a capacious concept like "Swaraj". This alternative ideological vision must not be tied to any one thinker or text. Instead, the constitution must become the key symbol for a counter-hegemonic ideology. Such an ideology would enable us to renegotiate some of the key issues that have been deployed by the Modi regime to achieve hegemonic status. This would also result in rethinking some of the key social and economic policies, such as redesigning policies of social justice beyond caste as the only criteria and reservations as the only mechanism or rethinking egalitarian economic policies to move away from an obsession with the state and allowing intelligent use of the market with sensitivity to ecological concerns. But let us focus on some of the key issues that need urgent and radical reorientation.

8.1. Recovering the lost ground of nationalism has to be a key agenda of counter-hegemonic politics. Nationalism continues to be the currency of politics in a post-colonial society as ours; allowing the Sangh Parivar to appropriate the nationalist plank is at the heart of the political setback for the idea of India. Thus, an unapologetic embrace of the legacy of the freedom struggle and proactive propagation of Indian nationalism as a distinct, non-chauvinist strand of the anti-colonial movement must be placed at the heart of the counter-hegemonic project. Instead of handing over the cultural legacy of nationalism to jingoism, we need to recover the idea of a nation centred around the people and their unity internally, and with other post-colonial societies externally.

Instead of simply decrying jingoism and critiquing shallow symbols of nationalism, we need to develop deeper, positive yardsticks of measuring nationalism: willingness to unite Indians across caste, region, and religion, sharing the pains and problems of all Indians, assertion of national sovereignty in the face of neo-colonial domination, and protection of genuine national security interests without bullying our neighbours. We also need a new concept for this form of nationalism – perhaps *desh prem* instead of *rashtra bhakti*.

8.2. This must be accompanied by a concerted attempt to reclaim the cultural heritage of traditions suited for our times. We must acknowledge that the westernised English-speaking elite – including liberal, left, and progressive sections – has done a disservice to the idea of India. We must give up the ignorance and suspicion of traditions that mark most modern secular Indians, invest deeply in multiple cultural and religious traditions, and be willing to engage in an open-ended conversation with traditions (not just an instrumental and selective appropriation of some elements that fit the modern imagination) and view these as building blocs of our own modernity. This must be accompanied by a shift in our cultural vocabulary and policy. A counter-hegemonic project would involve an advocacy of Indian languages including both non-scheduled languages and classical ones like Sanskrit, Tamil, and Persian, as well as support for an "Indianisation" of educational curricula that draw upon our context, our needs, and intellectual traditions.

8.3. A vigorous counter to the hegemony of majoritarian politics requires a recalibration of the politics of "secularism" so as to distance it from pro-minorityism and establish connections with the multiple religious traditions of India. We need nothing short of an open disavowal of a deracinated and culturally empty secularism. Secular politics must publicly distance itself from the exclusive demands of the Muslim leadership and focus instead on the insecurity, disadvantage, and discrimination in jobs, housing, and education that they suffer. Our secularism must draw upon syncretic traditions or traditions of religious coexistence and assiduously avoid the rhetoric that goes out of its way to offend sensibilities of followers of any religion, including Hindus.

9. Finally, counter-hegemonic politics needs a new political instrument. Clearly, none of the established political parties are fit for this

purpose. But the need is not merely to create a new party or a new alliance. What we need is a new kind of political formation that subsumes a party, which is a party but not just a party. Such a political formation will have to simultaneously perform several functions that are assigned to different organisations today. Contesting elections will of course be one of those functions, but not the only one. This will have to be accompanied by organising agitations and struggles, carrying out constructive work for realising an alternative vision, intervening in the politics of knowledge by way of creating new concepts, theories, and policies while also creating space for a meaningful relationship with the inner self of the political actor.

Index

Aam aadmi 208
accountability 33, 167, 175, 186, 194, 201, 227, 339–40, 342, 344
Adiseshiah, Malcolm 272
Adivasi(s) 19, 25–6, 28, 52, 77, 95, 179, 320, 361–2
Advani, L.K. 80, 84
Afrobarometer 282, 289
agriculture 15, 361
Ahmad, Imtiaz 307, 316
Akali Dal 60, 70, 319; movement 74
Alavi, Hamza 242
alliance(s) 26, 60, 77, 79, 81, 85, 210, 215, 242, 304, 314, 319, 357, 366; anti-BJP 357; Brahmin–dalit 77; building 304; Dravida Munnetra Kazhagam-led 215; JD–BJP 79
All India Anna Dravida Munnetra Kazhagam (AIADMK) 27, 60, 63, 97, 214, 319
All India Kisan Sangharsh Coordination Committee (AIKSCC) 361–2
Ambedkar, Dr B.R. 188, 335
Ambedkarite movement 218
American Political Science Review 151, 257
Andhra Pradesh (AP) 19, 60, 63, 65, 68, 76, 78, 87, 91, 95, 102–5, 206, 214, 218–19, 222–5, 227–8, 352, 357
antagonism 56, 68–9, 94
anthropology 238, 288, 309, 311–12, 317, 320
anti-BJPism: 356; Congressism 356; incumbency 172, 183, 215; Modiism 354–5; *award wapasi* 355; Muslim attacks 74, 154; Romeo squads 356, 359; Sikh riots 1984 35, 156
Argentina 134–5, 145–6, 148
Arunachal Pradesh 65, 76, 97, 103, 105, 228
Asom Gana Parishad (AGP) 19, 62–3, 69, 96
aspirations 17, 76, 88, 90, 112, 122, 130, 235, 239, 353
Assam 22, 51, 61–3, 65, 69–70, 76, 78, 91, 95–7, 102, 104, 182, 195, 218–19, 228, 230; foreigners' issue in 69; movement 70
assembly elections 19, 29, 61, 79–80, 82–3, 93, 102, 104, 106–7, 179, 184, 195, 200, 210, 214, 319; 1952–2003 102, 104, 106–7; 1991 93; 1993 82; 1997 35; 1999 319
Association for Democratic Reforms 186

Australia 109, 131, 134–5, 146, 148
Austria 119, 135, 146, 148
authoritarian/ism 8, 138, 140–4, 154, 349
autonomy 20, 25, 29, 33, 72, 117, 132, 188, 213, 221, 226–8, 231, 240, 242–4, 253, 313, 335, 343, 353, 358–9; extraordinary 25, 72; functional 20; institutional 353, 358–9; political 117, 343; regional 132; relative 242; subregional 221
Ayub, Mohammad 9

Babri Masjid (Mosque), demolition of 23–4, 35, 81
Backward Castes 15, 16, 81, 84, 210, 225, 268
Backward Classes 10, 14, 20, 73, 77, 81, 84, 268
Backward Classes Commission 10
Bahujan Samaj Party (BSP) 24, 26, 41, 62, 69, 81, 84, 93–4, 210–11, 214, 266, 319, 357
Bajrang Dal 155, 156
Bardhan, Pranab 242
Behaviourism 257
Belgium 112–13, 116–17, 120–5, 129, 135, 137, 146, 148; *1995 Belgian General Election Study* 124–5
Bengali Association 307
Bhambhri, C.P. 242
Bharatiya Janata Party (BJP) 1, 8, 16, 19, 23–4, 27–9, 35, 41, 60, 63, 68, 77, 79–82, 85, 92–3, 95–7, 132, 155–6, 208–11, 265, 268, 318–19, 329, 339, 350–2, 354–7, 359–60; electoral strategy of 155; rise to power of 8, 27–8, 209, 359
Bharatiya Jan Sangh 74
Bharatiya Kranti Dal 15
Bihar 16, 18, 20, 22, 24, 47, 61–3, 65, 69–70, 76, 81, 84, 87, 90–4, 102, 104, 209, 211, 218, 222, 224–5, 227–30, 250, 265–6, 351, 357
Biju Janata Dal (BJD) 27, 89, 95, 357
Bill of Rights 3
bipolarity(ies) 29, 70, 97, 228; Congress–BJP 97
Bodoland Development Council 221
Bofors exposure 79
Brahmin 77, 179, 210
Brazil 134–5, 140–1, 146, 148
Britain 3, 178, 200, 270
British India 218; Raj 3; rule 6, 34, 217
Bundelkhand 220
Bundesrepublik Deutschland (BDR) 119, 138
bureaucracy 5, 13, 21, 33, 82, 130, 189, 201, 335
Butler, David 266

Canada 112–13, 116, 120, 129, 131, 135, 145–6, 148
capitalism 82, 85, 241–2
casteism 11, 173, 180
caste(s) 5, 8, 10–13, 15–16, 20, 24, 26, 28, 36, 41, 46–8, 52, 69, 72–5, 80–1, 84, 86–7, 93–4, 129, 136, 142–3, 150, 153–4, 169–70, 172, 178–81, 185, 197, 199, 202, 206–7, 209–11, 219,

223, 225–6, 249, 264, 268, 288–90, 305–9, 311, 316–17, 329, 359, 364; agrarian 26; awareness 84; backward 15–16, 28, 81, 84, 170, 210, 225, 268; blocs 72, 181, 306; cleavages 81, 84; clusters 226; divisions 84; forward 81, 185; inequality 36; lower 16, 46, 52, 81, 225; middle 15, 225–6; mobilisation 47, 202; peasantry 73, 75; polarisation 69; politicisation of 12–13, 36, 249; politics and 12, 180–1; system 5, 26, 154, 223; upper 8, 13, 15, 20, 26, 28, 52, 69, 73–5, 81, 93–4, 150, 169–70, 209, 225–6, 268, 288, 305–6, 329
Census of India 128, 206–7, 274, 292; 2011 census 206; caste and 206, 207
central government 10, 22, 70, 87, 200, 226, 228, 330
Centre for the Study of Developing Societies (CSDS) 25, 133–4, 136–7, 141, 147, 251, 308, 315
Chandrashekhar 79
Chhattisgarh 76, 89, 92, 129, 225, 228–30, 291
Chile 140–1
citizen/citizenship/citizenry 3, 31, 126, 172, 174, 180, 185, 188, 199, 207, 335, 349; attitudes of 138, 156; equal 126, 180, 188, 335; informed 172; ordinary 33–4, 61–2, 69, 89–90, 199, 302, 321; politicised 109
civil society organisations 229
class(es): cleavages 82, 86; divisions 74–5, 181; dominant 227–8, 242; middle 25–6, 28, 79, 83, 85–6, 209, 329–31; political 44, 53, 199; ruling 241–2; under 353; upper 13, 52, 169, 305; working 179, 307
cleavage(s) 31, 41–2, 61, 66, 68–9, 72, 74–8, 81–6, 110–14, 116, 142–3, 180–1, 202, 306, 308, 321, 337; backward–forward 84; caste 81, 84; class 82, 86; communal 86; competing 72, 77; cross-cutting 75, 181; cultural 113, 116; generational 181; issue-based 77; linguistic 75, 113, 116; master 69, 74, 78, 83; national 85, 116; political 72; potential 72, 110; rural–urban 77; socio-cultural 111, 112; structures of 72
clientelism 173
coalition(s) 18–19, 25–6, 28–9, 47–8, 59–60, 65–7, 75–7, 84, 96, 177–8, 181, 196, 199, 203, 207, 209–11, 228, 250, 258, 293, 337, 345, 354, 356–7, 361; anti-BJP 354; governments 177, 203, 250, 258; Kshatriya, Harijan, Adivasi, and Muslim (KHAM) 77; localised 75; politics 47, 96; rainbow 19, 28, 66, 75, 207; short-lived 76; social 75, 77, 96, 178, 181, 337; temporary 209
Cold War 119
collective action 3
colonial/ism 38, 82, 174, 233;

power 5, 83, 280–1; rule 74; state 5, 11, 242
communalism 46, 63, 72, 80, 127, 169, 230, 265, 360
communist parties 19, 23, 24
Communist Party of India (CPI) 24, 130, 242, 304, 319
Communist Party of India (Marxist) (CPI[M]) 67, 96, 130, 210, 214, 319
Communist Party of India (Marxist Leninist) 30
community(ies): artisan 37; backward 14, 94, 185; cultural 126; dalit 185; dominant 185; linguistic 126; majority 73, 156, 356; marginalised 363; political 178, 220; politicisation of 36; religious 80, 120, 180, 308, 350; sub-regional 219–20; village 72, 328
comparative: elections 171, 193–4; engagement 54; politics 56, 213, 217
competitiveness 13, 56, 98, 150
conflict(s) 46; Naga–Kuki 307; social 46; socio-economic bases of 45; zones 291
Congress: dominance 10, 28, 54; movement 53; opposition system 19
Congress Party: catch-all character of 48, 52, 66, 68, 74-5, 92, 95; challenge to 79; comeback of 78; complacency of 208; decline of 28, 41, 49, 56, 80, 93, 96, 209, 319; defeat of 19, 79, 313; democratic background 50; dominance of 44, 53, 59; failure of 81; hegemony of 66; patterns of partisanship 91; politics of 78-9; social coalition of 77
Congress system 9, 42–3, 45, 49–54, 56, 63, 66–7, 70–1, 74–80, 83, 86–7, 89–91, 93, 96, 183, 228, 249; analysis of 45, 50; beneficiaries of 53; challenges to 50, 75–6; collapse of 79; critique of 53; decline of 78, 89; demise of 42, 67, 80, 91, 93, 183; framework of 51; reborn 77; redefinition of 78; return of 54; "two lives" of 43
consensus 2, 50, 52–4, 67, 86, 130, 132, 206, 229, 288–9, 301, 326, 328, 349; majoritarian 349; political 288, 289; spontaneous 67
Constituent Assembly 3, 132, 174
constitutional amendment 186, 196; 73rd Amendment 222; 73rd and 74th Amendments 184, 343; 91st Constitutional Amendment Bill 339
constitutional institutions 5
convergence 40, 64–9, 85, 89–90, 92, 94–8, 143, 228–9; bipolar 65–8, 92, 95, 228; multipolar 64, 68, 90, 92, 95; policy 69
corruption 10, 12, 17, 22, 169, 203, 235, 283, 341, 348, 359–60; ideological 17; political 203
Costa Rica 142
cow slaughter 23
criminalisation 33, 169, 240
cultural: boundaries 108, 111; community 126; differences 109, 119; diversity 109;

expressions 223–4; groups 113, 115–17; homogenisation 28, 35, 220; identity 108, 111–12, 114–16; inauthenticity 279–80; minorities 121; nation 114
culture 7, 22, 31, 112–13, 119–20, 128, 134, 215, 219, 222–4, 230, 235, 244–6, 256, 275, 278, 285, 290, 363; democratic 224, 230, 275; protest 31; shared 112

Da Costa, E.P.W. 269
Dalit(s) 19, 24–6, 28, 52, 77, 81, 84, 90, 93–5, 169, 179, 185, 188, 210, 222, 304, 306, 313, 335, 352, 359, 361–3
Darjeeling Hill Council 221
degradation 255
deinstitutionalisation 45, 348
delegitimation 113
Delhi 43, 59, 63, 67, 76, 91–3, 102, 104, 141, 155, 181, 205, 210, 228, 305, 307–9, 314, 318, 351
democracy(ies): achievements of 34; American 128; approaches to 6, 8, 113; aspects of 217; bourgeois 63, 71; breakdown of 154; "by-hearted" 31; character of 21; checklist model of 171, 279, 284; concept and theory of 259, 285; consequences of the game of 7; consolidated 117; contemporary 112; contingencies of 2; "creolisation" of 38; defence of 32; definition of 33; demise of 33, 167; design of 330; electoral 177, 182; equilibrium for 45; established 30; federal 122, 128, 131, 133–6, 138, 144–8; functioning of 37, 49; growth of 12; guided 9; history of 7, 12, 188, 335; idea of 6, 25, 30–2, 34, 37–8, 189, 290, 333–4; inclusionary 109, 112; Indian model of 1–3, 8–10, 13–15, 20–1, 30, 32, 34–5, 148, 152, 166–70, 175–6, 186, 188–9, 196, 198, 202, 207, 252, 256, 259, 321, 327, 330, 334–6; indigenisation of 39; industrial 188, 334; inner-party 339; institutional base to 13; insulation of 10; language of 17, 24, 31; legal-constitutional apparatus of 216; liberal 2–3, 10–12, 26, 32, 174, 176, 189, 198, 279, 333; low-intensity 33; model of 3, 189, 279, 284, 333; modern 9, 72, 284; Nehruvian 14; non-competitive 174; one-party 70; plural 1, 80; political 4, 33, 240; practice of 4; procedural 30, 33, 52; quality of 30, 202, 216–17, 221–2, 229; radical 39, 285; reform and 170; representative 20, 166–8, 170, 173–5, 177–8, 180, 186–8, 193–4, 199, 201–2, 349; sectors of 176, 198; social 201; sociological dimensions of 53; stability of 139; success of 38; supportive of 140–1;

survival of 4; "Third Wave" 141; United States and 12; "vernacularisation" of 38; vision of 3, 10; Western models of 2–3, 6–7, 38, 71, 175, 260, 334; working of 34, 166
democratic: authority 50; consolidation 117; cultures 223; decision-making 85; federations 152; institutions 8, 20, 115–16, 130–1, 138–9, 238, 327, 350, 353; invitation 9, 35, 334; liberal state 119; mobilisation 54; opposition 122; order 258; plebiscites 126; political process 80; principle 9; process 22; right 26; state nation 110, 137, 154; states 114; transition 2, 188, 225–6, 334
democratic politics 2, 6, 9, 15, 22, 29–30, 35–7, 42, 43, 53–6, 69, 71, 85–6, 90, 98, 115, 128, 167, 169, 186, 196–7, 215, 218, 225–6, 230–1, 254, 320, 329, 345, 350; Congress system 9, 12, 14, 19, 49, 65, 71, 207, 249, 259, 302; first phase 9–10, 12–13, 15, 18–19, 23, 52, 56, 303; incubation of 54; multiparty system 12, 28–9, 56, 177, 214; one-party-dominance system 12, 49; second phase 14–16, 19, 22, 25, 27, 303; success of 15; third phase of 8, 22, 24–5, 28
democratic theory 6, 8, 64, 171, 251, 259–60; contemporary 8; empirical 251; Western 6
democratic upsurge 25, 27, 30, 91, 167, 179, 184, 187–8, 293, 305, 331, 335, 342–3, 353; first 27; second 27, 30, 353
democratisation 2, 4, 17, 20, 26, 30, 32–3, 109, 117, 127, 168, 170, 189, 226, 281, 283, 287, 336, 342; comparative 30; Indian model of 2; process of 17, 20, 32, 117, 189, 336
demonetisation 354, 355
Desai, A.R. 242
Deutsche Demokratische Republic (DDR) 138
development: industrialised 16; Western-style 4; welfare-oriented 52
Devi Lal 7, 17, 91
difference(s): cultural 122; ideological 58; institutional 221; inter-regional 45; inter-state 77; linguistic 122; national 122; policy 68; socio-cultural 109
dignity 33, 62, 84, 94, 177, 185, 199, 201, 223
disparities 36, 361–2
dispute(s) 63, 78, 168–71, 182, 205, 236, 268, 278, 288, 301, 310–11, 316, 326, 340; electoral 182; factional 63; interpretative 168–70; methodological 278, 301, 310–11; Mizo 78
diversity(ies) 4, 13, 22, 35, 108–14, 116, 126–9, 132–3, 138, 148, 152–5, 207, 285, 348, 349–50; cultural 109, 132; ethnic 22; integration of 35; linguistic 109, 128,

133; politically activated 113; politicised 127–8; regional 13, 22, 35, 128, 133; religious 132; social 35, 127; socio-cultural 108, 110–13, 116, 154
dominance 12, 19, 28, 44, 49–51, 53–4, 57–9, 63, 69, 79, 94, 96, 98, 132, 171, 176–7, 182–4, 199, 225, 250, 332, 351–2; national 132; one-party 19, 50–1, 57, 59, 79, 177, 182–3, 250, 351; social 176, 184, 199
domination 47, 52, 64–6, 70, 79, 83, 225, 231, 285, 365; Congress 83; neo-colonial 285, 365; one-party 64, 70; patterns of 225
Doordarshi Party 266
Dravida Kazhagam 74
Dravida movement 219
Dravida Munnetra Kazhagam (DMK) 15–16, 27, 60, 62–3, 97, 215, 304, 319, 357
Dumont, Louis 244
Duverger's law 68

East Asia 282
East Asian Barometer 282
East Germany 119, 138
Economic and Political Weekly 48, 151
economic: changes 239; decisions 25, 30, 227; determinism 241; development 4, 37, 240, 349; globalisation 29; goals 5; growth 4–5, 8, 353; inequality 42; interests 11, 33, 37, 226–27, 231; issues 5; liberalisation 23, 29; policies 24–5, 30, 46, 63, 78, 82, 85–6, 94, 210, 226–7, 243, 289, 360, 364; processes 45, 221; reforms 23, 331; resources 227; sanctions 1; structures 42, 293; transformations 281
economy 4, 33, 36, 46–7, 69, 82, 85, 174, 221, 226, 238, 241, 243–4, 271, 282, 289, 292, 317, 325, 329, 331, 354, 360; command 46; globalising 69; Indian 33, 36; liberalisation of 85; market 82; market-oriented 46; political 47, 226, 238, 241, 243–4, 271, 317
education 15, 37, 109, 149, 151, 186, 197, 305, 348, 363, 365
Election Commission of India 147, 149, 182, 337, 339, 348
elections: forecasting 262; majoritarian 61; manifesto 7, 30; past and present 302; plebiscitary nature of 302; results 172; research methodology of 309; state-level 9, 213; studies 168, 171–2, 274, 302, 309, 317, 321; understanding of 312
electoral: choices 42, 172, 175, 320–1; competition 5, 41, 47, 61, 71, 86, 178, 193, 313, 316; democracies 177, 182; disputes 182; federalism 183; fraud 67, 71; mandate 195; outcomes 47, 172, 216, 275, 314; participation 179–80, 197, 224; politics 13, 26, 40, 47–9, 61, 67, 98, 114, 150–1, 171, 181–2, 185–6, 193,

196–7, 300, 304–6, 308–9, 312–13, 331, 358; process 147, 176, 199; realignments 43; reforms 328, 330, 336, 350; success 20, 211; turnout 179, 224; viability 57, 93; volatility 41, 43, 83, 184, 186, 196; waves 18, 213, 302–3; zone 267
electoral system 13, 60, 67, 69, 72, 77, 94, 99, 177, 197, 201, 264, 303, 328, 330, 337–8, 340; FPTP 67, 72; national-level 89
predictions 262–3, 264, 267; state-level 41, 89; verdicts 41, 85, 89, 207, 211, 216, 264
electorate(s) 18, 25, 59, 68, 73, 137, 151, 155, 172, 196, 209, 303, 307, 316, 319, 337–8; fragmented 18; joint 73; national 18, 137; single 73
electronic voting machines 320
Emergency, The 20, 21, 179, 195, 240, 250, 255–6, 348
empowerment 16, 210, 234
equality 34, 36, 199, 223
ethnic/ity: cleansing 112, 115; diversity 22, 86, 172; divisions 29, 175; minorities 8, 179; strife 62
ethno-federalism 116
ethnography 259, 293, 300, 320
Eurobarometer 133, 141, 282
Eurocentrism 276
Europe 41–2, 121, 129, 149, 155, 171, 197, 241, 246, 252, 256, 278–9, 281–3, 290; party competition in 41; social cleavages in 42
European Union 133, 282
exceptionalism 175, 302
exit polls 267–8, 275
extremism 56
ex-Untouchables 15, 19, 305

Fascism 21, 349
federalism 109, 112–13, 115–17, 119–20, 128–9, 131–2, 136, 155, 183, 186, 196, 200; asymmetrical 112–15, 131, 186, 196; "coming together" 117; electoral 183; Indian 129, 200; traditional theory of 117
federal structure 3, 44
federations 114, 117, 119–20, 152; "asymmetrical" 119; democratic 152; types of 119
First-past-the-post (FPTP) system 57, 61, 67, 72, 177–8, 196, 202, 264, 269, 328, 337, 356
foreign policy 8, 354
fractionalisation 58, 96
fragmentation 49, 58–9, 61, 68–9, 94, 96, 116, 173, 202, 209, 269, 340
France 108–9, 121
Frankel, Francine 46–7, 243; *India's Political Economy, 1947–1977* 243
freedom movement 73, 82
French Revolution 108
Friends of India 2
Frontline 267
functionalism, structural 257
fundamental rights 3

Gallup 283
Gandhi, Indira 8, 14, 16, 19–22, 34, 45–6, 53, 76–7, 79, 83, 195, 250, 302–4, 315, 357,

358; assassination in 1984 22, 46, 79, 156; defeat in 1977 21, 77; ideology of "Garibi Hatao" 17; political success 77; victory in the 1971 elections 250
Gandhi, Mahatma 10, 13, 73, 79, 132, 306, 352
Gandhi, Rajiv 23, 78–9, 82, 90, 156, 265, 268; assassination of 79, 265, 268; leadership of 78
Gandhi, Sonia 24
"Garibi Hatao" campaign 16–17, 208, 302, 304, 357
Gauri Lankesh 356, 359
Geertz, Clifford 244
gender 36, 181, 289–90; divide 36; gap 181; justice 36
general elections (*see also* Lok Sabha elections): 1967 elections 15, 45, 258, 300, 302–4, 306, 313, 318; 1967 to 1971 elections 314, 318; 1971 elections 18, 250, 300, 302–4, 315, 319, 357; 1977 elections 21; 1977 to 1989 267; 1980 elections 302; 1984 elections 302; 1991 elections 268; 1996 elections 25, 60; 1998 elections 25, 32; 2004 elections 318; 2014 elections 356; first elections 9, 27; fourth elections 9, 14; third elections 9
Germany 109, 119, 131, 134–5, 138, 146, 148
globalisation 29, 33, 37, 78, 189, 281–4, 289, 329, 331, 335
Global North 260, 275–6, 281, 285, 289
Global South 276, 281, 283–5, 288, 291, 293
Goa 48, 61, 65, 76, 97, 103, 105
Golden Temple, Amritsar 22
Goods and Services Tax (GST) 354–5
Goswami, Dinesh 328
governance 4–5, 21, 28, 31, 68, 85, 87, 145, 149, 176, 183, 187, 198, 207, 211–12, 218, 226, 230–1, 282, 329, 336, 342, 349, 355, 361; agenda of 68; democratic 31, 218, 226, 231, 336, 342; federal 87; institutions of 176, 198, 212
governmental: instability 56, 68, 83, 86, 169; stability 56, 331
Government of India Act of 1935 3
government(s): authoritarian 139, 140, 141; BJP 1, 35, 209; central 10, 22, 70, 87, 146, 149, 200, 226, 228, 330; coalition 177, 203, 250, 258; Congress 21, 23–4, 50, 80; democratic 139, 141; elected 10; form of 4, 7, 139, 140–1, 154, 194, 196, 263, 339; Janata Dal 23; Janta Dal (United)–BJP 209; LDF 226; Left Front 24; local 200; majority 177; misjudgement of 207; National Democratic Alliance (NDA) 205; non-Congress 21; Rajiv Gandhi 23; stability of 330; state 24, 88, 183–4, 186, 200, 201, 227, 343, 351, 361; survival rate of 186; United Front 82; United Progressive Alliance (UPA) I 204; United

Progressive Alliance (UPA) II 203, 207; V.P. Singh 81
Govindacharya 80
Gramsci 67, 242
Gujarat 16, 20, 22, 48, 59, 63, 65, 68, 76–7, 87, 90–3, 102, 104, 143–4, 155–6, 218–19, 222–5, 227–8, 250, 314, 348
Gujarat model 155–6

Habermas, Jurgen 138
Hardgrave, Robert 239; *India: Government and Politics in a Developing Nation* 239
Harijan(s) 77, 305–6, 313
Harit Pradesh 94
Haryana 7, 15, 61, 65, 76, 78, 81, 91, 97, 102, 104, 225, 227–30
health 37, 186
hegemony 23–4, 40, 64–7, 70, 75, 79, 89–92, 94–6, 98, 352, 359–60, 362, 365; Congress 90–2, 94–5, 98; one-party 79, 90, 96; unipolar 64–7, 70
heterogeneity, linguistic 120
Himachal/Himachal Pradesh 59, 63, 65, 68, 76, 91–3, 102, 104, 225, 228–9
Himachal Vikas Congress (HVC) 93
Hindi heartland 18, 21, 129, 185, 215, 219–20, 267
Hindu: constituency 74, 80; fundamentalists 1, 23, 155; nationalism 74, 77, 209; social hierarchy 19, 36, 179; social order 19; upper-caste 28, 150
Hindutva 47, 84, 209, 265, 318
homogeneity 109–10, 113, 128, 155
homogenisation 28, 35, 68, 86–9, 220; internal 87; intrastate 88–9
Human Development Index (HDI) 127
Human Development Report 2002: Deepening Democracy in a Fragmented World 127
human rights 20

identity/identities 13, 26, 35, 47, 73, 88, 108–9, 111–12, 114–26, 129, 132–4, 136–8, 153, 168, 172–3, 176, 180–2, 185, 187, 197–9, 202, 215, 219–20, 240, 306–7, 320; ascriptive 172; Belgian 123, 124; complementary 120, 122–3, 125–6, 133, 153; cultural 108, 111–12, 114–16; dual 121, 123, 126; exclusive 122, 134; French 109; historical 112; Indian 137; multiple 120, 122, 125–6, 153; national 109, 115, 119, 121–4, 136–8; plural 240; polarisation of 123; political 108, 116, 129, 137, 173, 185, 215, 307, 320;
politics 47, 202; regional 73, 132, 219–20; secular 198; social 176, 181–2, 187, 199; socio-cultural 111, 112, 116
ideological: cleavages 66; contestations 218, 223; differences 25, 57, 63; divisions 72; hegemony 24; legitimacy 351, 352;

mediation 26; mobilisation 88; persuasion 18; politics 62; preferences 12, 252; unsettling 24
ideology/ideologies 2–3, 12, 16–19, 23–6, 35, 57–8, 74, 82, 156, 172–3, 182, 197, 202, 210, 218, 222, 235, 237, 245, 250, 253, 352–3, 363–4; counter-hegemonic 363, 364; decline of 16; formal 57; high 17, 23–5, 57, 182; mass 3; nationalist 74; nation-state 35; Nehruvian 250; patchwork 16; political 17, 222, 235, 353; populist 17
imbalances, intraregional 45
imperialism 242
Index of Opposition Unity (IOU) 266, 267, 269
India/Indian union: aftermath of Partition 177; anti-colonial struggle 72, 137; as a state nation 126, 143; British division of 13; competitive politics in 12, 50, 55; contemporary 49, 96, 127, 137, 166, 171, 175, 186, 193–4, 212, 228, 234, 237, 245–6, 287, 325–6, 337; cultural divisions 13, 110–11; democracy in 137, 142, 144; democratic politics 2, 9, 53; electoral politics 150; established democracy 30; establishment of democracy in 7; human and income poverty 127; Independence 1, 6–7, 11, 13, 25, 29, 41, 53, 57, 64, 71–5, 132, 169, 179, 183, 185, 195, 204, 217, 222, 302, 315, 326, 339, 348, 351–3, 360; independent 3, 132, 155, 327; modern 3, 174, 272; Modi regime 351, 354, 355, 356, 357, 358, 359, 360, 361, 363, 364; partition of 4, 73; party system 40–1, 47–9, 54, 56, 58; political culture 7; political game in 45; political process in 47; political trust in 145; post-Independence 57, 64, 71, 204, 302, 315, 326, 339, 348, 351, 353; rural 16, 179, 181, 362; state nation 156; state politics in 42, 216
Indian constitution 3, 20, 131–2, 174, 177, 331, 334; Directive Principles of 3
Indian Council of Social Science Research 292
Indian democracy 1–2, 6–10, 13–15, 20–1, 30–5, 38, 70, 140, 148, 152, 166–70, 173, 175–6, 178, 186, 188–9, 193–6, 198–9, 201–2, 207, 231, 235, 252, 256, 259, 321, 327, 330, 334–6; achievements of 35; character of 15; decision-making in 9; design of 3, 186, 196; malpractices in 330; model of 2; Nehruvian phase of 13; performance of 34; problems in 334; second phase of 14–15; story of 6, 8, 169; successes and failures of 33
Indian economy 33, 36
Indian electoral system 173, 175–83, 193, 197–9, 201, 267, 300–3, 311; features

of 173, 199; specificity of 197
Indian Institute of Public Opinion 269
Indian model 2–4, 6, 33, 37–8, 132, 239–40, 251–5
Indian National Congress 9, 132
Indian National Lok Dal (INLD) 89
Indian nationhood 130, 133
Indian Parliament 1, 327
Indian party system 41, 47–8, 49, 51, 56, 67, 269; changes in 48–9
Indian political modernity 252–54, 259, 334
Indian politics 1–2, 6–8, 12, 14, 17–18, 23, 28, 40–1, 43–51, 53–4, 57, 81, 83, 86, 88, 98, 168, 173, 175–6, 198, 203, 213, 216, 228, 234, 236–7, 239, 243–4, 246, 249, 251, 253, 257–8, 260, 267–8, 272–3, 293, 302–3; analyses of 44, 47, 49, 243; distortions and maladies of 253; history of 2, 7, 83, 198; ideology of 18; socialism in 23; story of 8, 12, 176; study of 43, 249, 251, 258; theories of 48, 244
Indian polity 33, 129, 177–8, 245, 249, 258, 327
Indian states 4–5, 9, 11, 18, 68, 70, 82, 129–30, 133, 136, 143, 155, 196, 236–46, 250, 255, 352; disputes about 236; nature of 241; theories of 236–7, 240–1, 243, 246
India Today 267, 268
Indonesia 9, 131
industrial: growth 24; revolution 72
inequality 14, 24, 36, 38, 42, 91, 188, 201, 222, 335, 343, 353; caste 36; economic 42; social 24, 42, 91
information collection 310, 314
Inglehart, Ronald 133, 135, 146, 148
instability 56, 68, 69, 83, 86, 169, 183, 330–1; governmental 56, 68, 83, 86, 169; political 330
institutional: decay 8; edifice 21, 240, 348; fetishism 327; institutionalisations 8, 13, 131, 149, 239; mechanism 8; reforms 222
international: information order 2; relations 66
Ireland 3

Jammu and Kashmir 28, 31, 34, 64, 70, 97, 102, 104, 129–30, 136, 182, 195, 204–6, 220–1, 223–4, 228–9, 231, 348, 352, 356–7; misjudgement in 206; policy 204; UPA's mishandling of 205; withdrawal of special status of 28
Janata Dal (JD) 22–3, 26–7, 63, 68, 79, 89–90, 92–3, 95, 211, 265, 268, 318, 357
Janata Party 17, 21–2, 79; redistributive policies 17
Jan Sangh 16, 19, 74, 77, 85, 305, 318–19, 350
Janta Dal (United) 209
Japan 109
Jats 92

Jawaharlal Nehru University (JNU) 271–2
Jenkins, Robert 48
Jharkhand 61, 76, 89, 92, 94–5, 129, 222, 227–9
Jharkhand Mukti Morcha 95
John, Mary 338
judiciary 3, 13, 21, 32, 130, 144, 147, 153, 187, 329, 348, 358
justice 16, 36, 43, 74, 81, 218, 339, 350, 361, 364

Kairon, Pratap Singh 10
Kalelkar, Kaka 10
Kamaraj Plan 14
Karnataka 15, 19, 60, 63, 65, 68, 76–8, 91, 95, 102–5, 215, 218, 222, 225, 228, 318, 356–7
Kaviraj, Sudipta 243, 257
Kerala 10, 15, 19, 29, 51, 59, 61–3, 65, 68–70, 74–6, 78, 87, 91, 96–7, 102–5, 209, 214–15, 218, 222–3, 225–6, 228–9, 319, 344, 351–2, 357
Khalistan 136
Kishwar, Madhu 338
Korea 141
Korea Democracy Barometer 141
Kothari, Rajni 4, 6, 42–5, 49–54, 63, 174, 181, 239–40, 244, 249–59, 302; *Memoirs* 250; *Politics in India* 4, 43, 239, 249–52, 254–7, 259–60
Kumar, Nitish 209
Kumar, Ravinder 244

Lahiri, Ashok 266
landlords/landlordism 74, 242
land: ownership 11, 14; reform 11, 74, 271; laws 11; movement 74
language(s) 3, 7–9, 13, 16–18, 23–6, 31–2, 38–9, 45, 57, 69, 73, 109, 112, 119–20, 122, 128–9, 132, 171, 182, 198, 209, 219, 250, 252, 257, 277, 289–91; divide 73; French 119; Hindi 18, 21, 128–9, 185, 215, 219–20, 250, 267; Latin America 140, 282, 339
Latinobarometer 141, 282, 283
Law Commission 329, 341
leadership 3, 14, 44, 46, 50, 52–3, 73, 78, 81, 95, 97, 121, 132, 193, 205–6, 208, 214, 220, 223, 227, 292, 309, 321, 330, 357, 363, 365; central 46; charismatic 223; intellectual 292; national 205–6; nationalist 3; national-level 44; pattern 52; personalised 46; plebiscitary 53; political 121, 193, 220, 227; post-Independence 132; semi-charismatic 223; style 46, 53; upper-class 52; youth 363
Left Democratic Front (LDF) 59, 63, 68, 96, 215, 226
Left Front 24, 60, 62–3, 67, 96
left–right axis 57
legitimacy 11, 21, 27, 32, 50, 64, 67, 70, 120, 125, 130–1, 139, 147, 152, 180, 197, 225–6, 239, 240, 321, 335, 347, 351–2, 355, 359; ideological 351, 352; political 64; system of 50

liberalisation 23, 29, 37, 85, 288, 331, 353
Liberalism 38, 359
Liberation Tigers of Tamil Eelam (LTTE) 69
linguistic: cleavages 75; community 126; diversity 109, 128, 133; groups 180; heterogeneity 120; states 9, 13, 73, 129, 219
Lohia, Ram Manohar 10, 75, 328
lokayuktas 339
Lok Janshakti Party (LJSP) 211
Lokniti network 272
Lokpal 326, 328, 339, 359–60
Lok Sabha 1, 21, 27, 36, 47, 79, 81, 93, 95, 103, 105, 150, 178, 183–4, 195, 200, 207, 210, 213–14, 264, 351, 358; elections 21, 47, 79, 81, 93, 95, 150, 183–4, 207, 213, 264, 351, 358; 1989 election 79; 1991 election 79, 81, 93, 95; 2004 election 150; 2009 election 207; 2014 election 351; 2019 election 358; state-wise analysis of 47
Lok Satta 333, 341
lynching 355, 359

Madan, T.N. 244–5
Madhya Pradesh (MP) 48, 51, 59, 63, 67, 75–6, 91–3, 102–5, 219, 225, 228, 265–6
Maha Dalits 185, 208
Maharashtra 19, 47, 59, 65, 67, 73, 76, 87, 91–2, 95, 102, 104, 218–19, 221–3, 225, 227–30, 304, 319
Mahatma Gandhi National Rural Employment Gurantee Act (MGNREGA) 208
majoritarianism 223–4
malpractices 182, 330, 341
Mandal Commission 22–4, 27, 80–5, 87, 95, 185, 206, 208–10, 329
Mandir controversy 22–4, 27, 80–5, 87, 265
Manipur 61, 65, 76, 97, 103, 105, 136, 220, 228–30, 307, 318
Manor, James 339
marginal/marginalised groups 136, 142, 148, 152–3
Marxist(s) 22, 30, 67, 130, 210, 236–8, 241–3, 245, 249, 255, 310, 332, 357; superstition 332; theory 241, 243
Mayawati 82
Mazdoor Kisan Shakti Sangathan's (MKSS) 333, 344
media 194, 349, 358; debates 194; social 349, 358
Meghalaya 76, 97, 103, 105, 352
Menon, Nivedita 338
middle class 78, 82, 179
migrants 22, 69
minority/minorities 8, 19, 22–3, 37, 73, 79–80, 113, 119, 121–2, 136, 142, 154, 156, 177, 179, 230, 245, 355–6; cultural 121; ethnic 8, 179; personal laws of 73; rights 73; social 177
Mizoram 34, 61, 65, 76, 97, 103, 105, 130, 136, 143–4, 195, 218–19, 221, 228, 352
modernisation 5–6, 238–9, 256, 259, 279, 283

modernity 4, 35, 233, 244, 252–4, 256, 259, 284, 334, 352–3, 365
Modi, Narendra 349–61, 363–4
monarchy 122, 124–5
monopoly 14, 242, 340
MORI 283
Morris-Jones, W.H. 49, 238–9, 249
multiculturalism 35, 121, 129
multinationalism 127
multiparty: competition 49, 50, 60–1; systems 54
multipolar/ity: competition 68, 70, 96, 97, 228, 250; convergence 64–5, 68, 90, 92, 95
Muslim(s) 20, 28, 69–70, 73–4, 77, 93–4, 121, 136, 141–2, 150–1, 153–6, 177, 185, 268, 319, 338, 349, 352, 363, 365; representation of 185, 338
Muslim United Front, Jammu and Kashmir 70
Myanmar 113, 117
Myrdal, Gunnar 239

Nagaland 34, 64, 97, 103, 105, 129–30, 136, 182, 195, 218, 220, 229–30, 348, 352
Naidu, Chandrababu 95
Nandy, Ashis 245
Narayan, Jayaprakash 327–8, 334
nation building 4, 44, 108–9, 113, 115, 120, 132, 155; aggressive 120; French-style 109, 113, 115, 155; Indian model 132; process of 120; unitary 108–9, 112
nation state 35, 85, 108–15, 117, 119–20, 126, 131, 137–8, 145, 147–8, 154–5, 169, 174, 239, 244, 334; ideology of 35; Indian 169, 174
national: bourgeoisie 242; identities 121; independence movement 131; integration 4, 34, 126; movement 9, 36, 44, 72, 132, 174, 302, 305; opposition party 81; parties 8, 97, 184, 214–15, 258, 337; political community 22, 75–9, 82, 86, 199, 219; politics 1, 44–5, 51, 81, 87, 213–15, 224–5, 228, 291, 328, 336–7
National Advisory Council 208
National Commission to Review the Working of the Constitution 329, 333
National Democratic Alliance (NDA) 205, 214
National Election Studies in India 27, 196–7, 307, 315
National Sample Survey Organisation 292
nationalism 10, 74, 77, 82, 121, 127, 137–8, 209, 352, 356, 360, 363–5; Hindu 74, 77, 209
nationalist movement 5, 34, 72, 74, 76, 132, 222, 305
nationality 35, 79, 135
Naxalbari/Naxalite movement 14, 16, 22, 242
Nehru, Jawaharlal 8–10, 13–14, 43, 50, 53, 82, 110, 132, 254, 352; charisma of 53; leadership 50, 53
Nepal 291
NES 137–8, 140–2, 144, 150, 153
Netherlands, the 109

New Economic Policy 25, 227, 288
NGOs 32, 198
Norris, Pippa 144–5
North America 171, 197, 278–9, 281, 290
North East 31, 34, 61, 75, 97, 136, 223, 231, 320, 351
North India 73, 79, 81–2, 87, 91–2, 210, 269
nuclear: ambiguity 1; explosions 1, 8

one-party: closed 64, 70, 79; domination 12, 19, 49–51, 57–9, 64, 70, 79, 177, 182–3, 239, 250, 351; hegemony 79, 90, 96; pattern of 57; system 50, 64–6, 70, 79
Oommen, T.K. 244
Operation Blue Star 22
opinion poll/polling 122, 176, 199, 262–4, 267–8, 270, 275, 283, 285, 289, 291–2, 344, 352; commercial 283, 292; election-related 262; organisations 275; nationwide 263, 267; pre-election 315
opposition party 10, 53, 81, 302
Orissa 27, 51, 60, 65, 75–6, 91–2, 95, 102, 104, 218, 220, 225, 227–8
Other Backward Classes (OBCs) 20, 23–4, 26, 28–9, 73, 77, 81, 83–4, 90, 93–4, 151, 185, 206, 209, 222, 268

Pakistan 4, 7, 9
panchayat elections 179, 320, 341
Panchayati Raj (PR) 221–2, 258, 329, 337
parliamentary system 3, 10, 122, 186, 196, 200, 339
party competition 41–2, 44, 47, 49–51, 53, 55, 58–61, 67, 76, 85–8, 91, 98, 174, 193, 211, 218, 228–9, 302, 318, 349; format of 58, 61, 91, 228–9; hegemonic 76; ideological dimension of 51; models of 51; principle of 49; reconfiguration of 76; structure of 42, 218; system dimension of 53
party politics 47–8, 51, 207, 229, 258, 306, 314; regionalisation of 258; state-level 48
party system: changes in 40, 43, 49, 55; classification of 55–7, 61; dimension in 57; effect on 64; evolution of 71, 97, 340; model for 42, 54; national-level 45; nature of 40, 58, 340; reconfiguration of 83, 89, 91, 350; role of 55; state 44–5, 48; traditional classifications of 56; types of 42, 64, 70; typology of 43, 54–5, 71
Patel, Chimanbhai 90
Patil, S.K. 14
patriotism 112, 119
Pew Global Survey 282
plebiscites 18, 53, 126
pluralism 129–30, 155, 320
polarisation 12, 68–9, 70, 94, 123, 126, 360; caste 69; ideological 12; politics of 69; social 68
policy 3, 17, 30, 44, 46, 50, 52, 82, 85, 94, 108, 109, 111–12, 114, 122, 166, 176, 184, 196, 201, 210, 226–8, 235, 239,

288–9, 309, 332, 336, 360, 364, 366; affirmative action 3; anti-poverty 196; convergence 69; developmental 184; differences 68; divergences 69; economic 24–5, 30, 46, 78, 82, 85–86, 94, 210, 226–7, 243, 289, 360, 364; economic liberalisation 23; foreign 8, 354; governmental 336; initiatives 16, 354; issues 68; Kashmir 204; language 122; redistributive 17; responses 292; secular 8; social 196, 201; substantive 17

political: agencies 11, 27; agenda 8, 22–3, 32, 42, 78, 94–5, 98, 176, 187, 198, 229–30, 276, 326; attitudes 181, 276–7, 282, 284, 286, 289; behaviour 169, 181, 258, 276–7, 282, 284–7, 306, 320; boundaries 4, 111, 219; changes 5, 183, 318–20; class 44, 53, 199; coalition 26, 181; common sense 194, 325; consequences 9, 155, 330, 337, 355; crisis 8, 240; culture 7, 120, 215, 219, 222–3, 235, 278, 285; decision-making 29, 227; democracy 4, 33, 240; development 6, 14, 19, 27, 44, 148, 204, 238, 253, 281; discourse 23, 25, 80, 82, 85, 93; economy 47, 226, 238, 241, 243–4, 271, 317; efficacy 20, 149–50; elite 5, 10, 13, 20, 53, 229; events 11, 22; expressions 13, 26, 112, 116; formations 22, 25, 32, 62, 74, 84, 89, 214, 340–1, 366; ideology 17, 353; information 283, 342; innovation 3, 17; legacy 217–18; movements 13, 72–3, 136, 218, 222, 229, 234, 342, 353; order 217, 238, 246, 252; participation 25, 31, 179, 224–5, 283, 287–8, 305, 334; practices 98, 176, 189, 198, 224, 255, 259, 284, 286, 290, 330, 333; preferences 172, 180, 197, 226, 274; reality 29, 108, 115, 176, 198, 210–11, 236, 258, 269, 276, 288; representatives 31, 166–7, 170, 187; rights 20, 31, 230; stability 45; structures 176, 187, 198, 331; support 19, 306–7; system 6, 27, 43, 54, 122, 131, 153, 177, 199, 327, 349; theory 182, 257, 272, 286, 332; trends 89, 215; values 237, 258, 279, 327; wisdom 55, 108

political choice(s) 25, 42, 58, 62, 64, 86–87, 89, 98, 172–3, 175, 178, 183, 197, 202, 214, 219, 222, 224, 229, 231; fictitious 63; formal 173, 175; moderate 63; multi-party 65; nature of 58, 62, 65, 86, 214, 222; none 64, 70, 284; one-party 65; shallow 64; structure of 197; substantial 62, 69–70; substantive 90, 229; systematic 64; two-party 65

political community 4, 22, 34, 75–9, 82–3, 86, 112, 199,

212, 215, 219–20, 237; national 22, 75–9, 82, 86, 199, 219
political competition 16, 29, 41–3, 48–52, 55, 57–8, 60, 62–3, 66–7, 69, 70, 78, 80, 84–5, 86–90, 92, 95, 98, 175, 201, 217–19, 228, 318; bipolar 29, 59, 68, 95, 96, 178; Congress–BJD–BJP 95; Congress–BJP 68; Congress–Janata Dal 63, 95; Congress–TDP 63; consolidation of 175; democratic 41, 80; electoral 5, 41, 47, 61, 71, 86, 178, 193, 313, 316; format of 57–8, 70, 90, 92; forms of 51, 60; inter-party 50; intra-party 50, 302; LDF–UDF 68; multi-party 49, 50, 60–1, 302; multi-polar 68, 70, 96, 250; party 41–2, 44, 47, 49–51, 53, 55, 58–61, 67, 76, 87, 91, 98, 174, 193, 211, 218, 228–9, 302, 349; patterns of 41, 55; structure of 41–2, 48, 52, 55, 65, 80, 86, 89, 217–18; systemless 64–5, 71, 97; two-party 47, 59–60, 67; two-plus 60, 67, 95–6; types of 58–60, 67
political divisions 43, 71–2, 74–5, 180; class 74–5, 181; ideology-based 74; regional 76, 84; social 11–12, 28, 71–3, 76, 111, 174, 180
political institutions 5, 20, 33, 134, 137, 188, 238–9, 245, 253, 271, 325, 327–8, 334–5
political judgement 203–7, 211–12
political mobilisation 11, 19, 47, 52, 54–5, 62, 64, 69, 71–4, 80, 86, 88, 92, 95, 169, 185, 188, 198, 202, 209, 222, 230, 234, 240, 304, 326, 335–6, 356, 359–61; basis of 73; caste-based 169; cleavage-based 74; communist 74; competitive 52, 64; electoral 230; emotional 80; exclusivist 73; identity-based 198; ideological 88; mass 72, 361; patterns of 86
platforms of 72; radical 326; sectional 19, 92
political opinions 181, 272, 274, 276–8, 280, 282, 284, 286, 289, 321
political parties 5, 9, 15, 19, 21, 25, 28–9, 32–3, 36, 41, 58, 60–1, 63, 66–7, 71, 73, 78, 85, 139, 143, 147, 172, 174, 177–9, 183–4, 187, 193, 198–9, 201, 207, 214, 222, 228–9, 234–5, 240, 266, 291, 303, 306–7, 313, 320, 330–1, 339–41, 344, 353, 365; anti-BJP 356; changing fortunes of 55, 214, 303; dominant 57, 65, 70, 132, 207; identification 71, 172; national 121, 172, 313; non-BJP 356, 357; non-Congress 19, 21, 74, 95, 210, 270; proliferation of 148, 152, 169, 202, 331; regional 19, 22, 25, 210–11, 214, 231, 250, 258; single 1, 67, 269; small 58, 60, 331; socialist 93, 319; structures 64, 75

political power 15, 20, 29, 33, 64, 69, 81, 174, 183–4, 189, 195, 201, 221, 225–7, 234, 293, 336; decentralisation of 201; nature of 64, 65; transfer of 29
political processes 31, 33, 46–7, 78, 80, 136, 184, 207, 215, 313; contemporary 47; democratic 80; state-level 215
political reforms 188–9, 194, 201, 325–34, 336–40, 342–5; agenda of 188, 334; challenge of 334; measures of 343; old-style 340; radical agenda for 325–6, 329, 332, 337, 342, 345
political representation 129, 166–74, 178, 184–5, 187–9, 200, 335; mechanism of 188, 335; nature of 178, 187, 200; paradox of 166, 168
political will 36–7, 196, 201, 203, 221, 361
politicisation 12–13, 20, 26, 31, 36, 226, 234, 249
politics: accommodative 243; "all-India" 43; anti-Modi 355; anti-system 30; aspect of 172; authoritarian nature of 51; "backward class" 14; basis of 12, 78, 220, 351; caste and 11, 12, 180–1; cleavage-based 72, 77; coalition 47, 96; comparative 56, 213, 217; competitive 5, 11–13, 31–2, 36, 42, 50, 54–5, 72, 83, 90, 94, 97, 110, 132, 183, 188, 228, 334–5, 355; counter-hegemonic 362–5; criminalisation of 240; dalit–bahujan 188, 335; democratic 2, 6, 9, 15, 22, 29–30, 35–7, 42–3, 53, 54–6, 69, 71, 85–6, 90, 98, 115, 128, 167, 169, 186, 196–7, 215, 218, 225–6, 230–1, 254, 320, 329, 345, 350; economic limits to 11, 226, 350; electoral 13, 26, 40, 47–9, 61, 67, 98, 114, 150–1, 171, 181, 182, 185–6, 193, 196–7, 300, 304–6, 308–9, 312–13, 331, 358; identity 47, 202; inter-party 51; intra-party 51, 306; local 11, 177, 220, 313; mainstream 16, 18, 21, 205, 272; majoritarian 1, 80, 365; Mandalisation of 82, 210; Mandir 80–1; models of 287–8; modern 174, 182, 2520–3, 284, 310; national 1, 44–5, 51, 81, 87, 213–15, 224–5, 228, 291, 328, 336–7; national-level 43–4, 224; party 47–8, 51, 207, 229, 258, 306, 314; plebiscitary 21, 53, 303; representative 184, 186, 240; state 29, 42–9, 86, 98, 178, 200, 213–17, 224, 226–8, 232, 258, 319; subalterns in 180; transformative 43, 54, 67, 96, 98
Pondicherry 61, 103, 105
Poorvanchal 94, 220
populism 17–18, 186, 223
Portugal 109
Post-Congress polity 28, 43, 49, 57, 80, 89, 91

poverty 14, 16, 38, 76, 86, 127, 168, 186, 194–7, 205, 211, 239, 255, 353
power: centres of 15, 22, 33; devolution of 221; political 15, 20, 29, 33, 64–5, 69, 81, 174, 183–4, 189, 195, 201, 221, 225–7, 234, 293, 336; public 237–9, 241, 243–6; sharing 35, 221; social 85; transfer of 11, 226
Prevention of Corruption Act 359
primordial loyalties 12, 306
privatisation 25, 331
privy purse 16
progressivism 36, 241
protest movements 14, 22, 218, 250, 271
psephology 262–4, 266–7, 269; need for 264; package of 263, 267; pollstering and 267; post-mortems and 264; predictions and 262
public opinion 133, 176, 188, 197, 199, 222–4, 274–6, 282–6, 288–9, 291–2, 335, 344, 349, 351–3; agenda of 291; character of 286; collection of 292; formation 197; research 274–6, 282, 284–6, 291; survey-based 275
Punjab 10, 22, 35, 51, 60, 62, 65, 70, 74–6, 78, 81, 87, 102–5, 130, 135–6, 143–4, 182, 195, 218–20, 224–5, 228–30, 319
Purchasing Power Parity (PPP) 127

quality of life 37
Quit India movement 74

radical: agenda 25, 326; choices 63, 98; democracy 39, 285; democrats 33, 332; desire 5; expectations 4; opportunity 90; reform 327; social change 243; youth 14
radicalisation 25, 70
Rajasthan 51, 59, 63, 65, 68, 75–6, 91–3, 102–5, 222, 224–5, 228–9, 265–6, 304, 306, 313, 318
Rajya Sabha 184, 339–40, 348
Rama Rao, N.T. 17
Ramaswamy ("Periyar") 307, 314, 316
Ramjanmabhoomi agitation 80
Ram, Kanshi 24, 81–2, 90
Ram temple, Ayodhya 28
Rao, Chandrashekhar 205
Rao, M.S.A. 46–7
Rao, Narasimha 82
Rashtriya Janata Dal (RJD) 26, 89, 94, 211, 357
Rashtriya Swayamsevak Sangh (RSS) 74, 80, 84, 155–6, 350
Reddy, Y.S. (YSR) 205
regional: autonomy 132; diversity 13, 22, 35, 128, 133; divisions 72, 76, 84; identity(ies) 73, 132, 219–20; political parties 19, 78
regionalism 47, 87, 88, 220, 223
regional parties 19, 22, 25, 210, 211, 214, 231, 250, 258
religion(s) 24, 119, 128–9, 219, 302, 304, 307–8, 365
religious: communities 80, 120, 180, 308, 350; consciousness 219; diversity 132; groups 141

representative democracy 20, 166–8, 170, 173–5, 177–8, 180, 186–8, 193–4, 199, 201–2, 349; design of 178, 199; practice of 166, 187; reforms in 187
Republican Party of India (RPI) 307, 319
reservations 10, 81, 137, 268, 332, 364; caste and 10; jobs and 23
resources: control of 47; material 37, 216; natural 95, 227; unequal 342–3
rights: civil 230; democratic 31; individual 112, 116–17; minority 73
Roy, Ajit 242
Roy, Pranoy 266
Rudolph, Lloyd 243
rule of law 8, 33, 353
rural–urban divide 73, 77

Saberwal, Satish 245
Sachar Committee Report 185
Salwa Judum 291
Samajwadi Janata Party 266
Samajwadi Party (SP) 26, 62, 69, 81, 89, 93–4, 214, 319, 357
Samata Party 27
Samyukta Socialist Party (SSP) 16, 306, 319
Scheduled Castes (SCs) 69, 73, 136, 142, 150–4, 177, 185, 268, 305–6
Scheduled Tribes (STs) 37, 69, 136, 142, 151–3, 177, 268, 343
secession 109, 135
secularism 3, 244–5, 268, 350, 363, 365
Self-respect 36, 74, 353
Self-rule 4, 7, 26, 34
Shakdher, S.L. 328
Sikhs 22, 35, 136, 142, 150–1, 155–6, 348
Sikkim 76, 103, 105, 221
Singh, Charan 9, 16–17, 77, 79, 314
Singh, Manmohan 23, 82
Singh, L.P. 328
Singh, Mulayam 82, 84, 90
Singh, Rohit 307
Singh, V.P. 22–3, 81, 82
single-party dominance 59, 98
social: base 18, 29, 47, 179, 210; basis 78, 197, 225, 321, 351; churning 183, 209; cleavages 31, 41–2, 61, 66, 68–9, 72, 110, 180–1, 306, 308, 337; coalition 75, 77, 96, 178, 181, 337; change 42, 49–50, 54, 61–62, 69, 243, 336; cohesion 49, 337; communities 28, 34, 203; composition 20, 84; divisions 11–12, 28, 71–3, 76, 111, 174, 180; forces 19, 46, 75–6, 243; fragmentation 68–9; groups 19, 35, 62, 66, 71, 90, 98, 154, 185, 189, 199, 209, 231, 264, 293, 333, 336, 359–60; hierarchy 5, 19, 179, 197; imaginary 256, 285, 290; inequality 24, 42; justice 16, 74, 81, 218, 350, 364; order 19, 70, 185, 187, 217, 252; revolution 35, 170; support 29, 73; transformation 5, 42–3, 50, 54–6, 61, 92, 98, 183, 325, 336

socialism 10, 16–18, 23–4, 77–8, 82, 272; Gandhian 16, 77; indigenous 10; Nehruvian 16
society/societies: advanced 6; changes in 4; civil 32, 82, 194, 198, 229–30, 279; developing 283; diverse 4, 110; divisions in 74, 80, 175; heterogeneous 138; homogeneous 110; Indian 24, 31, 35, 73, 78, 80, 128, 134, 138, 173, 245; interests of 50, 241; modern 233; multicultural 111; multinational 111, 120–1, 131; non-European 6; orders of 7, 9–10, 24, 26, 305; pluralistic 131; post-colonial 71, 168, 174, 364; socialist pattern of 17; traditional 6
socio-cultural diversity 108, 110–13, 116, 154
socio-economic inequalities 45, 91, 293
socio-political: divisions 43; realities 115
South Asia 133, 149, 244, 263, 283
South Asia Survey 149
South East Asia 282
South India 74, 81, 87, 214
sovereignty 117, 174, 237, 244, 365
Spain 109, 112–13, 116–17, 119–23, 129, 131, 134–5, 137–8, 140–1, 146, 148
SRC (States Reorganisation Commission) 13, 205
Srikrishna Committee 206
Sri Lanka 113, 117, 337
Srinivas, M.N. 307, 309
state government 45, 183, 200, 226, 303
state nation 108–17, 120–1, 126, 130–3, 136–8, 143, 145, 147–8, 152–3, 154–6; concept of 110, 113; democratic 110, 137, 154; ideal-typical 120
State of Democracy in South Asia (SDSA) 133–8, 147, 149, 167, 169, 180
state politics 29, 42–9, 98, 178, 200, 213–17, 224, 226–8, 232, 258, 319; autonomy of 213, 226, 227; centre's intervention in 45; comparative study of 48; dynamics of 47; emergence of 43, 48; narratives of 46; studies of 45, 48, 215–17, 232
state/states: aspects of 237; classification of 46; consolidation of 77, 109; democratic 108, 110, 112–14, 116, 137, 144, 154, 174; ex-princely 51, 74; federal 109, 117, 119–21, 131, 147; formation of 87–9; liberal 119, 250; multinational 120, 136–7; post-colonial 242; princely 51, 74; reorganisation of 73, 215; repressive 230; socialist 119; typology of 47; unitary 113–14, 117, 119, 121
Sternberger, Dolf 138
Sukarno 9
survey/surveys: data 127, 148, 275, 278, 282, 287; practices 281; research 251, 258–9, 271–93,

301, 310–11, 313, 315, 317, 320
Swatantra Party 16, 74, 217, 304, 318
Sweden 109
Switzerland 110, 116, 119–20, 131, 134–5, 145–6, 148
systems theory 251, 257

Taagepera-Shugart index 58
Tamil Nadu 15, 18, 27, 48, 51, 60, 62–3, 65, 69–70, 75, 78, 87, 91, 96–7, 102, 104, 135–6, 143–4, 215, 218–19, 221–3, 225, 228–9, 304, 307, 319, 352
Tarkunde Committee 328, 337
Telangana 74, 96, 205–6, 220, 352, 357
Telangana Rashtriya Samiti 205
Telugu Desam Party (TDP) 19, 63, 68, 95, 214, 222, 357
Three M's (Mandir, Mandal, and Market) 22–3, 80, 83
Time magazine 2, 267
trade union 74, 314, 319, 362
Transparency International Survey 282
tribals 19, 75, 179
Trinamool Congress (TMC) 27, 89, 214
Tripura 19, 60, 76, 97, 103, 105, 214, 218, 228, 352
two-party system 29, 56, 66–7, 90–1, 93, 96, 175, 177, 327, 340

UK 128
Uniform Civil Code 28, 356
United Democratic Front (UDF) 59, 63, 68, 96
United Front 27, 70, 82
United Nations Development Programme (UNDP) 127
United Progressive Alliance (UPA) 203–5, 207–8, 214
United States of America (USA) 3, 12, 66, 117, 121, 127–9, 131, 134–5, 140, 146, 148–51, 171, 197, 242, 256, 278–83, 290, 338–9
universal adult franchise 5, 20, 26, 54, 72, 173–74, 175, 201, 331
Untouchables 15, 19, 154, 305
Upadhyaya, Deen Dayal 77
upsurge 9, 24–7, 30, 41, 43, 81, 84, 91, 95, 167, 169, 179, 183–4, 187–8, 293, 305, 331, 335, 342–3, 353, 359; participatory 9, 25, 41, 43, 169, 183
Urs, Devraj 77
Uruguay 140–2
USSR (Soviet Union) 22, 82, 116, 127
Uttarakhand 93–4, 225, 228
Uttaranchal 76, 89, 92–3, 129, 305
Uttar Pradesh 10, 15, 20, 35, 47–8, 59, 61–63, 67, 69–70, 77, 81–2, 84–5, 87, 91–4, 97, 102, 104, 210, 218–19, 222–5, 227–30, 264–5, 305, 307, 318–19, 356–7

Vajpayee, A.B. 204–5
Varshney, Ashutosh 155
Verfassungspatriotismus 119, 138
Vidarbha 220
violence 80, 109, 116, 156, 185, 230, 240, 363; anti-Sikh 156;

communal 80, 230; inter-group 185; militant 230
Vishal Haryana Party 15
Vishwa Hindu Parishad (VHP) 80, 155–6
vote banks 172, 180, 268, 306–8
vote of confidence 330, 339
voter(s) 16, 25, 55, 58, 62, 64, 69–71, 90, 97, 134, 149, 150, 172, 175–6, 179–80, 183, 196, 204, 206, 209, 211, 214, 264–6, 268, 270, 300, 302–3, 306–8, 310–11, 315–16, 320, 332, 350, 357; choices 300; individual 175; opinion 268; ordinary 16; Other Backward Class (OBC) 206; turnout 25, 149, 266; volatility 196
vote/voting 15, 18–19, 25–9, 58–9, 61, 70, 93–4, 102–3, 105–6, 148–53, 172, 179–84, 188, 197, 201, 214, 262, 264–72, 274, 303–4, 306–9, 311, 313–17, 319–21, 330, 332, 335, 337, 339, 341, 343, 356–7, 360; behaviour 172, 180–1, 271–2, 274, 303, 307–8, 311, 314–16, 320–1; change in 266; consolidation of 59, 357; dalit 93; individual 172; Muslim 93–4; OBC 93–4; opposition 267; pattern of 264, 303; preferences 270; share of 266, 268; swing 15, 18, 79, 215, 265–7, 293; turnout 149–51, 179, 197; upper-caste 93; valid 59

Weiner, Myron 44–6, 174, 216, 219, 249, 257
West Bengal 19, 24, 27, 29, 51, 62–3, 65, 67, 70, 74–6, 78, 87, 91, 96, 102, 104, 182, 195, 209–10, 214, 218–19, 221–2, 225–6, 228, 230, 319, 352, 357
Western democracy 6, 38, 175, 260, 334
Western Europe 149, 171, 197, 281, 290
West Germany 119, 138, 146, 148
West India 91–2
women 24–5, 36, 152–3, 181, 185, 197, 222, 268, 315, 332, 338, 361–3; issues of 36; movement 36; participation 36, 197; representation of 36, 338; reservation for 36
Women's Reservation Bill (WRB) 24, 338
Wood, John 45–6
World Bank 30, 282
World Trade Organization 23, 342
World Values Survey (WVS) 133–5, 144–9, 282
World War, Second 119

Yadav/Yadavs 24, 40, 48, 69, 92, 167, 169, 175, 178–80, 182–4, 332, 340
Yadav, Lalu 24, 82, 84, 90, 94
Yugoslavia 116, 126–7